The Greek Imaginary

The Greek Imaginary

From Homer to Heraclitus,
Seminars 1982–1983

Cornelius Castoriadis

With supplementary essay by Pierre Vidal-Naquet
Edited by Enrique Escobar, Myrto Gondicas, and Pascal Vernay
Translated by John V. Garner and María-Constanza Garrido Sierralta

EDINBURGH
University Press

Edinburgh University Press is one of the leading university presses in the UK. We publish academic books and journals in our selected subject areas across the humanities and social sciences, combining cutting-edge scholarship with high editorial and production values to produce academic works of lasting importance. For more information visit our website: edinburghuniversitypress.com

Ce qui fait la Grèce 1. D'Homère à Héraclite, Séminaires 1982–1983
(La Création humaine, 2)
Texte établi, présenté et annoté par Enrique Escobar, Myrto Gordicas et Pascal Vernay précédé de *Castoriadis et la Grèce ancienne* par Pierre Vidal-Naquet

© Editions du Seuil, 2004, 2024

English translation © John V. Garner and María-Constanza Garrido Sierralta, 2023, 2024

Edinburgh University Press Ltd
13 Infirmary Street Edinburgh
EH1 1LT

First published in hardback by Edinburgh University Press 2023

Typeset in Arno Pro
by R. J. Footring Ltd, Derby

A CIP record for this book is available from the British Library

ISBN 978 1 4744 7532 7 (hardback)
ISBN 978 1 4744 7533 4 (paperback)
ISBN 978 1 4744 7534 1 (webready PDF)
ISBN 978 1 4744 7535 8 (epub)

The right of Cornelius Castoriadis to be identified as the author of this work has been asserted in accordance with the Copyright, Designs and Patents Act 1988, and the Copyright and Related Rights Regulations 2003 (SI No. 2498).

Published with the support of the University of Edinburgh
Scholarly Publishing Initiatives Fund.

Contents

Foreword to the English Translation　　　　　　　　　　　　　　xi
　　　John V. Garner (2022)

Editors' Introduction　　　　　　　　　　　　　　　　　　　　xvii
　　　Enrique Escobar, Myrto Gondicas, and Pascal Vernay (2004)
　　　Translated by María-Constanza Garrido Sierralta

Seminars 1982–1983
　　　Cornelius Castoriadis
　　　Translated by John V. Garner

I. Seminar from November 10, 1982　　　　　　　　　　　　　　3
　　　Why the Greek world is of interest for us: summary of the themes of the seminar, p. 3. — Greek political and social thought can be seen more in the spirit of the institutions, or in the historians or poets, than in the great philosophical texts, p. 7. — How can we understand other forms of social life? p. 8. — The very possibility of judging and choosing is not present in every culture, p. 9. — Judgment and choice in the domain of art, p. 12. — Institution of society, the work of art, and the work of thinking, p. 13.

II. Seminar from November 17, 1982　　　　　　　　　　　　　15
　　　What relationship, other than a passive one, can we have with the past? p. 15. — Not every historical return is arbitrary; there can be a pertinent and fertile discussion about the meanings of a past society, p. 17. — On Gadamer and the hermeneutic perspective, p. 19. — To grasp the specificity of the historical object, one must posit imaginary schemas, p. 22. — The example of the signification of the *graphē paranomōn*, p. 23. — Why investigate the origin of democracy and philosophy? p. 25. — The birth of philosophy and politics in Greece: their indissociable character and originality with respect to other historical experiences, p. 25. — Q&A. On the historical scope of the inquiry: from the Homeric poems to the fourth century, p. 30. — The possibility and the will to understand other societies, p. 32. — Popperian falsifiability and the theory of epicycles, p. 33.

III. Seminar from November 24, 1982   35

    Homer and ancient Greece: an immense corpus with innumerable interpretations, p. 35. — Some chronological reference points, p. 37. — The world in which the Homeric poems were definitively composed was a world already familiar with the *polis*, p. 41. — "Influences": the old can be taken up into the new only with the signification the new gives to it, p. 44. — The selectivity of what one culture "borrows" from another, p. 45. — New forms: the example of mathematical demonstrations, p. 47. — Ideal space and the ideality of numbers, p. 50. — *Q&A*. The potentiality for an actualization is as valid as an actualization, p. 53.

IV. Seminar from December 1, 1982   55

    Two symmetrical naïveties in the study of the Homeric poems, p. 55. — Analysts and Unitarians, p. 57. — The specificity of the function of the poems in Greek culture, p. 58. — Their mode of composition, p. 60. — The era they refer back to, p. 63. — Certain elementary significations appear there that will play a central role afterwards, p. 65. — The Greek "sacred" text is not a sacred text, p. 66. — Creative imagination and memory, p. 67. — At the core of the significations of the poems one finds what is essential in the Greek imaginary: the tragic grasp of the world, p. 68. — Fate and transgression, p. 70. — Central to the *Iliad* is the experience of the inescapable given, which is death, p. 72. — Death suffered and death chosen, p. 74. — The tragic grasp: nothing is worth one's life; but if nothing is worth more than life, then life is worth nothing, p. 75. — *Q&A*. The classical text lends itself indefinitely to rediscovery, p. 77. — Hegel, the ruse of Reason, and tragedy, p. 78.

V. Seminar from December 15, 1982   79

    What we are looking for in the poems is the roots of the Greek grasp of the world; we must inevitably take account of what came along afterwards, p. 79. — Importance of the Homeric conception of *moira*, p. 81. — *Moira* and limits, p. 83. — Ulysses's choice, p. 85. — The coexistence of an impersonal law and the free decision of the human, p. 87. — Individuality, decision, and will, p. 87. — The "birth" of impartiality, p. 92. — *Q&A*. Will and choice, p. 93. — The enigma of Sparta, p. 94.

VI. Seminar from January 5, 1983   97

    On the difficulty of understanding Greek religion, p. 97. — The role of affect, p. 100. — The polyphony and profound unity of the Greek universe, p. 101. — Again, on influences and borrowings, p. 103. — The cult of divinities in the dominant current of Greek religion is a civic cult, p. 104. — The immortality of the soul and the crisis of democracy, p. 105. — What the Greek gods mean: the interpretations of Otto and Finley, p. 105. — The idea of anthropomorphism is at once true and false, p. 106. — There is no essential link between each Olympian and his or her domain, p. 108. — The gods are figures of the groundless, which is something as much outside man as in man himself, p. 101. — In Homeric religion we find different layers of religious significations rather than genuine incoherencies, p. 110. — Gods and men, p. 113.

VII. Seminar from January 12, 1983   115

The absence of revelation in Greek religion, p. 115. — This allows for the re-creation of myth in tragedies, p. 116. — In Greek religion there is neither a privileging of anthropogony nor an infinite distance between the human and the non-human, p. 117. — Digression on idolatry and divine "presence," p. 119. — A religion without promise or hope, p. 121. — The sense in which the Greek gods are "universal," p. 122. — The being of society and the monstrous in the episode of the Cyclops, p. 123. — The values of the Homeric world: what was disappearing and what would remain and be transmuted, p. 128. — The question of justice, p. 130. — The tension between the agonistic element and solidarity in Greek history, p. 133. — Q&A. "Monsters" and "barbarians," p. 134. — Believers and philosophers, p. 136.

VIII. Seminar from January 26, 1983   137

Myth is the figuration by means of a narrative of the meaning with which a given society invests the world, p. 138. — As distinct from a tale, myth is the carrier of an essential meaning for society, p. 139. — What is essential and universal in Greek myths is so for us as well, and not only as something coming from that tradition, p. 142. — These myths unveil a signification of the world that constantly presents meaning over a background of un-meaning…, p. 143. — … and one where there is no place to hope for a correspondence between our desires or our decisions and the nature of being, p. 143. — This vision conditions just as much the birth of philosophy as that of democracy, p. 144. — Chaos in Hesiod, p. 145. — Its two significations, p. 147. — *Peras* and *apeiron*: Anaximander, Plato, and Aristotle, p. 150. — Q&A. On the philosophical dimension of mythology, p. 154. — The meaning of the sacred in Homeric religion, p. 155. — The sense in which Greek mythology is true, p. 157.

IX. Seminar from February 2, 1983   159

The transcript for this seminar has unfortunately been lost (see p. xxvii).

X. Seminar from February 16, 1983   161

The two pairs of significations: *chaos/kosmos* and *hybris/dikē*, p. 162. — The principle the Milesians investigated is distinguished from every mythical conception by the fact that it is unrepresentable, p. 163. — This principle is, for Anaximander, the *apeiron*, p. 163. — Heidegger's translation of Anaximander's fragment, p. 164. — The verb *einai* in the fragment, p. 166. — Beings give themselves justice and punishment for their *hybris*, p. 170. — Existing itself is *adikia* or *hybris*, i.e. transgression, p. 173. — History of the tyrant Polycrates of Samos, who died by crucifixion, p. 174. — Q&A. *Chreōn* and *apeiron*, p. 175.

XI. Seminar from February 23, 1983   179

A scission that recreates itself constantly in the heart of philosophical questioning, p. 180. — The first formulations of the principles of ensemblist-identitarian logic…, p. 181. — … and the inauguration of a thinking that goes beyond that logic, p. 183. — The search for the minimal element that accounts for the maximum of observables, p. 184. — The rupture that Anaximander achieved, p. 186. — Thinking creates itself as an interest in itself and at the same time creates truth as unlimited interrogation, p. 186. — Xenophanes and the critique of the instituted representation, p. 189. — Heraclitus: appearing and being are not separated, p. 192. — Critical fragments and positive fragments, p. 194. — The equal participation of all in the *logos*, p. 195. — Q&A. Language and philosophers, p. 197. — *Chreōn* and creativity, p. 198. — Non-univocity and the foundation of the institution, p. 200.

XII. Seminar from March 2, 1983   201

Heraclitus's synthesis, p. 201. — The textual problem, p. 202. — One must be wary of interpretive overreach, p. 204. — The double critique of the tradition, p. 206. — Critique of the *idia phronēsis*, or private thinking, p. 207. — The relativity of every predication, p. 209. — A war that is also harmony, p. 211. — At the same time, being veils and indicates what it is, p. 212. — The slumberers and the *logos xynos*, p. 214. — The unity of all things, *logos*, and fire, p. 217. — Q&A. On fragment 108, p. 219. — How exactly to understand contrariety, p. 221. — The history of philosophy is a permanent deviation, p. 223.

XIII. Seminar from March 9, 1983   225

From the particular to the whole: Heraclitus and the constant work of thinking, p. 226. — The Parmenidean argumentation against multiplicity and the germs of theological philosophy, p. 229. — The critique of that: the refusal of the ontological privilege accorded to the purely thinkable, p. 231. — The double birth of philosophy and the *physis/nomos* opposition, p. 231. — Democritus and the arguments against the naturalness of language, p. 234. — Whether sensations are *nomō*, p. 236. — *Nomos* as self-constitution of humanity, p. 237. — Q&A. Heidegger and Greece, p. 239. — Again, on "influences," p. 241.

Supplemental Materials (1979–1999)
  Translated by María-Constanza Garrido Sierralta

Appendix A. Reports on Teaching   245
  Cornelius Castoriadis

Appendix B. Political Thought   249
  Cornelius Castoriadis (1979)

Appendix C. Castoriadis and Ancient Greece   285
  Pierre Vidal-Naquet (June–July 1999)

Index   300

Foreword to the English Translation

John V. Garner (2022)

The 1982–1983 seminars of Cornelius Castoriadis (1922–1997) at the School for Advanced Studies in Social Sciences (EHESS) in Paris are here translated as *The Greek Imaginary: From Homer to Heraclitus, Seminars 1982–1983*.[1] They were originally published in French in 2004, with expert editing and supplemental notes provided by Enrique Escobar, Myrto Gondicas, and Pascal Vernay. For basic introductory information on these seminars, their context, and their content, see their excellent Editors' Introduction which follows. For a general introduction to several themes prevalent throughout these seminars, see Pierre Vidal-Naquet's essay "Castoriadis and Ancient Greece," here included as Appendix C.[2] Such an eminent scholar's praise of Castoriadis's facility with the Greeks is especially noteworthy: "I could discuss Plato and Aeschylus with him on equal footing" (p. 285). For introductory purposes, I also humbly recommend my "Foreword" to *Democracy and Relativism*, pages viii–xvii of which address Castoriadis's relationship to ancient Greek

---

1. The general French title attaching to three volumes of Castoriadis's lectures on the ancient Greeks (i.e. the earliest three years of his seminars that have been preserved) is *Ce qui fait la Grèce*. It translates roughly as "what makes Greece," as employed in expressions from the seminars such as "What makes Greece is the question of *non*-meaning or of *non*-being" (p. 254). "Makes" here thus serves to attribute a characteristic feature, just as the word "were" functions in this case: "It is because the Greeks recognized that Greek is *only a* language [...] that they were Greeks" (p. 257, note 373). Since by means of such characterizations Castoriadis is elaborating his view that the Greeks have a distinctive "first imaginary grasp" of the world, I felt it acceptable—and preferable, because more natural in English—to use the main title *The Greek Imaginary*. (Castoriadis uses the exact equivalent expression in French occasionally.) Let it also be said here that, for Castoriadis, not all characterizations of something as "Greek" count as positive in value. For example, it is a characteristic of Athenian democracy to have failed to treat other *poleis* as being on equal footing to itself (p. 269). And, of course, Greece's failures regarding the status of women, slavery, etc. are all frequently highlighted by Castoriadis here and elsewhere.
2. In the 2004 French edition, Vidal-Naquet's memorial essay follows the Editors' Introduction at the beginning of the volume.

democracy and the relevance of his thinking for us today.³ I stand by those remarks, especially those on Castoriadis's non-ethnocentrism; but rather than repeat any of them here, I will focus only on matters of formatting and use of language which are specifically pertinent to this volume.

As for formatting, the reader should be aware of the various editorial marks and notes found in the seminars.⁴ The following may serve as a succinct guide:

- Markings in the main body of the seminars:
    - <words in angle brackets> – These brackets contain words added by the editors for clarifying or interpreting otherwise unclear statements. (See the Editors' Introduction for more information on their contributions.)
    - [words in square brackets] – These brackets contain clarifying words—e.g. French terms or language clarifying the context, which have been added by the translators as required for comprehension in English.
    - The bold heading "Questions" precedes questions raised by the seminar attendees, each rendered in italics. Castoriadis's responses are in the roman font just as in the seminar body.
- Markings preceding footnotes:
    - *Marg. C.C.* – This mark indicates a marginal correction, bibliographic reference, or other annotation added by Castoriadis. There were likely added in the early 1990s and were included in the French publication.
    - *Eds.* – This mark precedes a short bibliographic reference or a more substantive supplemental note added by the editors of the 2004 French edition. (In the French edition, the shorter notes were added to footnotes while the longer notes were contained in a separate Appendix. Here, they are all integrated into the footnotes.)
    - *Trans.* – Indicates a clarifying note added by the translators for this edition.

As for use of language in the seminars, several points may aid the reader in understanding this translation.

---

3. Cornelius Castoriadis, *Democracy and Relativism: A Debate*, trans. John V. Garner (New York: Rowman & Littlefield, 2019).
4. Slightly different formatting was required for the translation of Castoriadis's previously unpublished essay "Political Thought" (1979), which is included here as Appendix B. See the first footnote in that essay for formatting decisions.

First, Castoriadis's language in both the lectures and the question-and-answer portions is generally rather casual, witty, and sometimes abrupt or blunt. To capture these casual and oral features, I have used contractions throughout the seminars, and some of the French version's incomplete sentences have been retained, so long as comprehension is not thereby compromised in English. (The language of the other writings included in this volume is more formal.)

Second, beyond the standard problems in translating some French gendered terms into English, it is true not only that Castoriadis sometimes employs masculine pronouns when referring to persons generally, but also that he employs the term *homme* (man) to speak of *anthrōpos* (see p. 75). After considering a variety of options, I settled on generally retaining his use of gendered language. Importantly, Castoriadis was not unaware of the concerns that may be raised about gendered language.[5] But by retaining his usage, I aim to allow readers to judge the situation for themselves.

Third, all Romanized transliterations of the Greek alphabet are standard, with eta and omega indicated (*ē* and *ō*) and with diacritics used only in one case, to distinguish *bíos* from *biós* (p. 209).

Fourth, the reader should be aware that all quotations of philosophers by Castoriadis are translated directly from the French text of Castoriadis's lectures (unless otherwise indicated). Sometimes he translates from the Greek on the fly; at other times he employs French translations. On the other hand, when the editors' notes have supplied a quotation from a French translation of a classical work, we have substituted (and cited) a widely used English translation of the same passage. Also, more generally, the editors' references to non-English secondary works—as well as their use of quotations from them—have been replaced with English versions if available. If a quote is from a non-English work, and no English version is available, then we have translated the quote directly from the text's French.

Lastly, there are several key terms in the seminars that deserve special mention for clarification:

- "Ensemblist-identitary" is a descriptor conveying the French term *ensembliste-identitaire*, which is Castoriadis's own coinage. Sometimes shortened to just "identitary" or condensed into "ensidic" (*ensidique*), this term borrows from the French term for "sets" (*ensembles*), as in "set theory." Most generally it refers to the logic of determinate or determinable reality

---

5. See especially Castoriadis, *Democracy*, pp. 34–35, where Castoriadis clarifies that in cases like these his use of masculine terms is meant as inclusive.

as opposed to what is indeterminate.[6] In some contexts it refers specifically to the functional or instrumental aspect of human or animal life, which demands that objects have determinate meaning.

- "Germ" conveys the French *germe*. It might be better rendered as "seed," so long as one imagines a germinated seed. Castoriadis uses it as a metaphor to describe, for example, certain ancient Greek achievements, especially in democracy, which, while important for later developments, should not be considered by us as "models" or "paradigms" to imitate.
- "Meaning" and its variants in the English translation convey the French *sens*. This choice is wholly natural, but it might obscure for some readers the way that the French *sens* has shades of meaning overlapping with the English "sense" and also with "direction." Examples from the text: "meaning" (*sens*); "non-meaning" (*non-sens*); "un-meaningful" (*a-sensé*); and so on.
- "Positing" often conveys the French *position*. While this term is best translated as "position" in many cases, Castoriadis's meaning often requires an active and verbal translation, which Castoriadis himself links to the Italian *impostazione* and German *Einstellung* (p. 72). That said, in cases when "positing" proved too awkward, "position" was used (e.g. p. 8).
- "Signification" and its variants convey the French *signification*. However, the reader should keep in mind that "significance" might have been a better translation overall, were it not for the fact that Castoriadis frequently uses the plural, *significations*, and of course in English there is no plural for "significance." Likewise, in some cases the awkward-sounding "significancy" might have been acceptable; and while "meaning" frequently works, I have reserved the latter term for the French *sens*.
- "Understanding" and its variants convey the French *compréhension*. While this choice seems natural, nevertheless in cases when a negative prefix is used (e.g. *incompréhensible*), it was necessary to translate more directly (e.g. "incomprehensible").

In conclusion, I would like to thank above all co-translator María-Constanza Garrido Sierralta. Her excellent work on the Supplemental Materials and Editors' Introduction is properly credited below, but she is also responsible for drafting translations of the longer editors' notes (here included as footnotes preceded by *Eds.*). I learned enormously from collaborating with her. I should also note that our work on this translation was made possible

---

6. See Jeff Klooger, "Ensemblist-Identitary Logic (Ensidic Logic)," in Suzi Adams, ed., *Cornelius Castoriadis: Key Concepts* (London: Bloomsbury, 2014), pp. 108–116.

by funding from the University of West Georgia's Student Work Advisory Committee (under the Student Research Assistant Program, 2017–2018). Further funding was provided by the University of West Georgia's Office of Research and Sponsored Projects (through a Faculty Research Grant, 2021). I would also like to thank the anonymous reviewers for Edinburgh University Press for their helpful suggestions. Of great importance as well was the extremely generous assistance of Enrique Escobar, who was kind enough to consult with me about multiple issues of a textual nature and to offer minor updates to a few of the editors' notes. Lastly, I would like to extend a heartfelt "thank you" to my family—especially my wife Carly, daughter Eve, and son Simon—for their perpetual patience and love as I completed this rewarding but time-consuming project.

Editors' Introduction

Enrique Escobar, Myrto Gondicas, and Pascal Vernay (2004)

Translated by María-Constanza Garrido Sierralta

This volume, *The Greek Imaginary: From Homer to Heraclitus, Seminars 1982–1983*, covers the first five months of Castoriadis's teaching, in 1982–1983, at the School for Advanced Studies in Social Sciences (EHESS) in Paris. These months' unity of tone and topic seems to us to justify their separate publication. We will group in a second volume, *La Cité et les Lois*, the seminars from the remainder of that academic year and those from 1983–1984, which focus on the institutions of the democratic *polis* and in particular on the self-limitation of democracy as it appears, for example, in the political dimension of tragedy. This volume is first in chronological order among the full publication of Castoriadis's seminars (1980–1995). There is in fact no transcription for the years 1980–1982, and the few recordings found were unusable. Only the report that Castoriadis himself wrote for the School's annual publication (which we reproduce in the supplemental material [Appendix A]) makes possible a relatively accurate picture of their content.

See below the overall plan for the publication of the seminars, published under the title of *La Création humaine*, with the understanding that the order of the publication of the volumes will not necessarily respect the chronology and that the titles are not definitive.[7]

---

7. *Trans.*: The list of volumes below directly translates the state of publication in French as of 2004. The most important updates since then, for us, have been threefold: First, the second and third volumes listed were published in French in 2008 and 2011 respectively. Second, the third volume listed was in fact published with a series title matching the first two, i.e. as *Ce qui fait la Grèce, 3. Thucydide, La force et le droit* (Paris: Seuil, 2011). Third, the lectures entitled *Sur Le Politique de Platon* have been translated into English as Cornelius Castoriadis, *On Plato's Statesman*, trans. David A. Curtis (Stanford: Stanford

- *Ce qui fait la Grèce, 1. D'Homère à Héraclite* (1982–1983) [this volume]
- *Ce qui fait la Grèce, 2. La Cité et les Lois* (1983–1984)
- *Thucydide, La force et le droit* (1984–1985)
- *Imaginaire politique grec et moderne*, followed by *Sur* Le Politique *de Platon* (1985–1986)
- *Sujet et vérité dans le monde social-historique* (1986–1987) [published in French in 2002]
- *Temps et création* (1987–1988)
- *Validité de fait et validité de droit* (1988–1989)
- *Ontologie et modes d'être* (1989–1990)
- *Sens et significations philosophiques* (1990–1991)
- *Les Différent modes du faire théorique* (1991–1992)
- *Psyché et représentation, 1* (1992–1993)
- *Psyché et représentation, 2* (1993–1995)

In 1980–1982 Castoriadis deepened the idea, which had been at the center of his work *The Imaginary Institution of Society* (1964–1975), of the social-historical as a field of creation "that makes itself exist while making exist the institution and the social imaginary significations that incarnate it."[8] The seminars for the years 1982–1984 would study "the appearance of societies that challenge and call into question, even partially, their own institution" based on the concrete example of the creation of democracy and philosophy in ancient Greece, which, according to Castoriadis, were inseparable in terms of both their genesis and their meaning.[9] In *The Greek Imaginary: From Homer to Heraclitus, Seminars 1982–1983*, Castoriadis attempts to show that one can discern "even before the emergence of the *polis*" the germs of the dual creation of democracy and philosophy "in the first imaginary grasp of the world and of life by the Greeks, inasmuch as it is expressed in religion and myths."[10] It appears, whether in the *Iliad*, in the *Odyssey*, or in Hesiod's *Theogony*, as emergence from Chaos, as the arbitrary and transient character of all power, including the divine, as the definition of the monstrous by the absence of assemblies and laws, and as the refusal of the illusion of salvation in the

---

University Press, 2002). For general bibliographical information on Castoriadis, see the following websites (last accessed August 2022): Agora International, <https://www.agorainternational.org>; the Association Castoriadis <https://www.castoriadis.org>; and the bibliography prepared by Claude Helbling <https://independent.academia.edu/ClaudeHelbling>.

8. *Trans.*: This volume, pp. 245–246.
9. *Trans.*: This volume, p. 246.
10. *Trans.*: This volume, p. 247.

hereafter. (The reading of seminars VI, VII, and VIII will permit the reader to judge whether it is true that Castoriadis, as has sometimes been said, neglected the role of the gods in the institution of public space in Greece.) Regarding the inaugural phase of philosophy, the seminars focus on Anaximander and Heraclitus, who were "discussed at length both because they were the closest to the imaginary core of the Greek grasp of the world—with genesis and destruction being subject to a law that is beyond human meaning and non-meaning—and because they exhibit as of the sixth century the accomplished freedom of spirit."[11] These are the topics of the first five months of teaching, as summarized in the EHESS annual record. Yet, we will also find the guiding thread of this reflection in a few pages of a text drafted between 1979 and 1982, "The Greek *Polis* and the Creation of Democracy," in which the author himself explained the main ideas that had been at the center of his work at the EHESS since 1980.[12] We refer the reader to several pages where Castoriadis's argumentation is perfectly condensed.[13]

***

The unpublished document from 1979 that we reproduce in the supplemental materials, "Political Thought," announces and takes up more than one issue that the contents of the seminars of 1982–1986 would include. In an interview from October 1979 with the journal *Esprit*, Castoriadis announced, "Here and in what follows I'm summarizing a work on politics being drafted. The interested reader will find more information on the topic in the new Introduction to *On the Content of Socialism*."[14] The book never came to be. We have every reason to believe that the text we are publishing was a chapter. More than one reason may be advanced for its non-publication by Castoriadis. The fact that we are including it in the supplemental materials demonstrates that this is for us, to some extent, an "incomplete" text; and we will certainly find enrichments

---

11. *Trans.*: This volume, p. 248.
12. See Cornelius Castoriadis, "The Greek *Polis* and the Creation of Democracy," in *Philosophy, Politics, Autonomy*, trans. David A. Curtis (Oxford: Oxford University Press, 1991), pp. 81–123.
13. Castoriadis, "Greek *Polis*," pp. 101–105.
14. The "summary" refers to Cornelius Castoriadis, "Une interrogation sans fin," in *Domaines de l'homme, Les carrefours du labyrinthe II* (Paris: Le Seuil, 1986), pp. 253–259. The "new Introduction" refers to Cornelius Castoriadis, "Socialism and Autonomous Society," in *Political and Social Writings, Volume III*, trans. David A. Curtis (Minneapolis: University of Minnesota Press, 1993), pp. 314–331.

and also inflections or corrections in the seminars. It remains the case that, in terms of both the content of the ideas and the formulations themselves, many things were readdressed in what the author published in his lifetime. As a matter of fact, what counts is the very movement of ideas; and the text from 1979 is all the more interesting in this regard, for we see the knotting of two threads: the deepening of the political reflection nourished by the work of the republishing of his texts from *Socialisme ou Barbarie* in the course of the 1970s; and the philosophical interest in Greece. The two threads join together, of course, in "The Greek *Polis* and the Creation of Democracy," whose first draft is exactly contemporary with the interview from October 1979. It may seem a bit futile, especially when one is dealing with research spanning decades, to attempt to establish too rigorous a chronology, i.e. to determine when such a draft was first conceived, put on paper, or published. These are considerations that sometimes make up three distinct orders of reality for an author. As for actual philosophical reflection, while it is certain that he did not wait until 1970 to gain interest in Greece, it is from that date on that Castoriadis engaged in a systematic rereading of the great Greek texts, as part of the drafting of the second part of *The Imaginary Institution of Society*. Thus, this new unpublished work comes after about ten years of sustained research.

***

A few points deserve comment, above all the importance given across several years of teaching to the issue of what men were able to do or to think about more than twenty-five centuries ago in Greece. (In order to aid in the understanding of what is to follow, recall that for Castoriadis "Greece" was in general only an abbreviation for Greece from the eighth to the fifth centuries, i.e. that Greece which saw the creation of the *polis* and in some cases the institution of democratic *poleis*.) This choice might be surprising, as Castoriadis is a thinker whose reflection is oriented by the idea of the need for the transformation of *contemporary* humanity. The fact that we have something to learn from the Greeks is, nowadays, anything but obvious. Certainly, we have seen a multiplication of such books in the past twenty years, especially in France, on the theme "Greece and Us." This seems to be the case with most classicists' work, as they seem to be trapped in doubt with regard to the legitimacy, whether historical, social, or political, of their own domain. Globally, in this debut of the century, what seems self-evident (except in the increasingly sparse ranks of traditionalists, who have defended this or that dreamt-up version of Greece for the wrong reasons) is that we are a thousand times more inclined to doubt the interest in and the very existence of the Greek heritage. Furthermore, for a good portion of the public, even the educated ones, to accept as obvious that the Greeks looted their neighbors of all the things that they had claimed to have discovered seems to be an indispensable condition for being part of the "good" camp (anti-imperialist, multiculturalist, deconstructionist, etc.). The Greeks, moreover, practiced slavery, and among this [on this account] unremarkable people, women did not participate in political life. This would thus outright prevent one from talking about Greek "democracy," even at an embryonic stage. Should it be concluded that speaking of "democracy" in France in the first part of the twentieth century is absurd, since the majority of the adult population—women to be precise—were excluded from the electoral body? Or that only from April 1944 on did France *actually* become a democracy? But we must leave this discussion to the second volume of this series, where it is approached head on.

Consider Castoriadis's so-called "Hellenocentrism." Due to some inability to get rid of an inherited Eurocentrism, no doubt arising from his Marxist past, or also—and why not?—due to some sheer blindness of a sentimental order, Castoriadis [on this account] would have been the victim of a double mirage: first, that of the "Greek origin" of what we (Westerners) are; and, second, that of a false Western "universalism." On the first point, to assign to him motivations of a purely emotional order (Castoriadis was Greek, therefore...) does not seem very convincing. What has been said above will suffice to show that this is not a matter of intellectual tourism in the land of ancestors and that the only roots that are discussed here are those of the world itself, beyond that "misty Tartarus" of which Hesiod speaks.[15] Regardless of the very great attachment—on the whole rather banal as far as it goes—the man had with his native land, it must be clearly stated that Castoriadis, a French philosopher of Greek origin in the twentieth century, was led to be interested in ancient Greece due to the development of his reflections, both philosophical *and* political; and it would undoubtedly have been the same if he were named Dupont. "Those who believe that I am inspired exclusively or essentially by ancient history simply have not read me completely. My reflection began not with Athenian democracy (only in 1978 did I truly start working on it) but with the contemporary workers' movement. To cite the texts that, since 1946, put this reflection on record would be to cite the tables of contents of the eight volumes of my *Socialisme ou Barbarie* writings; in all these three thousand pages, there is but one allusion to Thucydides and another to Plato."[16]

---

15. *Trans.*: This volume, p. 148.
16. Cornelius Castoriadis, "Done and To Be Done," in *The Castoriadis Reader*, trans. David A. Curtis (Oxford: Blackwell, 1997), p. 414.

Moreover, Castoriadis would have burst out laughing if he were told he were on the side of the "ancients" in the various recent renewals of a very old quarrel [of ancients with moderns]. A text roughly contemporary with the incubation period of the developed themes in the seminars ("Social Transformation and Cultural Creation," 1978) is perfectly illuminating in this regard: Castoriadis *was not* nostalgic for any glorious past, and above all he did not believe that by cultural creation one must understand exclusively "learned" creation.[17] "Hellenocentrism?" What chiefly interested him was that sort of permanent critical work of society on itself which we know under the dual names of philosophy and democracy, which he saw as having a first birth in Greece. But this was no less obvious in his eyes than any other historical phenomena: the long "Renaissance" of the eleventh to the sixteenth centuries; the (ambiguous) heritage of the great rationalist tradition; and especially the workers' movement. And the lastest Castoriadis never ceased to see as it really was, despite its failures, namely one of the most prodigious attempts at the humanization of society that history has ever known. And, finally, there is the feminist movement, which represented an undeniable deepening of the project of social and individual autonomy and marked out the relative "superiority" of modern times compared with the Greek experience. These historical phenomena in fact represent, in relation to Greece, an assertion of the explicit instituting activity that goes beyond the sphere of the properly political, a sort of enormous enlargement of the base—human and institutional—of this project. And yet, this double rupture, "Greek" and "modern," for contingent reasons to be sure, never saw an equivalent outside of the Western cultural area. "Eurocentrism," then?

Castoriadis never ceased to reiterate that, in our own tradition, extreme and contradictory possibilities for the human being oppose one another and that our history should not be seen only as the development of the project of social and individual autonomy but also as the deployment of another imaginary meaning: the unlimited expansion of "rational mastery," which has wreaked havoc on a planetary scale. It is a history that has also been a monstrous attempt to subjugate—and that has destroyed and continues to destroy—many cultures. (That these cultures cannot be taken as a bloc and positively valued, nor sheltered from any and all critical judgment, is another matter, which he tackled in blunt manner in 1987's "Reflections on

---

17. *Trans.*: See Cornelius Castoriadis, "Social Transformation and Cultural Creation," in *Political and Social Writings, Volume III*, pp. 300–313.

Racism."[18]) Let us quote once more what he wrote regarding the attempts at an "ethnologization" of the study of Greece in the past century: "No doubt, this second attitude [the first having been the depiction of Greece, for centuries, as an 'eternal paradigm'] is formally correct. Not only, needless to say, *is there not nor could there be any difference in 'human value,' 'worthiness,' or 'dignity' between different peoples and cultures*, but neither could there be any objection to applying to the Greek world the methods—if there be any—applied to the Arunta or to the Babylonians."[19] But Castoriadis added, "The reasoned investigation of other cultures and the reflection upon them does not begin within the Arunta or the Babylonian cultures. [...] The keen interest in the other starts with the Greeks. This interest is but another side of the critical examination and interrogation of their own institutions. That is to say, it is a component of the democratic and philosophical movement created by the Greeks."[20] And there is also the following, which provides a justification of and a program for his four years of teaching devoted to Greece (1982–1986): "[Since] we know that this attitude is by no means universal but extremely exceptional in the history of human societies, we have to ask how, under what conditions, in which ways, human society was capable, in a particular case, of breaking the closure in virtue of which it generally exists."[21]

Let us avoid any misunderstanding here. Yes, there has been and there is more than ever a process of cultural integration at a global scale that is also (since it is not only this) the destruction of what makes for the originality of innumerable cultures. Thus, it is legitimate and even indispensable to recognize—and not only with lip service—the interest and value of everything that so many people could invent at various times in their history, without of course neglecting political forms and, very specifically, their different practices—which constituted Castoriadis's main interest—of debating their communal affairs. Since democracy, as has been wisely pointed out, did not fall from the sky upon Athens, it is always good to compare. One can see, through reading these seminars, that it would be difficult to accuse Castoriadis of ignoring the fact that other "democratic" forms, at the scale of the village or the tribe, had emerged since the dawn of time and survive to this day, and that they were at times already present in the first urban civilizations.

---

18. *Trans.*: See Cornelius Castoriadis, "Reflections on Racism," in *World in Fragments: Writings on Politics, Society, Psychoanalysis, and the Imagination*, trans. David A. Curtis (Stanford: Stanford University Press, 1997), pp. 19–31.
19. Castoriadis, "Greek *Polis*," p. 82, our emphasis.
20. Castoriadis, "Greek *Polis*," pp. 82–83.
21. Castoriadis, "Greek *Polis*," p. 83, translation slightly modified.

(This is so, although he was also interested in the paradox, which many great thinkers of the past were aware of, regarding the coexistence of these "local" democratic forms with the most despotic powers at the scale of the whole society.) Nor was he blind to the fact that reason and reflection are by no means the privilege of ancient Greece and that, as has been said and repeated for centuries (and in a more and more documented way, it is true), the Greeks were dependent in a thousand ways on civilizations that surrounded them. We must certainly be grateful that more and more studies have made us aware of the exact extent of this debt. We should not, however, pass right over what is essential. What Castoriadis obstinately asserted was that in this comparison there is a point beyond which one cannot readily go unless one simply asserts that there did occur in other places, before Greece—and this, despite all the limitations one might wish to specify (e.g. slavery, the condition of women, and so on, which nobody contests)—a critique (in action and done explicitly) of the foundations of the instituted order. It seems that today, as was the case twenty years ago, we are still waiting for the evidence of this. What sense does it make to believe, as some have contended, that every piece of the Greek heritage that one can (even with just an ounce of likelihood) trace back to an origin in Egypt, in Phoenicia, in Akkad, in Sumer, or even from extraterrestrials, represents a victory for the oppressed peoples of the Third World over "European arrogance"? European arrogance, in various frightful forms, has unfortunately and for a long time carried out other conquests over these peoples. If they want to wage different battles, with some chance of victory, they will sooner or later turn to what was born in Greece.

However, the ground of this quarrel may not lie there. In the polemic carried out especially in the United States in the past few decades against those whom Bernard Knox called (not without irony) *the oldest dead white European males*, is it truly the case that the anger is directed at a Greek "model," a dreamt-up Greece, a Greece made up of innumerable projections which nobody seriously defends? Short of seeking to oversimplify excessively a complex debate, we cannot help but think that what is often troubling is not really the idea that some things do indeed have historically and geographically *localizable* origins (and whether they were born at the meeting of the Tigris and the Euphrates, in the delta of the Indus River, on the Nile or the Mekong, and not in Greece, is hardly important). More or less obscurely, and ultimately, this has to do with something else, something bound up with the *definition* of what was born therein: namely, with the idea (which seems as scandalous today as it was twenty-five centuries ago even in the so-called "democratic" countries) of the real *instituting power* of the *dēmos*, of a *direct* intervention by the community of citizens in common affairs, but also with the idea of an unlimited critical questioning which is willing to accept that in certain moments one must *judge* and *choose*, which is something far from the relativistic flattening according to which all genuine comparison (and every choice) is impossible. In short, it has to do with democracy and philosophy, in the meaning these words carry in these pages. On all of these points, the seminars are sufficiently explicit.

Of a less general order, but still of interest to non-experts, is the question of the "Homeric man." On this topic, Castoriadis—as shown in some of the works we cite in the supplementary notes—would have rightly felt less isolated now than at the beginning of the 1980s. Castoriadis himself had criticized at length the idea of a singular human being as *"individual-substance,* an individual of divine right, of natural law, of rational law," and the "confusion over the category of the individual" (in 1981's "The Nature and Value of Equality"); he took care to distinguish between the individual as institution and the subject as project (in 1988's "Power, Politics, Autonomy").[22] He could not have been better positioned to criticize the "primitivist" conception, which had gradually been imposed in the study of the Homeric world following the works of Bruno Snell (but the origins of which date back even further). It is today more and more widely accepted that the veritable rift that some had believed they perceived between what we mean by responsibility or will and the notions that the Greeks could have had of it does not truly exist, even in the archaic period, within which the very existence of such notions has been questioned. This was not the case twenty years ago; we must recognize that since the beginning of the twentieth century, the "close and distant" *Iliad* (Vernant) has become extraordinarily distant.[23] Similarly, the relations between the problems entailed in selecting the authors studied— Homer, Hesiod, Anaximander, Heraclitus—seem in our day and age more obvious than in that era; and those who would be ready to subscribe to this selection, the best specialists among them, are probably more numerous now than before.

***

---

22. Cornelius Castoriadis, "The Nature and Value of Equality," in *Philosophy*, pp. 128 and 133; and Cornelius Castoriadis, "Power, Politics, Autonomy," in *Philosophy*, p. 144.
23. *Trans.*: See Jean-Pierre Vernant's preface, "Proche et lointaine *Iliade*," to James Redfield, *La Tragédie d'Hector: Nature et culture dans l'*Iliade, trans. Angélique Lévi (Paris: Flammarion, 1984).

What is the kind of "truth" about Greece that Castoriadis was striving to reach, considering that he never wished to work as a historian, but always tried to stick as closely as possible to the "facts"? What he said about the idea of Burckhardt and Arendt on the importance of the agonistic element in Greece could put us on the right path: this idea "is true—but not in the same sense as $E=mc^2$ is true. What does 'true' mean in this former case? That this idea brings together an indefinite class of social and historical phenomena in Greece that would otherwise remain unconnected—not necessarily unconnected in their 'causal' or 'structural' relation but unconnected in their meaning; and that its claim to possess a 'real' or 'actual' referent (i.e., one which is not just a delusion, or convenient fiction, or even an *Idealtypus*, an observer's limiting rational construction) can be discussed in a fecund way, though this discussion may be and, in the decisive cases, has to be interminable. In brief, it elucidates and initiates a process of elucidation."[24] Furthermore, with respect to everything pertaining to philology or pure erudition—it should be remembered that there is virtually no Homeric line to which entire libraries have not been devoted—Castoriadis applied the rule formulated by Paul Mazon in his *Introduction to the* Iliad: in presence of the facts, do as if one were the first to observe them and discuss them only with oneself, while knowing that there are few new ideas on some subjects, that it is futile to go back to their original formulation, and that it is good above all to try to present right ideas.[25] It goes without saying that it is sometimes difficult, for a thousand reasons, to stick too rigorously to this, and Castoriadis for his part did not hold back from sometimes discoursing about some privileged testimonials or interlocutors.

The work of the editors, by its very nature, obeys different rules. The "supplementary notes" by the editors [included here as notes preceded by the marking *Eds.*:] are intended to reinforce, supplement, or give nuance to a particular point Castoriadis was making; and they also signal in some cases that some excellent authors might have had completely different opinions.[26] They thus have the sole purpose of providing bibliographic supplements to the reader and will certainly not teach anything new to the specialists. As for the translation of quotations, we presumed, perhaps lazily, that, unlike ancient Greek or German, English is nowadays a universally known language.

---

24. Castoriadis, "Greek *Polis*," p. 86.
25. *Trans.*: See Paul Mazon, *Introduction à l'Iliade* (Paris: Les Belles Lettres, 1959).
26. *Trans.*: The supplementary notes in the French version were gathered in a separate Appendix. Here they are placed in the same format as the editors' smaller reference notes, i.e. as footnotes marked *Eds*.

We have, as is now standard, transliterated the Greek when it consisted of only one word or a few, following the most simple and transparent standards possible, approximating Castoriadis's habits, and continuing with the choices made for the publication of *Sujet et vérité*.[27] Thus, the iota "subscripts" are not transliterated; and with one exception, the rationale for which is obvious, we do not indicate accents. The lengths appear in the case of vowels such as *e* or *o* (epsilon = *e* / eta = *ē*; omicron = *o* / omega = *ō*). We resorted to Greek characters only for longer quotations that are offset from the body of the text; these passages are always translated and commented on by Castoriadis.

Our text has been put together from the transcriptions made by Zoé Castoriadis, week after week throughout the year. This is to say that without her this book would have not seen the light of day, since with one exception (Seminar XII) it was not possible for us to find recordings from the year 1982–1983. The transcript for Seminar IX (which according to some of Castoriadis's annotations was devoted entirely to Hesiod) is unfortunately lost. The transcriptions were reread, or, rather, skimmed through, at a later date (probably the beginning of the 1990s) by Castoriadis himself, who restricted himself to introducing by hand some marginal corrections and annotations. We have included those as notes [preceded by the marking *Marg. C.C.*:]; they are always preceded by [this marking] in order to distinguish them from our own interventions (such as bibliographical supplements, etc.), which are included as notes [preceded by the marking *Eds.*:].[28] With regard to the other conventions we used, they are the same as what we employed in *Sujet et vérité*: in other words, we have inserted our own interventions into the text only in places where an interpretation or an option for reading could occur, and these are marked with <angle brackets>.

In addition to including supplementary notes, we have also included Castoriadis's reports on teaching that were part of the EHESS annual publication (for the years 1980–1982 and 1982–1984) [here as Appendix A], as well as the unpublished article from 1979, "Political Thought" [here as Appendix B]. It seemed useful to include, as we did in *Sujet et vérité*, a table of contents with descriptive text. Michel Casevitz, Alice Pechriggl, Mats Rosengren, and Pierre Vidal-Naquet were kind enough to reread our work and helped in making it

---

27. *Trans.*: Cornelius Castoriadis, *Sujet et vérité dans le monde social-historique* (Paris: Éditions du Seuil, 2002).
28. *Trans.*: In the French edition, Castoriadis's marginal notes were indicated with Arabic footnote numerals and placed inside square brackets and marked by *Annot. Marg.* The editors' references were included as footnotes marked with angle brackets, while their longer, more substantive supplemental notes were gathered in a separate section at the end of the book.

less imperfect that it might have been. The last allowed us to reproduce his presentation as a sort of epigraph for all of these seminars on Greece [here as Appendix C]. This essay is a mixture of analysis and memories presented at the "Journées Castoriadis" that took place in June 1999.[29] We would like to thank him, as well as the journal *Esprit*, where his text was originally published.

---

29. Journées Castoriadis are organized by the Facultés universitaires Saint-Louis in Brussels, Belgium.

Seminars 1982–1983

Cornelius Castoriadis

Translated by John V. Garner

I. Seminar from November 10, 1982

The question I am going to take up this year concerns the importance of, and what's of interest for us in, the Greek world and the tradition one may call Greco-Occidental. To highlight its specificity properly, at times I will have to surrender myself to what is, in many respects, a very perilous exercise of comparing it with certain essential traits of the monotheistic tradition. To that end, I will comment on several aspects of the Old Testament, which, as you know, is the common root of the three monotheistic religions, Judaism, Christianity, and Islam. My thesis here—and those who have followed me up to this point can doubtless surmise it—is that there is an opposition between the monotheistic tradition as a tradition of heteronomy and the properly speaking Greek or democratic tradition as a tradition of autonomy.[1] We will therefore attempt to go to the roots of the Greek world, i.e. to what one may call the primary grasp of the being of the world and of human existence in the world by the Greeks, prior to all philosophical or political thematization. We will become familiar, thus, with the kernel of all the imaginary significations that are subsequently deployed and instituted in Greece. I would like in what

---

1. *Marginal Note by C.C.* (henceforth, *Marg. C.C.*): But there is no term-for-term correspondence here: there can be entirely heteronomous polytheistic society, obviously. — *Editors' Note* (henceforth, *Eds.*): See Cornelius Castoriadis, "The Greek *Polis* and the Creation of Democracy," in *Philosophy, Politics, Autonomy*, trans. David A. Curtis (Oxford: Oxford University Press, 1991), p. 105: "Unitary ontology, in whatever disguise, is essentially linked to heteronomy. The emergence of autonomy in Greece was conditioned by the non-unitary Greek view of the world that is expressed from the beginning in the Greek 'myths.'" But this non-unitary vision of the world expressed by Greek polytheism is a necessary condition—or rather "precondition"—but not a sufficient condition. The idea that there would be a direct link between polytheism as an expression of the diversity of the real and political pluralism—given that the decline of the city was correlated with the "ontological monism" stemming from Plato and the rise of monotheism—was defended passionately in the nineteenth century, with a language and arguments that bear the mark of their era, by an author who is today neglected, i.e. the Hellenist Louis Ménard, in works like *Du polythéisme hellénique* (Paris: Charpentier, 1863). On this remarkable author—an 1848 revolutionary and friend of Leconte de Lisle—it is useful to consult Gilbert Romeyer-Dherbey's introduction, "Louis Ménard ou le païen de rêve," in Louis Ménard, *Rêveries d'un païen mystique* (Paris: Guy Trédaniel, 1990).

follows to lay out in detail what, in this grasp, eventually came to be explicitly thematized and examined by philosophy, namely the three great oppositions that mark ancient Greek thinking: that between being and appearing (*einai* and *phainesthai*); that between truth and opinion (*alētheia* and *doxa*); and that between what we call nature and law. On the last, the translation does not allow us to understand what's at stake; for the Greeks this is the opposition between *physis* and *nomos*.[2]

We will also talk about the *polis*, about the city, about the creation of this form of collective life and of what accompanies it, namely the self-constitution of a body of citizens who consider themselves autonomous and responsible, and who govern themselves by legislating. Of course, this is not achieved in one day, nor peacefully. All told, it concerns the birth, not only of democracy but also of politics in the true sense of the term.[3] Before this there is no politics, there is no collective activity that aims at the institution of society as such. In Asiatic monarchy, for example, we have court intrigue, but not a collective activity of the people aiming to change the law. Next, we will occupy ourselves with democracy itself, with its most important characteristics in the *poleis*, the Greek cities, with the enigmas and the questions it poses, and especially with the fundamental question opened up by the creation of democracy in Greece, a question that, moreover, remains open. To put it briefly, starting with the moment when this rupture, i.e. the creation of the *polis*, came into effect, men posited themselves as authors of their laws and thus also as responsible for what happens in the city. From then on, the positing of the collectivity very clearly became the following: There is no extra-social, divine, transcendent source which says what is right, which says what is good or not, or what is just or not (and in the domain of politics the latter is what is at stake). But what, then, is the limit of humans' instituting activity or of the decisions they can make? What is the norm of the law, what is the standard, what are the criteria by which they can guide themselves since they have renounced saying (to put it metaphorically), "The norm of the law is what God said to Moses"? In Greece there is no God who has said whatever it may be to Moses. And recall that this is also the case for most of us, which thus already addresses the question of this seminar's relevance. The problem that presents itself now, then, is that of the self-limitation of the collectivity, or in other words of the means through which the political collectivity can put

---

2. *Eds.*: See Seminar XI, p. 179 and note 273.
3. *Translators' Note* (henceforth, *Trans.*): On the contrast between "politics [*la politique*]" and "the political [*le politique*]" see Cornelius Castoriadis, *Democracy and Relativism: A Debate*, trans. John V. Garner (London: Rowman & Littlefield, 2019), pp. 27–32.

curbs on its own activity. What curb, and why have any curbs for that matter? And this is also the question, of course, of the vainness of the perpetual search for curbs, for limits, or for guarantees that would stand every test, i.e. which could rescue the collectivity from itself.

From this perspective, we will begin with the birth of historiography—of history as recording, research, and critical reflection on the past—as coming to replace that which, in other societies, is the simple tradition *ne varietur*. Then we will reflect on tragedy as a properly (which is not to say exclusively) political institution. And here, I will repeat what I often say: Books get written on "Greek tragedy"; but that is absurd. There is no Greek tragedy; there is Athenian tragedy.[4] Not all of the Greek cities created tragedies, not even all the democratic cities. It's only in this one, where the self-creation of democracy culminates, i.e. in Athens, that tragedy appeared simultaneously. Doubtless this is also because in Athens the danger was the greatest. For, it's in Athens— due to its power and position—that something had to come about as a reminder of the fact that one is free but also, as Hannah Arendt has said, that even if one can engage in actions, one is never the master of their consequences.[5] And above all, since material consequences are not what is at stake—and these are not what tragedy talks about—we're not the master of their signification. This is what tragedy brings to mind constantly for the Athenian public. And, as you know, it was conceived in such a way that everyone, in a sense, participates in it; it was the grand, popular festival. Tragedy is an institution that has an absolutely fundamental political dimension, or rather that comes to play a fundamental role in the Athenian political institutions.

Then, after the problem of self-limitation, of the norm of the norm, of the law of the law, we will talk about a second problem of democracy that remains open within it, not only for the Greeks but also for us: that of equality. Greek democracy is based on the idea of equality; hence this paradox that we evoke in such a facile way: What does equality mean in a society that practices

---

4. *Eds.*: If it is true that nearly all the preserved tragic texts are by Athenian authors, tragic practices were able to emerge elsewhere than in Athens as of the seventh to sixth centuries; see Herodotus, *Histories*, V, 67 on the existence of "tragic choruses" in Sicyon, in the Peloponnese. But the idea that Greek tragedy was essentially "attic" is likewise the perspective of Albin Lesky, *Greek Tragedy*, trans. Henriette A. Frankfort (London: E. Benn, 1965). See also Harold C. Baldry, *The Greek Tragic Theater* (London: Chatto & Windus, 1971). For an opposed perspective, see, e.g., Brigitte Le Guen, "Théâtre et cités à l'époque hellénistique," *Revue des Études Grecques* 108:1 (1995), pp. 59–90, in which one will find, importantly, a recent bibliography on non-Athenian and "post-classical" theatrical (and tragic) production.
5. *Eds.*: Hannah Arendt, *The Human Condition*, 2nd edition (Chicago: University of Chicago Press, 1998), pp. 188–192, and more generally all of chapter 5, "Action," pp. 175–247.

slavery and where women have the status with which you are familiar? Honestly, these two points are of less import here than we typically say since what is essential here is the insoluble problem at the core of equality itself. Whatever we do, we never do anything other than what a democratic city would do; a certain collectivity decides we are equal, and there's always someone who's excluded from this collectivity of equals. Whatever you do, it will always be that way. If you all decide that children under thirteen don't have political rights, it's you who decide. It's thus always a collectivity that self-establishes itself as composed of equal members; this is the primary positing of a political collective. Of course, this problem deserves considerable elaboration.

We will move on subsequently to what may be called the recurrence and the victory of *hybris* in the democratic city, when democracy degenerates and collapses. Then we will approach the domain of political philosophy, which essentially means Platonic philosophy, particularly that which in Plato has to do with reflection on the city and its constitution. And we will discuss my thesis on the problem, namely that Platonic philosophy is essentially a response to the failure of democracy, a response which deduces from this failure—and Plato's conclusion here is very clear—that the human community is not capable of self-governing itself. This is one of the motivations, one of the nerves, of Platonic ontology. But it is not the only one. And there is, here, a very strange convergence. For, Plato is driven to elaborate his ontology by the need to fix an absolute point of reference that can, for instance, furnish a norm for the conduct of human affairs and for the constitution of the city. But, of course, he's also driven to this point by an internal quasi-necessity in political philosophy, which already starts with the Presocratics and, in any case, with Parmenides, i.e. the father, as Plato says (and a father one must kill, for that matter, as he also says). Thus, what's at stake here, independently of political considerations, is the search for an absolutely guaranteed point in being, which would be at once the foundation of the object of ontology and, of course, would at the same time secure a truth for human thought.

We are thus led to readdress from this perspective certain features of the history of Greek philosophy from the Presocratics to Plato by considering it as a sort of conflict, a sort of obscure battle between grand tendencies. On the one hand, there's something that begins with Parmenides and culminates in Plato, a search for an absolute anchoring point, which it finds in Parmenides's being, in the *eidē* (the "Ideas") of Plato, or in the *agathon*, the Good, which is beyond the Ideas in the formulation Plato offers in the *Republic*. This tendency, thanks of course to Plato, i.e. to the immense genius of Plato, comes to occupy the center of the Western philosophical tradition and thereupon dominates thought. On the other hand, there's everything that, as of the birth of Greek philosophy, exists as a second current. This is not a current that's coherent—neither is the former one, for that matter (and for this reason I speak of an obscure battle)—but it places the emphasis on *phainesthai* rather than on *einai*, i.e. on appearance rather than on being (or in any case on the gap); on *doxa* rather than on *alētheia*, i.e. on opinion rather than on truth; and above all on *nomos* rather than on *physis* (*nomos* means positing/institution/convention/law). This current is doubtless there in the Ionians; we can understand Anaximander and Heraclitus in this sense. It's certainly there in the great sophistical movement in the fifth century and in Democritus, who precedes Plato and is an approximate contemporary of Socrates. Subsequently it continues in a sense with the skeptics and the Epicureans, although this is a story we won't be able to tell. And we find it in authors who are not philosophers, which is very important.

On this point, I would beg you to pay the utmost attention to a methodological point. The first weakness, nearly always, of all reflections on ancient Greece is that they take philosophical texts (for example those of Plato or Aristotle) that talk about political subjects to be saying, "Ancient Greece, this is what it was." Yet, they're not dealing with facts in this case but with a universe of thinking, while failing to notice the prejudices that affect these texts. But the universe of Greek political and social thought is to be read in the spirit of the institutions, and we witness this infinitely better in the historians (Herodotus and Thucydides are fundamental from this perspective), in some Presocratics who aren't part of the grand Parmenidean-Platonic current, in tragedy, and even in lyric poetry. There we find some formulations that get as close as possible to the point of discovering the idea of the institution in its radicality, or the idea of history as creation, ideas that are totally absurd in the Platonic context. In effect, Plato's role in the history of philosophy was that of an enormous stone barrier that for centuries and centuries served to block the idea of creation in history, of the creativity of the collectivity as positing its institution, its proper *nomos*.

We will end with Aristotle, through an examination of his very peculiar position in all these respects. And I will comment on what I see as a fundamental historical paradox, which is that Aristotle, student of Plato (Plato: 427–347; Aristotle: 383–323), appears as the veritable philosopher of the fifth century and of the democratic city. One could write not one book but several on the thesis: Aristotle predates Plato. And this can be seen not only in his political philosophy (which is entirely opposed to that of Plato and according to which, when all is said and done, democracy, among all the realizable regimes, is the least bad) but even in his general spirit and, more surprisingly, in his ontology proper and in the whole of his philosophy. Although he went through Plato's school, he countered him. And we could imagine an Aristotle who would have lived in the fifth century and would have written approximately what he did write. So there you have it, our program for this year.

Let's begin today with the question of the choice of Greece in this discussion. The first evident fact is that our position—which involves interrogation and rational discourse and which I will call heuristic in the strong and true sense of the term—begins with the Greeks, with the city.[6] Second, quite evidently this very position forbids us from taking a historical culture or period, whatever it may be, as a paradigm, prototype, or model to follow. If I propose for us a discussion of Greece, we must fully understand that this is in no way in order to valorize Greek culture. We will very often run into sufficiently atrocious things, for example mass massacres. Rather, it's in order to consider it as a sort of germ—and I insist on this word, by opposition to model—that remains fertile for us.

Let's be precise. I will recite very briefly what I think about history and society and in particular about historical creation. History is the creation of total forms of human life, which is to say of instituted societies, in and through which human beings construct a world. And new forms, new essences, new *eidē* are posited each time by the activity of instituting society. How are we, who live in a determined society within one of these forms, then able to go out of it and understand other forms of social life, or anterior forms? And if we want to judge and choose between these different forms—and perhaps we are ineluctably so driven—how can we do it?

First and foremost, how are we able to understand? There's of course an essential difference here according to whether it's a matter of social-historical forms belonging to our tradition or those exterior to it. In the latter case—and this is obvious and banal—access will always be infinitely more difficult. Understanding of Chinese or Indian culture, or of so-called primitive or archaic cultures, demands that we try to penetrate into a world that is foreign to us by way of approaching it through certain of its dimensions, for example the functional-instrumental side (hunting, agriculture, etc.) or through certain aspects of its social organization. And if one wants to try to understand what this world means for those who constructed it, what the significations are that hold together all these particular institutions and arrange them by conferring on them a meaning, one will doubtless meet with considerable difficulties.

---

6. *Marg. C.C.*: Return to this. — *Trans.*: This marginal comment attaches to the term "heuristic."

I. SEMINAR FROM NOVEMBER 10, 1982

But what's surprising is that in general these difficulties allow themselves to be overcome and that, if we have access to sufficient documentary material, we do manage to understand how the constitution of the world was for that society. If the question seems a lot easier when it concerns societies that belong to our proper tradition, in such cases we are downstream. We come along after this creation, after the social imaginary significations that were posited by, for example, the people of the Renaissance or the seventeenth century or even, going up further, the Romans or the Greeks. These belong in a sense to the humus, to the texture of the social imaginary significations on which our proper world is constructed. But then another difficulty arises, i.e. false understanding due to a false proximity. It's not that we lack distance, but that we act as if the distance did not exist. We believe ourselves to understand, to reconstitute, or to penetrate into a world that belongs to our past because certain forms have remained the same, because the vocabulary has not varied much, because we find the creations of that world to be an element among those of our proper world. Of course, this illusion can be catastrophic. And this is precisely what happened and still happens very often when we seek to understand the ancient Greek world. Here, the similitudes, the apparent familiarity of the forms and the vocabulary, have led certain people to think that they truly understand what's at stake there, without seeing that these forms and these terms belong to a universe organized and oriented entirely differently. Understanding thus always poses problems, whether it concerns our tradition or not.

If we move on to the other question, that of the possibility of judging and choosing, things get complicated again. For, we live in the illusion that we could judge and hierarchize societies and decide that such and such a society is worth more than another, ours being better than the neighbor's or the inverse—it doesn't matter which. This illusion rests on the idea that philosophy could furnish us with the fundamentals for judging and deciding that such and such institution corresponds more than another to the idea or to the essence of the good society. But, independently of all the internal difficulties that we meet with here—among philosophers there's interminable discussion about how to define or found the good society—it must be clear that the very idea of judging and choosing, far from being universal, is part of the singular Greco-Western or European tradition. Quite evidently, such an idea does not exist and cannot exist within what one calls, for simplicity's sake, traditional civilizations or cultures, wherein the tradition categorically defines what is valuable or not, without being able to consider challenging either this definition or the tradition itself. Moreover, in a radical, profound sense, there is no place for the possibility of judging and choosing in monotheistic cultures. I remind you—we will return to this since it's important—that the cultures of the three monotheistic religions have at their basis either an instantaneous or a perpetual revelation and that they are singular in this regard. For, they are alone in asserting that what they posit as divine manifests itself from itself, in person, in a given moment, so as to speak the truth and the law. There is no revelation in polytheistic religions, in Greek, Roman, or Hindu religion, nor for that matter, in this sense, in Buddhism. Buddha is not a god. He saw the truth—that's it—even if he became divine subsequently. But this revealed speech radically excludes all possibility of judgment and choice since it posits from the start the foundation of judgment and choice as given by God, the source of being, of the world, of the institution, etc.

It's also a specificity of Greco-Western culture to call itself into question by itself through comparing itself to other cultures and other societies. Hence, the historical importance of Herodotus, the first to undertake an inquiry without being satisfied with saying, "Very far up north, there is such a people who produce amber," or with recounting mythical histories about the monsters from afar. For him, what's at stake is a systematic inquiry about the institutions, the morals, the gods, the customs, the ideas of the other peoples; and the one who carries it out never stops saying all along, "This is more reasonable than what the Greeks do…," or, "This is where the Greeks took such and such idea from…," and so on. A considerable relativization of the culture itself obviously results from this: We honor these gods, we speak this language, we have these customs; but other peoples have other ones…. And this will recur in the West, even if it's tricky to determine the exact moment. In any case, the movement is well under way in the eighteenth century. For, then not only do the descriptions of so-called savage peoples proliferate, but they do not hesitate to defend the equivalency of "savage," archaic cultures with European culture. Even so, this movement is not without a great degree of ambiguity—from the fifteenth century onward—since by comparison with these ideas the realities of history carry infinitely more force. I mean, of course, to refer to the conquest and the domination of the planet, and to the more or less universal imposition of Western culture, an imposition that is not for that matter necessarily violent. But this is a secondary question, even if forced Christianization evidently did take place. It remains like a guilty feeling which, while not stopping the West's millions of citizens from sleeping at night, nevertheless constitutes part of their culture. We'll thus be reminded that we've massacred the Indians, that we're involved in the subjugation of Africans and their deportation to America, and that still today we're destroying indigenous cultures. And it will be added that Western culture is too rational, too intellectual, that the truth is in Zen, or in Carlos Castañeda's

Mexican Indian who sees Being while smoking, and so on. From the silliest, folkloric aspects to the most profound reflections, the calling into question of Western culture by itself is always there.

There is, of course, another aspect that one cannot ignore: We're justified in saying that the Western tradition created politics to the extent that by this we mean struggle, political conflict, i.e. the conflict in which the stakes are not simply that group X and not group Y would take power, but rather stakes that concern the very institution of society. It doesn't matter here if one takes institution in the narrow political sense or in the larger sense; the conflict is there, and it traverses the ancient world. It then gets eclipsed with the Roman Empire and with what I call the rise of Christian barbarism. But then, starting in the twelfth and thirteenth centuries, it reemerged in the West. But what thus reappeared was the question of judgment and choice. One will always be able say that people judge and choose according to their interests or to their habits, but that matters little; *de jure* the question always poses itself from the very interior of that tradition. And indeed it takes on extreme forms because—recall once again—this tradition did not restrict itself to creating philosophy and democracy. Monstrous episodes can also be found there, like the massacre of the Melians by the Athenians, and that isn't the only one.[7] And further, there's Auschwitz and the Gulag; this is also there as the specificity of European history. It's true that atrocities have happened everywhere and always, and in all cultures. The Aztecs really did do human sacrifices. But the particular type of extreme monstrosity represented by Auschwitz and the Gulag, this is also one of the real claims to fame, as it were, of the West and of Europe. It's an entirely specific creation that has only appeared here. That is also something we must not forget. Deep down, which European tradition are we talking about?[8] As you know, one of the principal fascist

---

7. *Eds.*: This refers to an episode of the Peloponnesian War reported by Thucydides, *History of the Peloponnesian War*, V, 84–116. The Athenians, having refused the offer by the Melians, who wanted to remain neutral, ended by taking their city, killing all the adult men, and reducing to slavery the women and children.
8. *Eds.*: The question was asked in a recurring way from around 1990 on, in France and elsewhere. Among numerous publications, one may cite: Roger-Pol Droit, ed. *Greeks and Romans in the Modern World* (New York: Columbia University Press, 1998), with works by Brague, Brunschwig, Cassin, Castoriadis, Deguy, Detienne, Hartog, Ingremeau, Joffre, Lançon, Loraux, Mattéi, Morin, Nicolas, Olender, Peigney, Pépin, Polack, Sissa, Terray, Tourraix, Vernant, and Veyne. See also Barbara Cassin, ed., *Nos Grecs et leurs modernes: Les stratégies contemporaines d'appropriation de l'Antiquité* (Paris: Seuil, 1992), which stems from the colloquium "The Contemporary Strategies for the Appropriation of Antiquity," with works by Aubenque, Brunschwig, Narcy, Cassin, Chevalley, Thom, Alliez, Wolff, Deleuze, Derrida, Eco, Ricoeur, Deguy, Courtine, Buci-Glucksmann, Le Gaufey, Anscombe, Bubner,

micro-organizations in France calls itself Occident. It proclaims itself to be for the Western tradition, just like another group of "thinkers" elsewhere, on the extreme right, who use GRECE as their acronym.[9] It is certain that they and we are not talking about the same thing.[10]

Philosophy also encounters this problem of judgment and choice when it's concerned with questions that are not rational, or for which there exists little or no procedure for decision, or at least for reasoning. It appears for example in the domain of art. This is the topic of Kant's third *Critique*, the *Critique of the Power of Judgment*, which I urgently invite you to reread. In the impasse of contemporary political philosophy, there have been authors—and not the least among them, such as Hannah Arendt—who judge that the third *Critique* would allow for resolving, or at least for grasping more clearly than we have heretofore, the question of political law. In this work, Kant poses the following question: How can one form a valid judgment about what appears to be the object *par excellence* of arbitrary judgment, i.e. about the work of art? What is significant to me here is what Kant says about what the work of art is; and it's important because it focuses on the exact point where classical philosophy approaches quite closely the idea of creation as creation of *eidos*. Kant, speaking of the work of art, says that it's always the work of genius.[11] For him, clearly, small nuances are not so important: either it's a work of art, or it's nothing (and this is entirely true, by the way). Yet, he defines the great work of art as that which posits its own norms, which means that it's original in the sense that the work itself becomes the model, prototype, or norm for something else. And, for him, genius creates this work of art without being able to give an account of what it is doing or of why it is doing it. Thus, says Kant, it does not

---

and Irwin. And, lastly, see Marc Augé, ed., *La Grèce pour penser l'avenir* (Paris: L'Harmattan, 2000), which, along with an introduction by Jean-Pierre Vernant, contains contributions from the interdisciplinary colloquium of the same name, from December 2–4, 1996, with works by Augé, Descola, Motté, Romeyer-Dherbey, Quet, Mossé, Castoriadis, and Daraki.

9. *Eds.*: Formed in the late 1960s, the Groupement de recherche et d'études pour la civilisation européenne (GRECE) tried from the start to put forth—in a just slightly less crude form than in their original version—certain neo-conservative or traditional extreme right themes (having anti-egalitarianism as their common denominator) by means of journals like *Éléments* or *Nouvelle École*. On the origins of this movement, and on the surprising syncretism in which the evolution of its principal spokesperson, Alain de Benoist, culminated, one may consult Pierre-André Taguieff, *Sur la Nouvelle Droite: Jalons d'une analyse critique* (Paris: Descartes & Cie, 1994), which contains an important bibliography.

10. *Eds.*: On this problem and the discussion that it entails, see Castoriadis, "The Greek Polis."

11. *Trans.*: On this point and what follows, see Immanuel Kant, *Critique of the Power of Judgment*, trans. Paul Guyer and Eric Matthews (Cambridge: Cambridge University Press, 2000), §§46–50.

create it through calculation, through reasoning discursively, but as a nature, here referring quite evidently to the idea of *natura naturans* as opposed to *natura naturata*. In other words, it's nature in the sense of *physis*, what makes being, what makes things be born (*natura, nascor*), nature as a creative power that cannot account discursively for what it is doing, any more than the rose bush can say why and how it makes the rose. Such is his position, which for all that raises considerable difficulties. Kant and the Kantians think they have resolved the question of knowing why such and such work is great and another is not, or, more exactly, how to recognize genius. Kant's elaboration drives him to what he calls the judgment of taste. He posits that judgments of taste are not universals but generals, which is to say that I can make others see why I find such a thing beautiful. In fact, Kant's response is not really satisfying. I mean to say here that we cannot find in the third *Critique* any response to the question of knowing why, when so-and-so says that *Don Giovanni* is a great opera and "Viens, poupoule!" is a ridiculous, trite song, he's right. Nor why someone else can delight in "Viens, poupoule!" while *Don Giovanni* means nothing to him.

The problem thus remains intact and the way of approaching it—I'm not talking about the solution—must be entirely different. There remains another difficulty. If the great work of art is the work of a genius that is each time unique, and if it is a model and prototype, then what can it really be the prototype for since by definition its imitations as such count for nothing? There's a fundamental aporia here. We have to change optics and see in the work of art not a model or a prototype but an index, a sign, an indicator of something else.

If we turn back now to history, the similarity and the difference of the positions are the following. In history too we can say—in any case, I say—that every institution of society is a historical creation, a creation of form, of an *eidos*, and that in this sense it is comparable to the work of art. But be careful; I am not saying that the institution of society is a work of art. I am saying that there is an aspect that is comparable: the creation of a form, the positing of an *eidos*, of an essence. Otherwise, the difference is infinite. And I am evoking only one aspect; a society is in reality neither a prototype nor a model but a form that makes possible an entire series of creations. The institution of a society—Chinese society, for example—is this global creation within which an infinity of creations become possible, whether it's Confucianism, the Tao, the Legalists, Chinese painting, forms of administration, etc. An institution of society cannot be for us a prototype or model, and thus we have to change the terms of comparison and look not toward the work of art but rather toward the work of thinking. When we approach a great work of thinking from the past—Plato, Aristotle, Kant, Hegel, Spinoza, Marx, Freud, etc.—what are we looking for? Not for the revelation of a definitive truth. Nor for only some particular information that we can find there when we want to know, like Bergson for example, *quid Aristoteles de loco sensuerit*. We want to see what great thinking is, how it works—but not only that. We want to understand how, all while deploying its own forms, it posits forms that are not its own and that refer to something other than itself. And that is its great difference from the work of art. But the work of thinking, when it deploys new forms, does this so that something should be thought which is exterior to itself and which at the same time is not independent of it. This is the mystery of the relationship of thinking with its object. One cannot say that this object would be independent of the forms by which it is thought; and one also cannot say that it would be fabricated through and through by thinking.

II. Seminar from November 17, 1982

This year we're talking about the creation of democracy in ancient Greece. In one sense, this has to do with the past. Why are we interested in the past and in this past in particular? Before going into this question, there's another one with respect to which it is good to lay down some points of reference: What connection, other than a passive one, can we have with the past? On what basis and by means of what can we understand it? There's a response as old as the question itself, proposed since antiquity, and which has made a comeback over the last fifteen or so years, one upheld by very serious and very important historians. Simplifying or perhaps caricaturing it a bit, one could summarize it in the following way: There cannot be any authentic historiography, any history in the sense of an inquiry into and acquaintance with the events of the past. All historiography is thus arbitrary. This is more or less the position of Paul Veyne in a very interesting and very informative book, *Writing History*.[12] For my part, I think, as such, that this is completely unacceptable in the sense that it drags in a certain direction some considerations that, taken up individually, are completely right. For, in the historical past there are facts that are more or less obscure or more or less certain, but ones about which a rational, reflective inquiry is entirely legitimate and possible. Such an inquiry is neither arbitrary nor any more open to criticism than, for example, the works of anthropologists and archaeologists who, after having uncovered bones dating from four million years ago or even more, try to reconstruct the hominids to whom they belong. Or ones who ask themselves why, approximately sixty or seventy million years ago, the great dinosaurs disappeared, which allowed mammals to develop and dominate the emergent lands. This is an inquiry about perfectly legitimate facts, and it's entirely the same in the case of history, where there are also things to establish: These cuneiform tablets clearly belong to such and such an era; therefore, these people wrote, wrote certain things, and one has to decipher them. And, in general, we know how to decipher them. That's surprising, but there are few writings that we haven't

---

12. *Eds.*: Paul Veyne, *Writing History: Essay on Epistemology*, trans. Mina Moore-Rinvolucri (Middletown: Wesleyan University Press, 1984).

been able to decipher or understand: Etruscan; the Linear A in Crete; the writing from Easter Island.... And when there isn't any writing, there remain artifacts of every order, tools, vases, and so on. All of that didn't fall from heaven, and it refers—rearwards, forwards, and laterally—to something else. Moreover, as soon as there are written traces—which has traditionally been the criterion for history as opposed to prehistory—we have documents, testimonies, which are in themselves more or less critical, more or less rigorous, but which we can talk about, in the end. The dates are in general relatively easy to establish. That the Battle of Marathon took place in 490 BC, nobody, not Paul Veyne any more than anyone else, contests. By contrast, for a long while historiography situated the destruction of Corinth by Mummius in 148 BC, and it was only around the middle of the nineteenth century that we showed that it took place in 146. For all of these facts, all these events, all these acts—which are what the question of "how things really happened" focuses on (which, according to the great nineteenth-century German historian Leopold von Ranke, is the question that defines the very object of history)—the inquiry has a meaning.[13] And the responses aren't much more uncertain than for other branches of knowledge, including physics.

Yet, the true question obviously isn't there. There remains the exploitation of this extraordinary mass of facts and documents, with respect to which it's necessary to choose, to sort, to hierarchize, to interpret. This work doesn't have, so to speak, an end, even materially. Even now, on a terrain as worked over and revisited as the history of ancient Greece and Rome—and using texts that have been available for a long time—we manage to extract new information, sometimes allowing for corrections to be made. Moreover, the appearance of new manuscripts can change very many things, like the papyri discovered at Herculaneum in the eighteenth century or in Egypt in

---

13. *Eds.*: In the preface of his first major work, Leopold von Ranke formulated the principle that the role of history is neither to judge the past nor to prepare for the future, but to say, *wie es eigentlich gewesen ist*, "what really happened." See Leopold von Ranke, *History of the Latin and Teutonic Nations (1494–1514)*, trans. G. R. Dennis (London: George Bell and Sons, 1909). Arnaldo Momigliano detected in this statement an echo of Lucian of Samosata, *How to Write History*, 39. See Paul Veyne, *Did the Greeks Believe in Their Myths? An Essay on the Constitutive Imagination*, trans. P. Wissing (Chicago: University of Chicago Press, 1988), p. 109. We can also see hints of Thucydides, *History of the Peloponnesian War*, II, 48, 3: See the citation of Konrad Repgen (1982) made in Moses I. Finley, *Ancient History: Evidences and Models* (New York: Viking Press, 1986), p. 116, note 5; and, moreover, pp. 7–66 are particularly relevant to all the issues dealt with in this seminar. An English translation of Ranke's preface is found in Fritz Stern, *The Varieties of History: From Voltaire to the Present* (New York: Random House, 1973), pp. 55–58.

the nineteenth. And when we move on to the history of modern Europe, the documentary sources become nearly unexploitable. In a country like France, we will find municipal archives, land registries, or notarized acts from at least the eighteenth century. So, if you're making an economic and social history and you are trying to establish the Rouennaise standard of living at the start of the eighteenth century, you'll go and page through the notarized acts, draw out the dowry amounts, and so on. But you don't purely and simply go and recopy all the documents; you go and choose. How, and on what basis? The criteria of choice will depend on the interpretation which precedes and accompanies them. (This is a commonplace in epistemology, but it's necessary to repeat it.) For example, a Marxist historiographer—or the clichéd picture of a Marxist historiographer—preoccupies himself above all with collecting facts that will allow him to arrive at a conclusion about the state of the productive forces, the relations of production, the economic relations, the influence exerted by the economic facts on the remainder of social life, and so on. If one has another point of view, mine for example, then we will above all be interested in another question, only a part of which is the establishment of economic realities (which is in no way privileged, even if it is important), and one will seek to reconstitute the significations incarnate in the institutions of a society, which means the constitution of its proper world, whether it's a matter of ancient Greece, medieval France, contemporary Russia, or of an archaic society, per the case. Certainly, as those who have read me a bit know, the proper world of a society also includes for me its functioning; and these significations always also include a dimension that is ensemblist-identitarian, which means functional and instrumental. Entering into this are the production and the reproduction of material life. But in the end, all of that is, if I may say so, subordinate to my central preoccupation: reconstituting the significations and the institutions in which these significations are incarnate, by means of which each society constitutes itself as society and constitutes its world proper, which makes it such that it is classical Hebrew society, classical Greek society, or contemporary French society, and not a different one, no matter which.

How to try to reconstitute these significations? We will come back to this, but it's evident that here is where the radical skeptic or relativist jumps in and says: This reconstitution-restoration (which are two very unfortunate words, as I will show in a moment) can only be wholly arbitrary. This is where the slide starts happening. This reconstitution—which is in fact much more than a reconstitution—certainly depends decisively on the point of view of the one who "reconstitutes," and this is so to a degree wholly different than in any other science. But even in physics, for example, one can hold, and I for my part would hold, that there is also an interdependency between the categories of the scientist and the object on which he works. The latter isn't just given without further ado; it isn't organized by itself and from itself, to speak the language of the physicist. This dependency is even more decisive in the domain of history, but this does not mean that what I provisionally call "reconstitution" would be arbitrary. And this is so for two essential reasons. First, because a serious historian cannot say just whatever. Even if there is a large number of possible reconstitutions of significations of a society, a great variety of interpretations, which depend enormously in each case on the era when they are made—which is just another way of citing their dependency with respect to the one who enacts them—some limits are laid down by the material itself. Hence, nobody has yet come out and said that the Incan Empire is the prototype of democracy. Even so, in this same class of assertions we'd have to be careful since we've heard it said recently, in certain Parisian milieus, that Athenian democracy was the prototype of totalitarianism. It's true that this has to do more with the advertising industry than with thought or than with historical work. Remember that historical material, even if it says nothing rigorously certain about significations, assuredly is not silent.

On the other hand, to pretend that every reconstitution is arbitrary amounts to forgetting that the discussion—i.e. the confrontation between the interpretations of the significations of a past society—is precisely the condition for a better understanding. The situation here is the same as in many other domains of knowledge, where we are never dealing with the rigorous correctness aimed at, say, by mathematicians. Even in physics the opinions, the *doxai*, confront each other, without leaving us in arbitrariness. And a philosophical discussion is not a discussion between arbitrary points of view. Certainly, there have been people who'll say, who'll hold, for example, that all philosophies are equally valid. Why? Because they always have in mind the paradigm, the model—a false model—of an ideal rigor that mathematicians would supposedly possess; and this would imply that, as soon as philosophers discuss a problem, oppose one another, or diverge, all these debates have no authentic signification, with each person just expressing his point of view or whatever happens across his mind, without any possibility of deciding between them. It's a perspective that, once again, is perfectly false since it's enslaved to a narrowly scientific conception of knowledge. There is a possible and fruitful philosophical discussion; there is, at least we may hope, a possible and fruitful political discussion; and there is also a possible, pertinent, and fruitful discussion about the significations of a past society. We'll have a certain number of them, moreover, in the course of this year, and thus we will attempt to prove motion by walking.

For now I'll take up just one single example, which will return constantly during the seminars and the discussions that follow, which is the question of the individual in ancient Greek society, i.e. the category, the entity, the *eidos*, the form "individual," meant in a strong sense, in a modern sense. I already spoke about it last time and also last year. The discussion starts in the eighteenth century, with Adam Ferguson; it's made explicit by Benjamin Constant and then taken up again by Fustel de Coulanges in his *The Ancient City*, which asserts that the ancient Greek world was unfamiliar with what we call the individual, the latter being entirely absorbed by the collectivity. This is, in my view, a completely erroneous position; but we will try to discuss it, to look at the arguments from these people and those, and to show that we can reflect on this subject without playing heads or tails, and without choosing based on our personal preferences when deciding if there existed in ancient Greece something corresponding to what we call the individual in the strong sense.

There you have what could serve as an objection to this idea of the necessarily arbitrary character of all historical reconstitution. But there is still one other critique that I would like to mention briefly. It pertains to what has been called for thirty years now "the hermeneutical position," which goes back in what's essential to certain modern theologians (principally Schleiermacher), but which in recent times is above all associated with the name of the German philosopher Gadamer. (There are, I believe, some works of his translated into French, like *Truth and Method*.[14]) This position involves a full recognition of what one calls the "hermeneutic circle," which means that one who wants to interpret something—and here, it is essentially a matter of texts—never starts with an empty or virgin mind, and is always already within a certain "preconception," to use a term from Heidegger, to whom Gadamer was in a sense

---

14. *Eds.*: See Hans-Georg Gadamer, *Vérité et méthode. Les grandes lignes d'une herméneutique philosophique*, trans. Pierre Fruchon, Jean Grondin, and Gilbert Merlio (Paris: Seuil, 1976), in English as *Truth and Method*, 2nd revised edition, trans. revised by Joel Weinsheimer and Donald G. Marshall (London: Bloomsbury Academic, 2004). Also see the essays collected in Hans-Georg Gadamer, *L'Art de comprendre: Ecrits I et II*, trans. M. Simone et al. (Paris: Aubier Montaigne, 1982). For a complete list of Gadamer's work translated into French, see Catharin Collobert, ed., *L'Avenir de la philosophie est-il grec?* (Québec: Fides, 2002), pp. 230–231; and this work includes the French translation of a 1972 presentation, translated into English as Hans-Georg Gadamer, "The Relevance of Greek Philosophy for Modern Thought," *South African Journal of Philosophy*, 6:2 (1987), pp. 39–42, as well as studies on Gadamer (by Y. Lafrance, T. Grondin, F. Renaud). On the origins of modern hermeneutics, see André Laks and Ada Neschke, eds., *La Naissance du paradigme herméneutique (Schleiermacher, Humboldt, Boeckh, Droysen)* (Lille: PU Septentrion, 1991).

very close. And it's by means of this preconception that he approaches a text and makes it speak in a certain way. But the text resists and speaks perhaps in a different way than as imposed by the preconception, in such a way that the interpreter is led to modify it, to go back over the texts starting from this other preconception. As such, this circular movement gets set up between preconception of the interpreter and signification of the text, in the grip of which one always remains. This is a position that we are not going to refute here, and which moreover one cannot refute because it expresses something true and important. Put simply, what differentiates us in our work from such an outlook is, first of all, that the latter is concerned with *isolated* works within a tradition. It isn't clear that what is thus described, which holds for example when you approach one author, would hold in the same way if you were to approach a whole society, and even a whole tradition, and a tradition which is your own. And further, above all, hermeneutics, properly speaking, operates only on what one may call works and discursive works in particular. Yet—and I'm moving immediately into the position that will underlie all I'll say to you this year—what is important to us is not simply an interpretation of words but the project of total understanding (and I insist on the term "project"). Our interest goes beyond simple interpretation, which means beyond a simply theoretical task. When we approach the birth of democracy and philosophy, what is important to us, to express it briefly, is our own activity and our own transformation. And it's in this sense that the task we are undertaking can be called a political task. Put differently, if someone asks us, do you want to understand the ancient Greek world, then we will respond that, certainly, we want to understand it so as to understand it. We've thus made it such that understanding or knowing is already an end in itself, which doesn't seek further justification. But this coexists with understanding so as to take action and to transform ourselves. At the limit, even if at the end of this journey we remain the same, we won't be entirely so, since we will know or we will believe we know why we have decided to remain the same.

How and on what basis is there understanding? Certainly, at the start—and here we meet with the hermeneutic circle again—we will try to understand the ancient Greek world on the basis of what we ourselves are. But here the circle refracts and multiplies, becomes something more and other than a circle. It isn't even a torus; I don't know what topological figure one would need to invent here. For, it turns out that in the particular case of ancient Greece, what we are is inclusive, in a sense, of this object that we are going to examine. What we are, after all, is also our history; and it's on that basis itself and on that of its present result that we wish to think. This is just one of the aspects of the complexity of the question since—and I will return to this at length—this object itself, this history of Greece that starts with Greece, is what created this project of understanding that we are taking upon ourselves today. Put differently, we also want to understand how the very possibility of understanding in history was created, i.e. how it is, from an eidetic point of view, if I may call it that, that there appeared and came to fruition for the first time—for better or for worse, it's not important—<this absolutely new project, namely of understanding one's own history in order to transform oneself. We clearly see here what separates our task from every hermeneutical practice> and particularly from the grand interpretive traditions of the monotheistic religions. They find their boundaries explicitly posited for them in foundational texts. These are boundaries not to be transgressed, i.e. boundaries that determine them in themselves as interpretive efforts. I want to say here that for someone who is doing interpretation at the most elevated conceivable level, but who is interpreting *as* Jewish, *as* Christian, or *as* Muslim the Old Testament, the New Testament, or the Koran, then their interpretation cannot in any case be radical since a question remains forbidden to them by the very nature of their task and of their intention, a question that cannot and must not be posed. This is the question of the ultimate origin of meaning. The interpreted text presents itself as a source of meaning, as an assurance that with it things reach an end because behind the text's scribes, prophets, evangelists, and apostles there lies the source of all meaning become word. Here, therefore, there is a radical limit that rightly distinguishes a work of interpretation—however rich, subtle, and audacious it may be, like those of the Jewish, with the Talmud and Kabbalah, and the Christian traditions—from this project of understanding, which is at once radical and practical, in which we want to be engaged.

Finally, here's a last difference. In the hermeneutical perspective as Gadamer sees it and as it is generally seen, there is simply at best a discovery—or "unveiling," as Heidegger would say—of the meaning of the text by means of the interpreter's preconceptions and a discovery of the interpreter's preconceptions by means of the meaning that these preconceptions have allowed one to discover. But, in a certain sense, one can say that everything is there from the start, even if—at least this is how things are presented—there is in effect some work, some production of the meaning. However, the project of understanding that I speak about—and I contend moreover that things happen and have always happened this way, whether or not people have known it—contains, or should contain, at risk of being trivial, a moment of creation. We want to grasp this historical object, for example the Greek world, beyond the details, fragmentary connections, and trivialities pertaining to the ensemblist-identitary; we want to grasp it in its significations and its institution. It's thus infinitely complex (it's also fantastically polyphonic, but this is a different aspect). It's not just an assemblage of stones, unless it's refined stones, stones that speak, i.e. texts, acts, and so on. And regarding this object, as with every other analogous historical object moreover, we can ultimately say what Heraclitus said regarding the god of Delphi, namely that he "neither speaks nor conceals, but signifies."[15] And this is doubtless true of every object, which never says anything in an immediately transparent way. But in the end, this is true *par excellence* of a historical object, a historical universe: it does not conceal, it does not speak, it signifies. But what does it signify?

We cannot grasp this signification—or rather this magma of significations—except by positing an imaginary schema, or at least the matrix of such a schema, which will give to this historical object its inconceivable polyphonic unity, which will give back meaning to an innumerable host of manifestations, and which will make things visible that without it would remain invisible.[16] And this operation is never a reproduction nor a tracing of the object but a re-creation that, all while remaining related to the historical object, makes it appear anew to us in a sense that is full—meaning neither exhaustive nor rigorously demonstrable—as a world of significations. It's thus a creation by means of our capacity to posit a matrix of imaginary schemas, a matrix which exists in an otherwise indefinable, indescribable connection (some kind of relation, adequation, or fecundation) with what presents itself to us at first as a mass of materials that, again, do not conceal, do not speak, but signify. And

---

15. *Eds.*: Hermann Diels and Walter Kranz, eds., *Die Fragmente der Vorsokratiker* (Berlin: Weidmannsche Verlagsbuchhandlung, 1952), DK 22B93. Note that the Diels and Kranz volume provides the Greek text and German translation. Here and in subsequent seminars, it will be referred to as DK, followed by the section number corresponding to the thinker (e.g., 22 for Heraclitus), followed by a letter ("A" refers to testimonials, "B" to fragments, and "C" to imitations), followed by the fragment number. The English anthology by G. S. Kirk, J. E. Raven, and M. Schofield, eds., *The Presocratic Philosophers*, 2nd edition (Cambridge: Cambridge University Press, 2007), provides the Greek text along with the historical and critical elements, making it an indispensable tool. A French version (without the Greek) of the Diels–Kranz has appeared through the work of Jean-Paul Dumont, with the collaboration of Daniel Delattre and Jean-Louis Poirier, as *Les Présocratiques* (Paris: Gallimard, 1988), and is accompanied by an abridged version, *Les Écoles présocratiques* (Paris: Gallimard, 1991). Some of its translations have been debated, but this work is useful to those who cannot access the German work. Among the older works, the most useful remains John Burnet, *Early Greek Philosophy*, 4th edition (London: A. and C. Black, 1930).
16. *Trans.*: On Castoriadis's use of the term "magma" to characterize the non-deterministic nature of some levels of being and of social meaning, see Cornelius Castoriadis, "The Logic of Magmas and the Question of Autonomy," in *The Castoriadis Reader*, trans. David A. Curtis (Oxford: Blackwell, 1997), pp. 290–318.

what they signify is what we'll try to specify in a concrete way in our work this year. Nevertheless, to allow you to see somewhat better what I mean, I would like briefly to give you two examples at this time, and this is only so as to facilitate understanding, not to discuss them for themselves.

When we move into the heart of the matter and we leave behind, as Hegel might say, "the forecourt of the temple," I will speak to you about what I call the primary imaginary grasp of the world for the Greeks, which is there before philosophy and democracy, and which forms the nucleus of the Greek constitution of the world. Everything said by mythology and the Homeric poems takes its point of departure from within an understanding of the world as incomprehensible, from the world as chaos, as creating itself against the backdrop of chaos and on that basis becoming partially a cosmos (which means order, ordered universe) in which the understanding of the incomprehensible fully recovers its rights since the cosmos itself has at first no meaning, in the human and anthropological acceptation of the term. Speaking in a brief way, it isn't made for man, nor, for all that, against man. It's there, it has its order, and man is born and dies within it. And when he dies, that's the end. When we return to speak about this, I will do my best to show you that this really is the Greek first grasp of the world, and that a mass of texts or demeanors amply manifests it. And since those among you who have read me will perhaps say, "All this adheres too well to what you yourself think," we will return to discuss this.

The second example has to do with the other pole of interest, namely the political institution, and thus democracy. Very many aspects of it are already well known. Nevertheless—and I say this without arrogance—what is always striking to me (as I am neither an archaeologist nor a historian and I'm not someone who has discovered any new facts) is people's capacity to remain blind to the signification of what they have in front of their eyes. We may recall, of course, "The Purloined Letter" by Edgar Allan Poe. It's just like that for plenty of contemporary phenomena, for example the Russian military industry; a manifest fact is there but nobody notices its whole signification. They'll tell you, "Ah, you're talking about the Russian military *industry*; you're falling into economism!"[17] It's the same for a multitude of things having to do with Greek democracy. That's the case with the *graphē paranomōn*, which is a very important institution and one we'll come back

---

17. *Eds.*: See Cornelius Castoriadis, *Devant la guerre, 1, Les réalités* (Paris: Fayard, 1981), now also found in *Guerre et théories de la guerre* (Paris: Éditions du Sandre, 2016), pp. 71–348. — *Trans.*: The first section of *Devant la guerre* is translated into English as Cornelius Castoriadis, "Facing the War," trans. Joe Light, *Telos*, 46 (1980), pp. 43–61.

to revisit. People have been quite aware of it for a long time.[18] But we had to wait for Moses Finley to speak of it anew in his book on Greek democracy for the extent to which it is an extraordinary, fundamental institution to be clearly seen.[19] What does it involve? Every Athenian citizen may propose a law at the people's assembly, and the latter can potentially approve it. But any other citizen may subsequently haul the citizen author of the proposition before a tribunal and get him condemned for having led the sovereign body (the *ekklēsia*, the people's assembly) to vote in an unjust law. That's the *graphē paranomōn*. This is an extraordinary vacillation, an enigma of democracy, of an *autonomous* society! The fact was there, but nobody before Finley had seen its profound signification. We could also add other characteristics to those he indicates, and particularly the fact that this procedure refers to an explicit conception of democracy as a regime lacking any norm exterior to itself, in any case no legislative political norm. It thus falls on the citizens not only to make the law but to respond to the question: What is a just law, a good law? And this happens without them cracking open any sacred book or listening to a prophet; there is no prophet. Nor—and this is very surprising—do they consult the oracle. They consult the Delphic oracle to know what actions are necessary to undertake or not, e.g. to organize an expedition, to build a city, to choose where to build it, and so on. But they never had the idea of asking what law to establish.[20] Never. Now, based on all that, I would try to pull out

---

18. *Eds.*: Gustave Glotz, in *The Greek City and Its Institutions*, trans. N. Mallinson (New York: Routledge, 1996 [first French edition 1928]), was one of the first to focus on the importance of the *graphē paranomōn*, "the public indictment against bills contrary to the laws," as a "brake" that the Athenian democracy could impose on itself (see Glotz, *The Greek City*, pp. 125–128, 134, and especially 178–180). These pages can be compared with the rather trivial remarks of George Grote, *A History of Greece, Volume V* (London: John Murray, 1888), pp. 375–378.
19. *Eds.*: See Moses I. Finley, *Democracy Ancient and Modern*, revised edition (New Brunswick: Rutgers University Press, 2018), which is preceded in its French translation by an essay by Pierre Vidal-Naquet, which can be found in English as "The Tradition of Greek Democracy," *Thesis Eleven*, 60:1 (2000), pp. 61–86. Finley refers there to the "fundamental study" by Hans J. Wolff, "'Normenkontrolle' und Gesetzesbegriff in der attischen Demokratie," in *Sitzungsberichte der Heidelberger Akademie der Wissenschaften, Philosophisch-historische Klasse 1970* (Heidelberg: Carl Winter, 1970).
20. *Eds.*: In the archaic period, some texts, for example the "constitutional law" of Dreros (see note 42, p. 42), connect the law to the gods; but it is always the citizens, or rather the city, that decides on these laws. Herodotus, *Histories*, I, 65 reports on the tradition whereby the laws of Sparta were dictated to Lycurgus by the Pythia but were not a manifestation of divine intervention. However, many cities could seek endorsement of a law at the sanctuary at Delphi. Regarding the meaning that should be attributed to this process, see Marie Delcourt, *L'Oracle de Delphes* (Paris: Payot, 1955), pp. 114–115.

and reconstitute a host of significations that I consider as absolutely essential, as central for the idea of democracy and the project of an autonomous society. Here again, it would be only too easy—I want to anticipate this—to oppose me by saying, "You are doing nothing but finding what you cherish there, your own thinking," and so on. Certainly. Except that what matters to me—and this is why I am talking with you about imaginary schemas that one must posit as a moment of creation in this project of global understanding—is something that isn't given directly nor indirectly anywhere in the texts; it's precisely this contact that I am going to try to establish between chaos and democracy. According to this thesis, the primary imaginary grasp of the world as un-meaning and the absence of a transcendent source of meaning or of the law or the norm liberates the Greeks and allows them to create the institutions in which men give themselves, precisely, their own norms. In my view this is the heart of the matter. Perhaps it's completely false. But in any case, it's the schema, which no text gives nor could give, by means of which I am trying to grasp this historical moment.

Our work will thus have a strange status. It will be historical, without being so in the technical sense nor even in the profound sense of the term; it will also be theoretical, interpretive, and even more so political since on the whole the question is always: What interest does this have for us? And doubtless, in the end, it will also be something other than all of that or than the simple assemblage of all of that.

Let's go back to the question about why to reexamine, why to re-reflect on this tradition, and in particular on its moment of origin. There are two massive facts. I entitled my seminars this year "creation of democracy and philosophy," and I should have in fact entitled them "the creation of politics and philosophy in ancient Greece" since that's what they're about, and I will explain myself on this point now. As long as we are interested in philosophy, on the one hand, and democracy and politics, on the other, we are trying to revert to the very origin of these historical creations. Does this return to the origin of a phenomenon, of a creation, really teach us anything about its content? This is yet another question we will have to bear in mind and that we will be able to discuss in depth only at the end. That said, is there justification for situating this origin somewhere? Is there justification for speaking of a creation of philosophy and democracy—or, more exactly and more profoundly, in my view, of politics—in Greece? Those who took my seminars last year are familiar with the key features of my response: by politics, we mean neither court intrigues, nor the maneuverings of what we today stupidly call party politics—next March's municipal elections, for example, or things of that sort—nor even certain social conflicts that surpass group interest to attain a larger expression, wherein different groups try to modify their status in society, their economic position, and to correct certain injustices. We understand by politics an activity aiming at the institution of society as such. And, regarding such an explicit and autonomous activity, we do not know of—at least I do not know of—any example before ancient Greece. It is there that common affairs and the law become for the first time an object of collective activity that is explicit and, if I may say so, reflective in the sense that this activity is discussed as such. It's discussed not in its modalities, in its means, in its technical aspects, but in its very ends. This oscillation between politics and democracy—an oscillation or hesitation not in my mind but in the choice of the seminars' title—is easily understandable. Why? Because, evidently, politics conceived in this way cannot be dissociated from the fact that the collectivity decides to take in hand its own affairs, and not only the day-to-day affairs but what one might call in current language its legislation, which means, finally, its institution. The fact that this putting into question of the already-given institution, this taking in hand of instituting activity, remains partial—as has always been the case, by the way—and the fact that certain parts of the institution didn't get touched by this activity is absolutely evident and poses a problem. This problem is always with us, for that matter.

This is what we might call a first birth of politics, a first moment of its history. We may summarize it thus: Everybody has their word to speak regarding the law. It seems self-evident for us; but it's not self-evident in other societies and can even appear there as criminal or aberrant, or an indicator of psychosis. For the first time, this moment emerges, asserts itself, and gets incorporated to a considerable extent.

There is thus this first massive fact. The other one is, of course, the birth of philosophy, which means the birth of explicit interrogation calling into question the instituted representation about how the world is made and what the place of man or human society is in the world. This interrogation attains from the outset an absolute radicality that, as such, has never been surpassed; and for that matter it's hard to see how it could be. I say radicality because it calls into question not the content of this or that social representation, but the very status of representation, the very idea of knowledge and the foundation of knowledge, and through this, from the outset, grand interrogations that are still with us were articulated. I hold very strongly that they will always be with us as interrogations, not as problems that will one day have their answer.

We insist on this point: This specific relationship between the birth of philosophy and the birth of politics constitutes in no way, as one might believe, a common topic in the historiography of Greece. Historians are far from having measured all its depth. They've almost always confined themselves to juxtaposing, i.e. there's supposed to have been epic poetry, and then democracy, tragedy, philosophy, and then this and that. It's the Greek miracle. To which others have responded, "There are no miracles in history," and they cite the Babylonians, the Egyptian influences, and so on. But the deep, internal connection between these elements, in particular the inseparability of the birth of philosophy and of politics, or again of democracy and of tragedy, has generally remained unnoticed until the last few decades. It's necessary to emphasize in this respect the importance of the works of Jean-Pierre Vernant.[21] We will have to discuss them since, here again, unfortunately or fortunately, I find fault with the way in which the connection is made, particularly when he says that reason is the "daughter of the city."[22] For Vernant

21. *Eds.*: By 1981, Jean-Pierre Vernant had already published some of his main works: *The Origins of Greek Thought*, trans. anonymous (Ithaca: Cornell University Press, 1982); *Myth and Thought Among the Greeks*, trans. Janet Lloyd and Jeff Fort (New York: Zero Books, 2006); co-authored with Pierre Vidal-Naquet, *Myth and Tragedy in Ancient Greece*, trans. Janet Lloyd (New York: Zero Books, 1990); *Cunning Intelligence in Greek Culture and Society*, trans. Janet Lloyd (Chicago: University of Chicago Press, 1991); *Religion grecque, religions antiques* (Paris: Maspero, 1976); *Religions, histoires, raisons* (Paris: Maspero, 1979); and the volume co-edited with Marcel Detienne, *The Cuisine of Sacrifice among the Greeks*, trans. Paula Wissing (Chicago: Chicago University Press, 1989).
22. *Eds.*: "Greek reason is the type of reason that makes it possible to act in a positive, deliberate, and methodical manner upon men, but not to transform nature. In its limitations, as well as in the innovations it brought about, it was truly the product of the city" (Vernant, *Myth and Thought*, p. 397). A similar formulation appears, slightly modified, at Vernant, *Origins*, p. 132. And Vernant, *Origins*, pp. 124–125 indicates that Gregory Vlastos is responsible for establishing that the social experience is what "provided cosmological thought with the model of an egalitarian law and order in place of the all-powerful rule of the monarch." See especially Vlastos's 1947 essay, "Equality and Justice in Early Greek Cosmologies," in David J. Furley and Reginald E. Allen, eds., *Studies in Presocratic Philosophy, Volume I: The Beginnings of Philosophy* (London: Routledge and Keagan Paul, 1970), pp. 57–91. See, however, Werner Jaeger's comments on the "projection of the life of the city-state upon the life of the universe," in *Paideia: The Ideals of Greek Culture, Volume I – Archaic Greece: The Mind of Athens*, 2nd edition, trans. Gilbert Highet (Oxford: Oxford University Press, 1945), p. 161. See also the texts cited in note 268, p. 173 (Seminar X). On the accord between the Ionian "cosmological model" and the Cleisthenian "political model," see Jean-Pierre Vernant, "Space and Political Organization in Ancient Greece," in *Myth and Thought*, pp. 235–259; and see the essay by Pierre Lévêque and Pierre Vidal-Naquet, *Cleisthenes the Athenian: An Essay on the Representation of Space and Time in Greek Political Thought from the End of the Sixth Century to the Death of Plato*, trans. David A. Curtis (Amherst: Humanity Books, 1996). Vernant points out that these authors claim, like himself, that "Anaximander's type of geometric view of the world coincided with the political model of a city governed by *isonomia* such as the one Cleisthenes attempted to bring into being in Athens" (*Myth and Thought*, p. 247). M. Detienne went back to the same period to find the source of the idea of the city governed by isonomy, emphasizing the notion of "centrality" (*meson*). See Marcel

there would first be the political creation and, in a certain sense, the birth of philosophy would be a product, in the vulgar sense—a consequence—of the constitution of the political community. I will discuss this point in detail since it's very important. Let's say immediately that, for me, the constitution of the political community is already philosophy in action, which means that Vernant's phrasing applies only if we take philosophy in a relatively derivative or secondary sense. It will thus be necessary for us to reconstitute this political-philosophical connection, on the basis of an imaginary schema that will give it all its meaning.

There are two remarks to close with, ones I already made but which I'm keen to bring back. First, regarding democracy or politics we'll certainly find equivalents or approximations of democratic forms elsewhere than in ancient Greece or in prior periods, for example the democratic assemblies of warriors in certain tribes.[23] They do indeed hold discussions (very little, by the way, since they have an admirable terseness about them), they consult one another, and, in a sense, they decide based on a consensus. Likewise, we will find this in certain rural communities, like the *mir*, which greatly interested the old Marx, or the *zadruga*, or sometimes in Indian villages.[24] And doubtless there

---

Detienne, "En Grèce archaïque: géométrie, politique et société," *Annales*, 20:3 (1965), pp. 425–441, which analyzes, in particular, the question of deliberation in the *Iliad*. We will see in Seminar X (and in Castoriadis, "Greek *Polis*," pp. 101–107) the analogies as well as the differences between these analyses and those proposed by Castoriadis.

23. *Eds.*: These questions have attracted the attention of excellent authors, from Tacitus to Engels, and were the object of numerous anthropological works during the nineteenth and twentieth centuries. These have recently been rediscovered. See especially Marcel Detienne, ed., *Qui veut prendre la parole?* (Paris: Seuil, 2003), a work in which both the interest in and the limits of a certain form of comparativism are clearly shown. Detienne praises an anthropology "that feels completely free in going from culture to culture, drawing profit from any place where flowers are gathered and grow" in order to "escape from the claustrophobic space between the ceaseless repetition of the 'Greek Miracle' and the incurable obesity of 'Western Civilization'" (p. 12).

24. *Eds.*: On Marx and the Russian *mir*, see the texts on the rural commune and revolutionary perspectives in Russia: Karl Marx, "The Reply to Zasulich," in Teodor Shanin, ed., *Late Marx and the Russian Road: Marx and the 'Peripheries of Capitalism'* (New York: Monthly Review Press, 1983), pp. 123–124; see also Karl Marx and Friedrich Engels, "Preface to the Second Russian Edition of *The Manifesto of the Communist Party*," in Shanin, *Late Marx*, pp. 138–139. Engels alludes to the *zadruga* in Friedrich Engels, *The Origin of the Family, Private Property, and the State*, trans. Ernest Untermann (Chicago: Charles H. Kerr & Company, 1909), pp. 71–72. Let us remember that the Russian *mir* is a village community with a collective ownership of the land; the Balkan *zadruga* is a family group possessing communal economic activities. See Jean Gaudemet, *Les Communautés familiales* (Paris: Marcel Rivière, 1954), pp. 132–157. Since the nineteenth century, these two institutions

are lots of other cases. You'll find among these some collectivities that self-manage. What, then, makes the difference for what concerns us here? Life in such a collectivity is perhaps infinitely more agreeable or humane than—and perhaps it's more valuable in the absolute than—life in fifth-century Athens. It may be that an American Indian warrior, as a type of human individual, is absolutely unsurpassable (and I would be inclined to believe it). But that's not what I am talking about. In these self-managing communities, in which there is no differentiation of power between the dominators and the dominated, this self-management is carried out in a framework that's given once and for all, *ne varietur*, such that there's no question of modifying it. (Let's put aside, yet again, the question of the sexes, which is a dark history that is basically always getting sidestepped with regard to the Greeks, as for others.[25]) They manage the community as a function of the existing law. There's no question of explicitly having a legislative activity. Thus, when we're talking about democracy, let's have in mind not simply the existence of an assembly that deliberates and decides consensually, nor the absence of a domination in the factual sense of the term by a special group. The Greek creation of democracy, of politics, is a creation of an explicitly self-instituting activity of the collectivity.

We can make an analogous remark regarding philosophy. Speaking briefly, the interrogations that philosophical activity sustains are in a sense of course always there from as soon as there are human beings, and the response to these interrogations is supplied, as I already said, by the religious institution of society. We depend, moreover, on this response in order to reformulate the questions, which are never precisely made explicit. In this sense, one may say that religious thought is already a quasi-philosophic activity; but to call it philosophy would nevertheless be a terrible abuse of language since it's not properly a sort of critical activity. Elsewhere, outside of Greece, and emerging in approximately the same era—which Jaspers called *Achsenzeit*, i.e. the "axial age" of universal history between 800 and 200 BC, the time of the prophets in Israel, of Buddha in India, but also of the flourishing of Hindu philosophy and of Confucius in China—we have in other histories, in other traditions, particularly in India and China, something that is "like philosophy."[26] That's

---

have been the subject of numerous studies (particularly in Slavophile circles), which we will not be able to mention here.

25. *Eds.*: However, with respect to the considerable work conducted in the last twenty years on this issue, see the studies and the bibliography of Pauline Schmitt Pantel, *A History of Women in the West, I: From Ancient Goddesses to Christian Saints*, trans. Arthur Goldhammer (Cambridge, MA: Harvard University Press, 1992).

26. *Eds.*: Karl Jaspers, *The Origin and Goal of History*, trans. Michael Bullock (New Haven: Yale University Press, 1953). On the "Axial Age," see pp. 1–21 and 51–60.

indisputable. The subject is immense and would demand a separate discussion. But, briefly, what is it that differentiates this philosophy from that which was born in Greece and became, by means of European history, philosophy *tout court*? It's not simply the radicality of the interrogation. We'll also find some positions in the Daoist tradition, just as in Hindu philosophy, that are entirely as radical as certain Greek conceptions, i.e. a total critique of phenomena, of appearances, and extraordinarily subtle and very profound discussions about the arbitrary imposition by the subject and by language of distinctions and separations, organizations and pseudo-organizations onto a world that in itself knows nothing of them. There are, at that point, things that go just as far as one can go and that we cannot but admire. But this philosophy, at least in India—and in a completely different sense in China—remains in some sense a side activity. It's either a courtly philosophy, or a philosophy belonging to the sacerdotal class, or a philosophy of a solitary thinker. One never finds there the degree of implication in the activity of the social collectivity that one observes in Greece (even if, of course, there would be a lot to say about the whole social and political dimension of Confucian and Daoist movements in China). It's essentially at once speculative and, in India, complementary to sacred texts. Even when commentary gets very radical, i.e. even if it doesn't restrict itself to a simple interpretation of sacred texts as in other cases, it remains nevertheless an ancillary philosophy, to reemploy the medieval term. And I think that it's impossible to misrecognize the connection between this character of Hindu or Chinese philosophy—which, *in its own right*, as the English say, is a great philosophy—and the absence of a veritable movement of politics in these societies. For, they remained traditional societies, which at most experienced, as in China, only episodic, explosive social and political conflicts, which frequently took the form of peasant revolts and so on, but which were never articulated and never faced up in any direct way to the question of the institution of the political collectivity.

Questions

When you talk about a relationship between philosophy and politics in ancient Greece, you're referring above all to the fifth century, or even subsequently, to the Stoic schools and…

No, it's properly at that point that the relationship ceased to exist. I go back to the Presocratics and even before the Presocratics, to the Homeric poems. Here are some chronological points of reference. The moment when the songs that would become the Homeric poems were gathered and organized by one or two monumental poets is situated around the end of the eighth century BC. The Presocratics properly speaking, the very first of them, lived between the end of the seventh century and the first decades of the sixth. The famous eclipse that Thales would've predicted took place probably around 585. We thus have somewhat more than a century there where we find firstly Homer (and we're not going to ask whether there was one, two, or forty-eight Homers, which is a question that doesn't concern us directly). On the relationship between philosophy and politics, we will thus find some elements in Homer, in any case in the *Odyssey*, then others in Hesiod, and still others in the early fragments of the lyric poets, like in Sappho, which testify to a movement of representation and thought. We will also study the constitution of the cities according to a design famous even then, the signification of which has hardly been discussed from the point of view I take, namely that of the creation of the colonies. For, when one talks about the democratic movement, one is generally talking about Greek cities properly speaking or already established cities and the internal struggles that unfolded there. We already have an inscription from Chios that we can date to 570 BC, which talks about a *boulē* in a context that allows for understanding that it was a council elected by the *dēmos*.[27] After the colonization of the coasts of Asia Minor, which goes back to the eleventh century, there is a second large wave of colonization, directed above all towards the West (Sicily, Magna Grecia, and so on), where the first foundations date from 750. Yet, and this is most important, these Greek

---

27. *Trans.*: See inscription 8 in Russell Meiggs and David Lewis, eds., *A Selection of Greek Historical Inscriptions: To The End of the Fifth Century B.C.* (Oxford: Clarendon, 1969), pp. 14–19. For an English translation and study, see James H. Oliver, "Text of the So-Called Constitution of Chios from the First Half of the Sixth Century B.C.," *American Journal of Philology*, 80:3 (1959), pp. 296–301. — *Eds.*: The inscription known as the "Constitution of Chios" has been abundantly commented on since its discovery in 1907. A translation to French with commentary appears in Henri van Effenterre and Françoise Ruzé, *Nomina: Recueil d'inscriptions politiques et juridiques de l'archaïsme grec, I* (Rome: École française de Rome, 1994). With regard to the *boulē dēmosiē*, see Victor Ehrenberg, *The Greek State* (New York: W. W. Norton & Company, 1964), pp. 62–63 and notes pp. 266–267; and see also Anthony M. Snodgrass, *Archaic Greece: The Age of Experiment* (Berkeley: California University Press, 1981), p. 95. The idea that this was a "popular" council was called into question by Carmine Ampolo, in "La *boulē dēmosiē* di Chio: un consiglio 'popolare'?" *La Parola del passato*, 213 (1983), pp. 401–416, for whom the term *dēmosiē* simply means "public," an argument which has generally been found persuasive. Certain authors, all while accepting this critique, believe that it should not necessarily exclude the hypothesis of an early democratic experiment in Chios. See Eric W. Robinson, *The First Democracies: Early Popular Governments Outside of Athens* (Stuttgart: Franz Steiner, 1997), pp. 90–101.

colonies are not like the Phoenician colonies, or later the Jewish colonies of the diaspora, or even the Roman colonies, which are cases in which people carry with them the laws of their homeland. The Greeks, for their part, depart with some statues of their homeland's gods, they move in, and then they make their own laws or entrust that task to a foreign legislator. The movement of self-institution had thus already begun in the eighth century with colonization, which exists there as a first matrix for this self-positing of the political collectivity. On the question that interests us, there's a fascinating side to this phenomenon, but at the same time there's an enormous difficulty because the period is extremely obscure, the documents are very rare, and interpretive liberty—or even arbitrariness—in reconstruction becomes much greater. In any case, in my view the origin of the democratic *polis* is absolutely contemporary with the Homeric poems, i.e. with the time of their recording at least and not with the time the poet talks about, since that's a different story. On this point, I recommend to you to read an excellent little text by Pierre Vidal-Naquet, which was the preface to the paperback re-edition of the translation of the *Iliad* by Paul Mazon, which has some thirty pages that summarize the actual status of what has been called for two centuries "the Homeric question," and which talks also about the relationship of these poems to the society they describe.[28] You can read this very fine text at the same time as the Finley book that I spoke to you about already.[29]

We'll thus have to research the germs of democracy and of a reflexivity that calls into question the instituted representation going back even before the sixth century. The center of our interest this year will be the period from the Homeric poems to the fourth century (and especially philosophy there, i.e. Plato, Aristotle, and so on).

<Question about the possibility of understanding other societies.>

That's an enormous question. I can't talk about it now, but it's a subject that has preoccupied me for a long time. For now, I'll say simply that I believe that we can have understanding; and regarding what we don't understand, the

---

28. *Eds.*: Pierre Vidal-Naquet, "L'*Iliade* sans travesti," in *La Démocratie grecque vue d'ailleurs* (Paris: Flammarion, 1990), pp. 29–53. Also see, from the same author, *Le Monde d'Homère* (Paris: Perrin, 2002).
29. *Eds.*: Moses I. Finley, *The World of Odysseus*, 2nd edition (New York: Viking Press, 1965). One can find an annotated bibliography on Homer adapted to the French reader by Pierre Vidal-Naquet in the French translation: *Le Monde d'Ulysse*, trans. Monique Alexandre and Claude Vernant-Blanc (Paris: Seuil, 1990), pp. 223–244.

approach is: How is it that we can understand? I believe that there really is an access, which is not fallacious and is not arbitrary, not only to Eastern cultures but to primitive cultures and so on. That said, I do not think that an Aztec in the fourteenth century and someone Chinese from the same era would have attempted to achieve mutual understanding, one of the other. They could have had commercial or other types of relationships but would not have tried to achieve mutual understanding. For that matter, I also don't think that in our society this understanding of other societies would be evident for everyone. And what I've said here is perhaps a euphemism. Yet, it remains that this possibility, i.e. this willingness to understand other historical worlds—the will to go and look at how others live and not so as to say that they live like pigs or like savages—is itself one creation of our tradition, and we'll talk about it in relation to Herodotus, ethnography, and history. Why does our tradition give itself this possibility? First of all, because it breaks the total grip over us held by the imaginary significations of our society, in other words because there is from the start a relativizing of the world and of the institutions proper: We do things in this way; the barbarians do different things, differently. This is obviously just one condition of possibility; this will not allow us to truly understand. How do we get to that point? Ethnologists try to naturalize themselves into the cultures they study, to live on site. <I think that whatever> the radical skeptic <says>, there is no genuine solipsism of the interpreter; he can have an encounter with elements that were not in the corpus on which he was working at the start and which allow for a control. But all of that does not answer your question; these are nothing but common-sense considerations.

<Question about Popperian falsifiability.>

Sir Karl thought that because they did not answer to his criterion of falsifiability, certain disciplines such as psychoanalysis were not sciences. As for me, I would say the contrary of course, i.e. that it's precisely the very existence of psychoanalysis which condemns Popperian falsifiability, which is an impoverished and partial criterion without much interest. There are sensible discourses about which opinions differ, but which don't leave us with a throw of the dice nor with total arbitrariness. If you ask me in what case I would be ready to abandon my interpretation of ancient Greece, listen, it's horrible to say, but I can't see any case in which I'd abandon it. Perhaps under torture? More seriously, what strengthens me in this interpretation is that I find it fruitful. Every time I meet a new fact, or I happen upon a text that was unknown to me or about which I hadn't reflected, while being free of any desire to make them enter forcefully into my box, they pose perfectly sensible questions for me in relation to the central optic which is my own. You doubtless know what the partisans of the Ptolemaic theory did when it seemed contradicted by new observations of planetary movements. They added new cycles that we call epicycles. These supplementary hypotheses are the indicators of a moribund theory, even if in a sense it's the common lot of all scientific theories to fill out the starting hypothesis with complementary hypotheses. But as for what I'm concerned with, I don't believe I'm forced to have recourse to that.

III. Seminar from November 24, 1982

We will approach Homer today. We will have to go back and forth over things, sometimes making amplifications, which won't occur without repetition, and I request in advance that you excuse me. A preliminary methodological remark. You know this. It's a banality: The bibliography is immense; it has accumulated for two thousand years and continues to proliferate. Finley, in the preface to the latest edition of *The World of Odysseus*, observes that in twenty years the "swell of publications" in Homeric research has practically surpassed his capacities for reading.[30] He nevertheless believes he's read what's essential. I believe, I know, that I am far from having read not just "what's essential" but even just a good portion of the texts. Moreover, we're going to tackle a whole series of additional problems that are tied to the collectivity of discourse on Greece. I already mentioned one of them that's fundamental, i.e. the reinterpretation and, in the end, imposition of significations. It's an imposition that has nearly always been non-conscious, except perhaps in recent years and certainly in what we are trying to do here since we are starting out precisely from this idea of a reinterpretation, and we know that we are trying to re-create something. Within every era, of course, different ideological currents also coexist. If you read a certain set of recent literature on ancient Greece, you will behold, for example, that the constitution of the *polis* and of democracy comes down to an attempt to establish a *bürgerliche Gegenwart*, a "bourgeois" or "civic" presence.[31] We have here, in fact, a particularly subtle form of Marxism that I would call Lukácsian-Heideggerian. As for the other forms, the majority of Marxists will tell you that everything is explained by slavery. Let's not forget the professions, the philologists for example, without whom we couldn't say anything, but who sometimes say absolutely abominable things. There are also these surprising quarrels between archaeologists, philologists, historians, and sociologists. For example, and on the subject that concerns us today, take the one that began with Schliemann and his

---

30. *Eds.*: Moses I. Finley, *The World of Odysseus*, 2nd edition (New York: Penguin Books, 1979), pp. 9–11.
31. *Eds.*: Christian Meier, *The Greek Discovery of Politics*, trans. David McClintock (Cambridge, MA: Harvard University Press, 1990), pp. 53–81.

first excavations at Hisarlik in 1870. Up to his death in 1890 he remained persuaded that he'd found the vestiges of the world Homer described. This took place on a site near the entrance of the Dardanelles, where the ruins of some dozen cities have been unearthed. The stratigraphy was on the whole very well done, and this was one of the merits of Schliemann, who, as you know, was an amateur, a rich German merchant crazy about Homer who, against the positivist mentality of his era, wanted to show that the Homeric world had existed as it was described in the poems. Every time he discovered a new stratum, Schliemann sent letters everywhere proclaiming victory: "I've found Priam's treasure!" Then, he renewed the excavations and fell upon a more ancient stratum: "At last I've found the true Troy!" A German archaeologist, Dörpfeld, took over after the death of Schliemann, and the last great campaign of excavations was directed in the 1930s by Americans from the University of Cincinnati, with Blegen at the head, who later undertook excavations at Pylos in the Peloponnese.[32] Everything happened in this case as if certain archaeologists were rejecting the evidence, as if they had a *vested interest*, as one would say in English, i.e. a sort of particular interest that's very difficult to define—it's visibly neither financial nor professional—which was pushing them to show that what they had found corresponded well to the world described by Homer in the poems. And this was despite historical, philological, or sociological arguments that now abundantly prove—this is the dominant view among non-archaeologists—that the findings from Troy, Pylos, and so on—which certainly are very important, splendid, extremely rich with information (but that's not the question)—have nothing to do with the world described by Homer. It's not Agamemnon's treasure that Schliemann found at Mycenae; it's the treasure of a king of Mycenae.

 Beyond this first problem, the range of the interpretations extends, depending on the writer, from faith in the almost literal truth of the texts (which exists even now) to the total rejection of the accounts. We've also had since antiquity what we could call the "historical event" interpretation. With Euhemerus, who said that the gods were just superior men divinized after their death, the positivist type of interpretation began in the fourth to third century BC. It's the idea that all literary tradition, in particular the poetic, is only the embellishment, dilation, and deformation of a real core, of something that did actually take place. The relationship that then gets established between this dilation, deformation, or embellishment and this supposed real core will in a sense depend arbitrarily on the one who's talking. With regard to classical antiquity in general, you'll find the whole array of possible solutions,

---

32. *Eds.*: See Carl W. Blegen, *Troy and the Trojans* (London: Thames & Hudson, 1963).

from zero to infinity. Here's a single example so you see how far this can go. By around 1900, there were practically no more Plato dialogues. We have under Plato's name some forty texts, some of which are visibly inauthentic, i.e. pastiches written later which got included in the manuscript tradition. The beginning of the nineteenth century saw the birth and then assertion of the critical attitude, which rapidly became hypercritical, and the list of dialogues declared apocryphal lengthened little by little. Only exempted—and barely so—were the five or six that are cited by name by Aristotle ("like Plato said in the *Republic*," and so on). Despite everything, you couldn't declare that the *Republic* was inauthentic. Eventually, to get one's doctorate in philosophy in the nineteenth-century German university system there was a path entirely prepared, which was to demonstrate the inauthenticity of such and such Plato dialogue. That's when a more serious attitude appeared, founded on lexical and grammatical statistics, and they quickly ended up with the authenticity of nearly all the dialogues that were transmitted to us. This same method supplied the criteria for asserting the inauthenticity of a small number of dialogues, by showing where the pasticheur or plagiarist, trying to imitate Plato, slipped up or made a mistake.

In short, when you approach the literature concerning ancient Greece in general, and Homer in particular, you find yourself faced with an immense corpus, where opinions vary entirely on nearly all the imaginable subjects.[33] So it's necessary to form your own judgment, to inform yourself as best you can, and to take responsibility, even if you get denounced for having overlooked—which is completely possible after all—such and such decisive argument published in *Gnomon* in 1955.

Let's recall now some chronological points of reference. The first anchor—if one can call it that since very few things before the classical era are certain—is the arrival of the Greeks in Greece, which is important not, of course, from a racial or national point of view but because this collection of tribes, according to what we know, differed linguistically and culturally from the previous inhabitants. They brought with them a language, beliefs, and technical skills which make it such that we can speak of a new beginning, which evidently does not exclude contacts with the first occupants and even

---

33. *Eds.*: For Homer, see the very useful annotated bibliography cited above in note 29, p. 32. However, nothing can replace the great essay by Albin Lesky, *Homeros* (Stuttgart: A. Druckenmüller Verlag, 1967). Some substantial information on recent works can be found in the "Introduction" by editor Douglas L. Cairns, *Oxford Readings in Homer's* Iliad (Oxford: Oxford University Press, 2001); and see also the contributions in Robert Fowler, ed., *The Cambridge Companion to Homer* (Cambridge: Cambridge University Press, 2004).

presupposes (and I will come back to this) very important borrowings and no doubt also a mixture of populations to a good extent. It's a mixture perhaps preceded by another one, which arose in the course of the migration of the Greeks from out of the hypothetical formation place of Indo-European, probably somewhere to the north-east of the Black Sea, north of the Caucasus, and north-west of the Caspian Sea. In the course of this migration towards the south of the Balkan peninsula there were no doubt borrowings from other peoples, influences, and perhaps even additions and conglomerations. The dating of all of this got fairly shaken up some twenty-five years ago with the decipherment achieved by a non-philologist (which I point out just to be mean), i.e. the Englishman Michael Ventris, of a writing found on Cretan tablets—more tablets of the same sort were found later at Pylos in the Peloponnese—which we call Linear B. These tablets were dated to 1400 around the time of their discovery. And here, again, is a point that's worth mentioning, not only because it links up with what I said about the attitude of the different professions, but also because it's very beautiful from, let's say, an epistemological point of view. Why did Linear B remain for so long indecipherable? Due to the dominant ideology among philologists and historians as well as archaeologists, which was that the Cretan Minoan writing—and probably also the Mycenaean civilization—was pre-Greek, and that it wasn't Greeks who wrote those scripts. As you know, in cryptography, if you don't have a hypothesis about the language within which a script is written, you're entirely in the dark. They thus had these tablets in Linear B, and to decipher them it was necessary to start from a hypothesis about the language. Yet, one language was systematically excluded; it couldn't have been Greek. Things had been like that since Evans, the great archaeologist to whom we owe the discovery of the palace of Knossos. (You're aware that Evans's methods were criticized and that he was accused in particular of having taken certain liberties in his presentation of the results of the excavations.[34]) Thus, in 1952 Ventris, taking the view opposite to the generally admitted hypothesis, said: Let's suppose that it's Greek. And the decipherment was achieved (you can read its history in the Chadwick book); and it rather quickly met with

---

34. *Eds.*: A rather violent polemic (carried out in *Antiquity* and other specialized publications) was raised in the early 1960s by Leonard R. Palmer's critiques of the stratigraphy and datings by Evans. According to Palmer, Evans, reporting more than twenty years later on the notes taken by his assistant Duncan Mackenzie during the 1900 excavations, deliberately neglected, or erased, certain aspects of these notes. See Leonard R. Palmer and John Boardman, *On the Knossos Tablets* (Oxford: Clarendon, 1963); and see Jacques Raison, "Une controverse sur la chronologie cnossienne," *Bulletin de l'Association Guillaume Budé*, 3 (1961), pp. 305–319.

agreement from the specialists.[35] Even if lots of things remain obscure, as soon as one admits that it's Greek, the tablets make sense linguistically. Let's note as well, while I'm thinking about it, that it's a syllabic and not an alphabetic writing. So if one likewise takes into account a whole series of other archaeological givens, it dates back to the arrival of the Greeks in Greece in about the year 2000 BC (or 1950 according to Pierre Lévêque, and between 2100 and 1900 for others).[36] According to a contemporary Greek researcher, Sakellariou, there were perhaps two waves, with a first in about 2300–2100 and a second, more important one in the beginning of what we call the Middle Helladic, i.e. between 2000 and 1800.[37] In short, the Greeks probably settled in Greece in the beginning of the second millennium. A different civilization developed in Crete, i.e. the Minoan, and then in continental Greece after the sixteenth century and in Crete after the fifteenth century, i.e. the Mycenaean. This corresponds, no doubt, to a first cultural creation, but we cannot talk about that here. Let's simply point out two fundamental differences between this and classical Greece. The first is well attested; it has to do with social and political organization. The world that the tablets, above all those from Pylos, allow us to glimpse brings to mind an Asiatic type of monarchy. This is what has been called palatial civilization, with a monarch and an extremely important bureaucracy, with the administrative-political function of writing being distinctive there since it allows for control, i.e. for knowing what each village owes and what it must be supplied with. Beyond this initial difference, there's also another one, which is doubtless very considerable and has to do with religion. The question here is infinitely more obscure. One finds in the tablets, with about three or four exceptions, the names of nearly all the classical gods, even of those that were believed to have appeared very much later, like, for example, Dionysus. But the content of this religion is in all likelihood quite different from that of the classical religion or even the Homeric. The feminine figures—e.g. Sea Goddess, Earth Goddess—notably have a much greater importance there. This poses a considerable problem—but we

---

35. *Eds.*: See John Chadwick, *The Decipherment of Linear B* (Cambridge: Cambridge University Press, 1958); and Michael Ventris and John Chadwick, *Documents in Mycenaean Greek: Three Hundred Selected Tablets from Knossos, Pylos, and Mycenae* (Cambridge: Cambridge University Press, 1956).
36. *Eds.*: Pierre Lévêque, *The Greek Adventure: A Cultural and Historical Study of the Ancient Greeks*, trans. Miriam Kochan (Cleveland: World Publishing Co., 1968).
37. *Eds.*: Michel B. Sakellariou, *Le Peuplement de la Grèce et du bassin égéen aux hautes époques*, volume II: *Les Proto-Grecs* (Athens: Ekdotikē Athēnōn, 1980). On these questions, see the helpful contribution by Annie Schnapp-Gourbeillon, *Aux origines de la Grèce, XIIIe–VIIIe siècles avant notre ère: La genèse du politique* (Paris: Les Belles Lettres, 2002).

won't touch on it now—because the Greeks are Indo-Europeans; but the majority of Indo-European religions clearly privileged masculine divinities. This world was destroyed around the end of the thirteenth century, without us knowing exactly why.[38] It was destroyed in Pylos, in Mycenae about fifty years later, then in Crete. One of the Troys discovered on the supposed Iliadic site was also destroyed in this era, but it was a very small city, which could not correspond to the Homeric period. At that time, what we call the "Dark Ages" or the Hellenic Middle Age began, which runs from 1200 to the ninth to eighth century. We also have the periodization: Protogeometric (eleventh to tenth centuries); Geometric, properly speaking (ninth to eighth centuries); then Archaic Greece; and so on. As an aside, these periodizations are certainly very important from the archaeological point of view, but the archaeologists essentially base their work on the style of the objects they discover, especially ceramics, which is for us secondary relative to other elements that we want to take into consideration. Still, let's also note that in this period that which one traditionally called the first Greek colonization took place (migration is what one would call it today). It's probably then that the Greeks occupied, which they hadn't yet done, the eastern islands of the Aegean Sea and in any case the coast of Anatolia. This colonization thus took place in the eleventh and tenth centuries. The second wave, the genuine Greek colonization, which saw the Greeks swarm over practically the whole perimeter of the Mediterranean, begins in the eighth century; the first Greek colonies in southern Italy and in Sicily are from before 750. And in fact—a very important fact—the least uncertain dating we can do today for the Homeric poems (again, the Homeric question is an ocean of controversies) yields between 750 and 700 BC, with the date of 720 often being embraced. A supplementary question: There certainly is a temporal gap between the *Iliad* and *Odyssey*, a non-negligible gap (or else one must make other, much more unreasonable hypotheses), which can be proven well enough with the help of properly philological criteria— which have taken on an immense importance in Homer's case—based on criteria of content. It's certain, on the one hand, that there are differences between the world—the factual world, if I may say so, not legend, not narrative, intrigue, or anecdote, but the objective world, the social and material world—to which the *Iliad* refers and the one to which the *Odyssey* refers. But especially—and this has been noticed for a long time but perhaps

---

38. *Eds.*: The idea of a complete destruction of the Mycenaean world by a wave of invaders (which was common in the nineteenth century and is still found for example in Lévêque, *The Greek Adventure*) is no longer admitted today. See Schnapp-Gourbeillon, *Aux origines*, pp. 23–90.

III. SEMINAR FROM NOVEMBER 24, 1982   41

not sufficiently emphasized—there is, without doubt, a difference as regards the world that infuses the poet, the world in which he lives. I say "he," and that's another problem to which I will return in a moment. In any case, it's between 750 and 700 that the Homeric poems must be situated. They're thus definitively composed at a time when colonization had already begun, which entails in particular a certain political organization. The author of the Homeric poems lived in a world where the *polis* already existed, if not as a democratic *polis*, then at least as a clearly delimited place where free human beings—and of course also slaves—lived, who consider themselves a community independently of their internal divisions, social conflicts, politics, and so on (insofar as these things were already present in an articulated way). But, once again, the world in which the definitive composer or composers of the poems lived is a world already familiar with the *polis*. And shortly afterwards, there was Hesiod. Chronologically, the gap between Homer and Hesiod is no doubt very small; there is, for that matter, an ancient tradition—which is worth whatever it's worth—according to which there's poetic concourse (*agōn*) between them.[39]

The "hoplite revolution" also dates to this period. The hoplite revolution consists in the fact of moving from heroic combat—from the singular combat of some warriors assisted by archers or other combatants—to the phalanx, wherein the body of citizens fights precisely as a body, and in which this unity is materialized in the techno-military structure of the phalanx itself, i.e. in the capacity and material solidarity of those who are fighting, the assumption being that each one protects his neighbor with his shield. (With everyone seeking this protection, the phalanx "drifts toward the right," and thus it's the extreme left of the enemy that is most exposed to the strike.[40]) So, this is, if I may say so, the solidarity of the citizens in operation. There was a time when the undying realism of the interpretations wanted to make the *polis* the result of the hoplite revolution, which is in my view an aberration. I've thankfully noticed that Vidal-Naquet, in the article on Greece he wrote for the *Encyclopédie universalis*, which I didn't have a chance to read back in the day, says that the hoplite revolution must be taken as a consequence rather than as a cause of the constitution of the city, which is indeed for me absolutely obvious.[41]

---

39. Eds.: This is found notably in the anonymous Greek text *The Contest of Homer and Hesiod*, which can be found in Thomas W. Allen, *Homeri Opera, Volume V: Hymni, Cyclus, Fragmenta, Margites, Batrachomyomachia, Vitae* (Oxford: Oxford University Press, 1912).
40. Eds.: See Thucydides, *History of the Peloponnesian War*, 5.71.1.
41. Eds.: Pierre Vidal-Naquet, "By Way of Introduction: A Civilization of Political Discourse," in *The Black Hunter: Forms of Thought and Forms of Society in the Greek World*, trans. Andrew Szegedy-Maszak (Baltimore: Johns Hopkins University Press, 1998), p. 8: "The 'Hoplite

Again, witness to what extent the two interpretive mentalities can be opposed here. There are those who will say that a new technology must be invented such that a political form results from it. The technology, on this account, wouldn't really be that of the weapons themselves since the individual arms the hoplites carried don't present notable differences from the individual arms of the heroes in singular combat. The technological invention would rather be, as Marx could have said, the collective warrior, as one speaks about the collective worker. It's an analogical reasoning: as the division of labor offers a surplus of productivity relative to the labors of isolated individuals, the denseness of the phalanx of course offers a great surplus of military power, a firepower (that's the appropriate term) superior to the firepower of isolated combatants. So, this is indeed a technological invention since it has to do with the division of labor—of violence—and its re-composition. Alongside this point of view, there's also the contrary point of view, which is also my own, which says not that technological invention is the consequence in a causal chain of a change in the imaginary of the society in question, but rather that such invention is not possible *without* this change, which change such invention obviously incarnates and incorporates. It's a change in the imaginary, which means a creation of this imaginary schema of a community of co-responsible and consolidated men, and not simply an assemblage of individualities. The hoplite revolution, which we'll speak about again surely, is thus an aspect rather than a cause of the change.

Yet, it's near the end of the seventh century (we're unable to date it more precisely) that we find a law written with democratic elements at Dreros in Crete; the laws of Draco in 620 and the legislation of Solon in 592 in Athens, according to the dates most commonly accepted; and also the *rhētra* of Chios, about which we've already spoken.[42] Thus, it's not absurd to suppose—there isn't any genuine "proof" here, and it's a hypothesis I'm formulating based on certain indices and in particular on what we see in the Homeric poems—that, if near the end of the seventh century we already have democratic cities, then there must have been a beginning of the democratic institution a long time beforehand, in the cities of Ionia, which means in the eastern islands of

---

reform' at the beginning of the seventh century was both consequence and cause of a far-reaching political transformation." The above text is an abridged version of a text that appeared in *L'Encyclopaedia universalis, tome VII* (Paris: Britannica, 1970), pp. 1009–1018. Also see, by the same author, "The Tradition of the Athenian Hoplite," in *Black Hunter*, pp. 85–105.

42. *Trans.*: With regard to Dreros, see inscription 2 in Meiggs and Lewis, *Selection*, pp. 2–3.
— *Eds.*: The Dreros text is translated into French with commentary in van Effenterre and Ruzé, *Nomina*, p. 42. See also Snodgrass's discussion in *Archaic Greece*, p. 118–120.

III. SEMINAR FROM NOVEMBER 24, 1982   43

the Aegean and the Anatolian coast, right where the Homeric poems were born. There are other landmarks, like the reforms of Cleisthenes in Athens (508), which is a fundamental date because it marks the establishment of the great classical democracy. An extraordinary thing: Cleisthenes re-divides or reorganizes the people in order to make the divisions into tribes correspond to the necessities of the democratic regime, and not the reverse. This means "denaturalizing" and politicizing the distribution of the population. In 490–480 there are the wars of the Persian invasions; in 431–404 there's the Peloponnesian War, which in a sense signifies the historical defeat of the democracy. For, if democracy subsisted formally in Athens and in a lot of other cities during the fourth century and even afterwards, it's no longer the same thing at all. The "Funeral Oration" of Pericles in Thucydides, Book II, which is the fundamental text of Athenian democracy, was delivered during the first winter of the war, in 431–430. It's at once the apex and the beginning of the end.

So there you have the chronological markers with succinct commentary. Now here's some bibliographical information. For the initial period, the Minoan–Mycenaean period—what interests us is the birth of our tradition, which is found in the Homeric world and not in the Minoan–Mycenaean world (but what comes just before it must be understood)—look at the book by Ventris and Chadwick, *Documents in Mycenaean Greek*.[43] For the next period, there are two very important books: *The Dark Age of Greece* by Snodgrass and *Geometric Greece* by Coldstream.[44] These are debatable—Finley has a polemic with Snodgrass—but they are fundamental books where you can find the necessary elements of information.[45] For Homer himself, beyond Finley's book and Vidal-Naquet's preface that I spoke to you about, read the excellent book by Kirk, *The Songs of Homer*.[46] You can add in *The Greek Concept of Justice* by Havelock, the first half of which is on Homer exclusively, and you'll find very meticulous but not necessarily convincing discussions and interpretations of Homeric passages.[47]

---

43. *Eds.*: See note 35, p. 39.
44. *Eds.*: Anthony M. Snodgrass, *The Dark Age of Greece: An Archaeological Survey of the Eleventh to the Eighth Centuries B.C.* (Edinburgh: Edinburgh University Press, 1971); J. Nicolas Coldstream, *Geometric Greece* (London: Methuen, 1977).
45. *Eds.*: See Moses I. Finley, "Appendix I: The World of Odysseus Revisited," in *World*, pp. 142–158, especially pp. 154–157.
46. *Eds.*: G. S. Kirk, *The Songs of Homer* (Cambridge: Cambridge University Press, 1962), with an abridged edition, *Homer and the Epic* (Cambridge: Cambridge University Press, 1965).
47. *Eds.*: Eric Havelock, *The Greek Concept of Justice: From Its Shadow in Homer to Its Substance in Plato* (Cambridge, MA: Harvard University Press, 1978).

Before finally getting into Homer himself, let's mention a last problem of a general order, i.e. social-historical creation. We will encounter it here in the form of this quarrel between those who talk about the "Greek miracle," i.e. the absolute emergence of something with a complete newness and incomprehensibility in its genesis, and then, on the other side, those who see in Greece only the addition of Egyptian, Babylonian, and pre-Hellenic influences and so on. Last year, I expounded a general principle in this domain, namely that the notions of borrowing and influence become empty notions as soon as one leaves the purely descriptive and event-focused domain. The central idea in this regard is that the new can take up the old only with the signification the new gives to it. Or, to say it in reverse, the old cannot be taken up within the new except with the signification that the new gives to it. This is our starting point, which we speak about vertically (diachronically) or horizontally (synchronically), which means from the perspective of lateral influences. Put differently, only to the extent that there is a subject, an organizing principle, a pole for giving signification to what presents itself, can anything at all appear as an influence, a borrowing, a tradition, and so on. Without that, the new, the strange, the exterior, the other would be welcomed only as a noise, a perturbation, or an aggression to repel. This may certainly, in the latter case, lead to a modification of the subject, but it's a modification of an entirely different type. We've established this, as you recall, in our discussion of the living being.[48] Of course, there's a specificity of the human world, whether it's a matter of a society or an individual. For the living being—or for a computer, for that matter—what appears and doesn't immediately have a meaning gets dichotomized between what is totally deprived of meaning and thus exerts no influence and what, while still being deprived of meaning, is so very powerful that its influence is catastrophic, kills the animal, or breaks the computer. In effect, if instead of offering nourishment of the type of x that the animal, as one says, metabolizes or that the computer reconstructs as information, one bombards the one with doses of strong radiation or strikes the other with a hammer, then one will provoke a catastrophe, i.e. the collapse of the system that organizes a world. Quite clearly, in the human world, we are not left with just this dichotomy. Firstly, as I told you already, there's no noise; there can't be any noise. Whatever appears *must* be endowed with signification. Furthermore—and this returns to our problematic—there's a possibility, but simply a possibility, of a trans-social apprehension. Thus, as a first point, each society

---

48. *Trans.*: For a summary account (with key references) of Castoriadis's biological inquiries, see Suzi Adams, "The Living Being," in Suzi Adams, ed., *Castoriadis: Key Concepts* (London: Bloomsbury, 2014), pp. 135–141.

constitutes its own world. As a consequence, for it the other societies must be endowed with a meaning that its own constitution of the world confers on them. But at the same time there's something other: the possibility, in one way or the other, of passing beyond this cognitive informational closure in order to apprehend something that comes from elsewhere.

Each time, it's a concrete question of knowing whether such an apprehension is possible for the society in question and how far it goes, with the limit being that this apprehension tends towards an understanding. This includes the problems this understanding poses, of course, which we discussed during the seminars preceding this year's. Lastly, this question is just the generalization of the question, very much discussed by contemporary sociologists and ethnologists, of acculturation: How can an entirely different society acculturate—change in a cultural respect—with contact from the Western world? This isn't the only example, but it's the major example that has provoked such research. This limit—understanding—is what we tend towards in the type of relationships to other societies that have been created in our tradition (and which, here again, began with Greece). And then there's the other limit, which consists in saying: They're infidels; we're to cut their throats or ignore them. Between these two there lies the relationship to which one gives the name, bad as it is, of influence. Bad, because in general there is no pure and simple reception, or transferring, of social imaginary significations from one society into another. We will instead find in most cases a metabolization, an elaboration, a transformation of the received elements. The question of knowing what this elaboration and transformation is, how far it goes, how it forms, and what it signifies is precisely what serves as the hard kernel of this poorly named problem, i.e. the problem of influences and borrowings.

Here are some examples by way of illustration. Let's firstly note the selectivity of what one culture "borrows" from another. The Hebrews no doubt took an enormous number of things from peoples surrounding them and with whom they were in contact, which of course they transubstantiated into their own imaginary magma, as it's expressed in the Old Testament. During the period that corresponds to the classical Hebraic culture, astronomy underwent fantastic development, in particular in Babylonia, Syria, and so on. Yet the Hebrews absolutely weren't interested in it; there's nothing in the Old Testament that shows concern for this enormous segment of the ambient culture, except of course the presence of the stars or the story of Joshua asking the sun to pause.[49] Here's another very important example: Starting at what is doubtless a very ancient date, probably as of the fifth century but in any case in

49. *Eds.*: Joshua 10:12–14.

the third and second centuries and after, the Romans took in everything they could from the Greeks. They themselves said that the Greeks had civilized them, their barbarous conquerors. And this was the case in all domains, i.e. theater, poetry, lyric poetry, philosophy, and so on. The titles of Cicero's books are those of the dialogues of Plato, i.e. *De re publica, De legibus*, and the like. At the same time, the Romans were a people with a fantastically powerful, logical spirit by means of which they created Roman law, about which I've already written that it's the equivalent of Euclidean geometry in another field.[50] But there's not a single Roman mathematician. Across ten centuries of the history of Rome, you can't cite a single Roman mathematician. Why? In an era when Greek and then Hellenistic mathematics continued to flourish fantastically, they were cultivating themselves enormously, they had an extremely logically rigorous spirit, which is manifest in their juridical reasoning, but there are no Roman mathematicians; there's not even an attempt to copy the Greeks. This element isn't taken up; it's foreign. For what reason? How can one give an account of this exclusion of mathematics as such by the Roman imaginary, all while there isn't an exclusion of philosophy? One can say whatever one wants, e.g. assert like Heidegger that it's the crime of the Latins to have understood nothing of Greek philosophy, thanks to which all Western philosophy has understood nothing of Greek philosophy (which, by the way, isn't true). But, in the end, they do philosophy, or they try to do it. They don't even try to do mathematics. Here's a third example, which is of course the most massive, i.e. the rediscovery of Greece, of the whole ancient world for that matter, by the Europe of the Middle Ages. It's not a punctual or instantaneous event; antiquity is there the whole time, and, at the same time, it's not there. As of when did this European world begin to accord a different meaning to these remnants of antiquity, which were always there? Stones, Roman roads, aqueducts, manuscripts, sometimes Greek ones—from which derives the famous phrase *graecum est, non legitur* (it's Greek, we can't read it)—and in any case Latin ones. During a whole period these things were socially perceived as elements of a mythico-legendary past and, at the same time, for the Christians, as remnants of a diabolical era or one of sorcery. There are some very beautiful pages of Heine on this.[51] We can't say that there's a moment where every-

---

50. *Eds.*: See Cornelius Castoriadis, *The Imaginary Institution of Society*, trans. Kathleen Blamey (Cambridge: Polity Press, 1987), p. 120.
51. *Eds.*: Heinrich Heine, "Gods in Exile," in Havelock Ellis, ed., *The Prose Writings of Heinrich Heine* (London: Walter Scott, 1887), pp. 268–269: "[Popular belief] by no means declared the ancient gods to be myths, inventions of falsehood and error, as did the philosophers, but held them to be evil spirits, who, through the victory of Christ, had been hurled from the summit of their power, and now dragged along their miserable existences in the

thing topples over—there's almost no breaking point—and yet an enormous distance separates what's happening in the sixth or seventh century, in this respect, from what's happening in the fifteenth century, for example. But as of a certain point there is a *will* to borrow and imitate the ancient world, which gets manifest very clearly during the Renaissance and also in the seventeenth century. We know, moreover, that this furious will to borrow from the ancient world and to imitate it doesn't yield an imitation. It yields something different.

All of that gives us some landmarks for approaching this question of the Greek creation, be it a miracle or a simple addition of influences. And, once again, the question thus formulated translates a desperate naïvety. Of course, there is a Greek miracle. And then? There's also a Chinese miracle, a Japanese miracle, a Hindu miracle, Hebrew, Islamic, Inca, Maya, Tupi-Guarani, and anything you want. There's a miracle to the extent that, each time that a society constitutes itself, institutes itself—this is not a one-off event of course—there's an emergence of a new magma of imaginary significations and a creation of new institutions that incarnate them. And for this you cannot give a causal explanation; it's thus, if you prefer, a miracle. And, on the other hand, Greece, no less than any other culture, didn't suddenly spring up abruptly from the ground like in the story of Cadmus who saw warriors spring up where he had planted dragons' teeth. There were people already there, and also of course other peoples all around, and so on. The problem doesn't lie there. The problem, in this particular case, is precisely one of understanding these new forms. In his work on the exact sciences in antiquity, for example, Neugebauer concentrates on the mathematical knowledge not only of the Egyptians but also the Babylonians and on the borrowings by the Greeks.[52] But whenever one talks about borrowing in this context, one is talking of course about the contents of statements: the Egyptians already knew that the square on the hypotenuse of a right triangle is equal to the sum of the squares on the two other sides. The Greeks assuredly did not invent the content of this statement. All of that is well known, and it is surprising that we rediscover it periodically.[53] The essential question is that we find in the Egyptians and

---

obscurity of dismantled temples or in enchanted groves, and by their diabolic arts, through lust and beauty, particularly through dancing and singing, lured to apostasy unsteadfast Christians who had lost their way in the forest."

52. *Eds.*: Otto E. Neugebauer, *The Exact Sciences in Antiquity*, 2nd edition (New York: Dover Publications, 1969).

53. *Eds.*: In a work containing four pieces from 1996 dedicated to the "Orientalizing features" of Homer and others, the German Hellenist Walter Burkert, whose considerable role in the rediscovery of the topic forming the subtitle of his work—see Walter Burkert, *The Orientalizing Revolution: Near Eastern Influence on Greek Culture in the Early Archaic Age*,

the Babylonians statements that are based on a curious mélange of basic calculation and, above all, the empirical, i.e. observation, since there is an observational geometry. In the Greeks, this became something entirely different, i.e. theorems rigorously demonstrated.[54] Put differently, our problem is not one of knowing who was the first to see that for a right triangle, if one constructs a square on the hypotenuse and if one decomposes it into smaller squares, one could cover over the squares constructed on the two other sides; it's rather one of knowing who had the idea of rigorously demonstrating this proposition or other geometrical propositions. On this point, I direct you to Husserl's discussion in his text on the origin of geometry, which was translated into French for the first time and given a lengthy preface by Derrida.[55] And I'll limit myself here to reminding you of what Bourbaki said in the preface of the first volume of *Elements of Mathematics*: Many peoples have had mathematics, but it's with the Greeks that rigorous demonstration appeared for the first time. And, Bourbaki adds that every time mathematics has been in crisis, mathematicians have turned to the Greeks to find their examples of rigor.[56]

The essential question is that of the origin of the idea of rigorous demonstration and not that of the content of the theorems. Once again, in algebra the Babylonians were more advanced than the Greeks. The Chinese were too, and in this we wouldn't be able to talk about influences since there were barely any

---

trans. Margaret E. Pinder and Walter Burkert (Cambridge, MA: Harvard University Press, 1992)—is widely known, says the following: "After some decades of relative quiet, interest in ancient cross-cultural penetration has been rising again—not without uneasiness, and not only under the impact of Martin Bernal's *Black Athena*. Do we really owe some decisive development to the Greeks, and in what sense? Philosophy and science seem to be at the center of answers in the affirmative; but corroboration cannot be achieved without full view of the oriental background and alternatives" (p. 52). And: "Still, it was nowhere else but in Greece that philosophy in the form we know came into being. It may be to the point to recall the different social situation of the Greeks—no kings, no powerful priests, and no houses of tablets, which meant more mobility, more freedom, and more risk for mind and letters. In mathematics too the Greeks developed a new form of deductive proof in restructuring geometry" (p. 69).

54. *Marg. C.C.*: Since space is locally Euclidean, there exists an "empirical geometry" approximately "true" and constantly "verified" by ordinary physics, and even by the non-ordinary. Cf. Heisenberg.
55. *Eds.*: Edmund Husserl, *Origins of Geometry: An Introduction by Jacques Derrida* (Lincoln: University of Nebraska Press, 1989). Husserl's text is a fragment of Edmund Husserl, *The Crisis of European Sciences and Transcendental Phenomenology: An Introduction to Phenomenological Philosophy*, trans. David Carr (Evanston: Northwestern University Press, 1970).
56. *Eds.*: Nicolas Bourbaki, *Elements of Mathematics: Theory of Sets* (New York: Springer, 2004). See also Jean Dieudonné, *Pour l'honneur de l'esprit humain: Les mathématiques aujourd'hui* (Paris: Hachette, 1988), pp. 40–46.

contacts. It's one thing to measure the circumference of a circle with a thread, to carry this thread over to the diameter, and to notice that it passes over it three times and something; it's another thing to try to find the relationship between the circumference and the diameter, envisaged as the common limit of the areas of escribed and inscribed polygons. From then on, it's a question of understanding what this crossover into demonstration—which means into the absolute rigor of a logical implication—consists in. For, that is indeed what was created in Greece for the first time.[57]

But this goes even further. Implicitly, what's presupposed in this chain of rigorous implications is of course the existence of necessary relations in the object, in other words, laws. This is an issue not only of the laws of coherent discourse. This is not a matter of linguistic philosophy. The idea of law as such and even of laws in the object, of necessary relations, certainly isn't Greek. Without doubt, it has been there since the origin of humanity, for it expresses the idea of an unavoidable regularity. But there are two differences. First, this unavoidable regularity is more or less, each time, an assemblage of partial regularities that are simply *de facto* there. There is no connection, no attempt to establish a connection, between such and such partial regularities, nor to get them to be derived from something else. There is—which is something different—their mythical interpretation, which means imaginary. And, on the other hand, these laws are not impersonal: either they manifest the action of agents in the object, of agents conceived, if you will, projectively; or they are able to be, not avoided, but organized differently by the action of other laws, those to which magical action lays claim. (In this respect, the movement beyond magical thinking from the Homeric period onwards is a point on which Otto rightly concentrates in *The Homeric Gods*.[58]) Yet magic evidently is not at all the absence of laws; on the contrary, it relies on belief in rigorous chains of consequence. If I take your photograph and I pierce it with needles, something will happen to you. We see that there is, here, the idea of a necessary reaction. With elaborate magics, we are dealing with an enormous para-natural legislation that towers over, or conditions, the actions of simple natural regularities, but the action of these laws involves personal

---

57. *Eds.*: See Cornelius Castoriadis, "The Ontological Import of the History of Science," in *World in Fragments: Writings on Politics, Society, Psychoanalysis, and the Imagination*, trans. David A. Curtis (Stanford: Stanford University Press, 1997), pp. 342–373. See also G. E. R. Lloyd, *Magic, Reason and Experience: Studies in the Origin and Development of Greek Science* (Cambridge: Cambridge University Press, 1979), pp. 230–234: "[…] what is lacking from both Egyptian and Babylonian mathematics was the notion of proof" (p. 230).

58. *Eds.*: Walter F. Otto, *The Homeric Gods: The Spiritual Significance of Greek Religion*, trans. Moses Hadas (London: Thames & Hudson, 1954), pp. 7–10; 23; 37–39.

interventions of the mage. If there genuinely is a unification at the level of strictly imaginary significations, it cannot be a question of a rational unification of all of that.

So, the presupposition of rigorous demonstration is the existence of necessary relations in the object. But what object is Greek mathematics talking about? This is the second element, doubtless the most important: Greek mathematics begins as of the moment when there is this double creation of ideal space and of the ideality of numbers. The creation of this ideal and not merely abstract space is presupposed in the demonstrations as they are done, and it's made explicit (in a later text, but this shows that they were conscious of the nature of the problem) in Plato's *Seventh Letter*, which is often judged inauthentic (but it is in any case a text from the fourth century), where he says: We know very well that none of the real circles that we can draw, none of the shapes we spin out with the lathe, correspond rigorously to the definition of the circle as the place of all the points equidistant from another point.[59] So that's what is literally said in the *Seventh Letter*, i.e. that there's a difference between the ideal object envisaged by the definition of the circle and any circle we can construct. Aristotle says basically the same thing in *De memoria*, as in the *De anima* when he talks about the triangle as well.[60] As for the creation of the ideality of the numbers, it's already present in the argumentations of Zeno of Elea. In order to demonstrate the non-being of the phenomenal world, Zeno, as you know, tries to show that it cannot be conceived without contradictions. These are Zeno's paradoxes, the paradoxes of the continuum, or rather of the infinite. For example, take Achilles and the tortoise, where the argument is based on the divisibility-to-infinity of a line segment and also of any *unit* of measure. This, in a sense, presupposes in principle the existence of something that will never be able to exist, i.e. the nth-plus-one division of a line segment, whatever n may be. *Whatever it may be.* That's the only idea of the infinite the Ancients had, i.e. potential infinity and not actual infinity, which most of the time they rejected. Whatever n may be, there is always $n + 1$; and whatever n may be as a divisor, there is $n + 1$. Yet Zeno, of course, didn't move through the divisions; he simply evoked, by presenting his argument to his interlocutors, this infinite progression that cannot hold except in a space that's not a geometrical one, but a space of thought, of representation, i.e. entirely ideal, which means incapable of actualization, and

---

59. Eds.: Plato, *Letter VII*, 342b–c. Also, on the question of authenticity of the Platonic letters, see the useful clarification and references in Plato, *Lettres*, trans. with commentary by Luc Brisson (Paris: Flammarion, 1993), pp. 10–21.
60. Eds.: Aristotle, *De memoria*, I, 450a1–10; *De anima*, I, 1, 402b15–25.

in which the simple virtuality of the actualization counts as actualization. This is, in the end, the great implicit discovery: There exists a domain—a foundational one—*wherein the virtuality (abstract or representative) of the actualization counts as actualization*. An incredible thought, unknown elsewhere.

We have these two elements: the creation of a rigorous application and the rules of this application; and the creation of an object in which chains of rigorous applications would be possible through and through. And this object in which rigorous applications are possible through and through, which means one in which the statements bearing on the object are chained to one another rigorously, is both geometric space—in which all things (theorems, lemmas, corollaries, secondary properties, applied exercises) are regulated and correspond as such to concatenations of statements—and it is also of course numerical space, the numeric axis, in which everywhere equally there are rigorous chains of statements that correspond to necessary relations.

Here's a remark that's incidental—but is it really?—about what I have called ideality. Mathematical number and space, and not physical space nor physical number, are what's created in the space of ideality. In a sense, the representation by the Greeks of physical space absolutely does not correspond to this ideality, at least when we go to the limits. For, what is thus created as ideal space, the object of geometry, is what we call Euclidean space. And, likewise, what is created in the domain of numbers is what we could call in modern language a semigroup of the positive rational numbers. This Euclidean space, quite obviously characterized by the existence of indefinite straight lines, is also homogeneous and isotropic, i.e. characteristics that are at the basis of physics. It's isotropic, meaning without a preferred direction; it's homogeneous, meaning without different "layerings." The space is everywhere equally dense and non-dense, if I may allow myself this very bad image. Yet, the cosmic space of the Greeks absolutely is not Euclidean. From start to finish, from Hesiod to the Aristotle's *De caelo*, it's spherical; the cosmos is a sphere. And a sphere couldn't be Euclidean. For starters, the straight lines cannot go on to infinity; and also this spherical space of Greek physics cannot be called homogeneous since a natural place is privileged in it relative to all the others, namely the center of the world, the Earth, which the celestial bodies surround. Furthermore, the coexistence of these two representations—a Euclidean mathematical space and a non-Euclidean cosmological and physical space—is all the more problematic since for the Greeks mathematics and geometry, from beginning to end, absolutely are not an axiomatic game, as in the modern era, at least in the nineteenth century, wherein one posits such and such postulate and one constructs such and such geometry (and if one puts in a different postulate, one will construct a different geometry). No. The postulates at the basis of Euclidean geometry truly represent space, the very essence of space. The same goes for number, which while being indefinitely susceptible to division, never stopped representing for the Greeks—and not at the magical or numerological level but precisely at the level of an ideal of the mathematization of the universe—something that far surpassed human computations. For the Pythagoreans, number was sacred, and not only as a function of a numerological magic but because all physical properties correspond to numerical relations. Indeed, in the Pythagorean school—tradition attributes it to Pythagoras—it was experimentally established for the first time that the pitch of sounds emitted by a string is a function of the length of that string. In other words, if you divide the length in half, you obtain the same note at a higher octave. This profound correspondence between the arithmetical world and the physical world, or more precisely this indistinction, thus accentuates the cleavage—or the polyphonic representation—between a real world (i.e. that of cosmology, conceived as non-Euclidean) and an ideal world (i.e. that of geometry, itself conceived as Euclidean). And if these two worlds do not meet in a head-on collision, if the difference between these two principles does not manifest itself overtly, it's of course because space is locally Euclidean. In any case, we can work only under that hypothesis.

Let's conclude with the influences or the borrowings with regard to this example of mathematics. Even if one could show that all Euclid's theorems concerning the properties of figures or solids were already known among the Egyptians or the Babylonians, who would have transmitted this knowledge to Thales or to Herodotus, this would, strictly speaking, change nothing. For, the only thing that matters, and the true novelty, is the transformation of all of these empirical statements formulated in the pre-Greek world into statements bearing on *ideal* objects and their enchainment in a series of rigorous implications that ultimately makes a unity out of them, i.e. one that unifies space and that derives the cohesion and consistency of all of these properties demonstrated one after the other from a unique essence. Every time you prove a theorem of Euclidean geometry, you have the impression of having unveiled something that was *already there*. And this subjective impression moreover corresponds to what is entailed philosophically in this construction of geometry as a demonstrative science, namely that intuition in the philosophical sense (not in the sense of divination, but in the sense of *Anschauung*), inspection, and reasoning have brought you to discover a property *already there*.

Henceforth, originality (not in the journalistic sense but etymologically, in the sense of origin or source: *origo, archē*) is not the absence of foreign, borrowed, or received elements but the authentic taking up of these elements.

This is not like materials dominated by a form imposed in advance—that's not the image one should have in mind—but rather ones integrated under different dominant significations, as simple elements of signification. And this appropriation is possible only because there is a positing, a creation of a new imaginary schema. The later history of Greece offers us, by the way, a negative example of this. That is, as soon as the great phase of creation reached its end, as of the fourth century, elements that got taken up from outside universes were no longer transubstantiated within a new imaginary schema in the same way but tended to become, in a banal way, borrowings (which of course met up with certain preexistent elements of the Greek tradition). This was the case in a massive way with Eastern religions, beginning with Alexander's conquest; divine figures, magical ceremonies, mythical cults, and so on, got taken up but absolutely not transubstantiated. And in a certain sense, this precisely points to the decadence of classical Greek culture or at least the end of its great creative period.

Question

You said that the potentiality for an actualization is as valid as an actualization. Could you clarify?

When I do a mathematical proof, for example in the domain of what's called reasoning by recurrence, I do not need to traverse the entire series of numbers. If I show that a proposition, in holding true for the number n, also holds true for $n + 1$, then I stop. This is something we already find in Zeno, with the subdivisions to infinity.

IV. Seminar from December 1, 1982

Homer. The subject is, as we have seen, infinitely complex. The interpretations have proliferated contradictorily since antiquity, already from the time of Xenophanes and Plato, burdened sometimes with extreme naïveties. One of these is obviously the retrojection of what seems self-evident for the interpreter from such and such era, or the refusal to see the difference and even the otherness of what is deposited in these poems. This is a naïvety from which, as I told you in our first seminar, one can never totally free oneself. One always speaks starting from something, from one's era, from the society in which one lives. One may certainly criticize one's own prejudices, preconceptions, and so on, but how could one ever pretend to unbind oneself totally? There's another naïvety, symmetrical thereto and just as weighty, which is above all that of the moderns, and which comes down to dealing with the poems—or, for that matter, the entire Greek world—starting from prejudices of the positivist type, which I would almost be tempted to call "ethnologizing." Through a sort of variant of the enthnocentrist prejudice, they erase every difference between this Homeric world and the other bygone worlds we know of—and this was done by important authors—in order to treat it like a world that's primitive in the most naïve—I would say most mindless—sense of the term, i.e. a world that would be situated in the first stages of hominization.

If you think I'm exaggerating, I direct you to a very serious, relatively recent book, the reputation of which is quite high, i.e. *The Discovery of the Mind* by Bruno Snell.[61] There are two or three chapters on Homer in it, in

---

61. *Eds.*: See Bruno Snell's 1939 essay "Homer's View of Man," in *The Discovery of the Mind: The Greek Origins of European Thought*, trans. Thomas G. Rosenmeyer (Cambridge, MA: Harvard University Press, 1953), pp. 1–22: "Thus the early Greeks did not, either in their language or in the visual arts, grasp the body as a unit" (p. 7). "At first it might be suspected that *thymos* and *noos* are nothing more than the parts of the soul, such as we know from Plato's psychology. But those parts presuppose a psychic whole of which Homer has no cognizance. *Thymos*, *noos*, and *psyche* as well are separate organs, each having its own particular function" (p. 13). Snell's thesis was presented (and criticized) in *Philologus* and *Gnomon* starting in 1928–1930. Its most categorical formulation is in the 1939 essay quoted from above. His influence has been considerable, and we find traces of it in other diverse and important authors such as Hermann Fränkel (although his position is much

particular, where one finds this unreasonable assertion—which of course claims to be founded on philological givens and even on those of the plastic arts—according to which the Homeric world has yet to manage to conceive of a unity of the human being and in particular of his psychical powers. Since Homer obviously uses several terms—*phrēn, thymos, kradiē*—which no doubt represent metaphorical localizations, Snell thus envisions organs corresponding to different psychical faculties and goes so far as to say that there is, in Homer, no conception of the unity of the human being. We have to understand the enormous implications of what he's advancing there: It's a view not only that the human being of the Homeric texts would fall short of that of the most primitive tribe conceivable but also practically a psychotic view. Any infant achieves the constitution of what we call in psychoanalysis or psychiatry the unity of the image of the body, and thus also of the image of the faculties of the human being, between four and five years of age; and we will find no culture that doesn't possess this unity of the corporeal image of the human being and thus also of the human being as a seat of actions, of faculties, of affects, and so on.

I will turn now to the historical and philological problems posed by the poems. And, first of all, to the question—raised at least since the time of the Alexandrian grammarians—of interpolations and additions within the Homeric poems. Aristarchus, who managed the Library of Alexandria in the second century BC, practiced what one calls athetesis, which means he condemned as non-authentic certain lines of the transmitted text.[62] The

---

more nuanced), in *Early Greek Poetry and Philosophy*, trans. Moses Hadas and James Willis (New York: Harcourt Brace Jovanovich, 1975), pp. 75–85; as well as in E. R. Dodds; in Moses I. Finley; in Arthur W. H. Adkins, *Merit and Responsibility* (Oxford: Oxford University Press, 1960); in Jean-Pierre Vernant; in Jacqueline de Romilly; in Jan Bremmer; and so on. However, some warnings signs were noticed after the publication of books by Hellenists as reputed as Albin Lesky, *A History of Greek Literature*, trans. Cornelis de Heer and James Willis (Indianapolis: Hackett Publishing Company, 1996) and Hugh Lloyd-Jones, *The Justice of Zeus* (Berkeley: University of California Press, 1971), pp. 9 ff. More recently, and very vigorously, came works by Bernard Knox, "What Did Achilles Look Like?" in *Backing into the Future: The Classical Tradition and Its Renewal* (New York: Norton, 1994), pp. 50–54 and *The Oldest Dead White European Males* (New York: Norton, 1993), pp. 37–41. Similarly, see Bernard Williams, *Shame and Necessity*, 2nd edition (Berkeley: University of California Press, 2008). On the various contexts in which the concepts *phrenes, thymos, psychē*, etc. are used in Homer and other authors see also Richard B. Onians, *The Origins of European Thought: About the Body, the Mind, the Soul, the World, Time, and Fate* (Cambridge: Cambridge University Press, 2011), pp. 13–122.

62. *Eds.*: See Pierre Chantraine, "La tradition manuscrite de l'*Iliade*," in Paul Mazon, ed., *Introduction à l'*Iliad (Paris: Les Belles Lettres, 1959), pp. 30–33.

discussion underwent a new start in the eighteenth century; but it's above all a great German philologist, Friedrich August Wolf, who rekindled the whole debate in his *Prolegomena ad Homerum* and is the father of what we call the analytic school.[63] The "Analysts" consider that the poems such as we have them are essentially an assemblage of fragments that got taken up into the Greek epic tradition, which would have been formed quite late, at the latest in the sixth century. They did their best to show that such and such passage doesn't agree with the style of the others or breaks with the flow of the actions, that such and such other passage presents improbabilities too strong, and so on like that. There's always been an opposed school, i.e. that of the "Unitarists" or "Unitarians." It's still with us, by the way, and it's even enjoying a comeback among the Homeric philologists. The Unitarians think that basically the poems were, if not composed through and through then at least assembled, re-elaborated, and unified by one or two "monumental composers," to borrow Kirk's expression in the book I mentioned last time, which is one of the best I know of on this question in recent literature. We need not take sides in this discussion, which concerns us only on two points: the problem of the mode of composition and the approximate dating of the poems; and that of the world to which the poems refer. On the first point, I would simply say that, for my part, I am sufficiently convinced by the arguments of the, let's say, moderate Unitarians—like Kirk and even Finley or Vidal-Naquet—with regard to the existence of one, or more probably two, monumental composers who give a unity of structure and signification to an epic material that's already present, which was produced across centuries and transmitted orally. On the dating, as I told you before, there is presently a quasi-unanimity: the second half of the eighth century, with the barycenter of probabilities being 720.[64] But the

---

63. *Eds.*: Friedrich August Wolf, *Prolegomena to Homer*, trans. Anthony Grafton, Glenn W. Most, and James E. G. Zetzel (Princeton: Princeton University Press, 2016).
64. *Eds.*: The late dating (seventh or sixth century) defended formerly by M. L. West, and then by Minna Skafte Jensen in *The Homeric Question and the Oral Formulaic Theory* (Copenhagen: Museum Tusculanum Press, 1980), is, however, making a powerful comeback. See Gregory Nagy, *Poetry as Performance: Homer and Beyond* (Cambridge: Cambridge University Press, 1996), pp. 108–109 and 143–144; and see especially Alain Ballabriga, *Les Fictions d'Homère: L'invention mythologique et cosmographique dans l'*Odyssée (Paris: PUF, 1998), especially pp. 11–50). A different point of view can be seen in Irad Malkin, *The Return of Odysseus: Colonization and Ethnicity* (Berkeley: University of California Press, 1998); and Claude Calame criticizes the latter in his article "Odysseus, a Proto-colonial Hero? An Aspect of the Homerian Question," *L'Homme*, 164:4 (2002), pp. 145–153. Some of the strongest arguments in favor of a "low" hypothesis had already been presented in two books published at the beginning of the twentieth century and have been rather neglected since. See, in France, Michel Bréal, *Pour mieux connaître Homère* (Paris: Hachette, 1906);

position that I am going to develop in this seminar concerning the content of the poems, i.e. their signification, is compatible with any dating lying within the eighth century, even the start of the seventh century. And I would even say that, insofar as the position that I am going to develop is right, it confirms such a dating. I remind you that our interest in the text turns essentially around two axes: on the one hand, the text as a depository of nuclear imaginary significations which thus, since they were deposited there, were already present with the author or authors, no matter how many of them there were; and, on the other hand, the text as a source of these same significations for its listeners, at first, and then its readers. Put differently, what's important to us here is Homer *qua* educator or "instituter" of Greece.[65] This comes from the celebrated expression that Plato in the *Republic* cites while, of course, criticizing it.[66] What's therefore important to us is this formation which listeners and readers received by means of it, which was not necessarily conscious.

Let's make a digression here on the function of poems in the Greek world. First there were the lyric poets, i.e. poet singers who themselves no doubt went back into a distant past and were probably itinerant as of a certain point, were accompanied by an instrument, and improvised on given themes based on an oral composition formula. Then, as of the seventh century, there were rhapsodes, who traversed Greece reciting poems or delivering them accompanied by cithara in times of regular public festival or at other occasions. They regularly recited the Homeric poems in Athens at the Panathenaic festival (Athens played a large role here because the text was probably first fixed in writing there), in which the entire population participated (as with the performances of tragedies later in the fifth century), including women, children, and slaves since there was no discrimination in that respect. And as soon as these poems were written down, it was through them that one learned to read and made oneself literate. They were known by heart, constantly cited, and recirculated in the form of proverbs. Xenophon likewise recounts that Nicias, the Athenian *stratēgos* from the end of the fifth century, got his son to learn by heart the totality of the *Iliad* and the *Odyssey*. In other words, we're not dealing with a "literary" text. The relationship of Homer to Greek culture is not the equivalent of the relationship of Balzac, if you will, to contemporary French

---

and in Great Britain, Gilbert Murray, *The Rise of Greek Epic* (Oxford: Oxford University Press, 1960). One may find references to recent works in Cairns, "Introduction," pp. 1–12 and in Robert Fowler, "The Homeric Question," in Fowler, *Cambridge Companion*, pp. 220–232.

65. *Marg. C.C.*: Which the attacks of Xenophanes <DK 21B11–12>, Heraclitus <DK 22B42>, etc. reveal as well.

66. *Eds.*: Plato, *Republic*, X, 606e.

IV. SEMINAR FROM DECEMBER 1, 1982

culture. This is not a work reserved for a portion of society; it's something that people literally drank with their mother's milk and that they regularly returned to on innumerable occasions. The only analogous case would be for example in the Christian tradition—and also obviously in the Hebrew tradition—the foundational role of the Bible in a very believing Christian population that isn't satisfied with going to church and listening half attentively but follows the service and reads the Bible regularly, like for example in Protestant culture.

From this point of view, as soon as one doesn't give a too recent composition date, which is in any case impossible since we have solid enough cutoff dates (i.e. we cannot in any case consider the poems to be later than Hesiod, which means around 680), the remaining things—the mode of composition, the plurality of authors, and even the reality of the facts described, for example that of the Trojan War or the characteristics of the era Homer is supposed to have described—are relatively unimportant. Take the case of a cultivated English public, which is shaped by Shakespeare. The question of knowing whether what is described in *Macbeth* or even *Richard III* is historical has strictly no interest. What matters is the formation of spirit given by these texts. Furthermore, it's more or less the same with the Bible for Christians, or the Old Testament for Hebrews, or again the Koran for Muslims. There is, of course, a difference of scale: the relationship to the Bible or the Koran is a relationship to sacred texts, which establish their properly sacred character through reference to an event which is revelation. Belief in the reality of this event, and thus in the reality of everything said in it, is absolutely essential in this type of relationship with the text; but that is by no means the case regarding the Homeric texts. It is in fact the case that a crushing majority of Greeks believed in the reality of the content of the Homeric stories, but what's important is not this reality, nor even the intensity of this belief; what's important is the spirit and the signification of these texts. The episode of the Cyclops in the *Odyssey* will perhaps allow me better to make myself understood. What's important for us in this episode? It's certainly not a matter of knowing whether the Cyclopes existed and on what island, any more than it is of discovering the real fact that allowed for the interpolator, the "diaskeuast" of the Analysts, to weave his story. If this precision seems superfluous to us or even ridiculous, recall that a French scholar, Victor Bérard, who worked on the Budé edition of the *Odyssey*—which, by the way, he properly butchered, not hesitating to move around certain passages—believed strongly in 1930 in the possibility of rediscovering the entire geography of the voyages of Odysseus.[67]

---

67. *Eds.*: See in particular the four volumes of Victor Bérard, *Navigations d'Ulysse* (Paris: Armand Colin, 1927–1929).

The geographical illusion comes back around constantly in the interpretation of the *Odyssey*: We'll go and find Circe's island or the island of the Cyclopes.[68] This, let's confess, has hardly any interest from the point of view where we situate ourselves. What's essential is that in the episode of the Cyclops, there is quite simply the positing or the defining of what distinguishes human beings, i.e. a human collectivity, from what is not human, from what is monstrous, inhuman, or superhuman but not really divine. This is what we find in the episode of the Cyclops, and what—allow me to repeat myself— Greek children drank with their mother's milk. What this story is saying, in short, is: first, the Cyclopes have no *themistes*, which means laws; nor do they have any *agorai boulēphoroi*, or deliberative assemblies.[69] These terms go back to an implicit definition of what a human community is: A human community has laws, and it has deliberative assemblies in which things get discussed and decided. A collectivity that doesn't have this is monstrous. Obviously, if someone were, *per impossibile*, to prove that the Cyclops passage is subsequent to Cleisthenes—e.g. that a compiler from the close of the sixth century or the start of the fifth century would have put elements back into the *Odyssey* corresponding to the social imaginary significations of his era—we would be quite embarrassed. Yet, that isn't the case. The episode has attestations as of the seventh century, and it gives a definition of human society as a political society—the *zōon politikon* is already there in these *agorai boulēphoroi*—and as a community subject to laws, to *themistes*.

Now, here are a few words on the mode of composition of the poems. Today we think that at the basis of the poems there is a long oral tradition, spanning perhaps centuries, that was created and perpetuated by the lyric poets, the singers who didn't merely rehearse but introduced variations and additions each time, all while working within a framework and with means that are relatively fixed.[70] These consist of three elements. On the one hand, there are the epic *formulas*, these expressions that return continually in

---

68. *Marg. C.C.*: See the Bollack article. — *Eds.*: Jean Bollack, "Odysseus Among the Philologists," in *The Art of Reading: From Homer to Paul Celan*, trans. Catherine Porter and Susan Tarrow (Washington, DC: Center for Hellenic Studies, 2016), pp. 16–45.
69. *Eds.*: Homer, *Odyssey*, IX, 112. Also, see Seminar VII, pp. 123–128, as well as the commentary on this passage by Suzanne Saïd, *Homer and the Odyssey*, trans. Ruth Webb (Oxford: Oxford University Press, 2011), pp. 84 and 165–169.
70. *Eds.*: Here and in what follows, Castoriadis rearticulates, in its essentials, the status of the question as it is found, for example, in G. S. Kirk, *Songs*, or in other of his works, such as *The Language and Background of Homer: Some Recent Studies and Controversies* (Cambridge: W. Heffer & Sons, 1964), a work that collects texts worth consulting (especially E. R. Dodds's essay on the "Homeric question"). On the debates from the last twenty years concerning

Homer: Zeus as assembler of clouds, Achilles with quick feet, and so on. They are not solely commanded by an internal necessity (i.e. always to give the same qualification to characters), although they can have that function, but rather ensue quite simply from a metrical necessity. These are lines, half lines, or even smaller, which the lyric poet uses as rhythmical cells. One also finds constant themes, for example those of the battle of the heroes, who get presented in a sufficiently stereotypical way in the *Iliad*. On each side, a hero emerges from the mass of combatants, provokes the other, speaks about his own ancestors and their glory, and sometimes makes fun of his adversary. The latter most frequently responds: "No, my ancestors are more illustrious than yours." And at that point someone's lance strikes or doesn't strike the other one, who retaliates. A god perhaps intervenes to divert the lance. This type of duel returns very frequently with elements that include variations. The assembly of the gods and the deliberation in that assembly is another recurrent theme in the *Iliad* and *Odyssey*. For, there's an *agora* of the gods, and Zeus, while his power is eminent and predominant, by no means neglects the advice of the other gods. The third element, of course, is the legend as such, which means the Trojan Cycle, the set of its adventures, peripeteias, and events.

The recurrence of formulas in Homer has evidently always been commentated on, but it's only around 1930 that they decided to assign it an important role. The American Milman Parry pointed out the similitudes between certain essential traits of this formulaic poetry and those of other popular oral, non-written poetries.[71] The non-written is absolutely fundamental since the written destroys the memory of the lyric poet and popular singer as well as the *raison d'être* of the formulaic style. When you write, you go back over what's been done; you say to yourself: I already said that in this form, and you change such and such word. When you improvise in oral poetry, you work under the exactly opposite constraint, i.e. you rely on prepared formulas. The best comparison in contemporary culture would obviously be the interpretations by great musicians and singers of jazz. You find among them for example the *St. Louis Blues* theme, which corresponds to what I called the "legend" in these Homeric poems, but also formulas, standard agreements, which are remade and varied by the musician. Parry thus observes that among the South

---

"limits of the formulaic style," "typical scenes," and Homeric images, see the useful literary overview in Saïd, *Homer*, pp. 46–75. Also see, Cairn, "Introduction," especially pp. 33–56.

71. *Eds.*: See Milman Parry, "The Traditional Epithet in Homer" and "Homeric Formulae and Homeric Metre," in Adam Parry, ed., *The Making of Homeric Verse: The Collected Papers of Milman Parry* (Oxford: Oxford University Press, 1972), pp. 1–239. Also see Albert B. Lord, *The Singer of Tales*, 2nd edition, ed. Stephen Michel and Gregory Nagy (Cambridge, MA: Harvard University Press, 2001).

Slavs there was still in his time—he went there on site in 1933–1935—an oral poetry and popular singers who worked, like lyric poets, with a rhythmic constraint, i.e. with an equivalent of the Homeric dactylic hexameter (lines of six feet in which the fundamental meter is the dactyl, i.e. one long syllable, two short), or a decasyllable, with caesura after the fourth syllable. This constraint facilitates the work of the oral poet, who was accompanied, by the way, by a small sort of violin, the *gusla*. The formulas, which here described Serbian or Turkish warriors and so on, return quite constantly, and we also find the equivalent of themes. As for the legend, which plays the role of the Trojan Cycle here, it's essentially the "Battle of Kosovo" (1389) and what followed it, such as the exploits of Marko Kraljević. An entire epic cycle around the Battle of Kosovo existed still in 1933, when Parry went on site and started to record. We thus have here, in our times, an oral tradition, the study of which allows up to a certain point for the solution to the enigma of the composition and oral transmission of poems with 16,000 or 12,000 lines like the *Iliad* and the *Odyssey*. Of course, this wasn't achieved all at once; there was creation at the heart of a tradition (that of the lyric poets), successive accretions, and simultaneous stability and slow evolution, as with the most living forms of all truly popular art, of all folklore. The proof was thus attained that a lyric poet of this type could both deliver a very long poem and above all retain it. One of them, for example, at the request of Parry, delivered—across several days, in the rhythm of two hours in the morning, two hours in the afternoon—a poem of 12,000 lines, which Parry recorded, and which were truly improvised. (It's true that these improvisations had especially to do with added episodes that represented variations relative to the legend and that these were based in their essentials on the use of formulas, of hemistiches, or of whole lines that were already found in popular poetry.) This is thus a long tradition, which probably started at the end of the Mycenaean era, or perhaps even before. Let's recall, incidentally, that we can date this end with certainty; it coincides with the quasi-simultaneous destruction of a series of Mycenaean cities at around 1200 (Pylos was the last city to be destroyed, in 1190) as well as with that of the Hittite Empire. In short, starting then and going until the ninth century or perhaps even the eighth century, this oral poetic tradition developed, and then in the end very probably one or two monumental composers, around 720, gathered all this material and organized it into two great poems.[72] If in the *Iliad* there are almost none of what a modern would call, a bit stupidly perhaps, defects of composition, in the *Odyssey* there are things that seem a bit bizarre, i.e. the organic character of the composition certainly constitutes

---

72. *Eds.*: See note 38, p. 40.

a problem. Whatever the case may be, from that date on we are in our rights to suppose that the text remained more or less unchanged, except for some entirely minor elements.

Another important point concerns the era back to which the poems refer, which is not necessarily that to which the legend refers. The poems recount an episode, which is very brief for that matter, from the Trojan War and then the adventures of Odysseus and his return to Ithaca, the murder of the suitors, and so on. Did this war happen? No, by all probability, despite the fierce insistence—to which I alluded last time—of certain archaeologists. But the question that matters for us doesn't lie there. Even if the Trojan War is merely a legend, this legend is not situated in just any random place; the siege of Troy is not the siege of Stalingrad. By that, I mean that the poems speak to us of people who are armed and organized in a certain fashion. What interests us is the real world described through the poems. What era are we dealing with? Speaking abstractly, there are three possibilities. The first is that the poems describe the real world of their era. That is, the poet is in fact talking about what he sees around himself. (Think of a novelist today who would write about the wars of the Revolution or the Empire but in such a way that the characters would act within the framework of institutions that would resemble those of the Fifth Republic, and in which people wear leather jackets and have headphones over their ears.) This is a hypothesis to exclude, if one admits that the poems were composed in the eighth century or at the start of the seventh century or later since the Greek society of that era was very different from what is described in the poems. To take just one example, it's a society where the weapons are iron, while in Homer the weapons are always bronze. In this society, there are cities that have a particular organization—and this is so independently of the question of the emergence or not of democracy or of elements of democracy in that era—which is not the one we find in Homer. And, indeed, they are described in quite a schematic fashion there. One could advance a thousand arguments to show that we do not find, in the era when the poems are supposed to have been composed, the politico-social structures that are entailed by the heroic society Homer describes. Battle, for example, is no longer a duel between heroes but already a confrontation between hoplitic phalanxes.[73] Yet, this type of duel has nothing anecdotal about it; it refers to

---

73. *Eds.*: Since the 1980s some authors have relativized the role of the duel in the *Iliad* and have focused on the importance of collective forms of combat. See the "Annotated Bibliography" in Pierre Ducrey, *Warfare in Ancient Greece*, trans. Janet Lloyd (New York: Schocken Books, 1986), pp. 294–296, especially the references made to Joachim Latacz, *Kampfparänese, Kampfdarstellung und Kampfwirklichkeit in der Ilias, bei Kallionos und Tyrtaios* (Munich: C.

the totality of the social organization, i.e. to a society in which heroes, princes, and nobles occupied the forefront of the scene, surrounded by an anonymous mass that takes part in the combat but about which little is said. The whole emphasis in Homer is placed on the heroes.

A second possibility is that the society described by the poems is precisely the world to which the legend refers. Are we dealing with the Mycenaean world? Here we hit upon the question of the historicity of the Trojan War—but we don't need to go back into that—and especially of the conformity of the society the poems describe to Mycenaean society such as we know it. It's a long-debated question, to which Finley gave a response: The world of the poems is not the Mycenaean world. He used arguments for the first time that were not archaeological but based—and this is very important from a methodological point of view—on social analysis and also, to a certain extent, on significations. The first edition of *The World of Odysseus* is from 1954 and the decipherment of Linear B provided it with resounding confirmation. That is, the Mycenaean world, even independently of the arguments founded on material and archaeological givens and the like, showed up as very far removed from the world of Homer. One can advance diverse types of arguments here. One could say, first of all, that the Mycenaeans had a writing—Linear B, that is—and that Homer, actually, leaves out writing; only two lines make a vague allusion to signs, which are not necessarily writing.[74] Moreover, the geography of the Homeric world is not that of the Mycenaean world; it is not that the islands changed positions but that the regions described as important in the poems are not those that the excavations designate as such. Likewise, the social structure is not that of the Mycenaean world. The latter, as it appeared through the tablets—and this correlates entirely with the archaeological givens—is a palatial civilization, with a bureaucratic monarchy and scribes who record what the different layers of the populace must give and receive. Furthermore, in Homer—this is a very important aspect—cremation had replaced the Mycenaean practice of interment.

A third possibility was showcased by Finley with very strong and in my view convincing arguments.[75] The poems describe the real society of the era

---

H. Beck, 1977) and W. Kendrick Pritchett, *The Greek State at War* (Berkeley: University of California Press, 1985). But also see the chapter by Hans van Wees, "Homeric Warfare," in Ian Morris and Barry B. Powell, eds., *A New Companion to Homer* (Leiden: Brill, 1997), pp. 668–693.

74. *Eds.*: Homer, *Iliad*, VI, 168–169.

75. *Eds.*: Today, some historians contend that the poems reflect the institutions at the end of the dark ages (end of the ninth through beginning of eighth centuries) instead of those of the eleventh to ninth centuries and tend to focus on the presence of more recent elements

of the lyric poets; through successive contributions they constructed them around an inherited legend, the basic outline of which survived, although it itself didn't belong to that era. They describe the society of the *Dark Ages*, i.e. the dark ages of Greece between the eleventh and the ninth to the eighth century. Agamemnon and Achilles move about in a reality with whole aspects that belonged to these dark ages. Furthermore, this is a commonplace phenomenon. In *The Song of Roland*, for example, the legend makes reference to the era of Charlemagne, but what is described corresponds to an intermediate era, which betrays the constitution of the poem as emerging by accretion in an oral tradition. The same thing holds for the *Nibelungenlied* in Germany, and so on.

Let's add to this the fact that certainly, toward the end of this period and in any case at the time of the definitive composition by the monumental composer or composers, certain nuclear social imaginary significations—which would subsequently play a central, formative role in the Greek universe—were constituted or at least appeared for the first time. And I tend to think that the constitution of these significations, this new grasp of the world, probably got started very early on in this affair. It's as if for the Greek tribes there was a new start after the destruction of the Mycenaean world. For, this goes hand in hand with very important changes in numerous domains and in particular in the religious domain, which translates a different grasp of the world. As an index, I would only like to point to one central element, i.e. the signification attributed to death and the effect of this attribution on all the other significations. Yet, this signification and the entire sub-magma that organizes itself around it and is based on it is not borne out by this or that line which could have been added or interpolated by a rhapsode, a scribe, by Peisistratus, or by whoever you wish. This signification of death is borne out by the very organization of the whole of the *Iliad*. Remove 2,000 lines; it would still be there. In my view, this tends to show that an enormous change in the grasp of the world intervened, perhaps from the beginning of

---

in writing. See for example chapters 3 and 4 of Oswyn Murray, *Early Greece* (Cambridge, MA: Harvard University Press, 1993); and the works cited in Saïd, *Homer*, pp. 76–86, especially those of Jan Paul Crielaard and Kurt A. Raaflaub. For other authors—especially Anthony M. Snodgrass, "A Historical Homeric Society?" *Journal of Hellenic Studies*, 94 (1974), pp. 114–125—the "Homeric" society as it is presented in the poems is not coherent but, like Homeric language, is an amalgam of elements from various periods. On these questions, also see Kurt A. Raaflaub, "Homer und die Geschichte des 8. Jh.s. v. Chr.," in Joachim Latacz, *Zweihundert Jahre Homer-Forschung* (Stuttgart-Leipzig: Teubner, 1991), pp. 205–256; as well as Ian Morris's commentary in the reworked version of "The Use and Abuse of Homer," in Cairns, *Oxford Readings*, pp. 57–91.

the composition of the poems onwards, and that the creation to which they bear witness continued until the era of definitive composition. Not only does the episode of the Cyclops seem characteristic of a late period in this process, but the statements on justice at the end of the *Odyssey* introduce a rather new element in relation to the rest of the poem (and we'll come back to this). Here, in a sense, without disagreeing with Finley, we are going in a different direction. Finley is interested above all in the real world to which the poems refer. You need to read *The World of Odysseus*, which is a very fine book and, in my view, very true. We take separate paths to the extent that what interests us here is the ultimate depositing of these significations we find in the poems, which announce—and even more strongly, which are already the germs of— all of what would become the constitution of the classical Greek world. This is already sketched at the end of Finley's book but in a sense not wholly the same as my own.

Let's return now to what has been said so many times about Homer, educator of Greece, namely that he is the germ of all of what we find afterwards. It's an ancient commonplace, and it's strictly true. We can notice this even before starting the examination of the content of the poems, by observing what these texts are, i.e. their status. We can say this very succinctly: The "sacred" text of Greece is not a sacred text. This is already a fundamental difference relative to practically all the historical cultures with which we are familiar.[76] This text is neither religious nor prophetic; it is poetic. The author is neither religious nor prophetic; he's a poet, he's *the* poet. Or, if you prefer, the prophet of Greece is a poet who also is not a prophet. And in a sense when you've said this much, everything's been said. He is the *poet*, i.e. one who makes to be. And this poet forbids nothing, imposes nothing, gives no orders, promises nothing. He speaks. And in doing so, he reveals nothing, i.e. there is no revelation. He recalls. He recalls what was and, at the same time, what constitutes the lineament of what is, of what can be. He recalls this to the memory of men with the assistance of these daughters of Memory, of Mnemosyne, who are the Muses.[77] Before undertaking a short digression on

---

76. *Eds.*: See A.-J. Festugière, "Le fait religieux dans la Grèce ancienne," in *Études d'histoire et de philologie* (Paris: Vrin, 1975), pp. 11–21. In his view, we cannot place enough emphasis on the importance of the "lack, among the Greeks, of everything that would trace back to a literature of religious doctrine proper," the lack of a "Book, in the sense that we speak of the Bible, the Avesta, or the Koran," a lack that is due to the absence in Greece, except in very minority currents like Orphism or Pythagoreanism, of a "founder of religion, of an inspired man, or of a prophet-god who would go on to reveal to man a so-called true religion as opposed to others, a religion involving a creed, a morality, and a Church" (pp. 15 and 18).
77. *Eds.*: Hesiod, *Theogony*, 54 ff., 915 ff.

Mnemosyne, I am going to say something that's going to seem exorbitant to you. Quite obviously, all the mythologies of all peoples are significative and most frequently beautiful and even very beautiful. What distinguishes Greek mythology—beautiful or not, that's not the question—is that this mythology is true. The Greek myths are true. The myth of Ouranos-Chronos-Zeus is true. The myth of Oedipus is true. The myth of Narcissus is true. It's there—I mean, look in a mirror. The Muses preside over poetry in the strongest, most elevated sense: the creation of the beautiful. Yet, they are daughters of Mnemosyne; they are not artifacts of Memory, nor copies conforming to Mnemosyne. They are daughters. A daughter resembles her mother, but she is also something else than her mother. The creation of the beautiful—from what does it arise? From the creative imagination. And this creative imagination mobilizes all the powers of the human being and of the imagination, those of the radical imagination, i.e. the constituting imagination, as well as of the constituted imagination. It thus implicates memory in manifold ways, but it doesn't reduce to it. Muses and Mnemosyne are profoundly akin, but they are not one and the same thing. This truth that I claim today, in 1982, as *the truth* of human existence as far as the imagination is concerned, which means as far as everything is concerned, is thus deposited from the beginning on. As of the first hour, it's deposited there in this little fable—myth, tale, legend—call it what you want. The Muses are daughters of Mnemosyne. And there is more philosophical meaning in this little fable than in everything philosophers have been able to say on the imagination. For example, as you know—we've been talking about it for three years—the relationship of imagination to memory has been seen most of the time in philosophy (with some rare exceptions aside, i.e. Aristotle and Kant) as one of the derivation of the former from the latter.[78] The same holds true, in a sense, for the theory of the *mimēsis* of the imagination. What does that theory have to say, if we bring it back into the language of myth? It says that the Muses are not seen as daughters of Mnemosyne but as a little product fabricated by her. Which is it, in truth? It's obvious that the imagination, in its effective exercise, presupposes memory. That is, it always has to do with a magma of figures that are already there and, of course, are something completely different than an inert matter for it to recombine. But where do these figures come from? In order that there could be a deposit of figures that the imagination could use thanks to memory, it had to be that there was first a figurative activity, which means a creation of images, a formation of the unformed, or a formation with nothing,

---

78. *Eds.*: See Cornelius Castoriadis, "The Discovery of the Imagination," in *World in Fragments*, pp. 231–245.

i.e. radical imagination. We can here complete the myth, if I dare say so: The Muses are daughters of Mnemosyne, but at the same time they are daughters who make exist—this is a circle or paradox—the nutrients from which their mother is nourished and from which she already nourished herself before their birth, i.e. the water she drank and the air she breathed. These daughters are mothers of their mother. With this we are going beyond the myth. But it's still the myth that at once establishes the fundamental relationship between creative imagination and memory and establishes it not as derivative but as a profound kinship and at the same time an otherness.

So much for the character of the text. It's not sacred; it's a poetic text. The very fate of the Homeric poems allows one to see the reversal of the relationship. If they become "sacred," it certainly is not in a religious sense of the term but because they are this great text to which everyone refers, which even the law in Athens forbids one to modify as of the sixth century (since the rhapsodes were really taking too much liberty with it).[79] But it's the *poetic* text that, once again, becomes "sacred" because it's fundamental, and not the reverse.

And now, what do we find at the center of the poems' significations? Quite simply, it's what's essential for the Greek imagination, namely the Greek grasp of the world. With regard to what's explicitly said, the elements of this tragic grasp are already there in the two poems. As for action—*praxis*, as Aristotle will later say in defining tragedy—this tragic grasp is given, as I said a while back, with the very materiality and organization of what's recounted in the *Iliad*. It's not a commentary that has come to graft itself onto a history; what's tragic is the very structure of this history. Both in its action and literally the *Iliad* is a tragedy, and Plato saw this when he qualified Homer in the *Theaetetus* as a tragic poet.[80] This has been said before; it's not new. But we need to go further: It is, if you will, a meta-tragedy or a hyper-tragedy. And this is so in at least two senses. Firstly, and contrary to what will happen later with the tragic heroes, Achilles—as well as Hector by the way—knows from the start what awaits him. There's a beautiful phrasing from Anouilh's *Antigone* in which the chorus, announcing to the spectators what is going to happen (I'm citing from memory, old memories, and I haven't revisited the piece), establishes very clearly the distinction between tragedy and drama, i.e. melodrama. The

---

79. *Eds.*: According to a tradition with rather late attestation (first century BC), we owe to Peisistratus the writing down of Homer's poems. On this topic, see the critique in Mazon, *Introduction à l'Iliade*, pp. 271–282. Also, see the clarification by Jensen, *Homeric Question*, pp. 149–158, and a very meticulous discussion in Nagy, *Poetry*, especially chapters 5 and 6.
80. *Eds.*: Plato, *Theaetetus*, 152d.

chorus says that in drama there's suspense and then a whole series of accidents that could influence the action. Ah, if the police had arrived earlier! Ah, if the car had taken another route, then things would have happened differently! Tragedy does not depend on these junctions. It deals with the inexorable.[81] In classical tragedy, the spectators—like, for that matter, the listeners and later the readers of the *Iliad*—are complicit. They don't go to see *Oedipus the King* to learn what the story recounts. They know the story. Generally, they're even aware of several variants of it. Perhaps there's a bit of curiosity. They wonder which variant Sophocles will use, what occasional change he'll introduce. But they know. On the other hand, the tragic hero himself is not represented as knowing. It's even the contrary since the progression of tragedy is precisely the unveiling of the truth to the hero through horror—through blinding or murder—and not within the illuminated clearing of being. The hero doesn't know. Yet, in the *Iliad*, Achilles knows from the beginning. And Hector also knows from the beginning. And of course this prevents nothing, including in their own acts. And neither does this prevent—this is a very important point—the surprising coexistence of this anticipated knowing with the authenticity of the free decisions made and remade in the course of the action. Achilles, who knows in advance, dives again each time into a world in which he must choose to do or not to do. He is, as Aristotle will later say, *archē tōn esomenōn*, i.e. the principle of what will be, and fate—i.e. *moira* or *aisa*—becomes a reality throughout these free decisions of Achilles, which are freely made each time, but which change nothing of the inexorable.

The second reason why one may speak of meta-tragedy or hyper-tragedy is that, in fact, contrary to the classical tragedies of the fifth century, we're dealing with a story fragment that's autonomous in a sense or, if you will, autarchic. But, on the other hand, it's also a matter of a fragment of an action that was begun long before and that will continue long after. That the action was begun long before is also true of classical tragedy. But none of them start

---

81. *Eds.*: Jean Anouilh, *Antigone: A Tragedy*, trans. Lewis Galantière (New York: Random House, 1946). The chorus exclaims on pp. 23–24, "The spring is wound up tight. It will uncoil of itself. That is what is so convenient in tragedy. The least little turn of the wrist will do the job. [...] The rest is automatic. You don't need to lift a finger. [...] [Tragedy] has nothing to do with melodrama—with wicked villains, persecuted maidens, avengers, sudden revelations, and eleventh-hour repentances. Death, in a melodrama, is really horrible because it is never inevitable. The dear old father might so easily have been saved; the honest young man might so easily have brought in the police five minutes earlier. In a tragedy, nothing is in doubt and everyone's destiny is known. That makes for tranquility. There is a sort of fellow-feeling among characters in a tragedy: he who kills is as innocent as he who gets killed: it's all a matter of what part you are playing."

fully *in medias res*, as the Romans will later say.[82] The antecedents of the tragic action of the *Iliad* had been there for a long time. The hostility of Poseidon towards the Trojans, for example, refers—perhaps you know this already—to a dark story about a salary promised and not paid to Apollo and Poseidon by Laomedon, king of Troy, for the building of the walls of the city. From that day forth, Poseidon, the great god of the sea, avowed an inextinguishable hatred for the Trojans, and this element would play a permanent role in the action. And the whole story, moreover, dated back to another (rather small) story, i.e. that of the choice of Paris, who designated Aphrodite and not Hera or Athena as the most beautiful and gave her an apple (yet again an apple...). Thenceforth, Hera and Athena are sworn to the waste of Paris and his city. Lastly, this whole story, all these thousands of dead—we'll come back to this—resulted from this futility. And all of this was done in a sense without any genuine reason. This fragment of action, thus, is caught up in a hyper-tragedy that stretches upstream and downstream. Certain elements, upstream, are mentioned in the text; and what comes afterwards, which all the listeners and spectators know, will be taken up partly in the *Odyssey*. We won't find throughout all of this the *praxis spoudaia kai teleia*, as Aristotle will say, i.e. the serious and complete action that defines tragedy.[83] This does not close in on itself with a catharsis but refers to, and blends into, this hyper-tragedy that is the entire story of men and of the world.

A few words should perhaps be added here. We already saw that there is neither uncertainty nor expectation in the *Iliad*; on the contrary, that which is inexorable and the powerlessness of the human are what is on display, i.e. the ineluctable character of the realization of fate, of *moira*. Put differently, if the modern reader of Homer feels no suspense, then it's not because the poet was unable or didn't want to introduce any. This absence is homogenous and consubstantial with the underlying ontology of the poems. There cannot be any uncertainty.[84] We already have here the basis not only of tragedy but also of the entire Greek vision of the world. It should also be noted from this point of view that in the *Iliad*—and even in the *Odyssey*, though I will concentrate today on the *Iliad*—the twisting of action, the accomplishment of *moira*, of fate, is constantly conditioned by transgressions, by the surpassing of limits, by *hybris*. This element is there from the start. Agamemnon offends the servant of Apollo; Apollo sends the plague to the Greek camp. When Agamemnon

---

82. *Eds.*: Horace, *Ars Poetica*, 148.
83. *Eds.*: Aristotle, *Poetics*, 6, 1449b23–24.
84. *Marg. C.C.*: The genuine "novel [*roman*]" can only be born in a world that will have already partially abandoned this vision.

is obligated to return Chryseis, he does something he doesn't have the right to do. He takes a woman who was part of Achilles's plunder, Briseis. Achilles digs himself deeper into his anger in a way that one may call hubristic. And when the Trojans finally enter into the Greek camp, Achilles sends Patroclus against them, giving him the order not to move onto the offensive but to limit himself to repelling them. Patroclus goes beyond that, and Patroclus is killed. It's thus constantly *hybris* that brings on the new catastrophe and makes the action turn.

Here's another very important element. The end of the *Iliad* is not a catharsis in the Aristotelian sense. The end of the *Iliad*—that admirable Book XXIV—is, as you know, a reconciliatory end.[85] Achilles accepts to give the corpse of Hector to Priam. A very profound movement of empathy or sympathy sweeps away the two characters facing one another; it's not a confrontation. Both of them cry over the fate of humans, one while thinking of his son Hector, the other of Patroclus and his old father. Here there's a permutation, or more exactly a simultaneous communication, of significations and of affects between the two individuals who establish this *Versönung*, as one says in German (the French don't have a word that's really appropriate). This is a reconciliation which isn't like that between quarreling persons whom one manages to appease, but it's like a reunification of heretofore antagonistic elements, whereupon the poem draws to a close.

Finally, I'll comment on a point that is perhaps an effect of the historical stratification of the creation of the poems, although this matters little for us since our view of the text is here synchronic or structural, a view of the content such as it's given to a Greek from the year 600 BC. This is an aspect that has been noted only quite recently, and which had not been emphasized enough or seen in its profundity. It's that these poems which depict a heroic world contain at the same time the critique of this world. Take the speech of

---

85. Eds.: On the *Iliad* as a poem of not only war and death but also of "humanization" of the hero, see Kirk, *Songs*, p. 353: "It would be falsifying the balance of the poem to claim that it is the mental and emotional history of Achilles that chiefly matters; but the transformation of his pride and anger, first in the Embassy into doubt of the whole heroic code, then into indecision and the compromise that leads to Patroclus's death, then into self-reproach and grief, then into obsessional madness, and finally into some sort of reluctant acceptance of the basic laws of society and at least a similitude of generosity—all this is the moral core of the whole poem, and that which raises it beyond the level of reiterated cruelty and death to a more universal plane of pride, purgation and divine law. There is little doubt in my mind that this deepening of the themes of war is the work of Homer, the main composer of the poem." On this same subject, see the excellent "Introduction" by Bernard Knox to Homer and Robert Fagles, *The Iliad* (London: Penguin Books, 1991), pp. 58–64.

Achilles in Book IX of the *Iliad*, to which I will return in a moment. Achilles rejects Agamemnon's proposal to rejoin the fight in exchange for sumptuous gifts and says, more or less: This war has no meaning, and nothing is worth more than life. That's put into the mouth of Achilles, and it's done in a heroic context in which such an assertion is literally unthinkable. For, to say that nothing is worth more than life is unthinkable in the heroic world; but to say that this war has no meaning is even more unthinkable since the meaning of heroic existence is in fact war. Here, there's thus an immanent critique of the world that's described; and in my view we have to see the result of successive accretions in this. In any case, the final result for whoever reads or hears the poem—whoever read or heard the poem—could only be a tragic positing, i.e. *impostazione* in Italian, *Einstellung* in German. We are going to witness this immediately with regard to the most important issue in the poems, namely death.

At the core of the poems and particularly the *Iliad*, there's the experience of this inescapable given which is death.[86] And this given is there with no compromise, no consolation, no arrangement, no adulteration, no sugarcoating. Achilles says in Book IX (these are lines 400–409): Nothing is worth as much as life; nothing is *psychēs antaxion*. And he adds that one can seize cattle and fat sheep and buy tripods and horses, but the life of a man doesn't come back once it has passed out of his mouth. You're also familiar with the famous meeting in Hades between Odysseus and Achilles in the *Odyssey*,

---

86. *Eds.*: On the Greek experience of death, a rich documentation on the Homeric period is found in Emily Vermeule, *Aspects of Death in Early Greek Art and Poetry* (Berkeley: University of California Press, 1979). A general presentation is found in Laurence Kahn-Lyotard and Nicole Loraux, "Death in Greek Myths," in Yves Bonnefoy, ed., *Greek and Egyptian Mythologies*, trans. Wendy Doniger (Chicago: University of Chicago Press, 1992), pp. 105–112. But see also the work of Nicole Loraux on "beautiful death" and, on the subsequent period, see *The Invention of Athens: The Funeral Oration in the Classical City*, trans. Alan Sheridan (New York: Zone Books, 2006). And also see the articles in Jean-Pierre Vernant, *Mortals and Immortals: Collected Essays*, ed. Froma I. Zeitlin (Princeton: Princeton University Press, 1991). We would point out—see, for example, Karl Reinhardt, *Die "Ilias" und ihr Dichter*, ed. Uvo Hölscher (Göttingen: Vandenhoeck und Ruprecht, 1961)—that the *Iliad* is less of a poem about war, as has often been repeated, than a poem about death. See Jasper Griffin, *Homer on Life and Death* (Oxford: Clarendon, 1980), p. 94: "It is in accordance with this overriding interest in human life, in its quality as intense and glorious yet transitory, and its position poised between the eternal brightness of heaven and the unchanging darkness of the world of the dead, that the Homeric poems are interested in death far more than they are in fighting." On the place of the warrior's experience in these poems, also see James M. Redfield, "Warfare and the Hero in the Classical World," *Laetaberis*, 3 (1984), pp. 1–16.

about which I've already spoken a hundred times, where Odysseus evokes the glory of Achilles, who, like all the dead, is in Hades as only a shadow lacking *noos*, i.e. lacking mind or sense.[87] For only the divine Tiresias, by special grace of Persephone, keeps his mind and intellectual capacities in Hades. All the other psyches, all the other souls are shadows that float.[88] They know nothing, recall nothing, and must be made to drink blood so as to be able to hold "veridical discourse."[89] And Achilles responds to Odysseus: "Don't try to make death easy for me. I would prefer to be alive and a day laborer for a very poor peasant rather than to reign among the dead."[90] There you have the truth of existence in the poems. There's certainly a survival, but this survival is still more miserable than life on earth. It's even more miserable. As far as promise is concerned, that's all there is. And I could call up and comment here on other passages, like the speech Achilles offers Lycaon in Book XXI of the *Iliad*, when the latter pleads with him to spare his life for a great ransom. Achilles responds to him essentially with: "Why are you crying thus? Patroclus, who was far greater than you, is dead. As you look upon me, fine and tall, son of a goddess.... Alas, for me too, some day at dawn or at dusk or perhaps in full midday, Ares will take away all power from my body, and I will die. So die, you, as well."[91] And he kills him.

This grasp of death may seem bizarre in its very banality. For, you can say to me: "You're boring me with that, everyone knows that, and so on. Not only Homer and the Greeks, but everyone." Obviously, that's flat out wrong. Nobody knows it. Humanity spends its time telling stories about non-death in its different forms. The brutal fact has quite obviously always been occulted in the imaginary institution of every society. We can now ask ourselves the question: Where does this idea we find in Homer come from? It isn't visibly held by the Egyptians, who have a whole cycle of metempsychosis and so on, nor by the Babylonians, nor by the Mycenaeans.[92] It's quite simply that it just

---

87. *Eds*.: Homer, *Odyssey*, XI, 467–541.
88. *Eds*.: Homer, *Odyssey*, X, 491–495.
89. *Eds*.: Homer, *Odyssey*, XI, 148–149.
90. *Trans*.: Homer, *Odyssey*, XI, 488–493.
91. *Eds*.: Homer, *Iliad*, XXI, 100–115.
92. *Eds*.: Castoriadis could probably have recalled here certain aspects of the Sumerian-Akkadian conception of the afterlife, whose influence on the "composer" of the epic, whether direct or indirect, cannot be excluded. See Walter Burkert, "Orientalizing Features in Homer," in *Babylon, Memphis, Persepolis: Eastern Contexts of Greek Culture* (Cambridge, MA: Harvard University Press, 2004), pp. 21–48, and M. L. West, *The East Face of Helicon: West Asiatic Elements in Greek Poetry* (Oxford: Oxford University Press, 1997). On this conception, see the essay by Jean Bottéro, "The Mythology of Death," in *Mesopotamia: Writing,*

corresponds to reality. This is curious, but it's the case: It's the Greeks who discovered this fact that there is a final, definitive death—*telos thanatoio*, as the *Iliad* says time and again—i.e. that there's nothing to say about it, that we cannot give it any other signification, transubstantiate it, embellish it.

Here's a digression. We will find other peoples, for example the Hebrews before Isaiah, who seem not to believe in the immortality of the soul. But two elements come into the picture with them and contribute in some sense to attenuating the rigor of this matter. First of all, the man who's pious and God-loved will have a happy old age, like Abraham. He will die contented and full of days; these are the very terms of the Old Testament. That's inconceivable for the Greeks. They don't have heroes who die happy and filled with days. Even Hercules has an atrocious end (the Tunic of Nessus). Second, just as the damnation of God carries over across successive generations, divine benediction for the pious and God-loved man translates into the benediction of those whom he generates. This also makes no sense for the Greeks, for whom nothing is guaranteed regarding descendants.

But we should go even further and distinguish between a death one submits to and a death chosen.[93] If we restrict ourselves to saying that the Greeks—a surprising thing—are the first to discover that man is mortal in a

---

Reasoning, and the Gods, trans. Zainab Bahrani and Marc Van de Mieroop (Chicago: University of Chicago Press, 1995), pp. 268–286. It is true, as Georges Roux points out In *Ancient Iraq*, 3rd edition (London: Penguin Books, 1992), p. 100, that "such details of the Mesopotamian eschatology as we can extract from the myth 'Inanna's descent to the Netherworld' or the Sumerian cycle of Gilgamesh are scanty and often contradictory." Importantly, similar beliefs can be found in cultural contexts that are altogether different. Deprived of the hope of a Paradise, but promised a "wretched and dreary" afterlife, what the Mesopotamian, who felt periodically threatened by the order of things, sought, which holds true through the end of Mesopotamian civilization, was "to provoke the decision of the gods and secure their goodwill by performing age-old rites" (pp. 102–103). This is the meaning Roux gives in his interpretation to the Babylonian New Year Festival, explicitly taking up themes from Thorkild Jacobsen in Henri Frankfort et al., *The Intellectual Adventure of Ancient Man* (Chicago: Chicago University Press, 1946).

93. *Eds.*: In the 1976–1981 seminars at the Collège de France, Jean-Pierre Vernant tried to show that both the epic song (the celebration of the "beautiful death" of the hero, the choice of a brief life) and the funeral memorial translate the same "strategy with regard to death" that allows one to create, thanks to the memories of "exemplary deaths," the common past of a community of the living. See the texts gathered in Vernant, *Mortals and Immortals*, especially "A Beautiful Death and the Disfigured Corpse in Homeric Epic," pp. 49–74. See also Griffin, "Death and the God-Like Hero," i.e. chapter 3 in *Homer*, pp. 81–102. That said, while Vernant's contribution is certainly taken into consideration, Castoriadis is here pursuing a reflection on themes of his own. See Castoriadis, *Imaginary Institution*, pp. 315–316.

final and definitive sense, that would of course be interesting. But with that we would be stopping with simple awareness of an aspect of man's animality. Cattle die, horses die, humans die too. Or, at most we might move on to the more advanced point on this subject which is characteristic of modern philosophy, for example in Heidegger, for whom man is the only animal that knows that he must die. Obviously, what's essential in the Greek world goes beyond that. They're aware not only of the fact that we die but that we choose our own death and that we choose death. The two most striking characters of the whole Greek imaginary, the one in his origin—Achilles, a fictive hero—and the other in his culmination—Socrates, a character quite real and historical—both choose death.[94] Achilles knows that nothing matters as much as life, and yet he chooses death. He doesn't go back to Phthia but goes into battle, certain to find glory but also death there. The tragic grasp, here, is not the simple discovery of death, end of story, nor simply the fact that *Dasein* is *Sein zum Tode* as Heidegger would say, i.e. that being-there is a being towards death. No contradiction exists simply within being-towards-death. But the tragic grasp is the grasp of an ultimate contradiction, namely: Nothing is worth as much as life, but if nothing is worth more than life, then life is worth nothing. In the same vein, Socrates says that the *anexetastos bios*, the life without examination, the unreflective life—taking reflective in the strongest sense—is not livable. And likewise Achilles said that the *bios atimētos* or *akleiēs*, the life without glory, without renown, isn't livable. Here we have a contradiction in the object itself, which means in the texture of existence independently of subjectivity. And this contradiction in the situation of the human being is of course fully translated into the subjective plane, if I may use modern terminology. That is, man (*anthrōpos*) is necessarily torn apart by opposed motivations, which means, on the one hand, by the avoidance of death, or the consciousness that nothing is worth as much as life, and, on the other hand, by the avoidance of a life that wouldn't contain what makes it worthy of being lived. This tearing apart is moreover constantly present in the poems. If you reread them attentively, you will see that—contrary to what would be suggested by the inanities (they must be so called) of certain moderns—two times out of three the hero going into battle says to himself, "Am I not going to run away?" Ajax wonders, "Can I stay here? No, it's terrible, I'm going to run away." Odysseus says the same thing to himself, and Patroclus, and Hector, i.e. this Hector who rather

---

94. *Eds.*: See Plato, *Apology*, 28b–d, where Socrates cites the *Iliad*, XVIII, 113–123 (on the attitude of Achilles facing death). On the death of Socrates, see Moses I. Finley, "Socrates and Athens," in *Aspects of Antiquity* (London: Chatto and Windus, 1968), pp. 58–72; as well as Claude Mossé, *Le Procès de Socrate* (Brussels: Éditions Complexe, 1996).

than Achilles—and we will return to this—serves as the genuine hero of the *Iliad*. These beings who, they tell us, have yet to achieve an integration of their psychical faculties, or among whom the poet does not envision the integration of these faculties; these beings who are supposedly not persons since the person is—no?—a Christian invention; these beings who supposedly are not true individuals, who are just functions, shadows, symbolic predicates.... These beings, facing the enemy who is advancing, are continuously sweating from fear and saying to themselves, "Will I stay here? Will I go and fight or will I flee to save my sweet life?" It's after such an interior dialogue has concluded, which reoccurs in the *Iliad* at least a dozen times, that the hero generally—but not always—makes the decision to stay there, to fight, and eventually to get himself killed. This isn't always so, since there are some who flee, which happens to Menelaus and to Hector. It's not that Hector would be particularly cowardly. On the contrary, he's the bravest of warriors. Therefore, this dialogue of the soul with itself—to borrow the expression of Socrates and Plato—is not of such a kind as to be there only for décor or for style. The result of this dialogue is not predetermined, since there are moments when the hero abandons the field of battle. And when he stays, which obviously occurs in the great majority of cases (otherwise this wouldn't be a hero and there would be no epic poetry), it's after this deliberation has reached its end.[95]

95. *Eds.*: The question of the *decision* (and of the role of divine intervention) among the Homeric heroes has been the subject of many debates since the mid-1990s. It was already at the center of discussions on the Homeric "self," on which, see the texts cited in note 61, p. 55, to which we must add the famous work by Albin Lesky, *Göttliche und menschliche Motivation im homerischen Epos* (Heidelberg: Carl Winter, 1961), which is partially translated in Cairns, *Oxford Readings*, pp. 170-202, as well as James M. Redfield, "Le sentiment homérique du moi," *Le Genre humain*, 12 (1985), pp. 93-111. In 1993, philosopher Bernard Williams made an important contribution in *Shame and Necessity*, especially chapter 2 ("Centers of Agency"), pp. 21-49, the conclusions of which are not far from those of Castoriadis, despite the distance between their starting points (i.e. Williams belongs to the British analytic tradition); and Bernard Knox wrote a substantial review of this work, contained in *Backing*, pp. 220-243. One may also consult the work of Richard Raskin, "Do Homeric Heroes Make Real Decisions?" *Classical Quarterly*, 40 (1990), pp. 1-15 (also contained in Cairns, *Oxford Readings*, pp. 147-169); and there are additional references to the works of T. Jahn, A. Schmitt, H. Pellicia, and M. Finkelberg to be found in Cairns, "Introduction," pp. 12-24. See also Christopher Gill, *Personality in Greek Epic, Tragedy, and Philosophy* (Oxford: Clarendon, 1996). On the overall set of questions treated in Seminars IV-VI, see Bernard Knox's excellent "Introduction" to Homer and Fagles, *The Iliad*, pp. 3-64, the position of which overlaps with many of the points presented here.

IV. SEMINAR FROM DECEMBER 1, 1982

Questions

On the problem of the participation of the spectators: If they already know what they are going to find in the spectacle, why do they go?

In any case, they do not go for the suspense. Their attitude is not that of the modern spectator. What is a classical text, a piece of classical music, a classic scene? It's not something whose study has been approved by the Ministry of Education, which is regularly mistaken about it. Rather, it's a work that you can go back to ceaselessly, and you read it, see it, hear it even better. You listen for the thousandth time to a piece of great music, and you hear things you didn't hear before. You read a great text for the thousandth time, and you think beyond—and different things than—what you've already thought. I believe that in one's relationship with the Homeric poems, with tragedy, or in modern times with Elizabethan tragedy for example, it's this element that's determinative for the spectator, the reader, or the listener. This is doubtless also the case with Homer, despite the other factors there, which are in fact always present for us, e.g. "It's a different rhapsode there who's reciting the encounter of Achilles and Priam, so let's go see how he does it." Like when you go hear Berganza in the role of Zerlina, or Schwarzkopf in that of Donna Elvira, and so on. When it's a matter of tragedy, it's obviously something different since there—this is well known—the general framework is that of the legend. The text itself is presented for the first time to the Dionysia, and judges who are to a certain extent the representatives of the community, even if they are not elected, go on to award the prize. The interest, there, is in the treatment of the legend by the author; it's about the text properly speaking, the incidents, and the development that the author will give to that legend. And we know through certain examples that this development could be very distinctive. The story of the Atreidai treated by Aeschylus in *Oresteia* and by Sophocles in *Electra* are not the same thing. The same myth can be used in very different ways by Sophocles and Euripides. So, there's my response on the issue of the spectators of the tragedy. As for the poems, it's an issue of a relationship to a classical, monumental text, which lends itself indefinitely to rediscovery. And this hasn't changed, by the way. But let's not forget, in Homer's case, the more or less conscious perception of the fact that we are dealing here with our source text.

How do you situate yourself relative to Hegel's Ruse of Reason and the interpretation that Adorno gives to Odysseus?

I don't know.... A few moments ago, when I said that the free decision of the hero is, each time, a necessary link in the unfolding of fatal *moira*, I nearly cited Hegel and mentioned the Ruse of Reason and also what Adorno says about Odysseus and the "dialectic of myth and reason" in the *Odyssey*.[96] I didn't do that, in the end, because I believe we're in an entirely different context. By that, I mean that it doesn't make any sense, speaking of Homer, to talk of a Ruse of Reason, since in fact Hegel was only thinking of tragedy. For sure, he could read tragedy—in particular *Oedipus the King*—as a series of ruses of reason since we find in it an entire chaining together of acts that apparently have no purpose, or which have rather a wholly different purpose in the mind of those who accomplish them, and which all work together in the predetermined march of the process in its whole, even while—or, one could say, all the more so because—their manifest signification is opposed to their latent signification since the more an act seems to want to divert tragedy from its fatal path, the more in fact it approaches it. And one could think that tragedy is one of the sources of the very idea of a Ruse of Reason. But the retroactive reading, in my view, is not possible for the very simple reason that there is no reason in this affair. That is, we cannot talk of reason being a matter of destiny—*moira*—since the latter has precisely an a-rational character, which I will revisit next time, and it is an entirely essential element of the Greek grasp of the world.

As for Odysseus, it's evident that he's really an individual and that the *Odyssey*—we'll speak about this again—is the first Western novel, by contrast with the *Iliad*. It's a novel in the grand and strong sense of the word. But that's well known. And Odysseus doesn't have only that particular aspect. With him there is already a certain form of what we call modernity, or Westernness, if you will. Adorno himself sees in this one of the first manifestations of "bourgeois civilization." But that's a bit secondary here.

---

96. *Eds.*: See Max Horkheimer and Theodor Adorno, *Dialectic of Enlightenment*, trans. Edmund Jephcott (Stanford: Stanford University Press, 2002), pp. 62–68 and 77–126. We know that for Horkheimer and Adorno, the "lone voyager armed with cunning" is already a "*homo œconomicus*, whom all reasonable people will one day resemble: for this reason, the *Odyssey* is already a Robinsonade" (p. 48). They then wished to study "the dialectic of myth and enlightenment in the *Odyssey*, as one of the earliest representative documents of bourgeois Western civilization. It focuses primarily on the concepts of sacrifice and renunciation, through which both the difference between and the unity of mythical nature and enlightened mastery of nature become apparent" (p. xviii).

V. Seminar from December 15, 1982

I'll remind you of our approach. It's through our search for the roots or first elements of what we may call the Greek grasp of the world that we're interested in the Homeric poems. In our inquiry we thus inevitably consider what came afterwards. It's a tautology, if you will, but it has its importance; we need not conceal the fact that this is an attitude filled with dangers. Consider the example of the beginnings of a critique of the heroic world in Homer, in particular in the famous dialogue, or rather yelling match, between Odysseus and Thersites in Book II of the *Iliad*, a one-way yelling match, for that matter.[97] Thersites is a man of the people; he's truly the representative of the anonymous mass explicitly devalorized by Homer, including in his appearance: he's very ugly, he's squinting, he limps, and so on. He castigates Agamemnon, criticizes the conduct of the war and the war itself. We could say that we have here, perhaps, the first document written in which the exploited classes try to transform an imperialist war into a civil war, as one will later say (I'm only half joking). And it's Odysseus, filled with arrogance, who responds to him, who insults him, who strikes him with his *skēptron*, which is the insignia of royal power held by the one who is addressing other heroes. Thersites cannot—dares not—reply; he weeps from sadness while the masses laugh in a cowardly way at the spectacle of this poor simpleton. We see here an extremely entrenched opposition, and a dividing line in value, between the heroes and the *profanum vulgus*, the *polloi*, or as one will say later on, the *ochlos*, the *dēmos* (this term in Homer doesn't have the sense it will carry later on); only the heroes truly exist, and the others are just the mass that follows along.[98] Here, there's an aristocratic conception of the world—very obvious and very important in the poems—which will certainly survive subsequently. But it's self-evident that the origin of the Greek creation, in the strong sense of the term, of philosophy and of democracy lies in something else. For, there are other elements that coexist with this aristocratic conception. Now, you might say that we're wise after the event, aware after the fact. But the fact remains

---

97. *Eds.*: Homer, *Iliad*, II, 198–277.
98. *Eds.*: See Homer, *Iliad*, II, 200–206; and XI, 299–305.

that we're carrying out a historical inquiry, that we're thus perfectly entitled to be selective, and that we will already find elements in Homer that are wholly essential to what is for us the core of the imaginary significations and of the Greek grasp of the world.

I will review briefly the basic themes broached last time. Regarding the very definition of the Homeric poems, if they are the grand formative text of Greece, then they're by no means a revealed or sacred text. It's a poet who speaks, not a prophet. This fundamental point distinguishes Greece from all the other cultures, including those of the European area, where the invocation of revealed religion, of the Christian religion, is always present in the social and political struggles that unfold there from the eleventh century onwards, up to and including the American Revolution. The Preamble to the Declaration of Independence of the United States (1776): "We take these truths to be self-evident, that all men are created equal, that they are endowed by the Creator with certain unalienable rights [...]." The European world doesn't easily separate itself from this relationship to a revealed truth, supposing that it does manage to do so at all. In Greece, religion is something very important, which makes up a part of the *polis*, thus of the political institutions, but it precisely *makes up a part* and is never the source. No Greek would have ever imagined consulting the Delphic Oracle in order to know what the laws of his city should be, although one could ask about the choice of a prospective legislator, which is not at all the same thing.[99]

The second point, with which we concluded the last time, is that the fundamental signification of the poems, a certain tragic grasp of the world, is inscribed in their very texture, incarnate in the story recounted, the myth, the epic (the distinction between myth and epic is not an easy question, and I'll not discuss it here). And this expression is independent of the Homeric heroes' discourses. Even if one were to remove them all, the unfolding of the story would remain a tragedy, and even a meta-tragedy. For, what's at the heart of this tragic vision of the world is death, a universal experience certainly, but one lived among the Greeks—at least from Homer on—without any embellishment or compensation, which already constitutes an extraordinary singularity relative to other cultures. Even in the religions where there isn't direct immortality, for example with the Hebrews, divine benediction can extend to the following generations, if one has been well behaved. Lastly, in the most important episodes of the poems, death is chosen—and this is what distinguishes the Greek grasp of death from, for example, early Buddhism, even in its deepest, most sublime aspects. I reminded you on this

---

99. *Eds.*: See note 20, p. 24.

issue that the two characters to whom the specifically Greek representation of human existence applies—one in myth (Achilles) and the other in reality (Socrates)—both choose death.

Now, and so as not to get lost in the magma of all the significations contained in the poems, I would like to enumerate for you the themes that we're going to brush through, so to speak, since in the framework of this seminar we couldn't deal with them in depth. We begin with *moira*—not fate, not *fatum*, but *moira*; then, we'll talk about freedom, to use a modern term, and the individuation of human beings; then notions of universality and impartiality. After that we'll approach two very important aspects of the organization of the human world and of the fundamental descriptions that are posited there: on the one hand, *aristeia*, the supreme value, excellence; on the other hand, and with regard to the episode of the Cyclops in the *Odyssey*, the elements that herald the constitution of a political community at the basis of the democratic *polis*. Then we'll talk about Greek religion, not only in its relationship with society but in its very content. We'll try to take up all these threads so as to arrive at the global Homeric grasp of the world, about which we'll see that it's already implicit within the opposition, which is in my view essential for Greek thought, between chaos and cosmos. And we'll conclude by trying to see how the poems already contain the germs of a calling into question of the heroic world that they describe. As I already said, the world serving as the referent in the poems is effectively that of the "dark ages," after the disappearance of the Mycenaean world and before the emergence of the world of the *polis*. And we'll try always to distinguish the real universe to which the poems refer from the significations they carry, which do not concern the heroic world but the one within which the poet lives, which means that of the eighth century, perhaps the second half of the eighth century, around 720.

The term *moira*, recurrent in the poems, especially in the *Iliad*, is to be linked to the verb *merizō*, which means to partition, to divide.[100] *Moira* is thus the partition, the share, the lot, the draw. And the root **(s)mer-* immediately gives us the answer to the question: What is the *moira*, the share of man? His *moira* is *moros*, that is, death. Homer uses this word, derivative of *moira*; and the expressions *morsimon hēmar* or, in another context, *aisimon hēmar* (*aisa* is a synonym of *moira*) return regularly to designate the fatal day, the day of the death of a hero, the day that had been imparted to him, in the initial partitioning, as a boundary of his existence. It's important to concentrate on this signification of *moira* since this same word is used in some very concrete

---

100. *Eds.*: See Bernard C. Dietrich, "Chapter 7: Moira in Homer," in *Death, Fate and the Gods* (London: Athlone Press, 1965), pp. 194–231; and Onians, *Origins, passim*.

acceptations: a parcel of land, an army division, and even, in later authors, a political party, are also shares, *moirai*; but the *moira* par excellence is that of the human being, i.e. death.

In Hesiod, the *Moirai*, or Moirae, are three goddesses, daughters of the Night, who, like other pre-Olympian divinities, are formidable, vengeful beings for whom anger does not subside before they have punished those guilty of faults, gods or men.[101] That's how Walter Otto describes them in the last chapter, "Fate," of his excellent book.[102] And if we may assume relationships, negotiations, between these Moirae and men or gods, this is not likewise the case for Homeric *moira*, which is *not* a divinity personified but an impersonal force, a sort of supreme legality which imposes itself onto men as onto gods. There, where *moira* dictates its law, neither discussion nor reconciliation is possible. To whom would one address a supplication or sacrifice, given that *moira* is no one? Even the qualifier of merciless, which one can at least attribute to the Erinyes up through Aeschylus, would be too much here.[103] And one can also glimpse this quasi-abstract character of Homeric *moira*, borne out by recurrent expressions in the poems, through an illustration in two analogous and decisive scenes from the *Iliad* where Zeus, who nevertheless knows the decrees of *moira*, all the same wants to verify them. The first time, in Book VIII, while the battle had resumed between the Acheans and the Trojans, he deployed his golden balance to weigh out the fates, the *kēres* of the two armies, and the scale damns the Acheans.[104] The same scene, but more intense and more poignant, is repeated in Book XXII. Hector is pursued by Achilles and cannot escape him; they've already gone four times around Troy, and as they pass in front of the sacred fountains, Zeus again deploys his golden balance and places the *kēres* of the two heroes on it.[105] It's the pan containing Hector's fatal day, his *aisimon hēmar*, which is heaviest and falls, disappearing into Hades. Apollo, who heretofore had protected Hector, abandons him, while Athena comes and puts herself on the side of Achilles, whose lance will finally kill Hector. Every time, therefore, Zeus, the king of gods, must resort to a balance, a little machine—it's surprising that no structuralist has played with this yet—so as to know the decrees of *moira*. This impersonal all-powerfulness is neither Yahweh, nor God the

---

101. *Eds.*: Hesiod, *Theogony*, 215–222.
102. *Eds.*: Otto, *Homeric Gods*, pp. 263–286.
103. *Eds.*: Homer, *Iliad*, IX, 571–572, in Homer, *The Iliad of Homer*, trans. Richmond Lattimore (Chicago: University of Chicago Press, 1967): "[And] Erinys, the mist-walking, she of the heart without pity, heard her out of the dark places."
104. *Eds.*: Homer, *Iliad*, VIII, 69–72.
105. *Eds.*: Homer, *Iliad*, XXII, 208–213.

father, nor Allah; it's rather the idea of a law of the world that isn't personified and to which the gods themselves are subject. And we could maintain that all of that which, in rational thought, amounts to a search for irrefutable and inescapable regularities—whether it's a matter of physical or biological problems or of human affairs—is already there in germ in this construction of an impersonal, quasi-abstract *moira*, which imposes its decrees onto men as onto gods, and which is not a divinity that one might invoke or try to sway.

Here's another important point. The domain or reign of *moira* is that of limits, of bounds, of *perata*, to use a very weighty term in all of Greek thinking and in all subsequent philosophy. And, if I may say so, the central limit—this expression exists in mathematics but with a different meaning—is obviously death, *moros*, for all that lives. But within this limitation, there are more limits, the non-transgression of which *moira* also guarantees, and to which the Homeric expression *hyper moron* corresponds. That is, such and such character is unable to accomplish this or that action because, says Homer, this would be *hyper moron*. On this topic there are at least two cases that are worth recalling. First of all, in Book XVI of the *Iliad*, Patroclus, despite the warning of Achilles, pursued a furious combat. Three times he rose to assault the walls, and on this day, Homer tells us, the high-gated city would have perhaps fallen due to the blows of the Achaeans had Apollo not been there to repulse Patroclus. "Back off, you know well that it's not your *aisa* to take Troy, nor even that of Achilles, who is far superior to you."[106] Patroclus understood that with this he had pursued a battle *hyper moron*, but it was already too late, and he would be killed. The other episode is found at the very beginning of the *Odyssey*.[107] The gods have assembled to decide the lot of Odysseus, prisoner of Calypso, but Zeus starts by evoking the fury and folly of men, and especially of Aegisthus, who had been notified by Hermes that Orestes would kill him if he became the lover of Clytemnestra and the murderer of Agamemnon. It was thus in full knowledge of the facts that Aegisthus committed these acts of transgression and brought upon himself the afflictions that burdened him. In classical tragedy there's most frequently a progression of knowledge; for example in *Oedipus the King* the hero knows nothing and it's through the unfolding of the tragedy that he attains knowledge. In Homer, it's not like that. Patroclus and Achilles know; Aegisthus knows. The messenger of the gods himself had announced to him what would happen to him if he did what he wasn't supposed to do.

106. *Eds.*: Homer, *Iliad*, XVI, 684–711.
107. *Eds.*: Homer, *Odyssey*, I, 28–47.

The decrees of *moira* thus firstly have to do with death, the ultimate limit of existence, but also, within the realm of human activities, with certain limits that must not be transgressed. And this will remain a fundamental given in the organization of the world for the Greeks. A fragment of Heraclitus states that if the Sun, who is a god, were to divert from his course, the Erinyes would ensure that he respects his limits.[108] This fragment confirms for us that *moira* thus imposes itself also on the gods, who can do nothing about it. And we can even—though here things certainly become more obscure—interpret the myth of successive generations of gods in power as the consequence of a decree of *moira*. That is, Ouranos and Chronos wanted to perpetuate their domination and exterminate their children; they wanted to stop the natural course of time. They were thus likewise themselves condemned. The story extends even to Zeus himself, in the *Prometheia* trilogy, which is an incredible tragedy, one that perhaps appears even more incredible to us since only the second part (the first one, according to some), *Prometheus Bound*, has come down to us.[109] The Titan Prometheus, enchained for having given to humans what he was not supposed to give to them, fire, pits himself against Zeus. He knows that one day the latter will also be overturned by another divine power.[110] As such, no power is eternal, not even that of the gods. In eastern theocratic monarchy, power is given by the god who can withdraw it if such is his decision or if the king fails. But here it's a matter of the power of the gods which can be, which even must be overturned. We encounter again here the central theme of the famous Anaximander fragment, which we'll speak about in a few weeks: Since you have reigned, you can no longer reign; since you have been, you can no longer be. This limit, which Anaximander will call the "rendering of reciprocal justice among beings by destroying themselves or by being destroyed," applies just as much to gods.[111] In the third part, now lost, *Prometheus Unbound*, there was a reconciliation between Zeus and Prometheus. This theme is proper to Aeschylus, but, as you know, the myth is constantly reinterpreted and re-elaborated by the poets and in particular by the tragedians. Be that as it may, the threats proffered by Prometheus, which today we would call sacrilege, doubtless could not have been written by Aeschylus if they had not corresponded both to a certain mythical tradition

---

108. *Eds.*: Heraclitus, DK 22B94.
109. *Eds.*: On the place of *Prometheus Bound* in Aeschylus's trilogy, see Mark Griffith, "Appendix: The Trilogy," in Aeschylus, *Prometheus Bound* (Cambridge: Cambridge University Press, 1983), pp. 281–305; and in French, Suzanne Saïd, *Sophiste et Tyran, ou le problème de* Prométhée enchaîné (Paris: Klincksieck, 1985).
110. *Eds.*: See Seminar VI, note 166, p. 111.
111. *Eds.*: See Seminar X, pp. 164–174.

and to something that was perceived as self-evident by the Greeks. That is, as Chronos had overthrown Ouranos, and as Zeus had overthrown Chronos, a day will come when Zeus will likewise be overthrown. For, such is the *moira* of men and gods.

The third point on which I would concentrate, and which Walter Otto likewise saw clearly, is that *moira* is not a fate in the usual sense of the term, in the sense of *fatum*, of a predetermination and an absolute predestination. For, if *moira* does set limits, within these limits humans decide freely, in a sense. More precisely, they decide to transgress or not; and if they transgress, the nemesis will punish their waywardness. It's true that, in the poems, human decisions often have only the appearance of freedom, when the gods whisper to the heroes what they must do. And if this is sometimes good counsel, like with Athena *vis-à-vis* Achilles or Odysseus, most of the time they trick the humans and lead them into catastrophe and death. Yet, in the most crucial moments of the Homeric story—thus also for us the most characteristic ones—the heroes decide without assistance, incitation, or divine trickery. That's the case as we've just seen with Aegisthus, possessed by *hybris*, by that rage for transgression. But as for Achilles—and here I'm anticipating the next theme, human freedom (but I warned you about the extreme convolutedness of all these points)—his choices have no connection to limits to transgress or not; rather, they have to do with this dilemma: Must I go to Troy, bring glory on myself in combat, and die young? Or rather stay in my native kingdom to live a peaceful, but obscure and insignificant, life? He will confront this dilemma in the *Iliad* when, facing the embassy Agamemnon has sent him, he criticizes the absurdity, the nonsense of war and says that he's going to go back to Phthia to live and die there without glory but in tranquility. At the end of the day he—alone, freely, without there being any question here of limits to transgress—chooses renown and glory (*kleos* and *kydos*, which are two very important terms we will find again soon) and thus death.

Another hero also chooses death deliberately. It's of course Odysseus in the *Odyssey*. The nymph Calypso is in love with him. (Incidentally, there are lots of goddesses in love with men, but fewer than the cases of gods in love with women. And, by the way, Calypso complains to Hermes about the jealousy of gods, who will not put up with the goddesses' human loves even though they're always having a grand time with mortal women! This has been interpreted very uninterestingly, but let's move on….) Calypso had offered him immortality provided that he would stay with her. Odysseus thus has the choice between either immortality or the return to Ithaca followed by death. And he knows what death is, that it's worse than nothing. Having descended into Hades, he'd seen the miserable shadows wandering there. But he refuses

Calypso's offer.[112] A different element no doubt factors into his decision. Odysseus clearly knows that in any case he must die. He only has the choice between either an immortality that would throw into nothingness everything he was or a human death among his family in Ithaca. If he were to become immortal, he'd no longer be the same Odysseus, the one who with Calypso had longed to die, had dreamt of seeing "even if just the smoke" rising from his native land.[113] That's clearly spelled out in the poem, and one can only be astounded by the improbable profundity—no doubt unconscious, but regardless—that it achieves there.

Furthermore—and now we're getting into the paradox, into the aporia of this idea of a human immortality—how can an indefinite life be conceived? As growing old without end? That would be an absolutely horrible vision. But it is, by the way, at the center of another Greek myth, that of Tithonus. Tithonus, also a Homeric hero, is one of the sons of Priam. The goddess Eos, i.e. Aurora, has fallen in love with him. Previously she was infatuated with Ganymede, but Zeus took him away from her. In the guise of compensation, she asks Zeus to accord immortality to her new love. The years pass, and Tithonus grows older and older. He grows smaller, wrinkly, and decrepit, and finally Eos transforms him into a cicada.[114] Obviously, for a god immortality means eternal youth, but for humans it implies an entirely inconceivable temporality. How can one describe an eternal present which is nevertheless not immobile? And you find the same aporia in a form that is, it's true, a lot more vulgar in the Christian doctrine of the resurrection of the body. To what age will the stillborn child, the old dotard, or the mutilated soldier be restored? In what body? It's not known. These are mysteries of faith; they can't be thought.

To conclude, I come back to *moira*. So, while it is a matter of internal limits to existence, men are aware of them; and if they transgress them, it's because they are carried away by *hybris*. Man is this being possessed by *hybris*, by the rage for transgression. Homer reminds us constantly of this possibility which is up to men to decide on. We saw it for Aegisthus as for Odysseus. Hercules also chooses between virtue and vice.[115] And we find the same idea 150 years later in Solon, who addressed himself to the Athenians early in the sixth

---

112. *Eds.*: Homer, *Odyssey*, V, 214–221; and VII, 245–247.
113. *Eds.*: Homer, *Odyssey*, I, 58–59.
114. *Eds.*: On the myth of Eos and Tithonus, and the distinction between immortality and eternal youth, see the commentaries by Gregory Nagy, *The Best of the Achaeans: Concepts of the Hero in Archaic Greek Poetry* (Baltimore: Johns Hopkins University Press, 1979), pp. 196 ff.
115. *Eds.*: See the apologue by Prodicus of Ceos, as reported by Xenophon, *Memorabilia*, II, 1, 21–34 (= DK 84B2).

century, saying to them: "Don't complain about Zeus; you are yourselves, through your stupidities, through your meanness, the cause of what happens to you."[116]

Thus, there's no fate but rather an ultimate limit—death—and certain interior limits, within which man decides, alone sometimes, even if he dialogues with the gods and is very often under their influence. And this Homeric conception of *moira* is, in my view, fundamental. On the one hand, it announces and already contains what's necessarily at the basis of all rational research and of all rational reflection, which means that there exist laws that impose limits on all things, and which do not depend on some divine arbitrariness; on the other hand, as Aristotle will later say, man is *archē tōn esomenōn*, i.e. a principle and starting point of what will come. Man decides and decides at his own risk and peril and at his own cost, which is most often very heavy; at the end of the tally there's the final "cost/non-cost," i.e. death. This coexistence of an impersonal law and the free decision of the man facing it is, in my view, what liberates the Greek man for action in the practical, political domain as well as in the domain of thought.

I need to add some precision here regarding this decisive and central notion for the Greeks of the *archē tōn esomenōn*. For, if man is an origin and principle of what will come, at the same time he does not have mastery over the consequences of his acts, which Hannah Arendt, by the way, quite rightly emphasized.[117] In Homer this non-mastery is especially relative to concrete, factual consequences of human action, but in tragedy—we'll talk about this again in detail—it takes on an entirely different depth since it's not just the consequences of their acts that men no longer master but their signification. Of course, these two things are indissociable: the signification of an act is also that into which it gets inscribed, that which it goes on to yield. But in the end man does not master the signification. And this is what marks, in Greek tragedy, the limit of the human condition.

Two words now on individuation. First of all, there's the question of individual decision. Numerous passages in the *Iliad* as well as in the *Odyssey* very explicitly present the hesitations of the heroes, depicting them in the moment of combat, confronting opposed discourses within themselves, which is

---

116. *Eds.*: See Solon's famous elegy on "Eunomia," known by a quotation from Demosthenes, i.e. Solon, fragment 4, in M. L. West, ed., *Iambi et Elegi Graeci ante Alexandrum cantati, Volume II* (Oxford: Clarendon, 1972). See also Jaeger, *Paideia, Volume I*, chapter 8, pp. 136–149, and Fränkel, *Early Greek*, chapter 4, section 6, pp. 217–237, both of which relate Solon's words to Zeus's warning in the *Odyssey*, I, 32–43.

117. *Eds.*: See Seminar I, note 5, p. 5.

something Plato will later call "the dialogue of the soul with itself."[118] On this point, Homer uses for example the expression *dicha thymon echein* to describe the mind of the hero as split between two opposed parts.[119] And this decision-making is indissociable from an explicit introspection, from an examination of the reasons for and against, of motives that push for acting or not. All of this is perfectly clear throughout the poems. Yet, a contention arises here, however minor; but I wouldn't want to evade it. That is, it has been claimed that there would not have been any true decisions in the Greek world, at least not in the Homeric poems, but even beyond that, in Plato and Aristotle, because ancient Greece had no awareness of will.[120] Indeed, some still claim as much.[121] Certainly, the word *boulēsis* is absent in Homer—and even much later on—for designating the faculty or psychical seat that would make one choose this rather than that, or which underlies decision. But why conclude from this that the thing itself didn't exist? There's a confusion here between the unawareness of a word or the non-thematization of a notion by a language and the absence of the thing. It's almost as if one were to say that the Greeks didn't have an unconscious because they didn't have the word to designate

---

118. *Eds.*: See also Seminar IV, pp. 75–76.
119. *Eds.*: See Homer, *Odyssey*, XVI, 73, reprised and varied at XIX, 524.
120. *Eds.*: For example, Fränkel, *Early Greek*, p. 392, note 52: "'Will,' however, is a concept that is missing in the intellectual horizons of early and classical Greek thought. [...] Hence, there was no special word for will [...]." Also, see E. R. Dodds, *The Greeks and the Irrational* (Berkeley: University of California Press, 1951), p. 20, note 31, which points out that "Homeric man does not possess the concept of will," although he adds: "And it seems a little artificial to deny that what is described in passages like *Il.* 11.403 ff. or *Od.* 5.355 ff is in effect a reasoned decision taken after consideration of possible alternatives." The latter point serves to criticize Bruno Snell, "Das Bewußtsein von eigenen Entscheidungen im frühen Griechentum," *Philologus*, 85 (1929-1930), pp. 141–158. See also Lloyd-Jones, *Justice*, pp. 9–10 (and on the limits of lexical analysis, pp. 2–3 and 157–158). Also, see the references given above in note 62 on p. 56 and note 95 on p. 76 (especially, on the *ex silentio* argument in Snell, *Discovery*, p. 12, the fierce comments in Knox, *Oldest*, pp. 37 ff.).
121. *Eds.*: See, for example, Jean-Pierre Vernant, "Intimations of the Will in Greek Tragedy," in Vernant and Vidal-Naquet, *Myth and Tragedy*, pp. 49–84. "We are inclined to believe that it is as natural for man to make decisions and act 'as he wills' as it is for him to have arms and legs. And even where a civilization such as that of archaic and classical Greece has in its language no word that corresponds to our own term, we still have no compunction in endowing the men of that time, as it were despite themselves, with this function of the will that they themselves never named" (p. 50). And also: "In fifth-century Athens the individual, with his own particular character, emerged as subject to the law. [...] But neither the individual nor his internal life had acquired enough consistency and autonomy to make the subject the center of decision from which his actions were believed to emanate" (p. 82).

it! But what we should ask ourselves is why, up to a fairly late date, they did not *thematize the will*. As for me, I think that they didn't lack awareness of the concept but that, for them, the will was not a problem. Indeed, behind the thematization by the moderns of this notion, at its roots, there lies something else. A different theoretical lineage, the Jewish and Christian lineage, would have to be recovered there. For, it's on the basis of Christianity—but also certainly already of Judaism—that the human world is struck by an essential sickness, i.e. the sickness of the will. This has an evident onto-theological root, one indissociable from sin, i.e. one ought to do something, but one is perhaps incapable of doing it, and this is a fault. One imputes to oneself, here, the reason for this incapacity, in the form of a bad will or insufficient will. But with the Greeks there is no sin; there thus cannot be any thematization, any problematic of the will. The root lies there, and the culminations of it are in all modern literature, at least as of *Hamlet* through Benjamin Constant's *Adolphe* and the novelists of the nineteenth century: the wavering hero, full of ideas for remaking the world, but "it's awfully late, maybe tomorrow...". The whole of this nebulous thematic is absent from the enormous corpus of ancient Greek literature. There, we find dialogue with oneself, hesitation, questioning, then the decision to act or give in, but not—or only in a very marginal way—this supplementary moment of a deficient will. So, it's not a matter of a non-discovery of the will by the Greeks, but of the non-existence of the sickness of the will, or "sicknesses of will" (as the works of psychiatry from the nineteenth century say), and of the will as a sickness.[122]

On the other point, i.e. individuality, I believe it's hardly necessary to concentrate on it. If, in the poems, there's a fantastic quantity of secondary characters barely individualized, or individualized based on purely exterior attributes, it's absolutely obvious that the great heroes themselves are true persons. This includes Achilles, of course, but also Agamemnon, about whom I do not agree with my friend Vidal-Naquet, who sees in him only a function.[123] For me, Agamemnon is a very singular character, whose description even allows a critique of royalty to appear. For, in the end, in the *Iliad*, he's really just an enormous parasite. That is, he commands, certainly, but his orders are always mediocre, he is neither brave, nor valiant, nor capable,

---

122. *Eds.*: See the title of one of the most well-known works by the French psychologist Théodule Ribot, *The Diseases of the Will*, trans. Merwin-Marie Snell (London: Open Court Publishing Company, 1896).
123. *Eds.*: Vidal-Naquet, "L'*Iliade* sans travesti," p. 53: "Some characters are identified with a military or political function. [...] Agamemnon's function is the royal function." On this point, see also Fernand Robert, *Homère* (Paris: PUF, 1950), pp. 214–271.

and yet he's always the one who has the greater share of the spoils![124] But precisely, as such, Agamemnon is very much someone; he's not a function. Other Homeric heroes are also true persons: Hector, fantastically; Andromache, fantastically. The case of Helen is even more enigmatic and passionate. That is, she misses her homeland, but she doesn't want Troy to be destroyed; and if she loves Menelaus and is angry with Paris, she nevertheless agrees to make love to him.[125] You could believe you were in something by Choderlos de Laclos, with Aphrodite on top of that, which makes a difference. Homer composed a very modern person there, very mysterious, perpetually ambiguous and ambivalent, like in a great novel. Why did she leave Menelaus? Does she really love Paris? In the continuation of her story, which is not in the *Iliad*, she will help Odysseus when he infiltrates Troy.[126]

A bit of time is left for us to talk about what I called universality and impartiality. Hannah Arendt says, in an interview translated a few years ago in *Esprit*, that impartiality emerged into the world with Homer.[127] That's true, especially if we compare the poems with contemporary or prior texts. For, if it's absolutely clear that Homer speaks from the point of view of the Greeks (the "Achaeans" or "Danaans"), it is also entirely clear that this makes no difference with respect to value, in every sense of the term value, between the Achaeans and the Trojans. The former are never better, more beautiful, nor more divine than the latter. They nevertheless are not identical either, but their differences

---

124. *Marg. C.C.*: But there is an *aristeia* <of Agamemnon: Homer, *Iliad*, XI>. — *Eds.*: See the reproaches by Achilles (*Iliad*, I, 149 ff.), Diomedes (*Iliad*, IX, 33–49), or Odysseus (*Iliad*, XIV, 83–102).
125. *Eds.*: Homer, *Iliad*, III, 369–447.
126. *Eds.*: Homer, *Odyssey*, IV, 242–258; and Euripides, *Hecuba*, 239–250.
127. *Eds.*: Interview with Günter Gaus from October 28, 1964, contained as "What Remains? The Language Remains," in Hannah Arendt, *Essays in Understanding, 1930–1954* (New York: Schocken Books, 1994), pp. 1–23. An earlier formulation is found in "History and Immortality," *Partisan Review*, 24:1 (1957), pp. 11–53. See Castoriadis's comments in "Greek Polis." See also Simone Weil: "The human race is not divided up, in the *Iliad*, into conquered persons, slaves, suppliants, on the one hand, and conquerors and chiefs on the other. In this poem there is not a single man who does not at one time or another have to bow his neck to force. [...] Nothing precious is scorned, whether or not death is its destiny; everyone's unhappiness is laid bare without dissimulation or disdain; no man is set above or below the condition common to all men; whatever is destroyed is regretted. Victors and vanquished are brought equally near us; under the same head, both are seen as counterparts of the poet, and the listener as well. [...] There may be, unknown to us, other expressions of the extraordinary sense of equity which breathes through the *Iliad*; certainly it has not been imitated. One is barely aware that the poet is a Greek and not a Trojan." Simone Weil, "The *Iliad*, or: The Poem of Force," trans. Mary McCarthy, *Politics* (1945), pp. 324 and 329.

do not for Homer imply any hierarchy. It's been observed for a long time that the veritable hero of the *Iliad* could clearly be Hector rather than Achilles.[128] In any case, he's the most moving character, through and through tragic, with whom the reader necessarily enters into empathy. One of the two most deeply stirring scenes of the *Iliad* shows him saying his farewells to Andromache.[129] Hector, this awesome warrior, is thinking of his death; the tears of his wife mix with the laughter of his son. In this episode, the poet truly put all the humanity on the side of the Trojans. And then, in the last book, it's Priam who will go and beg Achilles at night to give him Hector's body so he can give him a decent sepulcher, and the humanity is equally partitioned between Achilles and Priam, who is an absolutely poignant figure, gripping in his truth.[130]

Finley, whom I admire a lot, thinks he nevertheless finds a small disequilibrium in metaphorical treatment in passages where the Trojans are likened to sheep fleeing at the moment of battle, and Vidal-Naquet follows him on this issue.[131] Finley says this is an image that Homer never uses for the Achaeans.[132] But we may also think that this image is called for in the context

---

128. *Eds.*: James M. Redfield, *Nature and Culture in the Iliad: The Tragedy of Hector* (Durham, NC: Duke University Press, 1994), notes, however, that Hector has been "neglected by the critics": "Of the more recent literary appreciators of Homer only Schadewaldt (1944) has devoted much space to Hector" (p. 249, note 1). Redfield's reference here is to Wolfgang Schadewaldt, *Von Homers Welt und Werk* (Leipzig: Koehler, 1965). But also see Jacqueline de Romilly, *Hector* (Paris: Éditions de Fallois, 1997).
129. *Eds.*: Homer, *Iliad*, VI, 390–496.
130. *Eds.*: Homer, *Iliad*, XXIV, 470–676.
131. *Eds.*: Finley, *World*, p. 43: "True, the poet denigrates [the Trojans] in small, but subtle, ways that easily escape the modern reader. The Trojan hosts, but never the Achaeans, are compared to a flock of sheep or a swarm of locusts." A similar point of view is expressed in Annie Schnapp-Gourbeillon, *Lion, héros, masques: Les représentations de l'animal chez Homère* (Paris: Maspero, 1981), *passim* and especially p. 31: "The author does not miss an occasion to subtly discredit the opponent." Pierre Vidal-Naquet, in "*L'Iliade* sans travesti," argues that collective comparisons "provide the decisive element," and in particular he discusses the "bleating sheep" passage from Book IV, 432–436. However, at this moment, the Trojans are not on the run but placed in front of the Achaeans. That is, Homer opposes their cries to the silence that dominates (except for the commands by the leaders) in their own ranks. The sole element that is explicitly asserted by the poet is the Achaean superiority in terms of military organization ("almost hoplitic"). See, in particular, *Iliad*, XVII, 364–365; or XVI, 210–220; or numerous examples in Book XV. On the question of Homer's "impartiality," Vidal-Naquet nevertheless concludes: "A beautiful ambiguity allows the reader, early on, to make Hector the hero of the *Iliad*" (pp. 48–49).
132. *Eds.*: Finley is too categorical here: In Book XV in the *Iliad*, the Achaeans are compared to sheep that are chased by wild animals (323–325) or to cows running away (631), while the Trojans are lions (593–594). In Book XXII, 308–310, Hector is compared to

and that there's no depreciatory intention there. In another passage, Homer lauds the heroism of a character by specifying that he's as brave as a fly.[133] And the comparison is by no means mockery. That is, a fly is very brave; you brawl with it, it comes back, it won't leave you alone. Only a modern who would have never seen a fly, a myopic German philologist perhaps, could see a disparaging image in that.

This "birth" of impartiality is an essential, foundational moment. The equal value of all men is like a first cherry in the basket, to which all the others are attached, i.e. philosophy, democracy, history, ethnography, self-contestation of the society's political institutions, and so on. As soon as others are worth just as much as us, we want to know them, know their institutions, their gods, to compare them to ours; interlocking with that is also a reflexive movement that bears on our proper institutions, so as to relativize them, criticize them, perhaps to change them. We will speak again at great length of all this later, but let's at least take note of this language by Herodotus, who begins his *Histories* with this sentence: "I am going to recount the lofty deeds of the Greeks and the barbarians."[134] Greeks and barbarians are thus placed on the same plane since the "lofty deeds" are identical in value in one group as in the other. And the word "barbarian" itself, you are well aware, is purely descriptive; it designates those who don't speak Greek. But, at least at the start, there is no pejorative connotation. The true difference in value is something we will see appear in the episode of the Cyclopes, who are not barbarians but monsters. And the boundary is indeed very strongly marked. What's not human in the Homeric world, what's exterior to it, these are the monsters, whether monsters with a human face, or monstrous humans. But we will take this back up in a later seminar.

Lastly, Homeric universality, impartiality, is also what allows for these profound moments and movements of identification with the other, of sympathy in the profound sense of the term and empathy, which are flagrant in the two scenes evoked above. There's an identification for the reader with the two protagonists in the deeply stirring farewells of Hector and Andromache. Still more, in Book XXIV of the *Iliad*, there's an explicit identification when Priam says to Achilles: You too, Achilles, have an old father like me, who's

---

an "eagle" that hunts "tender lambs or huddled hares." Yet he faces Achilles, who is not a lamb.

133. *Eds.*: Homer, *Iliad*, XVII, 570–573: Athena depicts Menelaus as having the "daring of that mosquito" (trans. Lattimore).

134. *Eds.*: Herodotus, *Histories*, I, 1.3–4

waiting for you without knowing whether you are alive or dead.[135] Perhaps that might seem to you to be fantastically banal, but I don't believe I've ever read any equivalent in Near East literature, nor in particular in the Old Testament. And then there's the one that's hidden between the lines of Priam's supplication, where Achilles is invited to put himself into the position of one who, while dead, would want his father to recuperate the body, and thus put himself into Priam's position, in the end. And precisely this movement of multiple identification, this so magnificent sympathy-empathy present in Book XXIV, would obviously be impossible without the universalization of the human that Homer orchestrates. In this respect, enemies are identical; each can put himself in the place of the other. Priam, king of Troy, imagines himself as Peleus, and Achilles identifies with the enemy he's killed, Hector. The root of this, of course, which is even more obvious in this last scene, is that we are all going to die. Death is the first universal, which posits the identity of the human condition through all appearances, all differences, and allows for accession to this universality. Perhaps this rapprochement would have pleased Hegel: it is indeed through the absolute and ultimate negation, death, that the universal of humanity is established in the Homeric poems.

Questions

<Inaudible, on will and choice.>

<In ancient Greece>, the moment of decision of course implies a will, but this will is not made autonomous; it's not a separate function that could then introduce this perpetual gap <in relation to reflection and to action> as is the case in the Christian world (leaving the Hebrews aside). I want to, but alas I cannot. Who truly wills? Who could will once and for all, for the whole world? God as the will? But the will for what? And what share of this will is imparted to man? We find here all the aporias of human free will and of its reconciliation with a divine will, an omniscience, an omnipotence, and so on. In Christianity man is a fallen being, a sinner, constantly confronted not with death but with his own renewed fallenness, with his incapacity to ever be worthy of the rule that gives meaning to his life. This is a rule that also incorporates into its very nature this fallenness; it cannot properly be applied, and thus man is necessarily miserable. One may as well demand from him that he should fly like a bird and then decide that since he isn't able he's thus culpable.

---

135. *Trans.*: Homer, *Iliad*, Book XXIV, 485–495.

This is what the great monotheistic religions are. But I simply want to show that the will does not present itself as *that* problem in the Greeks.

A question on Sparta, warrior city, which didn't take up certain elements of the Homeric poems....

While I claim to find in Homer a first deposit of significations entirely central to and decisive for what follows, I know well that it did not alone determine the Greek history to come. On the other hand, it's absolutely obvious that in the era of Homer the cities had already entered into this movement of self-institution, breaking with the royalty, the heroic world, and so on. In a sense, Sparta participated in this movement in the beginning. That is, among themselves, the Spartiates called themselves not equals but *homoioi*, identicals, by opposition to the *heilōtes*, the helots.[136] This is perhaps the first attested expression of equality that we have. These *homoioi* were purported at first to be the sovereign body; yet elements nevertheless subsisted that were both restrictive and oligarchic. The great movement began incontestably with the Ionian cities and encompassed Athens and a whole series of other cities, but not Sparta, which remained at the time like a kind of living fossil. That's how it was, and we don't know why.[137] Linguistically and in many other respects, Sparta is a Greek city, and one that didn't remain a heroic city; it was a military, hoplitic city, where one wages combat in organized and solidary battalions, and never for oneself. I remind you of the famous story of the Lacedemonian Aristodemus, who, having returned alive from the Battle of Thermopylae (480), kept his distance from Sparta, ashamed, rejected by everyone for not having been massacred like his companions.[138] He nevertheless took part in the victorious Battle of Platea (479), fought there like a lion, and got killed. But the ephors refused to attribute to him the posthumous recompenses

---

136. *Eds.*: On this issue, see Michael M. Austin and Pierre Vidal-Naquet, *Economic and Social History of Ancient Greece*, trans. Michael M. Austin (Berkeley: University of California Press, 1992), pp. 86–90, which discusses the status of the helots, and specifically the differences between them and slaves in Athens.
137. *Eds.*: See the pessimistic comments by Édouard Will, *Le Monde grec et l'Orient* (Paris: PUF, 2001), p. 57, note 1: "The Spartan bibliography is immense and continues to grow—without much profit being gained with regard to the advancement of the problems." See also the remarks in Moses I. Finely, "Sparta," in Jean-Pierre Vernant, ed., *Problèmes de la guerre en Grèce ancienne* (Paris: Seuil, 1999), pp. 199–212; and see also Vidal-Naquet, *Black Hunter*, pp. 168–188 and 147–156.
138. *Eds.*: Herodotus, *Histories*, VII, 229–231; and IX, 71.

accorded to dead soldiers at Platea since, while he had fought like a madman, he'd left his rank. We thus find in Sparta this idea of the primacy of the collectivity, central in the *polis*. We fight as group, neck and neck, without seeking individual exploits like Homeric heroes. But we don't find there this essential, fundamental element, which is present in Athens and in the Ionian cities, namely the possibility of changing the laws. In Sparta the laws are *ne varietur*; they are there always and forever.

<Inaudible question about the powers of the gods....>

Yes, it's true, the gods sometimes have this power, this privilege, of transforming a mortal into an immortal and divinizing him. There's Ganymede, Hercules, Castor, and also Pollux, in a way. But as far as I know, there's no example by which they rendered men immortal at the request of men themselves. And Hercules, the only one to have been divinized as compensation for an excellent, superlative life, was also of divine lineage, son of Zeus and Alcmene. Moreover, the properly Greek perception of his legend should be strongly emphasized. That is, the Hercules of the twelve labors, who was immediately divinized, is not at all the cardboard circus Hercules but essentially the virtuous man—very intelligent, by the way—who knew how to subdue within himself the base and vile passions. Yet, all the Greeks who read or heard the poems knew well what awaited the genuine Homeric heroes, Achilles, Ajax, Odysseus, and so on. The canonical lot of the most excellent individual was not Olympus but Hades.

VI. Seminar from January 5, 1983

Today we're going to talk about Homeric religion, and more precisely about what has been called the religious revolution in Homer. It's a subject that touches on the problem of Greek religion as a whole but more generally on the question of the possibility of our proper relationship—one of analysis, of understanding—to this particular religion, which is at once very distant from us and quite different (despite what has been said about it, particularly from the structuralist side) from a whole set of other religions, myths, or "archaic" beliefs.

It should be emphasized that for modern Western philosophy, Greek religion remains an enigma. About twelve or so years ago, I had just happened to read a book review on the subject in the *Times Literary Supplement*, in which they admitted to not understanding how a people who created philosophy, geometry, and tragedy could remain attached for the whole of its existence to beliefs so absurd, infantile, aberrant, and so on. Of course, the author of the article had forgotten that his own culture still remains attached to beliefs as absurd and infantile as an immaculate conception by a virgin saint or a being who's at once man and god, who ascends to heaven and redescends, i.e. in short, all these far-fetched stories, which are neither more nor less absurd than Greek religion or than whatever other belief. Such remarks simply manifest a total misrecognition of what a religion is. But there's something more to observe regarding the way to approach Homeric religion, or rather three things.

First, what almost always intervenes like a kind of veil over moderns' eyes, whether they desire it or not, is their preconception regarding religion. For, by religion they mean our religion; just as by civilization, they mean our civilization; by literature they mean our literature; by morality our morality; by good manners or politeness our manners or our politeness.[139] What I'm saying

---

139. *Eds.*: See the comments on the absence of a "true" Homeric religion by the authors (P. Mazon, G. Murray, and M. Bowra) cited by Dodds, *The Greeks and the Irrational*, p. 14. Especially see Mazon's famous observation (*Introduction à l'*Iliade, p. 294): "The truth is that there has never been a less religious poem than the *Iliad*" (an observation that, according to Albin Lesky, was a *Seltsamkeit*, an "oddity"—see Lesky, *Göttliche*, p.

here may seem very elementary and very stupid, but it's the case. Of course, this preconception is profoundly marked by monotheistic beliefs and by the entire onto-theology that accompanies them. We'll talk about this when we get to Greek philosophy. A tendency that I spoke to you about the other day is attached to this, i.e. this compulsion moderns have for introducing their notion of the will into their vision of the ancient Greek world, only to also state that it is absent from it.[140] The same goes for morality or ethics. One frequently has the impression that ancient Greek morality or ethics is being judged in light of the *Critique of Practical Reason*, of an ethics of *reine Gesinnung*, of the pure disposition of mind, in which one wants the good for itself, independently of any other motivation, as if this were the only criterion that allows for defining an ethics. But the appearance in the West of this type of attitude is rightly the product of Christianity, of an idealist philosophy like that of Kant, and so on. To say, for example, as some have dared to say, that for the Greeks there's no moral consciousness amounts in reality to saying that for them there is no consciousness that's unhappy about an inaccessible, unrealizable state. And the same thing holds for religion, which in Christian civilization entails a fundamental position defining the relations of man to God in terms of love. We love, we must love God. It's a love that, moreover, doesn't exclude fear, but therein lies the essential paradox. That is, how can an affect be the object of an imperative? That's the central rift; the Christian *must* love God in a sincere, spontaneous way while convincing himself that this is what he has to do. Furthermore, God loves you; he loves you on certain conditions. Sometimes, in its most noteworthy versions, his love is totally arbitrary (see the very specific relation of God to the Hebrews in the Old Testament). Yet, for the Greeks these two ideas are absurd, unthinkable. Likewise in Aristotle, as late as around the end of the fourth century, the word *philotheos* (one who loves God or the gods) appears only one time; and Aristotle says that it would be extravagant, absurd (*atopon*), to say that we love God.[141]

---

29). However, already there had been Ernest Renan, *Saint Paul* (London: The Temple Company, 1868), pp. 120–121: "If, as it can be maintained, the pre-occupation of death is the most important characteristic of Christianity and of modern religious sentiment, then the Greek race is the least religious of races."

140. *Eds.*: See Seminar V, pp. 87–89.

141. *Eds.*: Aristotle, *Magna Moralia*, II, 1208b30. The possibility of *philia* between man and God is likewise denied by Aristotle in *Nicomachean Ethics*, VIII, 1159a5: "[Much] can be taken away and friendship remain, but when one party is removed to a great distance, as God is, the possibility of friendship ceases." — *Trans.*: W. D. Ross and J. O. Urmson translation, in Jonathan Barnes, ed., *The Complete Works of Aristotle: The Revised Oxford Translation, Volumes I and II* (Princeton, NJ: Princeton University Press, 1995).

It's something completely different when in Aristotelian philosophy it's a question of a love that *physis* and all beings experience, which pushes them towards a god without any connection with the world, who is pure thought. What counts here is the difference between two Greek verbs, both of which the French render as "to love [*aimer*]," *philein* and *eran* (which yields *erōs*). Without going into the details, what the Christians call love, what the language of the Gospels calls *agapē*, and what the Vulgate translates by *caritas*—would correspond best with Aristotle's *philein*. *Eran*, for its part, has an erotic element, an element of desire for something. Yet, for Aristotle, this *erōs* that pushes beings and nature as a whole towards a God that, for all that, they're unaware of, is identical with the enormous attraction that the inferior experiences with regard to the superior. And if he writes that it would be absurd to say that a man loves Zeus (*philei Dia*), he doesn't even mention as a hypothesis—as it would be inconceivable, extravagant—that God could lower himself to love (in the sense of *eran*) humanity. That's the position of Aristotle, who is, though, a late author. Among earlier authors, the question isn't even posed; it's entirely foreign to their spirit. Notice, moreover, that the Greeks don't know of this infinite distance, this rigorous separation that the monotheistic religions tried to establish, without succeeding entirely, between the here and the beyond, between the human being and the divine being. There of course exists for them a difference, which is not simply quantitative but qualitative; but in a certain way it's not a matter of an ontological difference. The gods are excellent; they are infinitely superior to humans. But they don't find themselves on the other side of an ontological chasm that would separate them radically. This is conveyed, for example, by a fact that Hannah Arendt very rightly concentrates on, namely that the Greek gods are immortal but not eternal.[142] That is, they are neither in the totality of time—since they are born—nor even outside of time, as a rational theology would rightly prefer, in the case of Christianity.

Beyond this modern preconception that distorts vision, there are also two other very important factors, which have to do with the thing itself and not with prejudices. Both have, moreover, a reach that far surpasses the problem of the understanding of Greek religion. First of all, every social phenomenon unfolds, both for the individual and for the society concerned, in the three well known dimensions of current psychology. There exists a homology between the individual's representation (his image of the world) and a set of imaginary significations proper to this society; a set of aims or of vectors that orient social doing or acting in certain well determined directions; and then

---

142. *Eds.*: Arendt, *Human Condition*, pp. 17–21.

something still more mysterious, which we could call the affect of a society. Beyond simple metaphor, what's at stake is a certain, affectively colored way of investing the world and of living it, which we of course observe more easily at the level of concrete individuals, but which goes beyond them and saturates, so to speak, collective attitudes. Yet this affect, tied to the institution of each society, strictly depends on this society's way of living time, of constituting its own time. At the individual level, we meet with roughly two opposed modalities of investment of time: either it's what is going to bring about something better and it's filled with hope and positively colors the lived world; or it can only lead to diminution, impoverishment, and at the limit to catastrophe and death. From this come two types of the lived world of societies. Certainly, I'm speaking here with images and by an abuse of language; there is only a lived world of individuals, but this lived world is rendered possible and is oriented by all of what is deposited in the institution of the society and its significations. Yet, quite clearly, one couldn't speak of religion—no less than of any other social phenomenon—by making an abstraction from affect. Individuals and the collectivity have, regarding what is for them the divine or the sacred, an attitude that does not arise purely and simply from representation. A system of religious belief does not reduce to a system of ideas, still less to an ideology, as a stupid neologism that has prevailed for some time would wish. There's of course always this set of representations that constitutes the sayable and describable part of a religion; but there's also a way of being of the religious subject with regard to what these representations, precisely, are supposed to represent, which is of the order of affect. This is a fundamental reality for every religion. Here, we collide with one of the well known consequences of modern rationalism and pseudo-rationalism, the excessive intellectualization of history. One thereby aims to identify societies other than those of the observer with a set of productive forces and superstructures, with systems of representations—and thus with what can be said, described, and, in the case of the structuralists, arranged in a table to be filled with signs + or -, oppositions of yes/no, hot/cold, high/low, right/left, and so on. This is outrageously false. A society is—also by way of its representations, of course—a way of living the world and of creating its own time, potentially a way of destroying the world. A certain contemporary incapacity to grasp the totalitarian phenomenon is indissociable from this intellectualization of history. They want to make of totalitarianism a logical system that would be, for example, the aberrant culmination of certain philosophical, revolutionary, or other ideas—which generally opens up more or less banal deductions, even at their own level—and they don't see what's essential, namely that totalitarianism is a social-historical system that is both properly delirious and strongly invested with an affect that must be described as such. In the case of Nazism, there's an affect for victory that reverses immediately and visibly into a desire for death and for the destruction of others. All of that obviously also applies to religions. Even if one leaves aside the intellectualizing temptation, it's true that it's extremely difficult and in principle impossible to arrive at a true understanding insofar as one cannot live out the affect of others; but there nevertheless exists something called empathy and sympathy, even if these notions, when applied to a culture at a distance of several millennia, makes us face formidable enigmas. No matter what, the problem is there, and it comes back to the position of the historian: every great historian is like a creative or re-creative artist. He doesn't rest satisfied with describing events and analyzing social and historical situations; he's able to reconstitute (which is an enormous point for interrogation, i.e. how to control this reconstitution?) this indissociable whole, i.e. the representations, the aspirations of a society, and its way of living though the world and of living through itself, i.e. its affect. Certainly, very few historians have known how to do it (and even, in their way, very few novelists!). We can think of certain pages of Thucydides, or of Michelet on the French Revolution, or again of the *Paideia* of Jaeger, where we find in certain moments a reconstitution that is, in my view, very living and very "true."

The third difficulty pertaining to religion and in particular to Greek religion is this strange quality of the Greek universe, also present in other civilizations but perhaps in a less striking way, namely its extraordinary polyphony, or I could also talk in terms of magma. The principal components of it would be the past proper, resumed and re-created, re-elaborated, re-interpreted. In the case that interests us, this has to do with the religious elements anterior to the Homeric poems, then the exterior influences we've already talked about, and lastly a plurality of emergences at the very heart of this culture. Here, one must always be aware of traps and keep in mind the specific problems that all this poses.

Let's say one word, first, without lingering on it, about the presence of pre-Hellenic elements in Greek religion. For a long time, certain beliefs attested as in Greece in the early Bronze Age (or Early Helladic period) were likened to Anatolian beliefs, which means ones known to exist among the peoples of Asia Minor. The archaeological givens in this domain come essentially from the Cyclades islands and from Crete and date from before the fifteenth century. One of the most striking common traits is the existence of a central divine figure, an earth mother goddess, a master of game and animals.[143] (She

---

143. *Eds.*: Some recent works have called into doubt the real importance of such a figure, especially in Crete. See especially Lucy Goodison and Christine Morris, "Beyond the 'Great

will later become the Artemis whom Homer calls *potnia thērōn*.[144]) She's capable of begetting by herself, specifically of making a son appear, whom she subsequently makes her lover. In Greek mythology, this is the story of Cybele and Attis. The Phrygians called her Astronoë, or else Matar Kubileya, a name that is found in Greece in the form of Kubele, Cybele. A feminine divinity of this type thus plays a crucial religious role across a fairly large area, which doubtless extends beyond the Aegean basin. And this first stratum will coexist, up to a certain point, with elements that we could qualify with all the requisite prudence as Indo-European (see for example Dumézil on this point). We can certainly find analogies between the divinities of this era and the Homeric or subsequent divinities, but they are few and questionable. It's a matter of a "Zeus," an "Ares"; that's more or less all that one can say. All of that, when connected to a certain number of indices, particularly archaeological ones, corroborates the idea that Homeric religion really did represent a revolution.[145]

I spoke about influences, or in any case about similitudes. I'll give you some examples of them. In Syria they found at Ras Shamra, during excavations that uncovered the city of Ugarit, a set of epical-religious poems that go back to the second millennium, before a brutal destruction that is attested as of around 1100, and which is thus contemporary with that of the latest Troy and the Mycenaean palace. In particular, this text has to do with the god Baal, master of the earth, fighting against a god of the sea named Yam (the phonetic reconstructions are obviously uncertain). Another epic describes the victory of Baal over Mot, god of death, at the end of a fairly complex series of peripeties that include the death and resurrection of Baal. We thus have the three gods: Baal, Yam, and Mot, which we could place in parallel with Zeus, Poseidon, and Hades, even though—a crucial point—Baal is a god of the earth, which absolutely is not the case with Zeus. Through plenty of examples we find in another epic a striking analogy with one of the elements

---

Mother': The Sacred World of the Minoans," in their edited volume, *Ancient Goddesses: The Myth and the Evidence* (Madison: University of Wisconsin Press, 1998).

144. *Eds.*: Homer, *Iliad*, XXI, 470.

145. *Eds.*: See Finley, *World*, p. 136: "That we are faced here with a new creation, a revolution in religion, can scarcely be doubted. We do not know who accomplished it, but we can be sure that a sudden transformation had occurred, not just a slow, gradual shift in beliefs. Never in the history of the known religions, Eastern or Western, was a new religion introduced otherwise than at one stroke. New ideas may have been germinating for a long time, old ideas may have been undergoing constant and slow change, still other notions may have been imported from abroad. But the actual step of transformation, the creation of a new conceptual scheme, has always been sharp, swift, abrupt."

of the Odysseus myth, the story of Calypso. The goddess Anat, who covets the magic bow possessed by a hero, Aqhat or Aquehat, offers him immortality in exchange. He refuses and dies. An analogy? A borrowing by a Greek myth from the myth of Ugarit? We don't know. A common origin perhaps, drawing from an imaginary fund surpassing particular cultures.[146]

I just spoke about the triad of Baal, Yam, and Mot in Ugarit theology. Yet, we will see that in Olympian religion, in Homer, the three principal gods, Zeus, Poseidon, and Hades, have for respective domains the elements that surround the earth and limit it, with the earth itself belonging to all in common (we'll come back to this a bit later). This earth—primordial earth mother—is of course always a goddess; it's represented by Demeter. But she is not the central divinity, nor even a major divinity. As Finley has pointed out, Homer isn't concerned with her because he only mentions her six times in the poems, and never in a very important role.[147] Let's anticipate a bit what's going to follow. First, in a provisional manner, here's a quick array of Greek religion starting with Homer. Certain previous elements subsist, as we will see with Hesiod, even if they've lost importance; and it could be the case—but this is just a hypothesis—that the mystery cults are erected precisely based on them.[148] I'm thinking, for example, of the sanctuary and the rites of Demeter at Eleusis, and perhaps also of the Dionysiac cult and Orphic beliefs, which indeed involve a lot of obscurity. But what's essential is the upsurge, with Homer, of gods

---

146. *Eds.*: The texts that emerged during the 1929–1933 excavations were published for the most part by Charles Virolleaud starting in 1931 in the journal *Syria* and then translated in many other publications. One may consult the English translation by H. L. Ginsberg in James B. Pritchard, ed., *Ancient Near East Texts Relating to the Old Testament*, 3rd edition (Princeton: Princeton University Press, 1969). Similarly, see the fifteen volumes of Yves Calvet and Marguerite Yon, *Ras Shamra-Ougarit* (Paris: Éditions recherche sur les civilisations, 1983–2002), especially *Volume IV* from 1988 (by Dennis Pardee). For other parallels between the scenes of Homeric epic and Eastern literature—beyond, of course, those of Bérard, *Navigations*—see T. B. L. Webster, *From Mycenae to Homer: A Study in Early Greek Literature and Art* (London: Routledge, 2014), especially pp. 64 ff., which gives references for previous works. Also more recently, see West, *East Face*, and Burkert, "Orientalizing Features." On the problem of influence in general, see Seminar III, pp. 43–45. The issue of the relationship between Greek myth and Near Eastern mythologies is a domain in which arbitrary extrapolation and the most unbridled fantasy may sometimes run free. We may find a remarkably sober and prudent presentation in G. S. Kirk, *Myth: Its Meanings and Functions in Ancient and Other Cultures* (Cambridge: Cambridge University Press, 1970), especially pp. 172–251. See also chapter 11 ("The Influence of Western Asia on Greek Myth") of his book *The Nature of Greek Myths* (Harmondsworth: Penguin Books, 1974), pp. 254–275.
147. *Eds.*: Finley, *World*, pp. 136–137.
148. *Eds.*: Seminar IX, devoted in part to Hesiod, has been lost.

of a new character, the Olympians, and above all among them the sovereign triad Zeus–Poseidon–Hades, and, from another angle, Apollo and Athena. For the most part these are certainly political divinities, in the original sense of the term. That is, their cult is essentially civic, attached to the *polis* as a unity tending towards its self-government. By contrast, the gods of the mysteries are at once personal and social. Thus, at Eleusis, it was not necessary to be Athenian in order to participate in the cult; and as for what little we know of it, no difference was made between men and women, nor probably between free men and slaves. There was indeed a condition for admission: one had to be initiated. But with just that one caveat, the cult was aimed at everyone, which absolutely is not the case for Athena, civic goddess of Athens, for whom the cult was reserved for free Athenians (men and women for once).[149] Put differently, the Eleusinian rites, like the Orphic or Dionysiac cults for that matter, were aimed at everyone independently of the political integration of the individuals. But to come back to what we may call the central current of Greek religion, the magma of social significations that was created in the era of the final drafting of the Homeric poems (and through them) is contemporaneous, in my view, with the constitution of the *polis*; at the same time, it's the expression of the latter, through the adherence of the community of free citizens to the "political" values incarnated especially by their gods.

However, in this dominant current, we already find the idea—we could have mentioned it in regard to the episode of the Cyclops in the *Odyssey*—that the law is posited by human beings and by the political community, the *agora*. But there's also the idea that death, which can be chosen rather than suffered, is definitive, without hope of a beyond, and that there's thus nothing to expect from the gods after death, which frees up all sorts of possibilities for action. Opposed to this is a set of beliefs relative to immortality in the strong sense of the term, as something both persisting from the pre-Homeric fund but also certainly dependent on a continuous reemergence of elements of this type. It's not these phantom-like shadows that the dead are in the *Odyssey* when Odysseus (episode of the *Nekuia*) makes them go back up from Hades, but a full survival, implying metempsychosis sometimes, elements abundantly present in Orphism.[150] This goes hand in hand with the idea of

---

149. *Eds.*: On the role that daughters of Athenian citizens—first young girls, then adolescents—played in the cult of Athena Polias, see Nicole Loraux, *The Children of Athena: Athenian Ideas about Citizenship and the Division Between the Sexes*, trans. Caroline Levine (Princeton: Princeton University Press, 1994), pp. 23–24 and 48–49, with the references in notes 55 and 56.

150. *Eds.*: To understand the complexity of the realities in question (environment, beliefs, attitudes), see especially W. K. C. Guthrie, *The Greeks and Their Gods* (Boston: Beacon Press,

a retribution coming in a future life to recognize the good or the bad one has done, and doubtless also with—at least intellectually—a certain distancing of the individual *vis-à-vis* the political community. I would like, nevertheless, to caution you: What I am proposing here is just a hypothesis; and in any case we especially shouldn't believe in an absolute separation in reality. I remind you that I talked earlier about a magma, about a polyphony. We're dealing with two tendencies that coexist. And for both sides—the Homeric, Ionian, or political current, and Orphism and the mystical currents as of the fifth century—we find both a persistence of a heritage and a renewed creation. What one should ideally do—but we cannot take this on here—would be to study concretely the continuous interrelation of the two elements, their interpenetration in the unfolding of the Greek world. Be that as it may, one of the reference points for this hypothesis of course lies in the great crisis of the Greek imaginary at the end of the fifth century, with the collapse of Athenian democracy and everything accompanying it, which went hand in hand with a revival of beliefs in the immortality of the soul. For example, starting in the fourth century we find funerary inscriptions that mention another life, a retribution; these are things that, with some exceptions (an inscription found at Potidaea, which indeed dates from the last third of the fifth century), aren't encountered beforehand.[151] To say it in a provocative way, democracy would have to collapse for positive immortality of the soul to reappear.

Now, to get into Homeric religion itself, I will start off with some remarks on the world of the gods from the chapter on Homeric "Morals and Values" in Finley's book that I already cited, as well as the work of Otto, *Les Dieux de la Grèce* [*The Gods of Greece*], which in truth should've just as well been called "Homer's Gods."[152] These authors develop two opposed conceptions of Greek

---

1971), pp. 139–143 and 307–332; and see also, of course, the classic work of Erwin Rhode, *Psyche: The Cult of Souls and the Beliefs in Immortality* (London: Routledge, 2000). One may also consult Martin P. Nilsson, *Greek Folk Religion* (Philadelphia: University of Pennsylvania Press, 1972); Walter Burkert, *Greek Religion* (Cambridge, MA: Harvard University Press, 1985); and Jan N. Bremmer, *The Rise and Fall of the Afterlife* (New York: Routledge, 2002).

151. *Eds.*: See the epitaph for the Athenians who fell at Potidaea in 432 BC, in which we find the corrupted line: αἰθὲρ μὲμ φσυχὰς ὑπεδέχσατο, σό[ματα δὲ χθὸν], i.e. "The Ether has received their souls and the earth their bodies." See the text in David Lewis et al., eds, *Inscriptiones Graecae*, 3rd edition (Berlin: de Gruyter, 1981), Volume I, part 2, p. 1179. See also Guthrie, *Greeks*, pp. 290–291, where he notes its completely exceptional character for this period, in which epitaphs nearly always reflect the idea that glory is the sole form of immortality allowed to humans.

152. *Trans.*: The reference is to Walter F. Otto, *Les Dieux de la Grèce* [*The Gods of Greece*], which is a translation of *Die Götter Griechenlands* [*The Greek Gods*]. The English translation is in fact entitled *Homeric Gods*, cited above.

religion that are fairly representative of the principal tendencies of interpretation, with Otto's being, by the way, rather in the minority.[153] For Otto, Homer's gods are the sacred *par excellence*, in the sense of being radically other than the human being. For Finley, the essential trait of the Olympian gods would be their anthropomorphic character.[154] One may think that on a first analysis that's a common trait in all religions. After all, even when Christians want to distance themselves from what they call idolatry, they do nothing other (as so-called negative theology will say) than to confer on God attributes that are human, immanent, and in any case thinkable by humans; negative theology precisely rejects this, by asserting (following a Neoplatonic tradition represented in particular by Pseudo-Dionysius) that one cannot say what God is. On this issue, I recommend that you read the recent book entitled *God Without Being*, a compendium of this whole current of thinking by a believer, which is very well done and to which I will doubtless happen to return.[155] To sum it up briefly, one would need to get rid of ontology because it leads to idolatry. But at the end of his book the author makes, as if miraculously, by way of a definition-determination-attribute of God, love come about. It's as if love had nothing to do with a human affect, as if it were less idolatrous to define God by love than by being! (Let's leave aside the question of knowing whether, in the proposition "God is love," the copula "is" has an ontological value.) So, to say that the Olympian gods, or the Greek gods in general, are anthropomorphic doesn't allow us to get very far. This opposition between divinities according to their degree of anthropomorphism is doubtless only philosophical in appearance, or else it's so in the bad sense of the term, i.e. burdened by traditional philosophical categorizations. In my view, the best way to truly understand what the Greek gods signify is to see that they are what, in man, is more than man, or what imposes itself on the

---

153. *Eds.*: However, see the remarks in Lloyd-Jones, *Justice, passim*, and especially pp. 159–160, containing his defense of Otto with regard to Martin P. Nilsson's critiques. Otto's position may be likened in some respects to that of Jean Rudhardt, in the 1964 essay "Sur la possibilité de comprendre une religion antique," *Numen*, 11:3 (1964), pp. 189–211. According to him, in order to recover the experience of a "divine presence" among the Greeks, one must "see them live and imitate them, in imagination since we cannot do otherwise; one must imitate the manner of their thoughts, their affective reactions, and their behaviors" (p. 193). See also Jean Rudhardt, *Notions fondamentales de la pensée religieuse et actes constitutifs du culte dans la Grèceclassique*, 2nd edition (Paris: Picard, 1992).
154. *Eds.*: Finley, *World*, p. 132: "God was created in man's image [...]. The world of the gods was a social world in every respect, with a past and a present, with a history, so to speak."
155. *Eds.*: Jean-Luc Marion, *God Without Being: Hors-Texte*, trans. Thomas Carlson (Chicago: University of Chicago Press, 1991).

lives of men without them being able to control it, which means without them being able to control themselves.[156] We see very clear examples of it in the two poems, but especially in the *Iliad*, when a god penetrates the mind of the hero to panic him, to give him courage, to inspire him with an efficacious idea, or intervenes in his body to unleash his strengths or, on the contrary, to annihilate them.[157] One shouldn't deduce from this, as has been written to death, that the gods are only symbolic predicates of the human faculties. That would be absurd. They are a full presentification of what is inherent to man as well as of what is, in man, more than man, taken in the sense of a subject that is delimited, conscious, and master of his acts. By that, I do not want to identify the gods with the unconscious; I am talking about what surpasses man, in the most elementary and most profound sense of the term. With that laid down, the idea of anthropomorphism—providing that it is not limited to the exterior appearance given to the figures of the gods—is at once true and false. It's obviously true at a superficial level that the gods are represented in the image of men, both in their bodies (statues) and in their psychism (they speak to each other, get angry with one another, desire one another, or desire humans), and also in their social organization (which is something often rightly noted by Finley among others), i.e. assemblies, quarrels, power relationships with a preeminence of a unique sovereign, Zeus. But we're forgetting another very important aspect, i.e. that the gods are also made in the image of man in that

---

156. *Eds.*: See A.-J. Festugière, "La Grèce: I. La religion," in Maxime Gorce and Raoul Mortier, eds., *Histoire générale des religions, tome II* (Paris: Librarie A. Quillet, 1944), pp. 27–147, especially p. 41: "After Agamemnon's insult, Achilles drew his sword; but he placed it back in the scabbard; a superior power (*krēitton*) constrained him; it was a divine force, he recognized it, she grabbed him by the hair: 'Athena!' (*Iliad*, I, 188–201). When Teucer's bow was broken, he said, 'A daimon has broken my strength!' (*Iliad*, XV, 468). Having spoken of the power of Renown, Hesiod concluded, 'She is also a god' (*Works and Days*, 764). On the unwritten laws, Sophocles says, 'in them a great god resides' (*Oedipus Rex*, 872). To enjoy good fortune (*to eutychein*) is a god and more than a god (Aeschylus, *The Libation Bearers*, 60). The trembling of joy that comes when a friend returns after a long absence is a god (Euripides, *Helen*, 560). All that powerfully acts on man, envy, love, all that he strives for, wealth, wisdom, in a word, all that manifests as the superior effect of what can be made through human means, all of this is *theos*. Socrates exclaims *daimoniē* ('O divine') whenever the interlocutor expresses a thought that he could not find himself, which a god has whispered to him. And Plato creates a God of good beginnings, who in all endeavors guarantees success (*Laws* VI, 775e). A divine force is there: we felt her presence. This idea takes shape beautifully in Menander: 'Anything that prevails over us and surpasses us is regarded as a god.'"

157. *Eds.*: See for example Homer, *Iliad*, VII, 1–7 (Athena lends her strength to Diomedes) and 123–132 (she gives him instructions for combat); and *Iliad*, XVI, 698–704 (Apollo prevents the victory of Patroclus); etc.

they are subject to a fate. We'll come back to this. On the other hand, the anthropomorphic interpretation, at a deeper level, is false insofar as the powers designated by the term "gods" have by definition nothing to do either with empirical man or with "nature" (as per the interpretations that reduce Greek religion to a divinization of natural forces). Of course, in appearance, there's something true in that way of seeing it: Poseidon is the sea; Zeus is thunder; Hades is death; Demeter is the fertilizing power of the earth; Apollo is the sun, light, and so on. Yet, most basically, it's not really like that in Homeric religion, meaning the Olympian religion. Or, more precisely, it is true only for the minor gods, who are very certainly a residue. For example, in a celebrated episode of the *Iliad*, at the moment of Achilles's final assault, the river Scamander, which is a god, physically intervenes to stop his exploits.[158] It overflows its banks, inundates the plane, and almost manages to drown Achilles. The gods allied with Achilles and the Achaeans come into play: Athena calls on Hephaestus, god of fire, who throws flames on Scamander and burns the bed of the river, which ends by giving up and falling back. Scamander here acts like a river (i.e. it's in the nature of a river to flood) that would also be more than a river (i.e. it overflows intentionally). But, like all the other minor Greek gods, who are not one of the twelve great Olympian gods, he is fundamentally characterized by this essential, insurmountable trait, which is localization. Localization, here, is not to be taken simply in the geographical sense, even though this is the case for this river, the nymphs, the water divinities, and so on. We must understand localization as being in a point in time or space, thus as a limitation to an occasion of doing or to a property of things. And I agree with those who think we're essentially dealing, here, with persisting gods, and that Demeter herself—a very important goddess, personage of an initial goddess mother—belongs to a more ancient layer. By contrast, the Olympians cannot be identified with such and such zone or natural force. Each one of them disposes of a specific reign, or domain, which is something different. On this issue, I would like to turn your attention to a famous passage of the *Iliad* where what's at stake is the repartitioning of the powers among the gods.[159] We're in the middle of a phase favorable to the Greeks; Poseidon assists them no doubt beyond what is allowed, so much so that the combat risks taking a turn that doesn't correspond at all to Zeus's plan. So, Zeus sends the messenger of the gods, Iris, to tell Poseidon to stop intervening on pain of reprisals (the exact content of the threat remains hidden). Poseidon, very irritated, responds by denouncing Zeus's arrogance,

---

158. *Eds.*: Homer, *Iliad*, XXI, 200–384.
159. *Eds.*: Homer, *Iliad*, XV, 170–219.

and he recalls how each of the three great gods has obtained his share of sovereignty. This point is very important since it differs from the usual version of the myth, which one finds later in Hesiod as well as in Aeschylus. And this is what Poseidon says: "We're three brothers descended from Chronos, brought into the world by Rhea: Zeus, me, and thirdly Hades, who reigns over the dead. And everything was partitioned into three, and each one got [*emmore*, which is the root in *moira*, the drawing of lots] his appanage. As for me, I drew [*elachon*, from *lanchanō*] the gray sea to inhabit forever; Hades drew darkness; and Zeus drew as lot [*elachē*, again] the great sky with the Aether and the storms. But the earth and the grand Olympus are common to all three."[160] Poseidon concluded, "I will not let myself be intimidated." Iris tries to bend him by reminding him that the *esthloi* (the brave, the good people) can perfectly well change opinions, and he pronounces this decisive phrase: "You know that the Erinyes are always on the side of the elders." Yet the elder in this version is Zeus (in contrast to the Hesiodic, more well-known version, where Zeus is the last-born); and, after reflection, Poseidon yields.[161] What's remarkable in this story is that despite the priority of his birth, Zeus doesn't aim to monopolize the totality of the heritage nor even to decide alone regarding its repartitioning; this gets carried out by drawing lots.[162] I couldn't insist enough on the capital importance of this procedure, with such early testimony in this passage. In Athens, the choice of magistrates was done by drawing lots; and more generally, from Herodotus to Aristotle, the democratic regime defines itself by the allotment of magistrates or by the rotation of offices.[163] On the contrary, election is in the eyes of the Greeks an aristocratic principle—one elects the best—whereas in democracy everyone can be designated, and one has recourse to election only for functions that demand particular capacities, that of generalship, for example.

We should emphasize all of what is implied by this myth of the allotment of domains among the three great gods, namely that there exists no essential tie between each of these divinities and their domain. You hear it said that Poseidon is just the anthropomorphic divinization of the sea, or Zeus that of the sky and thunder, and so on. Yet here Poseidon is the god of the sea *by chance*; Zeus is the god of the sky *by chance*; Hades is the god of the dead and

---

160. *Eds.*: Homer, *Iliad*, XV, 187–193.
161. *Eds.*: Hesiod, *Theogony*, 453–506.
162. *Eds.*: On the influence of Mesopotamia on this point, see Burkert, "Orientalizing Features," pp. 35–37.
163. *Eds.*: See for example Herodotus, *Histories*, III, 80 (drawing of lots); and for a very complete table of the criteria of democratic government, see Aristotle, *Politics*, VI, 1317b19–20.

of the subterranean world *by chance*. Being a god, one must have a proper domain; but Poseidon, for example, is not the sublimation of the power of the sea. Of course, once this domain is attributed, his emblems tend to be marine or quasi-marine. We'll find perhaps that his statues have more curly hair than those of the other gods; we'll note that the horse, Poseidon's animal, has a part bound to the sea, and so on. In the same way, after the repartitioning Zeus will be represented by lightning, like a king of France or of England would be represented by any object relative to his domain; it's a banal metonymy. But the link between the god and his domain is aleatory, which excludes the hypothesis of an anthropomorphic representation of such and such force of nature. And to come back to this oscillation in the understanding of the Greek gods between the human and what is beyond man, it's true that these gods have nothing to do with everything that empirical man is, what he knows in a usual way, what he does and more or less controls. But at another level, what the gods stand in for is something human in the sense that men can have awareness of it in an exceptional way; that is what contact with the divine signifies. And the gods, above all, are figures of the groundless, the abyss outside of man as well as in man himself. We can, moreover, ask ourselves how, at the limit, we distinguish between what is in man and what is outside him, when we're talking about final things.

Nevertheless, the gods of course are neither omniscient nor all-powerful. They know more than men, but they don't know everything. So, they don't know all the future since it's Fate that decides on that, and we see Zeus in the *Iliad* weigh the lots on a balance. They are themselves subject to this fate, an impersonal force called *moira* or later *heimarmenē*.[164] One remark on this issue: Finley believes he has detected a certain incoherence between the idea of a fate imposing itself on all, men and gods, and that of a fate constructed by the gods, as seems to be the case sometimes in the Homeric poems.[165] After all, it would be surprising if there weren't any incoherency in beliefs; a religion is not a geometrical system. But, more profoundly, there's no genuine incoherency here. It's rather an issue of two different layers of religious significations. We in effect see the gods intervene in a domain that surpasses by far that of humans, over which they reign. They make being or prevent from being, or aid in being or destroy; but there exists a domain that concerns the ultimate lot of humans, in which the gods are not sovereign, any more than they are masters of their own domain. Here I'm risking an anachronism; I'm spanning three centuries since I'm finding this idea in Aeschylus's *Prometheus*

---

164. *Eds.*: See, for example, *Iliad*, VIII, 69–72; and *Iliad*, XXII, 208–213.
165. *Eds.*: See Finley, *World*, p. 134.

Bound. But, in my view, this is congruent with Homer's opinion. Thus, in the *Prometheus*, it appears that not only does Zeus not know everything since he sends messengers to Prometheus with the goal of having him reveal a future known by him but unknown to Zeus; but, through a certain number of statements and threats pronounced by Prometheus, we understand that there exists a fate that must impose itself on Zeus, which will provoke his destruction, his fall (and we'll come back to all this). Hesiod had already said that before Zeus, Ouranos then Chronos had been deposed. Prometheus alludes to these episodes in his threats. I remind you that Prometheus is a Titan; he thus belongs to the generation preceding the Olympians. At the same time, he's a renegade since he has helped the Olympians to vanquish his Titan brothers, who are of the generation of Chronos. Thanks to his relations with these very ancient divinities, Prometheus has a certain awareness of the future.[166] Not that he would be omniscient (he didn't foresee exactly what his proper lot was going to be as a punishment for stealing fire), but he has this knowledge relative to a *moira* that imposes itself on the gods and which risks provoking the fall of Zeus.

Finley brings up another incoherency between the absolute supremacy of Zeus and certain elements that come to limit him in the poems. So, in the *Iliad* we find assemblies of gods, but we cannot say that they engage in deliberation in the strict sense. And that's true of the *Odyssey* too, but the appearance of divine assemblies there is closer to a truly deliberative assembly, where the discussion takes precedence, and the sovereign won't make his decision until after having heard all the opinions. I believe we grasp an important difference here at a given point between the two poems; and I think it corresponds to two distinct historical layers. I'm not talking here about layers of writing but layers of significations. The assemblies described in the *Odyssey* should be compared with the presentation of the Cyclopes, who are defined as non-human because they don't have deliberative assemblies. These are two indices of the infusion, into the Homeric poems' universe, of the significations of the *polis* in process of constituting itself.

Let's pick back up and complete the array: These gods, at least the principal ones among them, even if they do acquire through drawing lots or otherwise some specific attributes, are in some sense universal, non-localized figures. And this new religion, or this new interpretive—and more than interpretive—creation incorporates anterior elements without concealing them entirely. This is proved by the survival, throughout the classical and post-classical

---

166. *Eds.*: In *Prometheus Bound*, Prometheus (873 ff.) says he owes his knowledge of the future to his mother Themis, whom Aeschylus identifies with the earth (209–211).

era, of purely local cults with which magical practices are sometimes associated. The *Iliad* and the *Odyssey* offer hardly any examples of magical practices linked to the gods. We find one in the sequence of the episode of Circe, i.e. the dialogue with the dead. Circe, who is a sorceress, shows Odysseus the magical act that will allow him both to conjure the souls of the dead and to make the seer Tiresias and the other shadows speak by making them drink the blood of animals killed for this purpose.[167] But this is very probably just something that has persisted—like the old cosmological myths one finds in Hesiod surviving in another form—all while, here again, we witness the creation of a new magma of significations. In parallel—and the archaeology gives us proofs of this—former cultic sites associated with elementary realities and representing at most vague sanctuaries (*shrines*, as one says in English) were progressively abandoned in favor of sites containing genuine temples, which testify to a certain degree of abstraction. For, the localization of a temple is not "natural" in the sense that the sanctuary of a river god or a wood consecrated to nymphs is, for example. At the same time, it's not totally arbitrary but *based on* a particularity of nature: the Parthenon on the summit of the Acropolis; Poseidon's temple at the extremity of Cape Sounion, a reference point for sailors; and so on. In other cases, we may wonder about the choice of site, like in Delos or at Delphi, where despite the majesty of the landscape we don't notice natural, organic, determinative links between the temple and its establishment.

The Olympian religion thus makes the magical-mystical elements retreat; at the same time, it marks the elimination of blood rites, even possibly of human sacrifices. Regarding the latter, here's an aside. Quite recently, a Greek archaeologist, Yannis Sakellarakis, uncovered in Crete a certain number of archaeological remnants dating from the Minoan or an even more recent period—around the fifteenth century—which very probably testify to the practice of human sacrifices, even acts of cannibalism.[168] There's no need

---

167. *Eds.*: We may add to this, in the same episode, Hermes's gift of the magic herb to Odysseus, thanks to which he resists Circe's sorcery (*Odyssey*, X, 281–306).
168. *Eds.*: See Yannis Sakellarakis and Efi Sapouna-Sakellarakis, "Drama of Death in a Minoan Temple," *National Geographic*, 159:2 (1981), pp. 205–222. Also see S. M. Wall, I. H. Musgrave, and P. M. Warren, "Human Bones from a Late Minoan IB House at Knossos," *Annual of the British School at Athens*, 81 (1986), pp. 333–388. Also see Albert Henrichs, "Human Sacrifice in Greek Religion: Three Case Studies," pp. 194–235, followed by a "Discussion" (Burkert, Heinrichs, Kirk, Piccaluga, Rudhardt, Vernant, and Versnel), pp. 236–242, in Jean Rudhardt and Oliver Reverdin, eds., *Le Sacrifice dans l'Antiquité* XXVII (Vandœuvres-Geneva: Fondation Hardt, 1981). Also see the rather skeptical point of view on the assessment of the archeological and literary testimonies presented by Dennis D. Hughes, *Human Sacrifice in Ancient Greece* (London: Routledge, 1991); or see those of

to tell you of the outcry that this discovery provoked in Greece, with all the pretended descendants of ancient Greeks crying out that their ancestors had been dishonored and so forth. On the side of myth, I remind you of the story of Iphigenia, whom Agamemnon is forced to sacrifice on the command of the gods with the aim of obtaining favorable winds that will allow for the departure of the ships towards Troy. This narrative incontestably makes up part of the Greek mythical corpus, but Homer doesn't mention it. The only Homeric reference to a human sacrifice is found in Book XXIII of the *Iliad*, when Achilles immolates a dozen young Trojans over the tomb of Patroclus, and the poet himself distances himself from this act.[169]

Let's say a few words now on the relationships between these gods and men. According to Finley, the Greek gods are devoid of all ethical qualities.[170] This is true, and it's fundamental. We could multiply the examples. Thus, in the *Iliad* we're struck by the constancy with which the gods lie and scheme. In the culminating episode situated near the end of the poem, the death of Hector needs logically to prove the heroic superiority of his adversary, Achilles. But if you read Homer, you will see that this absolutely is not the case. In fact, this death is due only to an infamous trickery of Athena, who, in the guise of the Trojan Deiphobus, persuades Hector to stay outside the outer wall of Troy, letting him understand that together they will triumph over Achilles.[171] Subsequently, in the course of the combat she gives back to Achilles the pike he had already thrown, and this is just one example among a hundred others. When I speak of infamy, of course, the term is completely inappropriate since, according to the Greek conception, there is no moral judgment to bear upon this genre of conduct. The gods intervene in the affairs of men in order to assist or destroy; each has their champion. But what we receive from them is linked to no particular merit, even if, of course, the gods would not lend a hand to a mediocre character. In any case, no human behavior has as a normal, predictable consequence the attraction of the gods' recompense or punishment. Likewise, the Homeric world—and the Greek world in general—obviously knows nothing of sin; it's familiar neither with expiation in the Christian sense of the term, nor with the reverential fear of

---

Pierre Bonnechere, *Le Sacrifice humain en Grèce ancienne* (Liège: Presse universitaire de Liège, 1994). See also the contributions by Stella Georgoudi, François Lissarrague, and Jean-Louis Durand, in *Archiv für Religionsgeschichte*, 1:1 (1999), pp. 1–106.

169. *Eds.*: See Homer, *Iliad*, XXIII, 175 ff.: "[...] and evil (*kaka* [...] *erga*) were the thoughts in his heart against them" (trans. Lattimore).
170. *Eds.*: Finley, *World*, pp. 137–138.
171. *Eds.*: Homer, *Iliad*, XXII, 227–231. But see the curious justification of the behavior of Athena in Otto, *Homeric Gods*, pp. 277–280.

the Christian towards his God. And to cite Finley once again: "Man turned to the gods for help in his manifold activities, for the gifts it was in their power to offer or withhold. He could not turn to them for moral guidance; that was not in their power."[172] The Olympian gods didn't create the world; thus they weren't responsible for it. There's a beautiful statement by Dodds, which Finley reemploys, that paints perfectly this type of relationship between men and gods: "Homer's princes bestride their world boldly; they fear the gods only as they fear their worldly overlords."[173] You will not find, in Homer or afterwards, this type of assertion that's always reappearing in the Christian, Jewish, or Muslim religion: "My God, I am unworthy of you, of your benefit; I'm but an earthen vessel," and so on. No Homeric hero, no Greek considers himself unworthy relative to the gods. It's just that he's weaker; if the gods are stronger, they're not essentially at another level of dignity. And, of course, this way of seeing things has a liberating effect for action and for the conscience of man. We can always wonder, like Finley—and I'll end with this—what's going on in Homer with the men who aren't heroes, i.e. with the masses. In effect, this distinction between hero and *profanum vulgus* is very precise in the poems, in any case in the *Iliad*. Finley rightly notes that the masses would have no more reason to fear the gods than the heroes. But what he doesn't say, and what's essential in my view, is that with the superiority of certain men over others not being guaranteed by any divine security, it necessarily rests either on a belief or on pure force. Yet, in a world where God is not there to speak the truth, where the truth is what's at stake in human effort, belief in the legitimacy of social power is going to dissipate. And we already see this in the *Iliad*, when Diomedes says to Agamemnon, the king of kings, "Yes, you are *basileus*, you have the scepter, but in reality, you are worth nothing."[174] Royalty is thus already criticized, and it will be more and more insofar as the common *logos* emerges (a process already at work in Homer). As regards force, once belief in the legitimacy of established powers is shaken, it of course belongs to the *dēmos*, to the majority, who will use it effectively to establish its power. In this sense, a religion such as the Homeric religion was of course not a cause of but was one of the conditions which permitted the simultaneous emergence of a free mode of inquiry and of a democratic collectivity.

---

172. *Eds.*: Finley, *World*, p. 138.
173. *Eds.*: Dodds, *The Greeks and the Irrational*, p. 29; quoted in Finley, *World*, p. 139.
174. *Eds.*: Homer, *Iliad*, IX, 38–39.

VII. Seminar from January 12, 1983

To begin, I would like to pick back up and conclude with Greek religion by specifying the four following points, formulated in a negative way: Greek religion is not a revealed religion; it does not accord any privilege to anthropogony; it contains no promise of immortality; its gods have no "national" character, i.e. they are posited as universals.

First, thus, Greek religion is not a revealed religion. For us this is no doubt something obvious, the recollection of which isn't pertinent except for those who live in the heart of a religion of revelation. But what's essential is the link between this absence of revelation and the primary imaginary grasp of the world in Greece. There's no revelation and thus no dogma, no truth *ne varietur* resting on a transcendent authority. This, for starters, allows for considerable variation in the theological tradition, the coexistence of different theogonies (Homer, Hesiod, and doubtless also other traditions), the local variations of numerous myths. There's a possibility for transformation, for movement, which would remain abstract were there not also human collectivities willing and able to make something of them. And, in effect, that's what happened; this abstract possibility became a discussion of social representation. We see here again the traps that are offered us by the causalist interpretations, the explanations that want to take things back to univocal factors in history. For, the absence of revelation and of dogma is not at all a special creation of the Greeks; it's even the most ordinary case, at least before Judaism. And similarly, nothing is more common than variations in the tradition, in the myths of each society. By starting with a Native American myth, Lévi-Strauss wrote the four volumes of *Mythologiques*, extending his analysis through innumerable transformations and variants into hundreds of other stories.[175] The simple variation of the representation as such would not be cause for a calling into question the social representation, in Greece any more than elsewhere. But with the

---

175. *Eds.*: Claude Lévi-Strauss, *Mythologiques*, i.e. the four volumes (1964–1971): *The Raw and the Cooked* (1983); *From Honey to Ashes* (1983); *The Origin of Table Manners* (1990); and *The Naked Man* (1990), trans. John and Doreen Weightman (Chicago: University of Chicago Press). Here, the topic is the Bororo myth of Geriguiguiatugo, the "capturer of birds" (*The Raw and the Cooked*, pp. 35–48).

help of other elements it does allow for its discussion and, in the end, for it to be called into question. To resume our confrontation with the monotheist tradition, we see that in the Hebraic world, despite the existence of different traditions, at a certain point the editors of what we call the Old Testament tried somehow to elaborate a coherent, univocal version. It cannot be such a thing, of course, as it's full or anachronisms and contradictions. But they tried nevertheless to manage it, and this is what would become the canonical text. Thenceforth, there was one sole possibility: not the overt calling into question of the world of social representations incarnate in the dogma, but rather interpretation. It's a work that surely started after the Exile, and which would yield that gigantic corpus collecting innumerable discussions and interpretations of the biblical text, the Talmud.

Thus, it's thanks to this freedom offered by the absence of revelation, the absence of the canonical formulation of a dogma—and also by means of another factor we will speak about later—that there was in Greece a perpetual re-creation of myth (and one could certainly speak of a reinterpretation, but this would not be sufficient, unless one takes the term interpretation in a very forceful sense). The most striking, most pregnant, most rich example of this re-creation is tragedy. We already spoke about tragedy and the fact that everything there is well known in advance, that there is no uncertainty; and, moreover, we asked ourselves what the interest of the spectator could be in this case. Yet, there truly is a waiting and an uncertainty, not regarding the events or what's going to happen in the end, but regarding the new signification that the myth takes on in each new work as the tragic poet re-creates it by virtue of changes, whether minimal or important, to the plot. And this allows us also to see just how far this freedom can go. For, what the poet thus presents makes up part of an official festival of the city, the Dionysia, and thus of the civic cult. We're in some sense dealing with an expression of the political community. And yet, we observe that the poet can alter important parts of the myth, above all by giving it, through relying on these sometimes-minimal alterations, a new signification. It would be hard to conceive of this without this first trait, i.e. the absence of revelation.

Let's move on to the second aspect. By contrast with the monotheistic tradition, Greek religion accords no privilege to anthropogony, to the creation of the human being. There isn't a fabrication, creation, or production by a superior power of a privileged and singular being that would be man. Man is a being like others. He possesses, of course, a particular status, which Greek reflection will return to tirelessly, and which we can already find in myth. But there isn't any ontological rift, so to speak, nor any specific act creative of man, at least in Homeric religion. Despite the enormous differences we spoke about, man is on a plane that isn't radically separated from that of the gods; and one couldn't express this better than Dodds does in the statement already quoted on "Homer's princes."[176] It would certainly be false to say that Zeus is only a super-hero, some Agamemnon to the *nth* power. But no abyss separates them; there's no ontological fracture.[177]

Here, a fundamental point is at stake, which demands that we be particularly attentive: we must try to understand well what this absence of separation signifies here. Take for example the most recent works on Greek mythology, this current that is brilliantly represented in France by Jean-Pierre Vernant, Pierre Vidal-Naquet, and Marcel Detienne. Among the last's books, I advise you to read, in particular, *Dionysos Slain*, as well as Vernant's introduction to *Gardens of Adonis*.[178] Vernant rightly concentrates on the fact that Greek mythology always established a rigorous distinction between three planes: that of non-human nature, i.e. of non-"humanized" beasts and plants; the plane of the human, including what humans have humanized (domesticated animals, cultivated plants, and so on, i.e. human complements that, as such, shouldn't be separated from them); and finally the plane of the divine. He shows that sacrifice is not uniquely destined to render homage to the gods but that it's also there to remind one—thanks to sorts of diacritical signs (they don't use this term themselves)—of the distinction not only between divine world and human world but also between the human world and what falls short of it. It's inconceivable, for example, to slaughter a wild boar for a sacrifice; they only sacrifice domesticated animals, oxen for example, and they offer cultivated grains to the gods. What's offered must belong to the human world, which detaches a part of itself to make of it a sacrifice to the gods.

We cannot but agree with the above. It's clear that the Greek world—and any other world for that matter—couldn't exist or would sink into madness if it were to live in an immediate and undifferentiated unity of the human, the pre-human, and the supra-human. It's necessary that there be articulation, and this articulation is marked by thousands of things. We'll see a sign of this—or rather a mass of entirely characteristic signs—in the famous story

---

176. *Trans.*: See Seminar VI, p. 114.
177. *Eds.*: On all of this, see an excellent 1966 essay by Jean-Pierre Vernant, "The Society of the Gods," in *Myth and Society in Ancient Greece*, trans. Janet Lloyd (New York: Zone Books, 1990), pp. 101–120.
178. *Eds.*: Marcel Detienne, *Dionysos Slain*, trans. Mireille Muellner and Leonard Muellner (Baltimore: Johns Hopkins University Press, 1979); and Jean-Pierre Vernant, "Introduction," in Marcel Detienne, *The Gardens of Adonis: Spices in Greek Mythology*, trans. Janet Lloyd (Princeton: Princeton University Press, 1994).

of the Cyclops in the *Odyssey*, where the distinction between human and non-human is marked in a categorical way, one entirely rich with significations. But if there is articulation, there isn't any cut-off. This is what one must properly see. There's no genuine transcendence, no infinite distance between the human and the non-human, whether this non-human were situated, if you will, above or below man.

The quality of this social representation—a world that's at once one and articulated (but, here again, there would be very important reservations to lay out, which we will return to with the notions of chaos and cosmos)—is very difficult if not impossible to grasp for us, i.e. we who have already been immersed, in this respect, in the universe of Christian theology. Despite the idea of the creation of man by God in his image, of grace, and of numerous other elements—and despite the anthropomorphism of the Christian (and even Jewish, which shouldn't be forgotten) God—there is, in the Christian tradition, this ontology of separation, of fracture, of the radical rift. And in one sense, we can wonder whether we're succeeding in effectively distancing ourselves from this vision of man's place in being, which was for centuries the one we were born with. Only work on the texts and the re-creative imagination allows us, perhaps, to approach this other view of the world, in which there's articulation and not separation; but nothing guarantees that we can attain it. This is a question that we could in no way respond to in advance. No matter what—and we will stick to purely negative remarks for now—it's clear that there's no radical separation, even if only because crossings between the three domains are always possible. Cases in myth where a man is transformed by the gods into an animal or plant are legion; the majority of Greek myths talk of such things. Even so, there are other cases—they are certainly rarer, but they exist—where some entirely exceptional human like Hercules or Ganymede is transformed into a god or demi-god, or into a divine being of another sort, a constellation for example. These passages are not, like the incarnation of the Christian God, at the level of a miracle. (There would, for that matter, be lots to say on the question of miracles....) In the second place, let's not forget the character—not anthropomorphic but, if you will, anthropic—of the gods, which I spoke about the last time. Finally, there's something more important, which takes us back to the question of anthropogony. Not only is man not a creature of the gods but all beings—stones, non-domesticated or domesticated animals, men and gods—emerge in a parallel and independent way through the course of a process and starting from an initial given which, for Hesiod, is chaos; and they're all subject to *moira*. With regard to this latter order of the world—i.e. emergence starting from chaos and the subjugation of all things to a *moira*—there's no particular status of the gods that differentiates them from men. We see here everything that separates us from Christian and even Hebraic theology.[179]

Now, here's a digression on idolatry. What's it all about? I permit myself, on this matter, to refer you to "Institution of Society and Religion" (the contents of which will certainly be familiar to those who have taken the seminar the last two years), in which I advance the thesis that all religion is necessarily idolatry.[180] For, in order to exist as a socially instituted religion, every religion must necessarily give a figure to what it calls transcendence—when it calls it thus—or to what we call Chaos, Abyss, or the Groundless. This figure may be a statue but also a story (since a story can also be a figure), a discourse, a word, or *the* Word. To say that God is Word is again, of course, idolatry. The only ones to have clearly understood this are the theologians of negative or apophatic theology, in which theology has precisely the task of the negation of all the attributes that man could conceive of for God. Indeed, we find in the Old Testament, and already with the prophet Isaiah, who is one of the most ancient authors, a critique of idolatry, of the cult of the *xoana*, as they say in the text of the Septuagint, which means material figures, a critique which appeals to a common sense which is rather voluntarian: How can one believe that these pieces of wood that one burns are gods, etc.? I haven't studied this question and I don't know if we can know what the genuine relationship was to their idols among the peoples surrounding Isaiah in the Palestine of his era, the Midianites or Moabites. Did they really believe that this piece of wood or stone was the god? It's an immense question about which, doubtless, there's no response. It's possible, and even certain, that there were societies in which some material object or another was the god himself, in person. But I think that with time inevitably a double situation comes about: The statue is no longer a fetish; it certainly has a sacred character and participates in the divine in an indescribable way, but it is not the god in person. It's a symbol of divinity—a venerable symbol—but one that does not incarnate it. Nevertheless, for an important part of the populace there probably subsisted a fetishistic dimension of this relationship with the emblems, the immanent representatives of transcendence.

How do things stand with the Greeks? I've never thought that the most common case, in Greece, was that of the faithful person, persuaded that such a statue—which everybody knows was just built by Phidias—was the god. But

---

179. *Marg. C.C.*: If there are also suggestions of "divine creation," these <do not play a> privileged <role>.
180. *Eds.*: Cornelius Castoriadis, "Institution of Society and Religion," in *World in Fragments*, pp. 311–330.

it matters little here what one is disposed to believe or not. I'm rather going to cite the words of Hippolytus in the piece by Euripides.[181] (One will object that this deals with a relatively late era, no doubt the last quarter of the fifth century, and that Euripides is the most "intellectual" of the grand tragedians, but nonetheless.) Hippolytus, addressing himself to Artemis, the goddess whom he venerates *par excellence*, says a very beautiful lovers' statement to her: "I'm with you, and we're trading words; I hear your voice, but I don't see your eye." (Here, *omma*, or "eye," is a metonym for "face.") Yet Hippolytus is on stage, facing the statue of Artemis. And facing that statue he says: "I'm with you, we're trading words; I hear your voice"—a statue doesn't speak—"but I don't see your face"—he sees it. This signifies very precisely that Hippolytus is well aware—and he says it, and the tragedian can say it in front of the Athenian public who consider it, if not self-evident, then at least acceptable—that when one is in front of the statue of the god, one does not see the god. We indeed see the double inversion: he is in front of the statue, but he does not see the goddess; the statue evidently does not speak, but he hears her voice. Evidently, the voice is the meaning, the discourse; he's in communication with the goddess. The goddess speaks to him, and he responds, but it's always a voice; it's not a vision. I believe it wouldn't be difficult to find other elements showing very clearly that when one speaks of idolatry, at least among the Greeks, one must not hold to the polemical vision of the Christian fathers of the first century and imagine that the faithful person would believe, without further ado, that the divinity would be there, in such a statue. No. There was a relationship mediated by the statue, without real presence but with sacredness.

It's true that there's also an experience of the divine "presence." I recently experienced this, which was a sort of "Pascal's night," if you will, but from the outside. I was in Israel during Christmas, and some friends encouraged me to go to Bethlehem. I was then able to go down into the crypt where the birth of the divine child was supposed to have taken place. The faithful were attending a mass there. It was exactly the same thing that I'd been able to observe on several occasions in India, seeing the faithful in front of the statues of Vishnu or Shiva: God was there. Sociologically, Christ was in that crypt. Not from the point of view of physical science, nor perhaps of philosophy, but from the sociological point of view, Christ was there; he was there all along, in process of being born. And the people who were there experienced that real presence of the divinity. It's perhaps an experience that you've had in the places where the Christina cult is associated with supernatural phenomena, whether in Lourdes or elsewhere. There's therefore a category of the faithful who by all

---

181. *Eds*.: Euripides, *Hippolytus*, 85–86.

accounts live out their relationship with the place—with what happened or is happening there—as a bringing to presence of the divinity. But the observer can reconstruct it only by perceiving the attitudes, gestures, and so on, and by attempting to abstract away from the presence of sellers of mementos. In the Bethlehem crypt, there are no sellers, and it takes you by the throat: for the believers, God is there.

What, finally, are we to understand by idolatry? It's impossible to think about a true religion having a social existence without there being transcendence somewhere "present" in the world and, at the limit, if it's not present in a cave, then it is present in a discourse, in a book, or perhaps quite simply for certain philosophers in the fact that they can formulate for themselves the categorical imperative. But it's present; it "announces itself."

Third point: In Greek religion there's neither promise nor hope. We have seen that, to the extent that there's immortality, it's something worse than a definitive death; it's the survival of miserable shadows without mind, meaning, or memory. (Recall the shadows of Hades in the *Odyssey*.) The condition of these beings is very much at the limit of the thinkable. Such is the attitude of the dominant current of Greek religion. It's true that probably from the sixth century on there were currents that arose in opposition to this, which one could if one wanted call mystical, even though the term is, in this case, quite bad. But these are marginal, atypical currents in comparison with the central current. They're represented especially by Orphism and then by the even more minoritarian Pythagorean sects. These currents were manifestly opposed to Olympian religion as one finds it in Homer. They present for example a different cosmogony, in which chaos is no longer the starting point of all things; they are quite markedly acosmic and in fact against the city, even when they don't explicitly say so. We know furthermore that in Orphism, anthropogony—the moment of the human being's creation—is absolutely central, which is obviously heavy with meaning. These sects preached, on the one hand, a wholly or partially vegetarian diet and, on the other hand, if not total sexual abstinence, then at least a sexual life subject to more constraints than what was then currently condoned. And the Orphics as much as the Pythagoreans rejected animal sacrifices and thus rejected this marker of articulation between human and divine.

Thus, what's explicitly formulated—Vernant's and Detienne's texts, which I just cited, are very rich and entirely probing in this regard—is the will to attain to a kind of divinization of the human being. It's about making man like the gods, not by defiance as in the story of the serpent in Genesis, but by ethical effort, in piety. It isn't surprising that these currents—certainly the Orphics and the strictest Pythagoreans—would be, at the same time, acosmic, apolitical, and even anti-political, against the city. For, it's obvious that if such an objective—i.e. divinization—is accessible, if one can propose it for oneself and pursue it, then taking interest in what happens here below becomes entirely derisory. And this conclusion is precisely where the Orphics and some Pythagoreans explicitly arrived; for this is the only place where a religion of transcendence, strictly speaking, can arrive. If one can truly *athanatizein*, divinize, then one can't see what interest the *agora*, the *ekklēsia*, tragedy, Salamis, the Persians, the construction of temples, or whatever else could offer. On the importance of these considerations for the retreat from the affairs of the world, see Pascal. Pindar responds to this very tendency of the Orphics at the start of the fifth century with those famous lines where he says that it's absurd to want to be immortal and that one must *thnata phronein*, i.e. to think, or to have a disposition of mind, that corresponds to the status of the mortal being.[182] And he also says that nothing is more vain or derisory than to despise what stands in front of oneself and to always aim at something that's far off and elsewhere.[183] These lines express an essential ingredient of the classical Greek attitude.

The fourth and final point concerns the "national" (or alternative) character of the gods. This is an intrinsically difficult problem, which demands that we bring in an enormous quantity of relevant givens belonging to the comparative study of religions. But it's doubtless not excessive to say that, on the aggregate—at least prior to the appearance of what was called the universal religions of salvation, Buddhism, Christianity, or Islam—every people makes a choice of gods, posits them as *its* gods, and opposes them to those of others. Yet, in this respect, I believe that we can propose that for the Greeks their gods are not "the gods of the Greeks" but quite simply *the* gods. Put differently, there are two aspects to this religion. On the one side, since Gernet and even before, Greek religion has been seen—and very rightly so since this certainly is a fundamental aspect—as a civic religion, as a religion of the *polis*.[184] The "political" cult has to do with the city, which

---

182. *Eds.*: See lines 59–62 of Pindar, "Pythian 3," in *The Complete Odes*, trans. Anthony Verity (Oxford: Oxford University Press, 2007): "Men should seek from the gods only what is consistent with mortal minds, knowing what lies before our feet, and the nature of our destiny. Do not, my soul, long for an immortal life, but make the most of what you can realistically achieve."

183. *Eds.*: See lines 23–25 of Pindar, "Pythian 3": "There is among mankind a very foolish breed, who disdain familiar things and look with longing at what is out of reach, seeking the impossible with hopes that will never be fulfilled" (trans. Verity).

184. *Trans.*: See Louis Gernet, *Anthropology of Ancient Greece*, trans. John Hamilton and Blaise Nagy (Baltimore: Johns Hopkins University Press, 1981).

accepts it, organizes it, regulates it, and sanctions its observance. Those who are responsible for certain ceremonies don't belong to a sacerdotal body that would self-perpetuate itself, designated according to particular procedures; they are named by the city. But, on the other hand, the gods to whom this cult addresses itself, even if they can have a privileged relationship with such and such *polis* (Athena and Athens, Hera and Argos, and so on), are not, for all that, gods who are exclusive to these cities; they aren't even gods who are exclusive to the Greeks but quite simply "the gods," the gods of all the world. This is what clearly appears in the *Iliad* as well as in the *Odyssey*. The Trojans don't have different gods; and the monsters like the Cyclopes can indeed despise the Olympians and refuse to render homage to them, these being the very same gods. They don't have different ones; nor do they say, for example, that the gods don't exist. Very powerful monsters believe quite simply that they can go as far as to face off with them. It's true that this observation cuts both ways since to those who say that in Greek religion the gods are posited as universals, one can always retort that the Greeks, whether they want to or not, do thereby impose these universal gods on everyone. It's in a sense an irrefutable objection, but that's not what's essential. What's important for us, in the context of our discussion, is that these gods are tied, each time, to a particular cult in the city; they don't have an ethnic or "national" character and are very much, in this sense, "universals." It's very significant in this respect that the Greeks always wanted to find equivalencies or to recognize borrowings, e.g., "The one we call Zeus, the Egyptians give him another name," or also, "Hercules was found in such and such form among the Egyptians, it's from them that we borrowed him," and so on. This attitude, already present in Herodotus, would be confirmed in what followed.

I'm coming now to what, in the poems and particularly in the *Odyssey*, is for me an assertion of the significations that concern the being of society and what a humanity that lives in society is, i.e. a humanity which, through that very fact, differentiates itself from the non-human, by opposing itself not only to the absence of certain human characteristics but also to the non-human as monstrous. We'll be interested particularly in the famous episode of the Cyclops.[185] It has been discussed endlessly since antiquity and indeed already by Plato and Aristotle.[186] And it's also a question of the Cyclopes in Hesiod's

---

185. *Eds.*: Homer, *Odyssey*, IX, 105–555.
186. *Eds.*: See Plato, *Laws* III, 680b1–8 (referring to *Odyssey*, IX, 112–115); Aristotle, *Politics*, I, 1252b19–24, and *Nicomachean Ethics* X, 10, 1180a28 (in both cases, referring to *Odyssey*, IX, 114–115). Sir James Frazer has studied more than thirty versions of the folkloric theme that serves as a starting point for Homer; see "Ulysses and Polyphemus,"

Theogony, though we're dealing with only a brief allusion there.[187] (In what follows, I have frequently benefitted from an excellent essay by a young École Normale student, Myrto Gondicas, in which certain significant points are very well indicated.) You're all doubtless familiar with the episode; I'll limit myself to recalling what's essential. Odysseus, disembarking with his companions onto the Island of the Cyclopes, is imprisoned by one of them, Polyphemus, a cannibalistic monster. After getting him drunk and jabbing him with an enormous stake in his single eye, Odysseus manages to escape by having recourse, in particular, to a celebrated ruse. He makes Polyphemus believe that his name is Outis, which means "nobody," and when the monster cries out for help from the other Cyclopes, they respond to him, "If nobody's doing you violence, you must be sick. Call upon our father Poseidon." This story is inscribed within the narrative of his adventures, which Odysseus tells while with Alcinous, the king of the Phaeacians. They belong to this group of adventures that one could call "exotic," i.e. non-Greek, and which take place—with one exception—among more or less fantastical beings, Lotus-eaters, Cyclopes, or Laestrygonians.[188] Those listening to these narratives, the Phaeacians, are at the hinge point between this exotic, even monstrous, world and the Greek world, the world of the Trojan War, which Telemachus recounts with Nestor and Menelaus. I won't dwell much on the Phaeacians (the word itself means "gray men"). Among their traits there are some that place them at the border of the visible world and the world of the beyond, but other traits mark out very strongly their belonging to a human, "civilized"

---

which is the appendix in his edition of the *Apollodorus: The Library* (Cambridge, MA: Harvard University Press, 1979), pp. 404–455. Also see Denys L. Page, *The Homeric Odyssey* (Oxford: Oxford University Press, 1955), pp. 1–20 (an "Analyst" reading). Also, see the "sociological" point of view (the episode as a reflection on the opposition of nature/culture or savagery/civilization) in recent studies such as chapter IV ("Nature and Culture: Gilgamesh, Centaurs and Cyclopes") of Kirk, *Myth*, pp. 132–171; as well as the 1970 essay by Pierre Vidal-Naquet, "Land and Sacrifice in the Odyssey: A Study of Religious and Mythical Meanings," in *Black Hunter*, pp. 15–38, especially pp. 18–26; and, finally, Claude Calame, "Mythes grecs et structures narratives: Le mythe des Cyclopes dans l'*Odyssée*," in Bruno Gentili and Giuseppe Paione, eds., *Il Mito greco* (Romer: Edizioni dell'Ateneo, 1977), pp. 369–392, as well as his 1977 essay "Myth and Tale: The Legend of the Cyclopes and its Narrative Transformations," in Claude Calame, *The Craft of Poetic Speech in Ancient Greece*, trans. Janice Orion (Ithaca: Cornell University Press, 1995), pp. 139–173. See also Alfred Heubeck and Arie Hoekstra, *A Commentary on Homer's Odyssey, Volume II (Books IX–XVI)* (Oxford: Clarendon, 1989), pp. 20–21.

187. *Eds.*: See Hesiod, *Theogony*, 139–146, where the Cyclopes are sons of the earth and not of Poseidon.

188. *Eds.*: The exception is the sack of the city of the Cicones, at Homer, *Odyssey*, IX, 37–61.

universe, as we would say.[189] They have, for example, a king who commands other "kings" with a *skēptron*, they have a kind of *agora*, assembly, and *kērykes*, heralds. The position of the queen in relation to the king is unique enough since she seems to play a role as important as his, which is not something Greek (in that era). Regardless, the Phaeacians are also anchored in the human world, which makes it such that Odysseus can be well received, can sit peacefully among them and recount his adventures before an audience for whom they are actually interesting.

Let's return to the Cyclopes. What's striking in the provided definition of them is that it proceeds essentially by negations. Of course, positive traits also intervene in their description, even if only in the presentation of the gigantic Polyphemus, who resembles a woody summit on a high mountain range. But at the outset, when Odysseus wants to make his listeners understand what the Cyclopes are, he tells them: "After our departure from the land of the Lotus-eaters, we resumed navigation and arrived at the land of the Cyclopes [Cyclops means "round eye"] *hyperphialōn athemistōn*." *Hyperphialos* is prideful in an exorbitant way, i.e. listening to nobody, being subservient to no one. *Athemistoi* are those who have no *themistes*, i.e. no posited laws, no institutions. (Bérard translates *athemestoi* as "without faith or laws."[190]) They arrived in the land of people who neither sow nor labor and who have neither *agorai boulēphoroi* (assemblies that issue, or support, or in which there are formed *boulai*, i.e. both opinions and decisions at once) nor *themistes* (i.e. institutions). Each one rules over his wife and children, *oud' allēlōn alegousi*, and they're without concern for one another or don't often socialize.

Here, we thus have the description of what we could call, if you will, a state of nature, except that it's done by antiphrasis or in an ironical way since this is a state of monstrosity. These are people who don't work, or in any case don't devote themselves to what for Greeks is the work *par excellence*, namely the cultivation of the land. For that matter, they don't have any need to; they trust in immortal gods and around them everything grows spontaneously. We should point out nevertheless that Polyphemus, for his part, does indeed have an activity. He's occupied with his sheep and makes cheese, which isn't something negligible. This is worth noting because the absence of genuine polarities or binary oppositions in this case could present problems for analyses of the structuralist type.[191] Nevertheless, we don't find among the

---

189. *Eds.*: See Homer, *Odyssey*, VI, 199–200.
190. Homer, *Odyssée*, trans. Victor Bérard (Paris: Armand Colin, 1942).
191. *Eds.*: See Kirk, *Myth*, pp. 169–170: "A certain understanding of the problem can be gained even by those who assimilate the myth in its present form: both nature and culture are

other Cyclopes any work or technique worth mentioning, although Odysseus and his companions do notice from afar some smoke.[192] We are, on the contrary, struck to observe the extent to which Odysseus envisions the world of the Cyclopes in a way that we could almost describe as technical when he tries to enumerate what they do or don't do and even highlights the possibilities for exploitation that these islands could offer to civilized people.[193] This is so much the case that some have been able to find a kind of call for colonization here.[194] But the point I want to concentrate on is this definition of what's properly human, which gets opened up by contrast when, as we've seen, Odysseus depicts these monsters by saying that they have neither deliberative assembly nor *themistes*. They've sometimes translated this latter term as "tribunals," but I believe that one must pay attention here to the root of the word. What's at stake is laws, posited institutions. It's true that it's said that each Cyclops *themisteuei*, i.e. lays down the law, for his children and wife. But it's added as well: without concerning himself with others. The Cyclopes are thus like sorts of *pater familias*, although the verb *themisteuein* excludes the idea that a Cyclops could kill in an arbitrary way his wife or his children. Another interesting aspect that we cannot dwell on here is that their monstrosity is relativized by the fact that they have speech, which in effect allows for there to be a story of the Cyclopes, for it not to be a simple trial, as when facing Charybdis and Scylla. But what's essential, let's repeat, is this: What, therefore, does a Greek child learn when listening to a rhapsode recite the *Odyssey*? It's that those who don't have any *agorai boulēphoroi*, any deliberative

---

seen to be ambivalent—and that is surely the key to the general dilemma. [...] It is not suggested that these opposed aspects are precisely mediated, in a strict Lévi-Straussian sense, in the myth of the Cyclopes, but rather that by bringing them into contact, by combining contradictory elements into a fantastic amalgam, the poets of the tradition gave expression, consciously or not, to ambiguities and complexities inherent in the concepts eventually stereotyped as *nomos* and *physis*, custom and nature. Particularly revealing is the demonstration of the relativity of one element to another. The other Cyclopes are civilized in relation to Polyphemus, uncivilized in relation to Odysseus and his companions, and in one respect super-civilized, akin to the Hesiodic golden race, in relation to mankind in general."

192. *Eds.*: Homer, *Odyssey*, IX, 167.
193. *Eds.*: Homer, *Odyssey*, IX, 130 ff.
194. *Eds.*: See Jacob Burckhardt, *Histoire de la civilization grecque*, tome 4 (Vevey: Éditions de l'Aire, 2002), p. 93: "The classic passage where Odysseus describes the island with the goats located in front of the Cyclopes' shore is presented exactly as if a man, having returned from travel, wanted to make a recommendation of this wonderful location to his city for the establishment of a secondary colony." See also Kirk, *Myth*, p. 165.

assemblies of the community, are monsters. That those for whom there aren't any *themistes*, any posited laws, are monsters and are not humans.

Certainly, we could be more nuanced. The *Odyssey* is not a theoretical text, and especially not a treatise in political science or geometry. The significations we're speaking about belong to a different order, and that's what contemporary interpreters often tend to forget. For, as we've seen, within non-humanity there are degrees, intermediate steps; it's not a chart with plusses or minuses. For example, during their voyages Odysseus and his companions reached the Laestrygonians, who are themselves rather monstrous beings, tall as mountains, and who are likewise cannibals. But these are social cannibals; they have a town, assemblies, and a king, even if they aren't "bread eaters" (the epithet "bread eater" is a formulaic, rhythmical cell in the *Odyssey*).[195] As for the Cimmerians, who feature in Book XI, they're a *dēmos*, they have a *polis*; and if, just like the Ethiopians (this other people that lives at the extremities of the world), they are more than human, they certainly are not monsters.[196]

We need to focus on this: We already find in the Homeric poems, from the beginning, the positing of the *agorai boulēphoroi* and *themistes* as characteristic elements of the human. (Let's note in passing that if there's ambiguity in the term *boulēphoroi*, it's not very different from what one finds in French with "deliberative" and that, in the end, what's at issue is not only a power to decide but also to reflect, to ask ourselves on what basis we're going to decide, or not.) But the theme of the *agora*—and this is directly interesting for our inquiry—also comes up again in other places in the poems. It's true that there's a clear enough difference between what the *agora* is in one poem versus the other, but it's perhaps a less decisive difference than has been suggested. In the *Iliad*, the *agora* is an assembly of free warriors—not only heroes—but it's only the heroes, the great nobles, who speak. We've seen that when Thersites, a man of the people, takes the floor, Odysseus insults him and strikes him with his scepter; he shouldn't have spoken up. If it's true that this *agora* is above all a sounding box for the discourse of the hero, it's also in certain cases a means for the leader to take the temperature of the "opinion." And the *agora* can then react, as in Book II of the *Iliad* when, in front of the assembly, Agamemnon pretends to want to lift the siege, and the warriors take him seriously and hurl themselves towards the ships.[197] But it's true that in the *Iliad* this active role of the *agora* is limited. In the *Odyssey* the situation is different, whether it's a matter of the *agora* of the gods or of that of Ithaca when Telemachus confronts

---

195. *Eds.*: Homer, *Odyssey*, IX, 100–134.
196. *Eds.*: Homer, *Odyssey*, XI, 14.
197. *Eds.*: Homer, *Iliad*, II, 86–156.

the suitors; in this case there is a genuine debate.[198] Still, this isn't the case in other episodes. For example, there's when Odysseus, having arrived with his people at the little paradisical island that stands across from the Cyclopes', calls forth an assembly (*agorēn themenos*).[199] He says to his companions that the bulk of the troops will stay there and that he, with a handful of men, is going to go over to the island to see up close who the men are who inhabit it, i.e. to see whether they are *hybristai* ("observant of no rule," but the word is honestly untranslatable), wild, and lacking justice, or whether they are hospitable and respectful of the gods. It isn't surprising of course that Odysseus and his companions, faced with dreadful trials, dream of finding a place where there would be people who are *philoxenoi*, hospitable. But it's interesting to note that this characteristic—hospitable and respectful of the gods (and particularly of Zeus, who protects strangers and supplicants)—is what first comes to mind for someone who wants to define those who aren't wild, unjust, and *hybristai*. Whatever the case may be, by all accounts we're dealing here with an assembly that seems to have been called forth only for announcing the decisions of the leader.

But in the Cyclopes episode we find, as we've seen, a different element, as if we are in a sense taking things up a notch. This is what's expressed by the use of the term *boulēphoroi*, deliberative—i.e. carrier of a *boulē*, a counsel, a decision perhaps—to qualify the assemblies. Some people will see in this, of course, one of the latest levels of accretion in the poems. That's quite possible; but as I said at the start, this changes nothing for us and even goes to strengthen what we're saying. For, it translates the fact that the poet, the monumental composer, is himself impregnated with social imaginary significations—political significations, in this case—which make their way into the poems, although this risks perpetuating an enormous social-historical anachronism by importing into what is supposed to be the heroic world—or what we call the Dark Ages—institutions belonging to Ionia of the eighth century, when the *polis* constitutes itself, with its *agorai boulēphoroi*.

To conclude this overview of the Homeric poems, let's look briefly within the poems at the *germs* that will be able to develop themselves in the subsequent Greek world and that we have not up to this point mentioned explicitly. But let's first ask what the elements of the poems' world are which end up disappearing in the Greek creation of the seventh, sixth, and fifth centuries. Above all, this of course has to do with the trenchant opposition—which

---

198. *Eds.*: On the *agora* of the gods, see Homer, *Odyssey*, I, 11–95; and V, 1–42. On the *agora* of Ithaca, see Homer, *Odyssey*, 2, 1–259; and see also XVI, 375–382.
199. *Eds.*: Homer, *Odyssey*, IX, 170–178.

forms an integral part of the values of the Homeric world—between the heroes and the *vulgum pecus*, i.e. this devaluing of ordinary beings, which is illustrated in a nearly caricatural way through the episode of Thersites. There are the warlords and then there are the others, and if a simple warrior gets involved in what doesn't concern him, he's entitled to baton or scepter blows. This element would disappear over time, even though political history offers us remnants of it in the assertion of certain values by the aristocracy or by the poets of the aristocracy, like Theognis or Pindar.

What will endure here, of course, is first of all a response to the question: What can a man wish for in a world that wasn't made for him and that, as such, contains no obvious answer? From the time of Homer and up through about Alexander, the response was *kleos* and *kydos*—renown and glory—as values that are, if not supreme, then at least entirely cardinal. It's these two elements that give to the culture, to the Greek creation, this agonistic character.[200] It's a character that some people have justifiably highlighted and that appears clearly in this assertion that we find twice repeated in the *Iliad*: At the end of the day, what's essential is to *aien aristeuein*, to always be in *aristeia* (*aristos*, superlative of "good," not only in the moral sense but as supreme excellence) and to *hyperochon emmenai allōn*, to be superior to others, whether this be in combat, as in Homer, or else in games, e.g. at Olympia or Nemea.[201] And we'll find this element again in the city, in the sense that the solidarity of the citizens or the existence of the community absolutely cannot be dissociated from the agonistic aspect, i.e. "Who's going to be the best?" Putting all questions of content aside, the tragic poets themselves wrote to win a competition; they wanted to be crowned, to have the first, second, or third prize. It's certain that this aspect is also linked in one way or another with what happens in the domain of knowledge properly speaking. Agonism can obviously become polemics or eristics, i.e. I know better than you, I can show that what you say is false, my discourse is superior to yours. Since there's no transcendent source of truth, no sacred law, no dogma (the gods don't speak except through the mouths of oracles, although the oracles are another story)—and since there isn't in fact any interpreter entitled to the truth, divinely inspired— the field is open to discursive competition, i.e. to whoever will speak better, will convince others better, will demonstrate more persuasion or have the

---

200. *Marg. C.C.*: See Burckhardt <*Histoire*>; Arendt <*Human Condition*>.
201. *Eds.*: *Aien aristeuein kai hyperochon emmenai allōn*: "always to be the best and to be preeminent above all." At Homer, *Iliad*, VI, 208, this is Hippolochus to his son Glaucus, on the Trojan side; and at *Iliad*, XI, 784, it is Peleus to his son Achilles.

strongest arguments.[202] It's significant, in this respect, that the classical expression for "the strongest argument" is *ho kreittōn logos*. *Kreittōn* is the comparative—when this word has to do with bravery or force—of *agathos*. *Ho kreittōn logos* is not only the argument that's stronger and more powerful; it's that which *imposes itself*. So, retain from all of this the central character of *kleos* and of *kydos*, which are inseparable, moreover, from honor (the *timē* that Achilles speaks of), i.e. from the high value acknowledged for the individual by the collectivity in which he lives inasmuch as he makes it his own. Let's finally point out another element that the Greeks of the classical period will place at the center of the citizen's attitude, but which one already finds in the *Iliad*, namely, *parrhēsia* or frankness, the fact of saying what one thinks, of not hiding one's opinion when it's a matter of important affairs.[203] There you have the positive elements, so to speak.

From a negative point of view, we can see—but I'm not going to focus on this—the beginnings of a critique of royalty cropping up in the poems, for example in Book IX of the *Iliad*, when Diomedes confronts Agamemnon with: Zeus gave you the scepter but he refused you valor.[204] It's really a critique, a dissociation between the royal function and the positive qualities that would justify the fact of being king. There's also the beginning of a critique of heroic morals, about which I already spoke, when in Book IX Achilles asks, "Why must the Argives make war with the Trojans?" and then he adds, "Nothing is worth one's life, I'm going to go back home." It's like a moment of questioning that bears on the *kleos* and *kydos* of the hero, i.e. "Why all of this?"

In the poems we also find—and this point is worth a longer pause from us—the first deposits of a certain conception of justice. We should really grasp the importance of this. Starting especially with Hesiod, it's true, we see a response to the meaningless state of the world appear, a human response, even if it's presented as the product of the will of Zeus. In relation to this first grasp of the world in which no meaning is proposed to man, where there's neither

---

202. *Eds.*: On the role of the "*agōn* paradigm" and the "competitive debates" in the development of the Greek science, see G. E. R. Lloyd, *Magic*, pp. 253–254 and 267. See also from the same author, *Demystifying Mentalities* (Cambridge: Cambridge University Press, 1990); and, on the will to "be the best," see Will, *Le Monde grec*, pp. 428–429.

203. *Eds.*: If the word is not found in Homer, the idea is often found in the *Iliad* through the way one is invited to "speak unerringly" (*nēmertea mythēsasthai*, VI, 376), to "tell without warping" (*atrekeōs agoreuemen*, II, 10), or to say things "according to reality, without warping" (*eteon* [...] *kai atrekeōs agoreu[ein]*, XV, 53). Elsewhere, in the context of public deliberations, one finds more than once the injunction to say "what seems best" (*hōs dokei arista*, IX, 100–103, XII, 211–215) to those who intervene.

204. *Eds.*: Homer, *Iliad*, IX, 37–39.

redemption nor hope unless it's the quasi-immortality of renown and glory, we see arise the idea that the world is not only this simple substitution of one being for another being, this sort of circulation of emergence and destruction that would be what's proper to what exists (we will return to this at length), but that there is also a *dikē*, a justice. What is this justice, precisely? Evidently, it's an enormous question, one that remains open still. But if it's true that this is explicitly formulated starting with Hesiod, we must also clearly note that this question of justice—i.e. the idea that there aren't only those things "that one does," appropriate things, or things that bring glory, but there are also just and unjust things (although, for all that, this latter distinction can't being founded definitively)—is already present in the Homeric poems. We have said and repeated that this element is already found in the *Odyssey*, and the fact is undeniable. In Book XXII, when the servant Eurycleia sheds tears of joy over the suitors' dead bodies, Odysseus silences her and tells her that one shouldn't triumph like that over these men, since it's the gods who've carried them off to punish them for their iniquities.[205] And there are many other passages where mention is made of the justice of Zeus.[206] And in these, those who respect justice and the gods are opposed to the violent and unjust.[207] But we'll also find entirely analogous elements in the *Iliad*, which is by all accounts anterior to the *Odyssey*. One could say once again that the lines we're going to discuss are extremely late accretions; but let's repeat that this poses no problem for us and quite the contrary. We'll take up here just one example among others, from Book XXIV.[208] After the death of Hector, Achilles not only refuses to allow his funeral to take place but attaches his body to his chariot every day and drags it around Patroclus's funeral monument. On the twelfth day Apollo revolts (lines 33–54) and accuses the assembled gods of being *schetlioi* and *dēlēmones*, cruel and malfeasant, reproaching them for having forgotten Hector's contributions. In his fury, Achilles doesn't constrain himself like everyone else to weeping over someone dear and thus to the conclusion of accepting what *moira* gives to everyone. He continues to commit offense against Hector's body, which is neither good nor beautiful. Must such

---

205. *Eds.*: Homer, *Odyssey*, XXII, 407–416.
206. *Eds.*: Homer, *Odyssey*, XIII, 213–214; XIV, 85 ff. and 259 ff.; and XXIV, 351–351.
207. *Eds.*: Homer, *Odyssey*, VIII, 575–576; IX, 214–215; XIII, 200–202; and XVIII, 141–142.
208. *Eds.*: See above all *Iliad*, XVI, 384–388, where Zeus punishes the kings who make "twisted" decisions of justice (*skolias themistes*), which are said by the poet to "expel justice" (*ek* [...] *dikēn elasōsi*), and also XVIII, 508; XIX, 180; and XXIII, 542, where *dikē* has different and more concrete meanings (sentencing rendered; reparations received from an adversary; a personal right one defends against others; etc.). See also the comments in the first chapter ("The Iliad") of Lloyd-Jones, *Justice*, pp. 1–27.

a thing be allowed? The intervention of the gods is common in the poems and isn't as such of interest to us. By contrast, what we should notice is that it must happen so as to respond to an excess relative to a just norm, or that there is at least the idea of such a norm, of a *dikē*, of something that "should be." This *dikē* is applicable even here, where it's not a question of a positive law. That there would be norms in the relationships between Greeks, e.g. that theft, murder, adultery would be under certain conditions forbidden, is obvious. But the issue at hand here isn't one of positive law; Achilles stands before the body of an enemy. What Apollo underscores is not that Achilles has violated a law but that his acts aren't "what must be," i.e. aren't just, in the sense of *dikaion esti*. It's an anticipation of the idea of a principle or a norm that, even if it isn't formulated in strict fashion like a written law, must guide and allow for gauging acts and conduct.[209]

Finally, here's one last germ, i.e. the surpassing of the heroic world as a world that is, if you will, individualist, i.e. in which everything is very explicitly centered on the hero, his exploits, and his fate. This is an idea that one already finds in the *Iliad*, in a line the obvious meaning of which has been called into doubt, in my view erroneously. The Trojan Polydamas points out to Hector that the *oiōnoi*, the birds, are saying that one mustn't pursue combat; the omen isn't good. And the hero responds: "The only good omen (bird) is to defend one's fatherland," i.e. *amynesthai peri patrēs*.[210] It has been said that one shouldn't attach too much importance the word fatherland, and that the idea of an obligation towards the community corresponds to a later phase.[211] I believe that if we place the term back in the context of the totality of the speeches that Hector addresses to the Trojans and the Greek heroes address to the Achaeans, it's difficult to escape the conclusion that in the poems there's

---

209. *Marg. C.C.*: Beyond the "positive law." See Sophocles, Antigone. — *Eds.*: See Castoriadis, "Greek Polis," pp. 94–121; and Cornelius Castoriadis, "Une interrogation sans fin," in *Domaines de l'homme, Les carrefours du labyrinthe II* (Paris: Le Seuil, 1986), pp. 254 ff.; and lastly Cornelius Castoriadis, "Aeschylean Anthropogony and Sophoclean Self-Creation of *Anthrōpos*," in *Figures of the Thinkable*, trans. David A. Curtis (Stanford: Stanford University Press, 2007), p. 19: "In obeying [worldly laws], *anthrōpos* must know that these laws do not determine absolutely what is permitted any more than they exhaust the range of the forbidden. Another element must exist next to the law instituted on each occasion— affirmative law, necessarily limited by its precise location in space and time, therefore relative—an element that needs to be interwoven with the worldly law, without dictating its content or cancelling it. It is this element that the poet, using the language and the representations of his city and his time names *theōn enorkon dikan*, 'the judgment/justice of the gods guaranteed by oaths.'"
210. *Eds.*: Homer, *Iliad*, XII, 243: *heis oiōnos aristos amynesthai peri patrēs*.
211. *Eds.*: For example, see Finley, *World*, p. 116, for whom the word simply denotes the *oikos*.

a genuine perception—which surpasses the simple consideration of the *kleos* and *kydos* of the hero—of the community, of this collectivity that is already constituting itself.

I would like to end by highlighting that the tension between these two elements will be present throughout Greek history. If you wanted to parody the Ancients, you could say that this is the source of the Greek world's good fortunes as much as the bad; but we won't dwell on that here. I'll limit myself to pointing out that, already there in this Greek creation there's a sort of well-regulated polarity, if you will, between, on the one hand, the *kleos* and the *kydos*, i.e. this thrust essentially attached to the individual and in which the agonistic element predominates, and, on the other hand, the solidarity of the *politeia*. Here's one last example to conclude. In the middle of the fifth century, in Aeschylus's celebrated epitaph, it's said (and this is formulated with an extreme beauty that the translation cannot convey): "It is Aeschylus, son of Euphorion, Athenian, who lies beneath this stone. He died in Gela (i.e. a Sicilian town), rich in wheat: His bravery (or: strength) efficient (or: well-proven), the woods of Marathon can tell, and the long-haired Mede too, who knows it quite well."[212] Whether this was written by Aeschylus himself or someone else doesn't matter; it's the epitaph that's appropriate to him. Aeschylus is excellent; he has a *kleos* and a *kydos*. Why? Not thanks to what he wrote (*Orestia, Prometheus*, etc.), but because he fought as someone brave among the brave men at Marathon. That means that he's excellent as an Athenian citizen and combatant. It's obvious that, considering the era in which this epitaph was written, there's definitely something like a provocation in it. Upon Aeschylus's death, they were still performing his great pieces in Magna Grecia; all Greece that wasn't lost in the darkest depths of the countryside knew who he was and what he did. And yet the epitaph says, like a sort of challenge: This won't be about tragedy; we're talking about the Battle of Marathon.[213] For those among you amused by this, there's a poem by

---

212. *Eds.*: See also the paraphrase in Pausanias, *Description of Greece*, I, 14, 5. The versions intended to be literal, with slight variants, have survived thanks to Plutarch and Athenaeus, as well as in the *Life of Aeschylus*, passed down in the Medicean Manuscript. A French translation can be found in Bernard Deforge and François Jouan, eds., *Les Tragiques grecs, I: Eschyle, Sophocles*, trans. André Wartelle (Paris: Laffont, 2001), pp. 91–93.
213. *Eds.*: But we could also see in Pericles's "Funeral Oration" the exaltation of Marathon at the expense of Salamis. See Nicole Loraux, *The Invention of Athens: The Funeral Oration in the Classical City*, trans. Alan Sheridan (New York: Zone Books, 2006), pp. 159–164 and notes on p. 404. Also see Pierre Vidal-Naquet's commentary on Pausanias, *Description*, I, 14, 5, in "Aeschylus, the Past and the Present," in *Myth and Tragedy*, p. 256: "To mention Marathon and omit Salamis might be seen as an ideological choice, a preference

Cavafy in which some young people from Sidon nine centuries later hear an actor recite Aeschylus's epitaph during a banquet. A young guest impassioned by literature rises up and cries out, more or less: "Look here, it's intolerable, writing what they wrote, limiting themselves to saying he fought at Marathon, as if it's just an anybody!"[214] Clearly we're in a period of decadence. For, what can properly be seen in this epitaph is the cardinal importance of belonging in the city, of solidarity with the body of citizen combatants.

Questions

<On the Greeks, the monstrous, and barbarians.>

There is, between "monsters" and "barbarians," an absolutely enormous difference, which we'll speak about with regard to Herodotus and the creation of ethnography. Put briefly, Homer's monsters are truly monsters, while barbarians, as everyone knows, are in the beginning just those who, instead of speaking Greek, make an unintelligible sound: *bar-bar*. I remind you that in Russian, the Germans are the *nemtsy*, the mutes. They don't speak Russian, so they don't speak. But Herodotus begins by saying that he's going to tell of the exploits of the Greeks and the barbarians. When one reads Herodotus, and already when one reads the *Odyssey*, it's impossible not to be struck by the extremely positive character of everything that is said about the Egyptians (this is indeed a constant feature among the Greeks). Yet, the Egyptians are barbarians, just like the Persians, the other people who always fascinated the Greeks. Parenthetically, you know that in Arnaldo Momigliano's book, which appeared in French under the title *Sagesses barbares*, the author was surprised at how one had to wait until the third century BC to find the first mention of the Jews and their religion in Greek texts.[215] With all due respect to the great

---

for the republic of the hoplites rather than that of the much more numerous sailors." See also Pierre Vidal-Naquet, *Le Miroir brisé: Tragédie athénienne et politique* (Paris: Les Belles Lettres, 2002), pp. 20–21. And see also the long critique of Loraux's position on this point found in Castoriadis's seminar from 1985, *Ce qui fait la Grèce, 3. Thucydide, La force et le droit* (Paris: Seuil, 2011), pp. 225–241.

214. *Eds.*: Castoriadis paraphrases the 1920 poem by C. P. Cavafy, "Young Men of Sidon (A.D. 400)," which can be found in Greek–English parallel in *The Collected Poems*, trans. Evangelos Sachperoglou (Oxford: Oxford World Classics, 2007), pp. 120–122.

215. *Eds.*: Arnaldo Momigliano, *Alien Wisdom: The Limits of Hellenization* (Cambridge: Cambridge University Press, 1990). Also see Castoriadis, "Greek Polis," pp. 81–88, as well as the discussion of Momigliano and Castoriadis in François Hartog, *Memories of*

Italian historiographer, it's his surprise that surprises me; it's not clear what would have driven the Greeks to take an interest in the Jews, unless it's just (starting from the moment when they effectively did so) to observe that their religion was decidedly very bizarre. The Greeks were, by contrast, literally obsessed by two other peoples, the Egyptians and the Persians. To move on quickly, let's say that for them the Egyptians embodied knowledge, the Persians state power (they're a people who knew how to create and conserve an immense state). Knowledge and power; those are the things about them that attracted the Greeks, who indeed ceaselessly return to this point. Herodotus attributes to the Persians things they couldn't have dreamt about, even up to the invention of democracy.[216] In Xenophon, and even later still, we find again this fascination for those people who knew how to constitute such an empire. (The Egyptians had also achieved this, but in the era when the Greeks began to speak about them, they were already a subdued people.) The Egyptians were aware, according to Plato, of everything that has come about on earth. The Greeks' admiration had no bounds.[217] Herodotus recounts that the Egyptians could go back into their past across more than 300 generations.[218] The historian Hecataeus of Miletus had bragged in front of the Egyptian priests about knowing his ancestors up to the fifteenth generation; at the sixteenth there was a god. Then, says Herodotus, the priests lead him into a hall of the temple where 345 statues of successive generations of kings of Egypt were found. And, if they didn't believe that a man could descend from a god, they said to Herodotus that there was a time when the gods themselves reigned in the land of Egypt. The Greeks, moreover, attributed to the Egyptians all sorts of mysterious esoteric knowledge and the like.

<Inaudible question.>

Very briefly—since I already spoke about it last time and we'll come back to it when we're dealing with the birth of philosophy and its elaboration—there

---

Odysseus: Frontier Tales from Ancient Greece, trans. Janet Lloyd (Chicago: University of Chicago Press, 2001), pp. 12–13. All the texts collected in this work are pertinent to the topics approached in these pages.

216. *Eds.*: See the famous speech of Otanes in Herodotus, *Histories*, III, 80.
217. *Eds.*: Plato, *Timeaus*, 23a: "Now of all the events reported to us, no matter where they've occurred—in your parts or in ours—if there are any that are noble or great or distinguished in some other way, they've all been inscribed here in our temples and preserved from antiquity on."
218. *Eds.*: Herodotus, *Histories*, II, 142–144.

is, for me, a nucleus of the imaginary grasp of the world by the Greeks, i.e. coexistence of a Chaos and a Cosmos, absence of hope for a better life after death, and so on, and this is the starting point for a liberation of action and thought. There you have what characterizes the principal current of Greek thought. It's true that marginally something else always existed—although, in the seventh and sixth centuries, it wouldn't be entirely clear.... Anyway, starting at a certain point, let's say the close of the sixth century and the fifth, there begins to manifest—a first element—this marginal tendency that I spoke about already, which is in effect searching for something other, something other that's not of this world, that's not in the city. We're of course talking about Orphism and Pythagoreanism. This aspect combines with—a second element—what we should rightly call the necessities proper to the philosophical movement, or rather its quasi-necessities. I understand by this that it isn't entirely by chance if, from Parmenides on, the awakening of philosophy leads into a sort of rational theology. This appears with clarity in Plato, although we can wonder whether the term "rational" is truly appropriate there. But, in any case, it's as of this moment that ontology begins to become onto-theology. A third element: At the end of the fifth and the start of the fourth century, we witness the defeat of Athens and of all that Athens symbolizes; in short, it's the crisis of politics. From that point forward, these marginal currents start to get the upper hand, not only among the philosophers, among those we would today call the <"intellectuals">, but also in society, with the increasingly important propagation of beliefs that promise immortality, the arrival of Eastern gods around which particular mysteries are organized, such as Sabazios in Athens or a Thracian Artemis called Bendis. This latter element is therefore the dissolution of the Greek world that had created the democratic *polis* and had placed at the forefront the values of creation, of doing within the world. And as soon as this element intertwines in some sense with the movement of philosophy, the affair obviously becomes frighteningly complicated. For, we have, on the one hand, the very trend of general social-historical evolution, which is introduced into philosophy in this context and gets transformed for it into a necessity of arriving at certain conclusions, I would say almost opportunistically. And then there's what unfolds from the necessities proper to philosophy, what arises in philosophy as a quasi-necessity of thought itself. To be a little less cryptic, in Plato's perspective, it must be, on the one hand, that there is a god as ultimate guarantor of human affairs; but also, on the other hand, in a more philosophical perspective and in a certain view of being, this being tends to become indifferentiable from what we call god.

VIII. Seminar from January 26, 1983

To finish up what's been said and introduce the subject that will occupy us now, I'll present some considerations about myth in general and, of course, about myth in Greece. Up to now we've essentially talked through the Homeric poems, the contents of which are profoundly interwoven with the mythical world. Our discussion is now going to take as its starting point (or as a bridgehead, if you will) the mythical figurations that Hesiod offers in the *Theogony*, figurations which will, furthermore, subsist for a long time afterwards. Another reason to reflect on myth is this historical problem, i.e. this historiography of knowing whether the birth of philosophy in Greece translates a radical break with mythology (a first position), or whether (a second position) it's merely a continuation. It's a discussion that has long occupied and still occupies, for that matter, the specialists.[219] I already suggested that I offer a response that refuses the two terms.

---

219. *Eds.*: See, for example, among recent publications, Richard Buxton, ed., *From Myth to Reason? Studies in the Development of Greek Thought* (Oxford: Oxford University Press, 1999), containing contributions by R. Buxton, G. Most, S. von Reden, J. Bremmer, W. Burkert, J. Gould, C. Calame, G. Lloyd, A. Griffiths, F. Hartog, D. Lenfant, J. Steru, A. Henrichs, P. Murray, C. Rowe, T. Johansen, M. Bélis, F. Graf. The position of those who see in philosophy a radical rupture is nicely presented by Burnet, *Early Greek*. But there have been many other authors with this view before him (to name the most famous ones, Grote, Zeller, Gomperz) and after him. See also Wilhelm Nestle, *Vom Mythos zum Logos. Die Selbstentfaltung des griechischen Denkens bis auf die Sophistik und Sokrates* (Stuttgart: A. Kröner, 1975). The thesis of essential continuity has been defended, in particular, by F. M. Cornford, member of the "Cambridge ritualists," who tried at the beginning of the twentieth century to build bridges between Hellenism and ethnography. See Francis M. Cornford, *From Religion to Philosophy* (Princeton: Princeton University Press, 1991); and *Principium Sapientiae: The Origins of Greek Philosophical Thought* (Cambridge: Cambridge University Press, 1952). See also Vernant, *Origins*, pp. 100–118, as well as Vernant, "The Formation of Positivist Thought in Archaic Greece," in *Myth and Thought*, pp. 317–398. See the critique of Cornford (and Vernant) in chapter 12 ("From Myths to Philosophy?") of G. S. Kirk, *The Nature of Greek Myths* (Harmondsworth: Penguin Books, 1974), pp. 276–303. For Kirk, "[There] were not one, or two, but several critical steps in the evolution of that systematically rational and wide-ranging thought that we call philosophy. [...] The development of philosophy in Greece was not the result of a sudden 'discovery

Contrary to what is asserted by what I will call the dominant ideology in sociology and history as it's expressed especially in structuralism, myth's meaning or function does not consist in carrying out a logical organization of the world, and particularly not according to a logic of binary oppositions (raw/cooked, honey/ash, etc.). We can indeed find a binary logic in myth, but it is, if you will, merely an instrument. This has nothing surprising about it since, after all, this binary logic is quite simply the fundamental form of what I call ensemblist-identitarian logic or, if you will, an instrumental logic. I mean a logic of classification and of separation which thus proceeds always by A/non-A, yes/no, and which sometimes takes what the logician would simply call contradiction (A/non-A) and pushes it towards a polar opposition (A/"the thing at the extreme conceivable opposite of A"), which is not at all the same. In short, myth, if it contains binary logic, is far from exhausting itself with that. The most perspicacious authors—Vernant, for example—understand this perfectly and show the role of ambiguity in this logic of polarity. In my view, all of these constitute timid efforts to get some distance from the structuralist or logicist straitjacket and to draw closer in some sense—if this isn't too much of a stealing of the spotlight—to a logic of magmas. The genuine organization of myth is in effect that of a magma. Even if it necessarily bears an ensemblist-identitarian dimension, without which any assertion would no longer be possible (i.e. if I assert the identity of A and non-A, then at the same time I necessarily posit their absolute distinction, otherwise my statement would no longer make any sense), there's a different dimension that's specific to it. If you want to represent this concretely for yourself, you can—while being very careful since this type of transition is always risky (it's an analogy, not a homology)—compare myth to what Freud called the formations of the unconscious. Not that myth would be a formation of the unconscious; that's something entirely different. Rather, it's a formation of the social imaginary, which is neither conscious nor unconscious in the sense that these terms have in psychoanalytical theory. But what draws these together is the plurality of levels at which the explication as well as the signification of myth unfolds. And there's also the fact that throughout this plurality of levels myth makes, significations exist that are not coordinated among themselves as if they were obeying an ensemblist-identitarian logic. I would say, for my part—and this is a definition—that myth is the figuration, by means of a narrative, of the

of the mind,' a dramatic unleashing of reason over five or six generations. It was closer to a spiritual and emotional Odyssey lasting for many hundreds of years, in which storytelling, social preoccupation, migration, literacy, conservatism, and religion all played their part" (pp. 300–302).

meaning with which a given society invests the world. Or, if you will, myth puts into act this meaning, this signification imputed to the world by a society, by giving figure to it through a narrative.[220] More specifically—but summarizing a lot since my aim is not now to talk about myth for itself—if we push the Freudian analogy further, there's essentially one and even several manifest meanings of myth legible in its figuration, i.e. in the presentation of a story or a narrative; and then there's what we can rightly call a latent meaning, namely what the myth signifies about the world and about men.

Let's thus admit that we're considering myth in this way. Indeed, in my naïveté I don't see how one could consider it differently; I cannot see how a society could exist without giving meaning to the world and to itself in this world. And, then, we know very well that it does not start out by offering this meaning through philosophical discourses, which for that matter don't offer it and which, even once philosophy does exist, only touch on a tiny part of society. If one poses the question like this, one can obviously no longer approach the relationship between mythology and philosophy according to the traditional alternative of radical rupture or simple continuation. For, myth, as primary depository of the central imaginary significations of a society, of course contains in germ something like philosophy to the extent that it does respond to the question *about meaning*, a response that is obviously given without there being explicit questioning. That is, we read the question in the response, in the fact that a response is given. Here, there's a question that could appear out of place: Why, then, does this deposit of significations form itself into precisely this form of myth and not into that of a discourse, of a systematic exposition? Why must it be that the response to the question of the signification of the world of society, of the acts of men, and so on, takes the form of a figuration by a narrative, the elements of which are acts? We cannot not ask this to ourselves, but we know immediately that there exists no response to this question, at least not an a priori response. Rather, as such, humanity begins—and continues, for that matter—in this way, by embodying signification in a figuration. And discourse as we conceive of it—i.e. that which tries and tends to extricate itself from every figurative element—is quite obviously a later creation, which originates, at least with regard to the current of history in which we're found, precisely in Greece.

Another incidental question: What's the difference between myth and tale? This is a far from negligible question since an author as important as Georges Dumézil, who devoted fifty years of his life to reflecting on mythology and made essential contributions in this field—I enthusiastically

---

220. *Marg. C.C.*: See Ricoeur now?

advise you to read everything of his that you can get hold of—admitted even in 1970 that he was never able to understand the difference.[221] To illustrate what's at stake, we could ask ourselves what separates, let's say, the myth of Oedipus from the tale of Hop-o'-My-Thumb. Obviously, it's not by accident that after Oedipus I mention Hop-o'-My-Thumb, but there are doubtless better examples. I believe quite simply that the response to Dumézil is that myth is a bearer of an *essential* meaning for the society under consideration and of a meaning that at least for this society is *universal*. I will not comment on these two terms, which intersect; in this context the essential is to a very large extent universal. That's quite obvious. After all, a tale is a story that one recounts for children, and it's unimportant whether one could or couldn't give an analysis, psychoanalytic or otherwise, of Little Red Riding Hood. What counts is that apart from precisely those significations which a psychoanalytic interpretation purports to unveil, this tale says nearly nothing to the people familiar with it, i.e. nothing essential or universal at least, or otherwise just trivialities of the type "Don't trust the wolf." Now, if this response stands to reason, why then hesitate to offer it? Doubtless it's because to assert that myth is the bearer of a universal and essential meaning for the society in which it emerges implies the abandonment of all formal criteria of distinction. One can no longer find in the form of the narrative, in the syntax or the terms utilized, a criterion of differentiation. Even a well programmed computer would be incapable of deciding whether such and such narrative is a tale

---

221. *Eds.*: On this admission, see Marcel Detienne, *The Creation of Mythology*, trans. Margaret Cook (Chicago: University of Chicago Press, 1986), p. xi and note 69, p. 163. We know that for Lévi-Strauss the difference is only one of degree; the tale is built on weaker opposition and the role of arbitrariness is greater. See Claude Lévi-Strauss, "Structure and Form: Reflections on a Work by Vladimir Propp," in *Structural Anthropology, Volume II*, trans. Monique Layton (Chicago: Chicago University Press, 1976), pp. 115–145. Also, G. S. Kirk—in *Nature*, pp. 31–33 and 35–36—recalls that the difficulty of establishing a rigorous distinction between myth and tale had already been pointed out by great anthropologists such as Franz Boaz (1916), Ruth Benedict (1930–1935), and Edward Evan Evans-Pritchard (1967). He observes, however, that if the myth is "a traditional tale," then, in order to become this traditional narrative, it ought "to possess both exceptional narrative power and clear functional relevance to some important aspect of life beyond mere entertainment"; myths must be "bearers of important messages about life in general and about life-in-society in particular" (pp. 28–29). See also Walter Burkert, *Structure and History in Greek Mythology and Ritual* (Berkeley: University of California Press, 1979), p. 23: "myth is a traditional tale with secondary, partial reference to something of collective importance." And see Fritz Graf, *Greek Mythology. An Introduction* (Baltimore: Johns Hopkins University Press, 1993), p. 7, for whom the difference between tale and myth lies in the "cultural centrality" of the myth. Lastly, see Jan N. Bremmer, *Greek Religion* (Oxford: Oxford University Press, 1994), p. 57: "traditional tales relevant to society."

or a myth; from a formal point of view, they are similar. The criterion that we've applied implies that we—we who are speaking, or the inquirer or researcher—take on the responsibility for saying: Look here, in such and such myth there's an essential and universal meaning for the society under consideration, which one cannot find in such and such tale. For, the latter relates a story that's of course always endowed with meaning (otherwise we wouldn't tell it), a meaning that's perhaps important, but not an essential, organizing meaning of the world. At the same time, all while assuming this responsibility, we accept that there can be uncertainty, that tale and myth are not necessarily separated by an iron curtain, that there can be hybrid beings, intermediate cases. If you read the *Iliad* or the *Odyssey*, you will constantly pose for yourself the question: Is this a myth or a tale? And you will be able to respond only in accordance with a number of decisions, of non-arbitrary postulates, which will have emerged step by step from the investigation and will have become discriminating criteria of what the formative significations of the Greek world are. And, in many cases, you'll hesitate over the classification. Moreover, as soon as we consider things in this way, the classification loses its importance.

Let's go back to the relationship between myth and discourse. Myth, thus, presents the figuration in a narrative of essential significations for the society under consideration. Discourse, for its part, will extract these significations in accordance with a new creation by explicitly positing a questioning to which it wants to give reflective responses. Thus, we're now almost immediately in the order of philosophical discourse. And what permits one to explicate why and how this transition comes about is that—in a certain number of cases and in particular with the Greek myths—we're dealing with essential and universal significations, which don't hold only for the society that has generated them. To take an extreme example, the American Indian myth that forms the starting point of the four volumes of Lévi-Strauss's *Mythologiques* is a pure object; it tells us nothing. It shows at most (if one assumes Lévi-Strauss's interpretation) how these tribes incarnated within a narrative that which is for them the distinction between nature and culture, or, to move more quickly, between the raw and the cooked. It's a distinction one finds everywhere, including in Greece; this is precisely the object of Vernant's and Detienne's book *The Cuisine of Sacrifice among the Greeks*.[222] It refers back to the fact that society differentiates itself from the pre-social world or from what it believes to be such and that it tells this story in the form of a myth (or "tale") about the passage from raw to cooked (civilization is a system in which one cooks what

---

222. *Eds.*: Marcel Detienne and Jean-Pierre Vernant, eds., *The Cuisine of Sacrifice among the Greeks*, trans. Paula Wissing (Chicago: University of Chicago Press, 1989).

one eats, in which one doesn't eat those like oneself). But the reach of the American Indian myth doesn't transcend the society under consideration or, if it does surpass it, then this has to do, if not with a triviality, then at least with a very general and abstract truth such that it doesn't teach us much of anything.

The case of Greek mythology is different. I said to you earlier in the year that the Greek myths are true, an assertion that might appear provocative, but which signifies exactly the following. What's essential and universal in the Greek myths is likewise so for us as well, and it is so not merely *qua* issuing from this tradition; it is so for all. And here we have an enormous point for investigation. I posit (this is a postulate) that we can recognize everywhere—whether it's directly or *qua* inverted, or even *qua* denied, it's not important—something on the order of the problematic of narcissism, or of the Oedipal problematic; but it's not only in Greece that one will find the myths of Narcissus and Oedipus. What counts here is that myth goes far beyond a simple figuration of the opposition nature/culture or even permitted/forbidden; it posits a grasp of the world and carries a magma of significations. And then—a second point (to which I'm certainly particularly sensitive, in accordance with my philosophical preoccupations proper)—the Greek myths are true because they unveil a signification of the world that one cannot reduce to any type of rationality, a signification that constantly presents meaning over a depth of un-meaning, a depth of non-meaning, or a non-meaning as everywhere penetrating meaning.

The risks of misunderstanding are multiple. To make myself better understood, I will cite the example of a researcher as subtle and fecund as Marcel Detienne, who, at the start of his book *Dionysos Slain*, fights against what he calls a humanistic Hellenism (which was in effect more or less that of the nineteenth century), because this Hellenism would have seen—and this is correct—in Greek mythology an initial figure of rationality.[223] Historiographically, the remark is justified; this is one of the retrospective projections performed on Greek antiquity by a rationalist and positivist West, considering itself as the representative *par excellence* of rational humanity and as the inheritor across the Western tradition of the glorious "Greek miracle." In this vision, Greek mythology *must* already be rational, which guarantees its specificity (our ancestors were no savages!). We have here, in broad strokes, the clichéd picture of a certain attitude of humanist Hellenism. Detienne and others fight against it, and they're completely right. But they place themselves on a ground that is, in one sense, entirely false. For, what Greek mythology precisely unveils, with regard to its signification, is not a rationality. What

---

223. *Eds.*: Detienne, *Dionysos*, p. 18.

unveils itself there as an ultimate signification of the world is the un-meaningful; and meaning emerges as a figure, starting from or over the depth of this un-meaning, but it's always condemned to return to it. And this is what serves to kick off or, if you will, what constitutes the nourishing soil of the Greek social imaginary; it's what will allow for the creation of philosophy as well as of democracy.

To illustrate this, I'll return to an element that from the point of view of the sequencing of philosophical reasons is not primary, but which very much is so from the anthropological point of view, specifically the Greek attitude towards the world as it is revealed in its way of envisaging hope. This is a question I've already approached, and I'd like to go back to it briefly, highlighting the relationship that it presents with the creation of philosophy and democracy.[224] To do this, let's review, here, Kant's three famous questions regarding the interests of man: "What can I know? What must I do? What may I hope for?" On the first two, I don't have a response wholly prepared. I would simply remind you that the discussion is inaugurated by the Greeks. But on the third question, I have a response: *nothing*. And I maintain that this response is at the origin of the Greek grasp of the world. Naturally, one should make the term hope more precise; hope or hopefulness has two senses. On the one hand, a current, empirical—ontic, as Heidegger would say—meaning refers to the fact that in daily life one has, *vis-à-vis* reality, a certain number of limited or delimited expectancies in relation to our activities. One is expectant for the sun to rise anew tomorrow, to find fish in the sea, to see wheat spring up, and for a child being born alive, and so on. This hope indeed refers to a whole series of very important problems of both a cosmological and a psychological order. How does it happen that we have these expectancies, and rightly so? (For we can in effect assert against all the skeptics that the sun will rise tomorrow, and so forth.) This issue gathers together essential problems from the theory of knowledge. What's at stake here is a presumption of a certain regularity in things, and in particular one having to do with phenomena whose regularity makes them positive for men, or in any case relatively "manageable." By contrast, nobody would say that we hope for our death, though the event would be entirely of the same order of probability as the rising of the sun, if not as to the moment, then at least as to the fact. But hopefulness or hope also has another sense—not ontic but ontological, even "destinal," to employ the term of the French translators of Heidegger—which is the idea of a fundamental, ultimate accord beyond all possible contradictions and oppositions between our most profound aspirations and what's going to happen.

---

224. *Eds.*: On what follows, see Castoriadis, "Greek *Polis*," pp. 101–105.

It's the idea of a sort of harmony between the world, the cosmos, and what we are, i.e. what we are as inclusive of the privileged way that we desire, of course. This hopefulness thus implies that the order of the world—this cosmos of the cosmos, if you will—includes the response to our own aspirations. Such a representation is found in many societies, perhaps in all of them. This is, in my view, the fundamental monotheistic position. Yet, it's completely absent from the primary Greek attitude, at least up to the fifth century, and this is what appears in the myth of Pandora in Hesiod, which we'll speak more about.[225] You know that Pandora comes to men as a gift of the gods, but this gift is a trap, and they should've refused it. Pandora opens the famous jar, from which escape all the ills familiar to humanity. When she re-closes it, hope remains within. Thus, there you have the Greek view of the human: an abundance of ills of every sort and an absence of hope, i.e. this hope enclosed in a box that one can no longer open.

We thus have a world that emerges from chaos, in which existence itself appears as an excess, a *hybris* (this is the meaning of the famous fragment of Anaximander that we will read later), and at the heart of this world is a human being who, for every case of being expectant, can only count on, after death, a life that's worse than death, as we've seen with regard to the Homeric poems. Yet, I repeat, this vision conditions in an essential way the birth of philosophy as much as that of democracy. For, if the initial position consists in saying that the world is signification through and through, there's no place for philosophizing; or at minimum one will philosophize once and for all, one will erect a system that will translate into our language that which is, for us, the meaning of the world. Likewise, if the world is only chaos, there's no longer a place for philosophy. The historical possibility of philosophy depends on the fact that the world both is and is not thinkable at once. And also, of course, it's due to there not being a God who has revealed the truth of the world; otherwise, instead of philosophy one would have at most an interpretation of the divine word. And this holds true for the totality of the human world. I mean that the political activity of men, the explicit aim of an institution of society by a

---

225. *Eds.*: Hesiod, *Works and Days*, 53–105; see also *Theogony*, 558–612. Also, according to Jean-Pierre Vernant, "The Myth of Prometheus in Hesiod," in *Myth and Society*, pp. 183–202, the double nature of the figure of Pandora "is, as it were, the symbol of the ambiguity of human existence"; and the "fundamental ambiguity of Pandora is matched by the ambiguity of *Elpis* (hope) [...]" (pp. 199–200). See also Pierre Judet de la Combe, "La dernière ruse: 'Pandore' dans la *Théogonie*," in Fabienne Blaise, Pierre Judet de La Combe, and Philippe Rousseau, eds., *Le métier du mythe: Lectures d'Hésiode* (Villeneuve-d'Ascq: Septentrion, 1996), pp. 263–299; as well as Dora Panofsky and Erwin Panofsky, *Pandora's Box: The Changing Aspects of a Mythical Symbol* (New York: Pantheon Books, 1956).

collectivity that institutes itself by itself, also itself presupposes the absence of a predefined ideal order of human things, but also the absence of a simple facticity such as the pure reign of force. It's a matter of establishing a certain cosmos in a human world that, without excluding all forms of order, isn't ordered all by itself through and through. Put differently, two elements must be posited simultaneously. There exists no social law known or imposed in advance that would be valid once and for all; law is to be established against the chaotic, hubristic elements of the human world. At the same time, these elements are not such that they would render impossible the establishment of a law, in the same way that what exists isn't a simple non-meaning but meaning over a depth of non-meaning or shot through with non-meaning. By means of this we're harnessed to a task that's not infinite, as philosophers have sometimes said, but interminable.

I'm now coming to the signification of the pair of opposed terms *chaos* and *kosmos*, which—along with the other pair of *hybris* and *dikē*, which we spoke about quite at length—have a fundamental importance in the Greek grasp of the world, in my view. The second opposition isn't entirely homothetic with the former, but it has a profound kinship with it. And if I draw them near to one another here, it's because I think that there are two dimensions within the problematic that they open up, namely the properly philosophical dimension and the anthropological dimension, which I alluded to in what I was just saying.

Let's take the philosophical dimension. We start with the *chaos*. The first text in which we find it is Hesiod's *Theogony*. How far back does it go? Once, they dated Hesiod (and likewise Homer) quite far back, towards the middle of the ninth century. According to the dating generally accepted at the present time—with which, inasmuch as I can have an opinion, I would be more in agreement—one would need to place Homer in the second half of the eighth century and place Hesiod, who is visibly posterior, towards the year 700. Indeed, we have testimonies that go in this direction.[226] In any case, after the Homeric poems, it's the most ancient text that we possess.

---

226. *Eds.*: Herodotus, *Histories*, II, 53, says that Homer and Hesiod had lived "not more than 400 years" before him, which gave rise to different calculations. The traditional dating (middle of the eight century) is accepted by Paul Mazon in his edition, i.e. Hesiod, *Théogonie, Les Travaux et les jours, Le Bouclier*, trans. Paul Mazon (Paris: L'Association Guillaume Budé,1928), pp. xiv–xv. G. S. Kirk is in favor of a later date (second quarter of the seventh century) in *Songs*, pp. 285–287, and in "The Structure and Aims of the Theogony," in *Hésiode et son influence: six exposés et discussions* (Geneva: Fondation Hardt, 1962), pp. 61–62. Richard Janko comes to the same conclusion in *Homer, Hesiod and the Hymns: Diachronic Development in Epic Diction* (Cambridge: Cambridge University Press,

146   THE GREEK IMAGINARY

After an initial invocation of the Muses, which is much longer than what we find in Homer and which is in itself very interesting, we read in the *Theogony* this surprising assertion that, prior to everything, *Chaos genet(o)*.[227] I regret that we can't here dive into a reflection on this extraordinary expression. If we want to be direct, we should read it as: "first the Void became," or "first came about the Void." Of course, you can quibble and say that if Hesiod isn't using the imperfect of the verb *einai* (to be [*être*]) but rather the aorist of the verb *gignomai* (to arise [*advenir*] or to become [*devenir*]), this choice is determined by metrical reasons. But that doesn't matter really because the text is there: first became—arose—the Void. After Chaos arose *Gaia eurysternos*, the Earth of broad sides or with broad breast; it's a certain basis, says Hesiod, offered perpetually to all that exists. And, thirdly, Eros.[228] Here we more or less have independent elements. From this, genealogies follow; these entities will generate other things. Thus, from Chaos, Erebus (total darkness) and the black Night come out; then from Night, Aether and Day; and so on.[229] The Earth generates, by parthenogenesis, a being that is its equal, Ouranos (the Sky). She sleeps with him—the first incest recorded in all Greek history—which produces the generation of the Titans, and from there I think you're familiar with what follows.

Regarding the initial Chaos, one should firstly avoid a misunderstanding. The temptation exists to identify it immediately with what we designate by

---

     1982), pp. 188–200. In favor of an earlier dating (between 750 and 720), see M. L. West, ed., *Hesiod: Theogony* (Oxford: Clarendon, 1966), pp. 40–46.

227. *Eds.*: Hesiod, *Theogony*, 116.

228. *Eds.*: For Castoriadis, therefore, as for other authors—for example, Paul Mazon, Clémence Ramnoux, and, more recently, Reynal Sorel, *Les Cosmogonies grecques* (Paris: PUF, 1994), pp. 24–25—verse 119 ("[…] and Misty Tartaros in a recess of broad-wayed earth […]") is an interpolation. Among the proponents of authenticity, see above all G. S. Kirk in Kirk, Raven, and Schofield, *Presocratic*, pp. 34–35, whose translation was just used; and see West, *Theogony*, pp. 193–194, where he writes, "Tartarus comes in oddly at this point, since it is really on the other side of Chaos from Earth (814). At the same time, since Earth has no lower limit that can be seen or definitely imagined, both Chaos and Tartarus could be considered as something not separate from Earth, but deep inside it and part of it. Cf. 841, *tartara gaiēs*. It is possible that Hesiod originally began with the trio Chaos, Earth, Eros, and inserted Tartarus later, when he came to the Titanomachy and realized that an important part of the universe had been omitted from the cosmogony" (p. 194). Alain Ballabriga—in chapter 4 ("L'Univers et l'Abîme") of *Le Soleil et le Tartare, l'image mythique du monde en Grèce archaïque* (Paris: Éditions de l'EHESS, 1986), pp. 257–290—likewise supports line 119 but by placing *Tartara* in accusative case, i.e. making it the object of the Olympians' sovereignty and not a "primordial element" on the same level as Chaos, Earth, and Eros.

229. *Eds.*: Hesiod, *Theogony*, 123.

this term, namely a formless mixture. Yet, it's well established that the name *chaos* is akin to the verb *chainō*, which signifies "to gape" (whence "gap"). We're thus dealing with a hollow, a void. We have numerous passages that attest to this meaning, and we know that the term will only much later adopt the sense that we're familiar with for it, which Greek would render by *kykeōn* (formless mixture, soup). For this you have to wait until the first century.[230] But in line 116 of the *Theogony*, the word Chaos without any doubt has its primary sense, i.e. that of void. And this void refers to a substratum, a primordial matrix. We have here an example of what Olof Gigon calls Hesiod's "surprising power of abstraction."[231] Everything must arise on the basis of void; being comes about starting from the essential non-being of the void. Here, I'm translating Hesiod into modern, Platonic, and post-Platonic philosophical jargon.[232]

Nevertheless, in the *Theogony* there's another signification tied to Chaos, even if Hesiod doesn't call it by its name. It interests me primarily because—I say so candidly—what I'm pursuing here are the antecedents of the idea of chaos, abyss, groundless, in the sense that I give to these terms.[233] And we find this at the end of the narrative of the struggle between the Olympians

---

230. *Eds.*: On the word and notion of Chaos, see Pierre Chantraine, *Dictionnaire étymologique de la langue grecque: Histoire des mots. Nouvelle édition mise à jour* (Paris: Klincksieck, 1968). But see also: Olof Gigon, *Der Ursprung der griechischen Philosophie. Von Hesiod bis Parmenides* (Bâle and Stuttgart: Schwabe & Co. 1968), pp. 28–29; Fränkel, *Early Greek*, p. 101; Kirk in Kirk, Raven, and Schofield, *Presocratic*, pp. 34–41; and in the commentary in West, *Theogony*, pp. 192–193. The differences between these authors perhaps traces back to what Gigon calls the "contradiction" (p. 30) between Hesiod's philosophical intention and his means of expression. Castoriadis essentially follows Gigon's interpretation here. See also an early formulation by Castoriadis in 1979's "Political Thought," found herein pp. 263–265; and see also Castoriadis, "Greek *Polis*," pp. 103–105.
231. *Eds.*: Gigon, *Ursprung*, p. 29: "It took a surprising power of abstraction to rise to this concept [i.e. Chaos seen as a formless space pre-existing both earth and heaven]. For Hesiod, the origin must be that which is most indeterminate and most impalpable."
232. *Eds.*: On this difficult question, see above all Gigon, *Ursprung*, and Fränkel, *Early Greek*; and see the (somewhat critical) discussion of Fränkel in Clément Ramnoux, "La nuit de la cosmogonie," in *La Nuit et les enfants de la Nuit dans la tradition grecque* (Paris: Flammarion, 1986), pp. 84–86. See also Jean-Pierre Vernant, "Mythes cosmogoniques: La Grèce," in Yves Bonnefoy, ed., *Dictionnaire des mythologies* (Paris: Flammarion, 1999), pp. 501–502. The former can be read with the French translation (based on West's edition) of the *Theogony* by Annie Bonnafé (Paris: Rivages, 1993), pp. 12–14. Finally, see also Sorel, *Cosmogonies*, pp. 26–31.
233. *Eds.*: See above all Cornelius Castoriadis, "Institution of Society and Religion," in *World in Fragments*, pp. 311–330. See also Cornelius Castoriadis, "The Imaginary: Creation in the Social-Historical Domain," in *World in Fragments*, pp. 3–18; and Castoriadis, "Une Interrogation sans fin."

and Titans.[234] I remind you of the genealogy: Earth (*Gaia*) and Sky (*Ouranos*) generated the Titans. The youngest of them, Chronos, seizes supreme power by castrating his father. (The *Theogony* already gives the meaning that Freud's *Totem and Taboo* gives to the primitive myth in 1914: Why does the primitive father castrate his children? Response: To avoid being castrated by them. This is the circularity of myth.) After this, to avoid the same lot Chronos doesn't "devour" his children; he simply swallows them whole. But his wife Rhea, who is also a figure of the Earth, hides the last born, Zeus, who when all grown up will make Chronos spit back out his brothers and sisters. The Chronos clan then take their place on Olympus, from where they fight against the Titans, who are on Mount Othrys. Zeus will prevail thanks to the gift of fire by the Cyclopes and with the aid of three monsters, the Hundred-Handers (Cottus, Briareus, and Gyges), who will throw the vanquished Titans beneath the Earth, into Tartarus, where they bind them.[235] This place is described by Hesiod as being as far from the Earth as Earth is from the Sky, enclosed by a wall of bronze, with an opening surrounded by a triple row of shadow; and "above, the roots of the earth and the unfruitful sea have grown through" (verses 727 ff.; I'm using the Mazon translation to go faster).

What does this passage tell us? We're not trying to lay bare the contradictions, to extract a system. We're dealing here with a magma of figured and represented signification. What was in the mind of the poet and in the social imaginary of his era? First, there's the idea of a chaos as a void that comes about, as that from out of which come beings, at first sub-beings like Gaia or Eros. And at the same time the signification-representation of a place/non-place (Tartarus) above which the roots of the earth grow through. I'm putting myself into the point of view of the signification, without offering commentary of the aesthetical or other type. This Earth, of which we're told that it came about after Chaos and doubtless from out of Chaos, is here presented as having its roots, in a sense, in Tartarus. And this is where they enclose the Titans, monstrous and hubristic gods, in this sort of primordial, unspeakable matrix. Tartarus here plays the role of a chaos in the second sense of the term. It's not simply a void, even if, obviously, a void is also necessary in order to put the Titans in there. This second sense is thus present in Hesiod himself. Another passage comes just afterwards (lines 736–819) that describes Tartarus in great detail. One should know that modern philologists

---

234. *Eds.*: For the episode of struggle against the Titans, see Hesiod, *Theogony*, 629–746. For the Olympians gaining the advantage thanks to the help of Cottus, Briareus, and Gyges, see 711–717. For the Titans being thrown into Tartarus, see 717–756.
235. *Eds.*: Hesiod, *Theogony*, 713–745.

almost unanimously consider it as not being from Hesiod's hand—or mouth, if you will—but an interpolation added to the poem at an unknown date. Insofar as I can judge, not being a specialist, the arguments in support of this thesis seem very solid. But nobody contests that this passage or other similar ones represent a tradition that existed alongside Hesiod, before and after him. Here again, what interests us is not to establish the authenticity of these lines in the philological sense of the term but to know to what extent they make up part of the tradition of the era and what significations they translate. On this point, there isn't any doubt; it's not an addition from the fifth century or the Alexandrian era. Yet, what does this description of Tartarus say to us? We read there for example that there are, found there, the sources and the extremities of all things, of the Sea, of the Earth, of the starry Sky; these are "places frightening and musty, which strike fear even for gods, an immense abyss, the ground of which one could not reach."[236] ("Abyss" here is *chasma*, a word related to *chaos*.) And therein are unleashed endless wind gusts, perpetual whirlwinds that would fill with fright even the gods, says Hesiod. "There stands the frightening dwelling of the infernal Night, which somber clouds envelop."[237] We can see that the author of the passage is not lacking in images or epithets to describe this place to which, once again it's explicitly said, the roots of all things that exist descend, a place that therefore in a sense nourishes these existents, and which at the same time is described as total disorder, total obscurity, and terrifying. We thus have here an image of the basis of being, or of beings, which is quite clearly laid out.

With regard to this originary matrix, this substratum, we are dealing, at the end of the day, with two ideas, two significations. The first is that of line 116, i.e. the Chaos as Void, as Abyss. The world emerges *ex nihilo*. Being itself is first of all a void. If I translate into my terminology, we have here the idea of a radical creation, of a creation from out of nothing, and of a creation of the nothing itself from out of a hyper-nothing. The second signification is expressed both in the lines on Tartarus which are Hesiod's (essentially lines 727–728, and more broadly lines 720–735) and, even more so, in the interpolation that I just summarized for you. It's the idea of a *kykeōn*, of a formless, terrifying mixture, which contains all things and nourishes all things. Yet, this second idea—this is quite surprising and I can merely posit this thesis here—is the one that's called forth to play the most important role in the development of Greek philosophy.

---

236. *Eds.*: Hesiod, *Theogony*, 739–740.
237. *Eds.*: Hesiod, *Theogony*, 744–745.

We see emerge here on the spot, in a living and immediate connection, an essential philosophical signification from out of mythological significations that already contain it. It's the idea of a chaos-abyss in the sense of a formless mixture in which all the forms to come coexist, and which is in every case the effective condition of possibility and reality for forms (which is what the image of the roots signifies, i.e. the nutritive element contained in this substratum). Yet, this signification appears from the beginning of philosophy onwards, with Anaximander's *apeiron*, i.e. that famous principle posited, as Aristotle will put it, as the *archē*, as the primordial element. Our principal source is here a passage from the commentary of Simplicius on Aristotle's *Physics*, written a thousand years later.[238] Anaximander, thus, says that the *archē*, the principle, the origin of beings, is the *apeiron*.[239] The word *apeiron* is linked to *peras* (limit, end, completion). *Apeiron* will of course come, in the Greek philosophy of the era of Aristotle and afterwards, to signify "infinite." But its fundamental sense, which we must absolutely have in mind, and which is most important for Greek philosophy and for the history of philosophy (i.e. a sense systematically concealed for twenty-five centuries) is not that of the infinite but of the *indeterminate*.[240] This emerges very clearly from all the oppositions that we find in Greek texts, including among philosophers, between *peras* and *apeiron*. Moreover, here there would be other etymological stakes to draw out: *peras* is near to *peira* (experience, knowledge, familiarity with). The indeterminate is thus also the unknowable, that which is without limit or end, but not, once again, in the sense of a mathematical infinite. It's a question of end in the sense of de-finition, de-limitation, de-termination (in determination you have "term" or *terminus*).

We'll speak in detail about what precisely Anaximander understands by *apeiron*, but the witnesses to the persistence and role of this signification do not cease with him, far from it. We thus read in Achilles Tatius, an astronomer and philosopher from the third century AD, that Thales and Pherecydes of Syros posited water as the principle of all things (a fact that was known from

---

238. *Eds.*: Simplicius, *Physics*, 24, 13 (= DK 12A9 and B1). Also, see the English translation, Simplicius, *On Aristotle's* Physics *4.1–5 and 10–14*, trans. James O. Urmson (London: Duckworth, 1992), which generally employs Hermann Diels, ed., *Commentaria in Aristotelem Graeca IX* (Berlin: Verlag Georg Reimer, 1882). On the fragment itself, see Seminar X.
239. *Eds.*: On the *apeiron*, see Seminar X, pp. 163 ff.
240. *Eds.*: We should give credit to Nietzsche for having proposed *das Unbestimmte* where Diels was satisfied with *das Unendliche* and Burnet with *the Boundless*. See Marianne Cowan, "Introduction," in Friedrich Nietzsche, *Philosophy in the Tragic Age of the Greeks* (New York: Simon & Schuster, 2012), p. 20 (and p. 47).

other sources, in the case of Thales) and that Pherecydes also called water "chaos."[241] This demonstrates well the presence in this era of the second signification of chaos, not that which derives from *chainō* (void), but that which shows it as something undifferentiated, containing possibilities for differentiation. We will find analogous ideas in Anaxagoras. And from Xenophanes there also exists a fantastic quotation—some have seen the founder of the Eleatic school represented here—namely fragment 28 of Diels–Kranz, where he says: "We see the end (*peiras*) of the Earth here, near our feet, where it borders the air, but toward the bottom, it goes on to the infinite (*eis apeiron*)."[242] I would also like to point you to a fragment of a late Pythagorean, Philolaus (end of the fifth century), where he says that *physis* put itself together, coordinated itself, organized itself (*harmochthē*, a Greek verb from which comes "harmony") within the ordered cosmos (*en tō kosmō*) *ex apeiron te kai perainontōn*, i.e. from out of the infinite-indeterminate and the finite-determinate, from unlimited and limit.[243] And he says the whole world and everything in the world is always made from *apeiron* and *perainon* (or *peras*), i.e. always contains *apeiron* and *peras*. We find this same signification again in the two great philosophers of the Greek world, in Plato and Aristotle, where it plays a fundamental role. It's striking to observe the persistence of this signification, the impossibility of ridding oneself of it, in Plato, i.e. someone who conceived of being as *idea*. I would say that he knows we cannot rid ourselves of it. In the *Philebus* (16c), he cites, he says, an ancient and true discourse according to which all that can be said to exist is made from one and many and possesses in itself (*symphyton*: growing with it in its being and in its becoming, co-native, if you will, taking "native" in the ontological and not empirical sense) *peras* and *apeiron*. All that is can only arise to being containing constantly at once *peras* and *apeiron*, determined and indeterminate, definite and indefinite. The *Philebus* is one of the latest dialogues of Plato. But what's even more striking is to observe the fundamental role that this signification of a chaotic substratum plays in the *Timaeus*, that great dialogue which in a sense collects at once his cosmology and his ontology, a decisive dialogue for entering into his thinking. It's a late one, but not one of the very last ones. In my view it comes just before or just after the enormous dialectical explosion of the *Parmenides* and *Sophist*. In a way, it's opposed to the problematic of the two dialogues, but dialogically opposed. Everything happens as if in the *Parmenides* and *Sophist* Plato, at sixty-five or seventy years old, starting again right from the beginning, kills

241. *Eds.*: DK 7B1a
242. *Eds.*: DK 21B28.
243. *Eds.*: DK 44B1.

the father Parmenides and remobilizes his theory of the Ideas and his conception of what can be a truth or a true statement, all while in the *Timaeus* the approach seems entirely opposed. However, I have a tendency to believe that one doesn't always write things one after the other, although perhaps this is just a projection due to my bad habits. I think that Plato could've had half of the *Timaeus* in his drawer while writing the *Sophist* and *Parmenides*, or the reverse, or both at the same time. And in the *Timaeus*, everything happens as if Plato were asking: Fine, if we now take account of what we can plausibly and reasonably say about being and the world (these are, by the way, more or less Timaeus's formulations in the dialogue), what would we say? And he says… the *Timaeus*. Moving quickly: There exists a "demiurge," an artisan who fabricates the world or the *kosmos* by imposing order on a preexisting substratum. He contemplates the model of this order in what Plato calls the eternal living being, an idea or a system, an "organism" of ideas. The demiurge tries to make of the world something that comes nearer, as much as possible, to this eternal living being. Once this task is achieved, he doesn't declare that it's good, as does the God of the Bible, but he delights in looking upon this world that's compared to an animal. There you have what the demiurge is for Plato.

Yet this *kosmos* depends on the imposition of an order on a substratum that, as such, is a rebel against order. This idea returns several times in the *Timaeus*. I don't want to expand on this, but we find it in the passage (48e–53b) where Plato discusses what he calls the receptacle or the *chōra*, which means something intermediary between space and a space filled with matter. He describes here something that exists in itself, independently and in advance of every form, which can receive every form without for all that being organically adapted to it: there's no harmony. And this absence of harmony is translated by Plato's expressions when he says, repeated several times, that the demiurge imposes an order on the world *kata to dynaton*, as far as possible. There is something that is superior to the power of the demiurge, which is the resistance of the substratum to letting itself be defined by an order through and through. The limit of this divinity is precisely the being-thus of a substratum that manifestly is not the pure creation of a personal God. And this is why in the final analysis there isn't any theodicy in any ultimate sense in this conception. It's because there's this initial duality and because the rational and sensible action (to use modern terms) of the demiurge can exert itself only upon this rebel substratum.

I think, for my part, that Plato himself had, in the domain in which one would least expect it, i.e. in mathematics, the experience of this insubordination of the substratum. <We know that the existence of irrational numbers> posed a major problem to Greek thought. Their existence flows, moreover, immediately from the Pythagorean theorem since the relationship of the diagonal of a square, or of the hypotenuse of a right triangle with the two sides equal, isn't rational. We know that if the side has value 1, the hypotenuse has the value of the square root of 2, which is not a rational quantity. What appeared like a scandal there deeply unsettled Greek thought and made it enter into a period of intense fermentation from which it would emerge with Eudoxus of Cnidus, who regulated the problem of irrationals more or less in the same way that Dedekind would later do so, i.e. thanks to a theory of proportions and approximations. What's important, for Plato, is that he has just lived through a major conquest in the mathematics of his era, the achievement of the construction of regular polyhedra, and at the same time the demonstration that these regular polyhedra are five in number. There exists an infinite number of regular polyhedra in two dimensions, but there are only five regular polyhedra in space, namely with four, six, eight, twelve, and twenty faces. Plato, furthering a thought that goes back to the Pythagoreans and continues into the present time including in fundamental physics, wanted to establish a relationship between mathematics and physics. This meant that he wanted to be able to make a connection between what he considered to be the elements of matter (earth, water, etc.) and what appeared to him to be elementary unities of being and what is thinkable as they are present in stereometry, that is to say, the regular polyhedra. Thus, he assigned to each element a regular polyhedron and said, for example, that fire is constituted of tetrahedra—the exact attribution doesn't matter—and so on and so forth, reserving one of the forms for the global figure of the cosmos. He then tried to construct these regular polyhedra from out of triangles, which is entirely plausible since the triangle is the elementary shape in a two-dimensional space. And there he discovered that he couldn't do it according to rational relations. This means that if one posits an equilateral triangle, for example, as the element for the construction of these polyhedra, there isn't a rational relationship between the side of this triangle and the sides, the faces, the volumes, and so on, of the generated polyhedra. When he put himself in the position of the demiurge, Plato thus himself encountered in this research that character of the substratum that's irreducible to the rational. And here, it's not even an issue of a material substratum; it's already a rational—purely thinkable, mathematical—substratum.[244] This is why he several times employed the turn

---

244. *Marg. C.C.*: More precisely, it's even richer: The substratum of mathematics is space, and space contains in itself the irrational, the *arrhēton*, in the form of the square root of two, for example. Whence comes the "irrational" character of the *chōra*.

of phrase *kata to dynaton*, i.e. as far as possible. That is, the demiurge cannot rationalize through and through the world he constructs.

And this aspect is found again in Aristotle, for whom in matter there is an *apeiron*, which is the limit of the conceivable, i.e. that which would be absolutely deprived of form and determination.[245] This signification would persist in Greek philosophy, in total opposition to modern onto-theology, which evidently stems from a different signification, i.e. that of a rational, absolute creator God, for whom, in a sense, there can't be an ultimate irreducibility in what he's created. From this comes the idea of mathematization, which is not modern (it's Greek), but which takes on an entirely different look, in particular with Descartes and following from him, and finally the modern illusion of a system, unknown with the Greeks. Aristotle never wrote a system. The Middle Ages did violence to the texts in order to present them as systematic. This modern illusion is obviously the homologue of the illusion of a rationality of being through and through.

Questions

I don't agree when you say that the system is a modern illusion. It's really the Stoics who are the first to have said that what is, is rational through and through...

You're entirely right, even if this would lead us into the third century.

So you're going to start modernity in the third century BC?

I wouldn't be the first person to do so! One could effectively assert that modernity begins with the third century. And modernity in the sense of the search not simply for a system, but also for a transcendent salvation. That starts even with the fourth century since it's then that these Orphic and Pythagorean currents that show up in the sixth century—which I already spoke to you about—flourish. But you're perfectly correct to say that the Stoics bear out the aim for a rigorous systematization, with, for that matter, an ontology that is in its essentials a theology.

In mythology what are the elements of rationality that announce the coming of philosophy? What is the philosophical dimension of mythology?

---

245. *Eds.*: See Aristotle, *Metaphysics*, VII, 10, 1036a9; and *Physics*, III, 207a25.

The philosophical dimension evidently is not in the way of proceeding, in the mode of exposition. It is, as I tried to say, in the significations. Today, I focused on this essential signification, i.e. chaos, and on its two acceptations. Of course—and this is what relates to the *Theogony*—at the same time we find the idea of an imposed or existing order, one that is identified, as we see later with Anaximander, with *moira*, this law of partitioning, supreme and impersonal, which is the same for all. I think it's in the conjunction of these two significations—chaos and this impersonal law that's imposed the same on all—that one should look for the roots, the prime matter, the terrain on which philosophical reflection could be born.

Can we speak of a sense of the sacred in Homeric religion?

We already touched on this subject last time. Everything depends on what we mean by sacred. If we take up the meaning I give to this term, i.e. presentation of the Abyss in the world, obviously there is something sacred in Greek religion. This notion, certainly, isn't simple. I previously cited the case of the cave in Bethlehem. What does the presentation of the Abyss in this world involve, and how far can it go? It incontestably meets with a limit that one could call, if one wanted, fetishism, which is present everywhere. The icon, seen as an object like a painting one can scrape to make a healing potion out of it, has existed for centuries, and it's always there. Yet, this icon is a sacred object; only, the faithful man who venerates it is conceiving of what I call Abyss, which for him is called by another name, and which becomes real in itself in a mode that is not entirely the same for a Muslim or a Jew. For, they refrain from representing God, all while they cannot go without a certain number of holy endowed places, like the Wailing Wall, which have a fundamental privilege in their reality itself and not merely at the symbolic level. I believe it would be vain to want to go beyond this definition according to which the sacred is that which, for those holding to a religion, makes present the Abyss in this world. We would find, once again, an extraordinary range of nuances between fetishism pure and simple, represented in nearly all religions, and the most sublimated form, in which the faithful person thinks, at the limit, that the presence of transcendence in this world is nothing other than a discourse. There is, of course, a fantastical difference between these two extreme terms, but this discourse is itself also sacred; its status cannot be called into question in any way.

You say that in myth the response makes the question appear, in some sense. But we could wonder where the question comes from....

I don't know. But it's like this: the human being, humanity, cannot exist without making the question of signification arise.

What do you think of Vernant's response, which relates this to the organization of the city?

Here, I fear that you're mixing up several things. I'm talking about significations that were there long before the city was, before reason in the proper sense of the term. Vernant says that reason is daughter of the city; he's not talking about signification in general. How to define reason? This is yet another abyss. Let's say that it's an issue of this movement of thought that reflects, that self-interrogates, that calls itself into question. Yet a mythology does not by itself call itself into question. And in this sense mythology is not reason. For Vernant, this also means that philosophy, mathematics, history, and so on, are "daughters of the city." I already said, all while agreeing in general with this formula, that I nevertheless find it a bit unilateral. My position is that philosophy and democracy are born together and from the same movement—one can say of reason that it's daughter of the city only if one takes reason in a very secondary sense. The birth of the *polis* is at the same time the birth of a generalized calling-into-question. Reason in the primary sense is this. Or, to say it differently, the constitution of the *polis* and of a community that poses for itself the question of the law is already a philosophy in act, not a philosophy in words but a philosophy enacted, which raises the question of what one should do and at the same time the question of the criteria in accordance with which one will respond to it.

Regarding the myth of Pandora and hope, Aristotle says that one cannot be courageous if one lacks hope, that a coward is a man without hope.[246] Is there not a valorization of hope there?

Aristotle forgive me, but this is really a consideration that is, I wouldn't say fleeting, but a bit secondary. For, even at the psychological level where he's positioned, it's only true *hōs epi to poly*, as he says himself, i.e. *most of the time*

---

246. Eds.: Aristotle, *Nicomachean Ethics*, III, 7, 1116a.

there cannot be courage without a certain hopefulness, but it doesn't get to the bottom of things. For, one can speak of the courage of unhope, of the courage of the one who knows that all is lost; we know that this exists. It's indeed something that's well known, particularly by way of the Greeks. This interpretation of Aristotle thus remains at a descriptive, secondary level. To get to the bottom of things, it's because there isn't any hopefulness that the Greek universe can signify.

You say that the Greek myths are true because they unveil a signification of the world, and that this signification is not rational. But I wonder if the term itself, unveiling, doesn't imply that there would be something that exists to be revealed. Alternatively, one could say that the Greek myths construct significations that didn't exist before them. All of this is obviously tied to the problem of truth and of its unveiling.

The questions that you draw out go very far. Myths create significations; the significations are created. This is my fundamental starting point. In relation to this, and in relation to everything that is a historical creation according to my way of speaking (i.e. the psychoanalysts *and* the shamans, modern physics *and* magic, the law or tribunals *and* the absolute power of the monarch, and so on), are we going to be satisfied with saying (as has been said and as they say on all sides, from Lévi-Strauss to many others) that, on this matter, there are only productions of such and such a culture, with each culture drawing a lot, as Lévi-Strauss writes, for such and such combinations rather than such and such other ones? And there's nothing else to add? With this position, you evidently can assert neither that the Greek myths are truer than others, nor that Western science differs by nature from archaic representations of the world. I will spare you the too-easy rehashing of this argumentation against Lévi-Strauss himself since his discourse on the impossibility of making a value judgment about other cultures is also the product of a culture, which is valid only for this culture, and so on. I believe that we can go much further, all while knowing that there isn't any definitive response to this problem. For, we can always refer a social-historical world, created each time, to something that surpasses it. At an entirely elementary or trivial level, it's obvious that even the most "primitive" tribes subsist by means of a fantastical quantity of practices by referring themselves in an adequate way to something that is not entirely created by the tribe. One can make a spark fly by rubbing together two pieces of wood: that's an invention. But that fire burns—and that this property allows or forbids certain things—is something that no tribe has created *ex nihilo*. Here, man is working upon what I call the first natural stratum, a reality that allows him to live and on which he is parasitic, if you will, but in relation to which certain things work or don't work. If he wants to warm his food, fire is needed; if he wants calves, he must lead the cow to the bull, not a mule to an elephant. These are practices in which one encounters something other than the pure and simple creation of society, and which translates a logic inherent in the organization of nature. But, as I've said a thousand times, all of this tells us nothing about what a society is, apart from banalities.

Now, let's place ourselves at the other extreme of the same line of interrogation, namely the calling into question of the instituted significations. This is when, for example, we ask ourselves in what sense the discourse of modern Western science has a different character than archaic beliefs; or whether our interrogation about justice is something different than and more than a singularity, a cultural idiosyncrasy; or again under what conditions we can express a true statement (since this is, in the end, the question that you are posing). I think that we're then in a different position, which is precisely dependent upon this rupture. In this social-historical creation of opening, of calling-into-question, of interrogation, we are no longer enclosed within such and such sphere of the social-historical world without ever being able to look outside.

This surpassing of our proper social-historical institution is certainly very enigmatic. It's even doubly enigmatic, above all in its conditions of possibility, since it is itself socially-historically instituted: we learn while growing up, at least a certain number of us, that we can believe nothing that we haven't previously ourselves put to the question. And this is instituted; it's doesn't spring spontaneously from the soul of the human, which would rather tend to the exact opposite. But also in its achievement, we cannot, at this level, do without a discussion that is each time specific to what's at issue: What is Western science? What is the Catholic religion? What is philosophy? And to think is, at once, to take responsibility for saying, for example, "The world—being—is chaos." It's to take this assertion to be true, to argue for it. And if I meet with a mythology, Greek mythology, which in effect represents being as chaos and meaning as emerging over the ground of non-meaning, I can then maintain that this mythology is, in this respect, "true." Of course, for Descartes–Spinoza–Leibniz, for whom being obviously is not chaos, this mythology is the very type itself of an insufficient thinking, in which the imagination prevails over good reason; and then to say that being is chaos is not only false but, above all, absurd.

IX. Seminar from February 2, 1983

The transcript for this seminar has unfortunately been lost (see p. xxvii).

X. Seminar from February 16, 1983

Ἀναξίμανδρος [...] ἀρχὴν [...] εἴρηκε τῶν ὄντων τὸ ἄπειρον [...], ἐξ ὧν δὲ ἡ γένεσίς ἐστι τοῖς οὖσι, καὶ τὴν φθορὰν εἰς ταῦτα γίνεσθαι κατὰ τὸ χρεών· διδόναι γὰρ αὐτὰ δίκην καὶ τίσιν ἀλλήλοις τῆς ἀδικίας κατὰ τὴν τοῦ χρόνου τάξιν, ποιητικωτέροις οὕτως ὀνόμασιν αὐτὰ λέγων (DK 12A9/B1).[247]

247. *Eds.*: Anaximander fragment DK 12A9/B1 is extracted from the commentary on Aristotle's *Physics* by Simplicius, who takes it from Theophrastus. See the translation by G. S. Kirk in Kirk, Raven, and Schofield, *Presocratic*, pp. 107 and 118: "Anaximander [...] said that the principle and element of existing things was the *apeiron* (indefinite, *or* infinite), [...] from which come into being all the heavens and the worlds in them. And the source of coming-to-be for existing things is that into which destruction, too, happens 'according to necessity; for they pay penalty and retribution to each other for their injustice according to the assessment of Time,' as he describes it in these rather poetical terms." Also, in what follows, be aware that some of Castoriadis's handwritten marginal notes which are, unfortunately, far too elliptical to be used here, refer on several occasions to W. K. C. Guthrie, *A History of Greek Philosophy, Volumes I–VI* (Cambridge: Cambridge University Press, 1962–1981), especially *Volumes I* and *II*, as well as to some of the studies gathered in David J. Furley and Reginald E. Allen, eds., *Studies in Presocratic Philosophy, Volume I: The Beginnings of Philosophy* (London: Routledge, 2018), which includes work by Cherniss, Cornford, Vlastos, Popper, Kirk, McDiarmid, Guthrie, Lloyd, Hölscher, Heidel, and von Fritz. He also refers to Alexander P. Mourelatos, ed., *The Pre-Socratics: A Collection of Critical Essays* (Princeton: Princeton University Press, 1993), which includes works by von Fritz, Heidel, Kahn, Fränkel, Cornford, Kirk, Guthrie, Hölscher, Furth, Owen, Reinhardt, Mourelatos, Furley, Solmsen, Long, Vlastos, and Kerferd. As for more recent works than those Castoriadis used, see A. A. Long, ed., *The Cambridge Companion to Early Greek Philosophy* (Cambridge: Cambridge University Press, 1999), although its bibliography unfortunately privileges works written in English. In French, see the studies collected in André Laks and Claire Louguet, eds., *Qu'est-ce que la philosophie présocratique?* (Villeneuve-d'Ascq: Septentrion, 2002), which provide some useful clarifications on some questions. On the Anaximander fragment, one should consult Marcel Conche, *Anaximandre: Fragments et témoignages* (Paris: PUF, 1991), which provides the Greek text but also various interpretations. One should also see Charles H. Kahn, *Anaximander and the Origins of Greek Cosmology* (New York: Columbia University Press, 1960), in which we find an in-depth analysis of the fragment (specifically in chapter 3, "Anaximander's Fragment: The Universe Governed by Law," pp. 166–196), the conclusions of which do not always align with those of Castoriadis.

Before entering into discussion of this fragment of Anaximander, I would like to remind you of what it is that we're in the middle of. We spoke about two pairs of significations: *chaos* and *kosmos*, on the one hand; *hybris* and *dikē*, on the other hand. I told you how they're similar, in my view. If there isn't an identity or strict term for term equivalence, there's certainly a very profound kinship. This kinship is nowhere spoken of as such—unless implicitly in this fragment of Anaximander, at least in the way I interpret it—but it is supported by everything we know about the Greek imaginary grasp of the world.

The explication of this non-rigorous homology drives us to distinguish on the anthropological plane between two levels of the meaning of the pair *hybris/ dikē*. At the most profound level, the opposition itself erases itself to make way for something that is simply chaos, a law of annihilation reigning over the world. In the originary Greek conception of the world, there is no *dikē* for man, no retribution, no relationship between his acts, his merits, and his fate. What reader of, what listener to the *Iliad* could imagine for a single second that there exists a correspondence between what Hector, Andromache—especially Andromache—are and what must ineluctably happen to them? At this level, man is a being like any other, thus subject to the same determinations; and there is no cosmic "formula" stating right, unless it's that which announces, once and for all, one and only one right, i.e. death, which obviously is not a right. We must keep this in mind to understand these words by Anaximander, who isn't writing in the void and doesn't fall from the sky, in contrast to what Heidegger would like. Anaximander writes in *a* historical and social context, and his ideas are rooted in *those* imaginary significations.

Now, at a second, social or political level there is indeed a *dikē*, posited from the beginning in Homer, which would undergo a considerable blossoming in Hesiod, especially in *Works and Days*. This *dikē* is that which regulates inter-human affairs and which would culminate in the conception of a law established in and by the city.[248] In the middle of the fifth century, Sophocles would speak of "established passions" in the famous chorus of *Antigone*, where the poet celebrates the creative power of the human being, who teaches himself language, thinking, and the laws that the cities establish.[249] When the moment comes we'll speak again about this tragedy, but we should clearly see that this praise of man, this conception of the human being as creator, is the trace, the clearest deposit of something that shapes the Greek cities and world from at least the start of the seventh century. There you have the second

---

248. *Eds.*: See Seminar VII, pp. 130–131.
249. *Eds.*: Sophocles, *Antigone*, 332–375, particularly 353–375. See also Castoriadis, "Aeschylean Anthropogony."

meaning—more limited perhaps, but more important of course from the point of view of political activity—of *dikē*, and of the opposition *dikē/hybris*.

Here are some clarifications regarding context, before turning to our fragment. Anaximander passes for having been the friend and student of Thales, the first of the Milesian philosophers, the first philosopher. And this makes us highlight here one of the essential points that marks the birth of philosophy and the rupture that it represents: With the Milesians, we put aside the stories of cosmogony referring to "intuitable," perceptible, visible entities in order to focus on the research on and the positing of what Anaximander, according to Simplicius, calls *archē* or *stoicheion*. This means a principle, an origin, or an element that would be beyond what is given, beyond *phainesthai*, i.e. appearances, as we would say in more modern language. And this distinguishes itself from every theogony or any mythical conception by the fact that it is *unrepresentable*. This rupture is so grand that it will be operative in two stages. With Thales, first, for whom the *archē*, the principle, the origin of beings would be water; but this is a water, if I may say so, that has ontological weight, i.e. an *Urwasser*, a primordial water, of which the empirical water we drink and bathe in are merely an embodiment. Then, immediately afterwards we have Anaximander, for whom it's precisely the *apeiron*, the indeterminate/indeterminable—and unrepresentable—that is the principle of all things. And the *apeiron*, i.e. that which has no limits (*peirata*), is also that of which one cannot have any experience (*peira*, a word akin to *peiras/peras*).

We have no text from these authors, who are known to us only by fragments, quotations, or allusions of commentators and doxographers. For Anaximander, the principal fragment, which will occupy us today, is drawn from the commentary by Simplicius (sixth century AD) on Aristotle's *Physics*. Simplicius himself borrowed it from Theophrastus, a disciple of Aristotle. He presents Anaximander as the successor and disciple of Thales, and as the first to have called *apeiron* the *archē* of beings, i.e. this principle and origin of all. Not "water nor any other of the elements one says exist," but *heteran tina physin apeiron*, i.e. "another infinite—indeterminate—nature," from which everything arose. Simplicius comments that Anaximander could not use one of the four classical elements—water, earth, fire, air—as the substratum, the *hypokeimenon*, since they are given to us and are transformed one into the other; for him there would need to be *allo ti para tauta*, "something other beyond that," beyond the physical and the perceptible, namely the *apeiron*, the indeterminate. The elements will result by separation from this *apeiron*. At the end of the fragment, Simplicius, or Theophrastus, adds that Anaximander expresses his thought with "rather poetic words," which is doubtless pointing to expressions like *dikēn kai tisin tēs adikias*.

There also remains to us a fragment of Pseudo-Plutarch, which he also took from Theophrastus, which explicitly says that the *apeiron* is the cause of the birth and corruption of all things.[250] It then asserts that for Anaximander time is infinite, in the quantitative sense: *ex apeirou aiōnos anakykloumenōn*, i.e. an entire circular movement of genesis and corruption from infinite time and, no doubt, for infinite time. And this principle, *apeiron*, is itself "immortal and indestructible (or incorruptible)," as Aristotle writes in the *Physics*.[251] There you have the context.

As I had already begun to tell you last time, one could, by neglecting a number of elements, give this statement by Anaximander a superficial interpretation, positivist in some sense: the *apeiron* would then be a sort of reservoir of matter, which all phenomena and entities would leave from and return to.[252] One could also read it in a way that is, let's say, more respectful and noble, like Jaeger does for example, whose interpretation is quite close to—or at least not foreign to—what I will propose to you today, but which is not radical enough for my taste.[253] And then there's Heidegger, who re-translated this fragment term for term and whose commentaries are, in my view, more of commentaries on Heidegger by Heidegger than they are on Anaximander by Heidegger.[254] I'm going to present—very briefly—the translation with which he ended up, but I fear that it will seem incomprehensible if you haven't already read this author.

After having separated (following Burnet in this) the part of the statement that goes up to *eis tauta ginesthai* as probably unauthentic—all while recognizing that Anaximander, for all that, doubtless must have said something equivalent—he ends up after many detours with this translation of what remains, according to him, as the original text of Anaximander.[255] His translation is: "…along the lines of usage; for they let order and thereby also reck belong to one another (in the surmounting) of disorder."[256] *Chreōn* is

---

250. *Eds.*: Pseudo-Plutarch, *Stromateis*, 2 (= DK 12A10).
251. *Eds.*: Aristotle, *Physics*, III, 203b10–13 (= DK 12A15).
252. *Eds.*: In Seminar IX (lost).
253. *Eds.*: Above all, see Werner Jaeger, *The Theology of the Early Greek Philosophers* (Oxford: Clarendon, 1947). See also chapter 9 of Jaeger, *Paideia, Volume I*, especially pp. 156–165.
254. *Eds.*: Martin Heidegger, "The Anaximander Fragment," in *Early Greek Thinking*, trans. David Farrell Krell and Frank A. Capuzzi (San Francisco: Harper, 1984), pp. 13–58.
255. *Eds.*: Heidegger, "Anaximander," pp. 28–29. See also Burnet, *Early Greek*, p. 52, note 6.
256. *Eds.*: Heidegger, "Anaximander," p. 57, which translates the Greek: "… κατὰ τὸ χρεών· διδόναι γὰρ αὐτὰ δίκην καὶ τίσιν ἀλλήλοις τῆς ἀδικίας." — *Trans.*: The English version quoted in the main text is always the Krell and Capuzzi translation of Heidegger's 1946 essay "Der Spruch des Anaximander," in *Holzwege* (Frankfurt: Vittorio Klostermann,

translated by *Brauch*, which already presents multiple problems. In German, *ich brauche* means I utilize, I need something. Heidegger, for his part, aligns *Brauch* with the old German *bruchen* and the Latin *frui*, which signifies "to enjoy" something.[257] In the end, he arrives at the following interpretation of *chreōn*: "to hand something over to its own essence and to keep it in hand, preserving it as something pres*ent*."[258] That's pure, twenty-four-carat Heidegger! As for the expression *didonai dikēn*, which means to render justice to someone, in the sense of him undergoing a punishment, it's translated as "to let order belong."[259] To carry this out, Heidegger has to enact a syntactical dissociation between the elements that go together. He makes the *allēlois* (one to another), which depends on the *didonai dikēn*, bear uniquely on the word *tisin*, which he translates, by a philological error (and I'll come back in a moment to the etymology of *tisis*), as "reck."[260] In short, in Heidegger's version, everything happens in the accord of beings among themselves; but this is at the price of the introduction of an expression that we don't find in the text, i.e. precisely the "in the surmounting"—which in German is *im Verwinden*—a term which, despite what the French translator says, is not opposed to *überwinden* but signifies practically the same thing, namely "surmounting." Under these circumstances, what's at issue for beings is to accept and to correctly estimate the existence of the other by surmounting *adikia*. In short, we're in full Heideggerian pastoral, despite the indications in the contrary direction by the author.[261] What are the beings doing? They're in accord, the ones with the others, they recognize one another; and they have

---

1977), p. 372: "... *entlang dem Brauch; gehören nämlich lassen sie Fug somit auch Ruch eines dem anderen (im Verwinden) des Un-Fugs.*" Castoriadis's text follows the French translation, *Chemins qui ne mènent nulle part*, trans. Wolfgang Brokmeier (Paris: Gallimard, 1986), p. 448, which reads: "... *tout au long du maintien; ils laissent quant à eux avoir lieu accord donc aussi déférence de l'un pour l'autre (en l'assomption) du discord.*"

257. *Trans.*: Heidegger, "Anaximander," pp. 52–53.
258. *Trans.*: Heidegger, "Anaximander," p. 53. See *Holzwege*, p. 367: "*etwas seinem eigenen Wesen aushändigen und es als so Anwesendes in der wahrenden Hand behalten.*" And compare *Chemins*, p. 443: "*délivrer quelque chose à son déploiement propre et le maintenir, en tant qu'ainsi présent, en ce maintien sauvegardant.*" (The italicized emphasis placed on the word "pres*ent*" as quoted in the main text follows Castoriadis's emphasis. However, this emphasis is lacking in the Brokmeier, although the latter does italicize the term in this way throughout much of the essay.)
259. *Trans.*: Heidegger, "Anaximander," p. 44. See *Holzwege*, p. 357: "*den Fug gehören lassen.*" And compare *Chemins*, p. 435: "*laisser avoir lieu accord.*"
260. *Trans.*: Heidegger, "Anaximander," p. 47. See *Holzwege*, p. 360: "*Ruch.*" And compare *Chemins*, p. 434: "*déference.*"
261. *Eds.*: For example, Heidegger, "Anaximander," pp. 431–432.

a correct estimation, not of injustice, but of discord. Heidegger's arbitrary invention comes apart in the way that it introduces a word that doesn't exist in the fragment, and which says exactly the contrary of what the context offers for understanding, i.e. "by surmounting" the *adikia*. He's inserted a sign that means "not-A" into a statement that says "A." The mysteries of contemporary hermeneutics.

Let's go back to Anaximander. An initial thing is striking, which to my knowledge has not been sufficiently underscored, which is the *gar*. *Gar* is "since [*car*]" or "because [*parce que*]" in French, *for* in English, *denn* in German; but the Greek word can also signify "in effect." In any case, we remain within the domain of explanation or justification. In French, if one writes "*p* since *q*," one may also write "*q* therefore *p*"; the logical implication is the same. He ate *since* he was hungry; he was hungry, *therefore* he ate. But the logical order of consequence uses the construction with "therefore." Now, we should read Anaximander's statement by going from the second part towards the first: One to another the beings give justice (*dikē*) and pay for injustice (the *tisis* for the *adikia*), and it's for this reason (i.e. *gar*, reversed for the logical consequence) that, from the same things and to the same things (*eis tauta*), the arising and the destruction—or generation and death (*genesis* and *phthora*)—exist for the beings. As we will be ceaselessly obligated to do a back-and-forth between the second and the first part of the statement, I ask you to carefully keep in mind this logical articulation, this implication, quasi-implication, of the second part in relation to the first.

The subject of the second part of the statement is *auta*, that is, *ta onta*. How are these *onta* qualified in the rest of the fragment? It's as those to whom *genesis* (arising) and *phthora* (corruption or destruction) belong. This is their essential attribute. These *onta* are likewise present in the first part of the statement in the plural dative, *tois ousi*, with all of these occurrences being declined forms of *on*, i.e. the present participle of the famous—of the terrible, wretched, sinister—verb *einai*, to be [*être*]. And if we may translate this *on* by a being [*étant*], as does Heidegger, we must never forget that it draws together the two significations of *einai* and of *on*, i.e. of "being [*être*]" and of "a being [*étant*]." And this ambivalence is essential for the whole history of philosophy, including Heidegger. When the classical philosophers Plato and Aristotle pose the ontological questions, they ask, *ti to on*, i.e. What is being/a being? They don't ask, *ti to einai*. Aristotle frequently uses the form *to einai*, i.e. the infinitive preceded by the article, as a subject in numerous formulations, but his ontological question, like that of Plato, is *ti to on*, What is being/a being? We therefore have in this statement an implicit opposition between, on the one hand, the *onta*, the beings [*êtres*], who are presented as plural—and which are necessary to it since they come and go, appear and disappear, i.e. there isn't just one of them—and, on the other hand, something which is not there, the *on*, which according to Anaximander (or what we believe we know of him) would be the *archē* or the *stoicheion*, the genuine being [*être*], *aidion anolethron*, permanent, eternal, and indestructible, and which he thus calls *apeiron*.

Without discussing for its own sake the question of the verb *einai* here, it's necessary nonetheless to say a few more words about it. In this fragment, indeed, this verb is all the more enigmatic since it shows up in three forms. First, *tois ousi*, as we have seen, is the dative of *ta onta*. Second, *esti* is the third person of the indicative present—*est* in Latin, *is* in English. And, lastly, it's there in the form of *ginesthai*, "it arises," "it takes place," which is homologous to *esti* and cannot in this case signify something different: *genesis esti* and *phthoran ginesthai* are identical constructions, two attributions. With *tois ousi*, we have what, when I learned grammar in school, we called a characteristic dative, i.e. something is for someone, to someone. It expresses an appropriative relation, which can be simply descriptive—*est mihi puer*, as one would say in Latin (There exists a child for me; I have a child)—but which, in this fragment, is an essential attribution. Anaximander here tells the ultimate truth about what is and how it is: *esti tois ousi genesis*; it is for beings to arise; arising belongs to beings. And the whole rest of the statement goes on to develop this essential qualification.

Let's pause now on the verb *einai* itself, even if only to respond to certain Hellenists, particularly Havelock. In the book I already told you about, *The Greek Concept of Justice*, he judges that we put significations into ancient Greek texts which existed only later, and that the verb *einai* doesn't take on its full force until Plato. I believe, for my part, that from Homer onwards, we can distinguish three levels of signification of the word. First of all, we have what we would call in modern languages the logico-mathematical significations, i.e. belonging: The French *are* men; the set "French" belongs to, is included in, the super-set "men." Then there's also identity: two terms or concepts have a single referent; there's no point in examples here. These senses are obvious, or in any case abundantly attested to. We have the impression sometimes, when reading certain modern philologists, that the Greeks in the time of Homer didn't know how to say or think that something is something else, that something belongs to a class. Yet, there's no tribe, however wild or archaic it may be, that couldn't say or think that.

In the second place, "being [*être*]" is to exist. Something is; this is. And I don't think that we can distinguish this existential sense from what modern philologists like Kahn have called the *veridical* sense <i.e. "verifying," or

asserting the truth of something>: the two are identical.[262] In Homer, of course, the assertions of existence are there everywhere, in the present as well as in the past or the future. We find expressions like *essetai hēmar*, "there will be a day" (when Troy will be destroyed, etc.); and we recall the famous description of the divine Calchas, of whom Homer says that he knew the *eonta* (the present beings), the *essomena* (the beings to come), and the *pro eonta* (the beings that were). This is a description that has been abundantly annotated, particularly by Heidegger.[263]

Certain philologists would like to separate a locative sense from this existential sense: Something *is there*; and here we meet up with almost the entire Heideggerian interpretation of being as presence. I believe that logically as well as philologically this independent locative meaning does not exist, except in compositional forms. When being, *einai*, provides locative determinations, the existential sense is always presupposed. That is, to say that a thing is there, is also, forcibly, to say that it is, in the sense of existing. As for knowing whether a thing can be said to exist without being there, somewhere, this is a very profound philosophical question, which we cannot discuss right now.

Havelock, for his part, distinguishes the existential sense from a sense of status: "being more courageous than," for example. This is, in my view, a logical error: this sense of status is in fact an attributive sense, which we may formalize in a logico-mathematical way by making it enter into these three varieties of being as a determinative, attributive copula. The discussion is muddled only because one gets set on finding cases in which "being" becomes a simple logical copula. This never happens; "being" remains always taken up into the three sub-significations or sub-usages of belonging, inclusion, or identity. *Is*, in "A is B," would be a logical copula only if one were to remain within vague thoughts; as soon as one reasons, the contents are immediately different.

The third meaning of "being"—which marks the emergence of philosophy—is *ousia*, essence. Essence, which comes from the Latin *essentia* (from the Latin verb *esse*), and *ousia*, which comes from the Greek *eimi*, *einai*, express—that is, Plato gave the term this meaning—the same relation. And this meaning appears when one asks, for example: What is justice? One is no longer asking about existence, and one is looking beyond logical attributions.

---

262. *Eds.*: Charles H. Kahn, "The Greek Verb 'To Be' and the Concept of Being," in *Essays on Being* (Oxford: Oxford University Press, 2012), pp. 16–40. See also Nestor-Luis Cordero, "Appendix I: La signification du verbe *einai* dans la littérature préparménidienne," in *Les Deux chemins de Parménide* (Paris: Vrin, 1997), pp. 215–233, as well as the works cited in note 345, p. 229.
263. *Eds.*: Heidegger, "Anaximander," p. 415.

Now, is this a legitimate or even a possible line of questioning? Perhaps not. Perhaps we will never be able to say what the essence of something is. Perhaps one must rest satisfied with showing that it is included in, that it belongs to, or that it is identical to such and such other. In any case, this is the task which philosophy—at least its dominant current—assigned for itself: to say the *ousia*, to say what the essence of things is. This goes as far as to turn the question back on itself—an extraordinary redoubling, which some would deem delusional—in order to ask oneself what the being of being is, the *ousia* of *ousia*. What does one mean when one says that something *is*, beyond simple existence?

But this species of turning the question in on itself is, in my view, not uniquely, not essentially even tied to an evolution, enrichment, or alteration of the meaning of *einai* in Greek philosophy. It emerges in fact in a configuration in which the word *einai* is not the most important one. The fact that this has not been seen goes back to this annoying tendency of philologists and philosophers to consider that the most important words in the language are the substantives, and secondarily the verbs. We can see this in our fragment with the all-too neglected *gar*, and we will see it again with the *ex* and *eis*. In the same way, in the philosophical question *par excellence*, *ti to on* (What is being/a being?), it's the pronoun *ti* that expresses what's essential in the questioning and suddenly therein takes on an extraordinary profundity. For, it's a completely different thing than asking oneself *tis*, i.e. "who" is so-and-so? It's Mister X or Mister Dupont. The *ti* is in a sense undefinable; to make it precise or elucidate it, one can only return to the ontological question itself. French is deceptive since it translates *ti to on* by "what *is being*?" [*"qu'est-ce que l'être?"*]. But the English *what is?* or the German *was ist?* fully recapture the Greek enigma and constrain one to rendering the ontological question precise.

Let's go back now to the statement and more precisely to its second part. Anaximander tells us that the *onta*, the beings, *didonai allēlois*, give themselves one to another, *dikēn kai tisin*. *Dikē* is justice, which one may also translate as "adjustment" or, by Heideggerizing a bit, "reestablishment of an order that was disturbed." As for *tisis*, Heidegger translates the word as "reck" by pretending that its "essential and original" signification is "esteem."[264] He makes it derive from the verb *tiō*, to honor (which yields *timē*). But this is to confound quite simplistically two words. More than fifty years before Heidegger wrote his text on Anaximander, Schulze had already brought attention to the fact that one should distinguish between an etymological family from which *tiō* or *timē* come, in which the essential signification is "respect," and a different one, from

---

264. *Eds.*: Heidegger, "Anaximander," p. 432.

which *tinō* or *tisis*, come, in which the essential signification is "punishment."²⁶⁵ We will find examples of *tisis* in this sense in Homer, in particular regarding the "*tisis* of Atreus," the compensatory punishment by which Orestes avenges his father, or again in Hesiod, and cases are numerous in Herodotus.²⁶⁶

But what do these *onta* give themselves justice and payment for? For *adikia*, for "injustice." Here again, Anaximander isn't writing in a void; he doesn't use words arbitrarily but according to a meaning already fashioned by Homer, by Hesiod. Both of them, as we saw, speak of *dikē*. Well, *dikē* opposes itself forcibly to *adikia*, certainly, but also more frequently to *hybris*. The two words are, if not identical, then at least closely allied; there's a reciprocal reference between *adikia* and *hybris*. Thus, the *onta* give themselves justice and punishment for their injustice or for their hubris. But what *hybris*? This is obviously *the* question. Remember: We already spoke, regarding Homer, about *moira*, this fate, this lot imparted to each man and each being, and the limits of which he must not surpass. When Patroclus wants to mount the assault on the walls of Troy, Apollo stops him. You can do nothing that would be *hyper moiran*, beyond your lot; you cannot transgress the limits that have been imparted to you. And in Greek mythology, in Homer, in tragedy subsequently, which beings are the ones at issue other than these beings *par excellence* which are humans, who try constantly to transgress their *moira*, to go *hyper moiran*, beyond their lot? I don't believe that it would be forcing the interpretation to see an innate, quasi-consubstantial tendency in this human *hybris* and to deduce from it that the *hybris*, the *adikia* of Anaximander is likewise natural and common to all beings. But we'll come back to the signification of this *hybris*.

Let's pursue the reading of the second part of the statement. Rendering justice and payment for *adikia*, for *hybris*, occurs *kata tēn tou kronou taxin*, i.e. according to the order of time. For many, this part is posterior to Anaximander since it has a Stoic consonance. It is perhaps in effect a later addition, which in effect appears even to enunciate something obvious, a platitude; there is of course an order of time. But this precision takes on its whole force if one links it to *kata to chreōn*, "according to what is necessary," "according to what is due," from the first part of the fragment. The beings give to one another

---

265. Eds.: Wilhelm Schulze, *Quaestiones Epicae* (Hildesheim: Olms, 1892/1967), pp. 355–356. See the commentary by Émile Benveniste, *Dictionary of Indo-European Concepts and Society* (Chicago: Chicago University Press, 2016), pp. 342–347.
266. Eds.: Homer, *Odyssey*, I, 40; but see also *Odyssey*, II, 76; and *Iliad*, III, 288–290 (with commentary in Benveniste, *Dictionary*, p. 322–347) and XXII, 19; as well as Hesiod, *Theogony*, 210; and Herodotus, *Histories*, VI, 84, VII, 8, and VIII, 76.

justice and payment for their injustice, for their *hybris*, according to the order of time; this is why (*gar*, inverted), *kata to chreōn* (according to what is due) *genesis* and *phthora* (generation and corruption) take place from the same and to the same. We are here at the very heart of the mystery of this statement. The word *chreōn*—which is not the Heideggerian *Brauch*, and even less so his translator's *maintien*—belongs to the same family as the impersonal verb *chrē*, "it's necessary," which also yields *chreai*, "usage," "necessity"; but it is linked equally with *chreos*, "recompense," "debt." Anaximander thus seems in this part of the statement to comment on the signification of the term *chreōn*, which assures the link between *dikē-tisis* and *adikia*, on the one hand, and *genesis* and *phthora*, on the other hand. What one must pay for would be *genesis*, birth; and what is due would be *phthora*, death. But we will take this up again later.

We come now to the essential and final lines of questioning: "This is why according to what is due, according to what it is necessary to pay, it belongs to beings to arise and there arises for them a corruption, *ex hōn* [...] *eis tauta*, from these things to these same ones." *Ex* and *eis* here refer to a same, to a something, but a something in the plural. And this plural presents a problem. Translating literally: The "things" out of which there is generation for beings, towards these things there also arises their corruption. The fragment of Pseudo-Plutarch is, as we saw, much more explicit: It is from the *apeiron* that everything comes, and it is to the *apeiron* that everything returns. But if the *apeiron* were at issue here, we would have a singular: *ex hou* (and not *ex hōn*) and *eis touto* (and not *eis tauta*). Perhaps Simplicius was wrong; but in any case, what he gives us has a meaning. And even more than *hōn* and *tauta*, the two prepositions *ex* and *eis* are what's enigmatic. I told you that we too often have, in a general way, the tendency to neglect the importance of prepositions, to consider their significations as obvious. And we're wrong: they're perhaps what is most mysterious in the language. What does *à* or *de* mean in French? It's much simpler to give examples of their use than to define them. The same goes for translating them; between two languages, the approximate equivalencies for substantives, adjectives, and verbs are common, but between prepositions they are rare. So, Anaximander's *ex*, close to the Latin *ex* and perhaps also to the French *de*, has at once a signification that's locative, temporal, and to do with "origin"; it's the place where, the time from which, and the principle, i.e. the ancestors. As for the *eis*, which would be the Latin *ad*, the French *à* or *vers*, it also has a locative and temporal sense, but it still expresses an idea of limit, of measure—up to, so far as—as well as a signification of relation, of intention.

These precisions allow us to give the end of the fragment a first interpretation, which is certainly coherent with what we know elsewhere from

Anaximander. The *ex hōn* (…) *eis tauta* would be the great ontological reservoir already evoked, another way of naming the *apeiron*, from which all arises and where all returns. Indeed, Anaximander has already been made into a sort of father of the principle of the conservation of matter.[267] By analogy with what we said in the preceding seminars, the *apeiron* would take on the role of *chaos*, and the *onta* would be what makes the *kosmos*, an ordered universe in which there are differences, beings, and—whether this portion is authentic or not—a certain order of time. This interpretation is supported both by the literality of this part of the statement and by what we know of Anaximander's *apeiron*, *archē*, and *stoicheion*, origin, principle, and element. That is, it's the reservoir, the ontological provision from which there can arise a *kosmos*, which is destroyed anew into the *chaos*, whence comes another *kosmos*, and so on. We would have a sort of movement that's cyclical and instantaneous, permanent, with *chaos* becoming *kosmos* and *kosmos* becoming *chaos*. But if we remain there, the statement as a whole no longer makes any sense. We absolutely don't see why the *gar* would link together the fact that the beings give to one another justice and payment for their *hybris*, with the fact that it is their due that they return into the *apeiron* whence they departed. The *gar* no longer makes sense and neither does the *chreōn*. We then have no need to make the *hybris* and *dikē* intervene so as to express either a universal principle of conservation of matter-energy, or the idea that there is an element or an *archē* from which everything derives and to which everything returns. There's no necessity to invoke this idea to end up with this conclusion. The conclusion can be drawn from itself or perhaps argued differently; but it cannot be argued starting from this. It is not because there is *hybris*, and that *hybris* is paid for, that matter is conserved.

Thus, I will propose for you another interpretation, which seems to me to correspond much better with what is written in this part of the statement and permits one above all to take account of the fragment as a whole. For this, I need to translate the *ex* and *eis* with "according to": according to the same principle, or from the same necessity. I could tell you, of course, that nothing guarantees that Simplicius here gives us the very terms of Anaximander, that we have here some Greek from the sixth century AD. The first part of the statement, for its part, is written in an almost trans-temporal Greek, which remains the same from Plato to Simplicius, i.e. fine philosophical Greek with

---

267. Eds.: Samuel Sambursky, *The Physical World of the Greeks*, trans. from Hebrew (London: Routledge, 1963), pp. 7–9: "A second conception which the Milesian School bequeathed to future generations down to our time is to be found in its linking of the idea of primordial matter to the law of conservation of matter."

its symmetry and so on. Is this Anaximander's Greek? Nobody knows. It shouldn't be hidden, however, that my choice is somewhat arbitrary; but with this interpretation the meaning of the fragment lights up: The beings give to one another justice and payment for their *hybris*, and this is why, as it is due, it is according to the same necessity, the same principle, that they are born and that they perish. What, then, is the principle? Quite simply—and this is the final reversal—it's that to exist itself is in a certain way *adikia* or *hybris*, transgression.[268] The *adikia* is not, as has been said, the persistence in existence beyond one's time, the simple *hyper moira*. Here is where Anaximander goes further than Homer: The *adikia* is existence itself. And this existing must be destroyed according to the same principle that produced it. There prevails in the end a kind of ontological justice which abolishes the *hybris* implied by particular existence. This is perhaps where we encounter the primary signification: since every particular existence implies a delimitation, *peiras*, term, it must each time return to the indeterminate.

If we now take the whole of the fragment, we have a first part that comments quite simply on Anaximander's general thesis. Everything comes from the *apeiron*, and everything returns there; and beyond the concrete *onta*, there is the *on* which is *apeiron*, the being that is unrepresentable, indeterminable, and so on. But this primary signification is found inserted into, mixed with, a second one—without there being any identity, contradiction, or opposition between them—which alone allows one to give meaning to the articulation of the statement, i.e. to the *gar* and to the *kata to chreōn*. It tells us that the *hybris* or *adikia* for which the beings must pay the price is their very

---

268. Eds.: But see Jaeger, *Paideia, Volume I*, p. 159: "Existence in itself is not a sin—that is a non-Greek idea. The words are a personification of the strife between things, which is compared to a lawsuit among men. We must picture and Ionian city-state. There is a market-place where suits are heard and decisions are given; and the judge sitting on the bench to ordain (*tattein*) the compensation to be paid. The judge is Time." An implicit critique of Jaeger is found in Gigon, *Ursprung*, pp. 81–82: If it is true that to see individuation itself as sin is an Indian and not a Greek idea, then, on the other hand, what is Greek is "the idea that the fact of existing itself implies an irremediable guilt (see, for example *Théognis*, 327 ff.) and that whoever purports to transcend it demonstrates presumptiveness, *hybris*, and thus renders himself guilty. We must not forget that with Anaximander we find ourselves in the first half of the 6th century, a period of great social instability in which more than one person (in Miletus and elsewhere) would rise unscrupulously and cause his own downfall. Any attempt at transcendence leads to excess, and any excess must be corrected anew. All this is necessary, χρεών." For Gigon, "according to the order of time" here refers to becoming itself. The judge could not be Time; such a personification is hardly conceivable. Rather, it is the things that do each other justice, not a judge placed above all of them.

existence. For, it's the *same* principle—existing and annihilating existing—which presides over their generation and their corruption.

Since the start of these seminars, we've been talking about the relationship between the primary imaginary grasp of the world by the Greeks and the origin of philosophy, and I hope that the discussion of this Anaximander fragment has helped you better understand what I understand by it, namely the generative relation and rupture between—and the kinship and divorce between—philosophical significations and mythological significations.

By way of conclusion, to allow you to breathe a little bit, and also to shore up the final interpretation that I gave you, I would like to tell the story of Polycrates of Samos, who died crucified, as it's reported by Herodotus.[269] This doubtless is not a "true" story in the historical sense, but it was invented in a precise historical culture, and as such its truth is much more profound, i.e. it's that of a view of the world. Think of the crucifixion of Christ; whether it was historical or not is not most important. What's most important is that it would be, and how it is, recounted. Polycrates took power around 540 and died in 522 BC; he thus lived a generation after Anaximander. This was a remarkable man, a protector of the arts and letters, and in particular of the poet Anacreon. If we are to believe Herodotus, no other tyrant could compare to him in magnificence. Don't forget that the tyrant, in Greece, was not the oppressor, the modern dictator, but the leader—in general, the leader of the *dēmos*—who seized power by force, during this phase when the aristocracy was unstable and when the *dēmos* could no longer establish its proper power. We could amuse ourselves by comparing his situation to what the Marxists–Leninist–Trotskyist tradition calls "Bonapartism." Polycrates was thus tyrant in Samos, and everything was successful for him: his court was brilliant; thanks to his fleet he figured out how to make Samos powerful; he was allied with the pharaoh Amasis. Yet, this perfect success was unsettling to Amasis, who let it be known to Polycrates: Everything is going too well for him; what he's living is *hyper moiran*; doesn't he fear the jealousy of the gods? Polycrates acquiesced and decided, in order to entreat the latter, to sacrifice a very precious good, an emerald that was set in a ring, which he went on to throw into the water, far from the bank. Several days later, a Samos fisherman offered the tyrant an enormous fish. The servers opened it and discovered the ring. When he learned of this, Amasis understood that Polycrates was condemned, that the gods had not accepted the offering, and he broke off every relation with him in order to not have to be saddened by the fall of a friend when the ineluctable affliction would occur. And, sometime later, the

---

269. *Eds.*: Herodotus, *Histories*, III, 39–47 and 120–125.

catastrophe in fact arrived *kata to chreōn*: Polycrates fell into the trap laid for him by a Persian governor and met, Herodotus says, with a "miserable end." Fine story, you'll say to me, but what's of interest to us in it? What's of interest to us is this question: What is Polycrates at fault for? Where is the *hybris* in all of this? For there isn't, at first glance, anything hubristic in his comportment or, if you prefer, nothing particularly hubristic for a Greek tyrant in his era. His *hybris* is quite simply to have brought his being to a full completion. It's too perfect a success, without mixture of goods and ills. And this goes contrary to *to chreōn*, contrary to what is due. He has to pay for this injustice. He's thus destroyed.

I'll stop here to respond to your questions. We'll speak next time about being and appearance, truth and opinion, and about *physis* and *nomos*, "nature" and "law."

Questions

The chreōn *you're talking about would thus be a sort of* fatum, *blind law?*

There's definitely blindness, first in the sense that nobody knows in advance, although all men know that there is this *chreōn*, except for those who are crazy, imbeciles, or precisely the *hybristai*. But, more profoundly, in the primary imaginary grasp of the world by the Greeks, the ultimate law is itself blind. It's what it is, emergence and destruction; it has no reason and isn't rationalizable. In this viewpoint, there's a prevalence—a subjective or anthropocentric element perhaps intervenes here—of destruction, of the perpetual crushing by this meta-law, the *chreōn*, which leads to *katastrophē*, to *phthora*, corruption, and so on. And therein a cosmos can emerge, always conceived however as passing, cyclical, that which establishes itself, gets dissolved, establishes itself.... But as for *chreōn*, you cannot explain it by referring it to other words. Like "being," for example, it makes up part of those other words. You cannot explicate them by other words; you can only speak starting from and through a return to them. A language uses these without us knowing directly how to define them truly. This is especially so in the case of Greek, a language, as we've said, that's "spontaneously" philosophical.

What's the relationship between Anaximander's apeiron *and the Milesian cosmology? Is this* apeiron *due to the new image of the world?*

Due to—I don't think so. There is, in this conception of the *apeiron*, a sort of intuition that goes beyond all cosmology. Let's try to reflect together. Someone suddenly asserts that the *archē*, the origin and principle of all things, is the indeterminate. How are we to understand such an assertion? While it can obviously be argued or reinforced by means of particular conceptions about certain classes of phenomena, it essentially relies on a radical transformation that I would qualify, for my part, as an invasion by the unrepresentable. To say that the *archē* is *apeiron* is to say that it is inaudible, invisible, and also incalculable not only quantitatively since it's infinite, but also insofar as it is intrinsically indeterminate. Now, what would the bridge be between this central intuition-grasp of Anaximander and his cosmology? Perhaps (and indeed we've already proposed this) it has to do with what he says about the four elements, which would be formed by separation and recombination from out of the *apeiron*; one might thus try to understand how one can obtain concretions from out of the non-concrete, the non-determined…. What I would take, for my part, from the cosmological conception of Anaximander is that it already introduces the principle of sufficient reason. It says, in effect, that the Earth rests suspended, without being supported by or relying on anything, and that it doesn't fall because, situated at an equal distance from all things, it is not more drawn towards high versus low, nor to the side.[270] This is to invoke a principle of symmetry which is still the daily bread of contemporary physics. Moreover, several doxographers relate to us that Anaximander conceived of the worlds as innumerable.[271] And here I won't resist the temptation to direct you to this month's edition of *Scientific American*, in which we learn—the latest word in matters of contemporary cosmology—that our universe would be but one of 10^{78} universes which resulted from the initial explosion.[272] This number is in no way infinity, but it nevertheless makes for a lot of universes. It seems thus that we have passed from a conception in which the visible universe would have resulted from the Big Bang to the idea that at the moment of the Big Bang and for 10^{-35} seconds an enormous quantity of

---

270. *Eds.*: Castoriadis is referring to reports by Hippolytus (DK 12A11) and Aristotle (DK 12A26). Also see Gigon, *Ursprung*, p. 87.
271. *Eds.*: There are numerous controversies on this topic. For certain authors, innumerable worlds succeed each other (Zeller, Cornford); for others, these coexist (Burnet); for others, lastly, the attribution to Anaximander of a theory of plurality of worlds is erroneous and anachronistic (Kirk, Kahn). See references and commentaries in Burnet, *Early Greek*, pp. 60–66; Kirk, Raven, and Schofield, *Presocratic*, pp. 122–126; and Conche, *Anaximander*, pp. 100–126.
272. *Eds.*: "Science and the Citizen," in *Scientific American*, 248:2 (February 1983), p. 76 ("The Inflationary Universe").

phenomena were produced, a single one of which is "localized," i.e. our little universe. This perhaps truly has no relationship to Anaximander, but it does have a unity with the idea of the indeterminate.

What place could time have in the interpretation of Anaximander that you just gave us? Would it be more of a modality of the indeterminate, or rather a way of passage between the indeterminate and being, in the sense of presence, of being-there? For, it's obviously not by chance that Heidegger spoke about being and time....

This is an excellent question, to which I cannot respond in a head-on way. Once again, there is, here, the *to kata tēn tou kronou taxin*, which a majority of philologists agree in speaking of as a later addition. Other doxographers, other fragments talk about a time *aidios*, eternal, interminable. And *taxis*, moreover, evokes the idea of order that rather runs counter to the *apeiron*. I cannot talk to you more about it at the moment, but your question, as well as the one about the *chreōn*, give me occasion to insist on an important point. It's that in Anaximander's thinking we already have what I would call the poison of philosophical bifurcation, which means the fact of never being able to definitively remain anywhere. When he posits the *apeiron*, the indeterminate, the latter is, for all that, determined in a sense *kata to chreōn*, i.e. subject to a determination that is, itself as well, universal and irrefragable. We thus have a principle that establishes the ultimate substantial consistency of being, which is philosophically determined as *apeiron*, but which, at the same time, is subject to another determination, *kata to chreōn*, or *chronos*, which doubtless at this level is secondary, more external, more superficial. The *chreōn*, what is due, that which should be, is a necessity that imposes itself on the *apeiron*. Even if one says that it's just a phase of the *apeiron*, it's also something else since if there were only *apeiron*, there wouldn't be *chreōn*. Forgive me this comparison, but the "launch" of philosophy is a bit like that of a rocket: the first stage—to posit a principle, the *apeiron*, in this case—constrains it to think the difference between what is and that according to which it is. This is, indeed, philosophy's *pons asinorum*; and it's the reason why the drift towards rational theology appeared so early on in its history, with the idea of a philosophical god that's at once being and principle, a law of its own being. But we'll return to all of this.

XI. Seminar from February 23, 1983

What we must constantly have in mind when we talk about ancient Greek philosophy—or ancient Greece in general, for that matter—is that this philosophy doesn't emerge in some sort of clearing of Being but comes to light as a permanent struggle against what we may aptly call a nightmare, the nightmare of non-being, of generation and corruption, and more generally of the inconstancy of what is. This struggle, in the end, comes down to three oppositions: between what is and what appears, which we'll speak about at length today and doubtless also next time; between opinion and truth; between nature and law, or rather *physis* and *nomos*. These oppositions should not, by the way, be kept separate, otherwise the first two become trivial. Although the third (*physis/nomos*) won't be formulated explicitly until a bit later, around the middle of the fifth century, we find the first deposits much earlier, and in a sense already in Hesiod.[273]

We spoke about Anaximander, and we saw that the fragment we were discussing can't truly make sense unless we connect the being of beings [*être des étants*], or their existence, to being [*être*] in the sense of essence, and unless one also connects this existence with a universal, impersonal law, i.e. the *chreōn* that Anaximander talks about, which is a law of constant generation and corruption. This *chreōn* responds in this fragment to an *adikia*, i.e. to a *hybris* which in the end we're obligated to make coincide with the very fact of

---

273. Eds.: See Felix Heinimann, *Nomos und Physis* (Damstadt: Wissenschaftliche Buchgesellschaft, 1980); Marcello Gigante, *Nomos Basileus* (Naples: Bibliopolis, 1993). And see Cornelius Castoriadis, "Value, Equality, Justice, Politics: From Marx to Aristotle and from Aristotle to Ourselves," in *Crossroads in the Labyrinth*, trans. Kate Soper and Martin H. Ryle (Cambridge: Cambridge University Press, 1984), pp. 260–339; *"Phusis* and Autonomy," in *World in Fragments*, pp. 331–341; and "Done and To Be Done," in *The Castoriadis Reader*, trans. David A. Curtis (Oxford: Blackwell, 1997), pp. 361–417. On the debate from the fifth century onwards, see Guthrie, *History, Volume III*, pp. 65–134; as well as chapter 11 ("Sophistic Relativism") of George B. Kerferd, *The Sophistic Movement* (Cambridge: Cambridge University Press, 1981), pp. 83–110.

existing. We're obligated in this way because Anaximander doesn't talk about certain beings who would be particularly unjust or in some way or other malfeasant. He doesn't say for example that the beings who would like to persist in existence beyond the time imparted to them must pay for this exorbitant pretension; he speaks absolutely, in a universal way: all the beings, *ta onta* (*tois ousi* in the plural dative). Of course, we can also see in this assertion the first formulation of a statement that bears on the totality of beings in order to qualify it: it's characterized by *genesis* and *phthora* and subject to *chreōn*. I'm also saying that there implicitly appears with this fragment what one may call the divorce, the scission, the dehiscence that re-creates itself constantly in the heart of philosophical interrogation, i.e. this ultimate duality, at once inescapable and insurmountable no matter what one does. On the one hand, there are (*esti*) beings [*êtres*] (*onta*), and one may qualify them, give them attributes, even try to define their essence according to the third sense of the verb to be, which we spoke about last time. But there's also that according to which what is is *kata to chreōn*, which means the law, which is not simply a qualification of beings as such but a regularity, a general norm, a necessity which everything must obey regardless of its particular qualification. That's what *chreōn* is. We thus find ourselves facing a sort of split, an inevitable duality between being and the principle or the law of being.

I'm now going to go into the discussion of the three oppositions (which in fact aren't truly so, as we'll see): to be/to appear; truth/opinion; *physis*/*nomos*. These aren't truly oppositions because even if thinking unfolds in this inaugural phase by strongly asserting these antagonisms—and this is what allows it to be singular, i.e. to surpass the instituted social significations—there's never an absolute rupture between the two terms. That's what, in part, constitutes the depth of the problem since if there's opposition between, for example, being and appearing, nevertheless being would be nothing if it didn't appear, and appearance can never be pure appearance, i.e. there's the being of appearance. (I'm anticipating here something we'll return to later.) Yet, this is implicitly present in the interrogations, in the responses (i.e. responses that at times precede the interrogations), in the very aporias aroused very early, from the sixth century on, in the thinking of the first philosophers. We can say the same thing, for that matter, about the opposition between truth and opinion, *alētheia* and *doxa*. In any case—for us anyway—*alētheia* can appear only in a human *doxa*. If *doxa* is in principle what is opposed to *alētheia*, in one way or another this *doxa* cannot be totally deprived of *alētheia*. And we could say something analogous about *physis* and *nomos*, although in this case the dialectic, if you will, presents itself in a rather different way. Put differently, there is, between these two terms, an equally profound opposition and relation; and *polarity* is doubtless the word needed here, the two poles being at once opposed and indissociable.[274]

But before going further, allow me a long digression—which of course isn't entirely one—on what we may call the extraction and elaboration of ensemblist-identitarian logic in this philosophy. Let's take randomly, or almost so, a fragment of Heraclitus, who as you doubtless know is a philosopher from the sixth to fifth centuries, straddling them. We place his peak, his years of maturity—his forties, according to convention—around 505. He's thus a contemporary of Cleisthenes and the reforms establishing democracy in Athens and also a contemporary of Pindar. He comes after Xenophanes and a bit before Parmenides. If we randomly take up a fragment of Heraclitus, we chance upon statements in which the same thing is presented as having contrary properties, contrary properties in the absolute or with respect to, i.e. in relation to, something or someone. This can seem at times (for us) to be an awful banality. We moderns (here's a digression within the digression) are in this way very unfortunate—and this is so whether it has to do with Heraclitus or any other Presocratic, but it's particularly the case when dealing with Heraclitus—since he has fragments that are truly dazzling and of an uncanny depth, like lightning in a Cimmerian night, or as if we were witnessing the condensation of a nebula, or like stars that start to blaze on a dark night. In short, it's very hard to interpret Heraclitus as an imbecile who says that nice weather is preferable to rain. Yet, with him we find statements that, for the moderns we were mentioning, just express at first sight certain banalities: "It's not even possible that Heraclitus could have said that! He must have said something different." Thus, there begins this process of the trituration of the text, of wholly bizarre or singular correction or interpretation of such and such a term to try to extract from it a signification that's more striking and unexpected in the same fashion. Heraclitus, for example, talks quite stupidly in a fragment I'll come back to: The sea is the source of life for fish, but it's fatal for men.[275] This is doubtless true, and everybody knows it and has known it as of the first man who took a swim in the sea some thousands of years ago. Do we

---

274. *Eds.*: See Fränkel, *Early Greek*, p. 54 and the commentaries found in the systematic index, pp. 525–527, as well as G. E. R. Lloyd, *Polarity and Analogy: Two Types of Argumentation in Early Greek Thought* (Cambridge: Cambridge University Press, 1966), p. 11, which quotes the most important of his predecessors. Lloyd points out (p. 90, note) that Wilamowitz was one of the first to compile a list of "polar expressions," in his *Herakles*. See Euripides, *Herakles*, ed./trans. Ulrich von Wilamowitz-Moellendorff (Cambridge: Cambridge University Press, 2010).

275. *Eds.*: DK 22B61.

really need the philosopher Heraclitus to teach us this or other things of this order that we indeed find in these fragments?

What even is there behind this type of statement? What moderns tend to forget in all of this is that they are themselves perched atop an enormous pyramid whose edifice has endured twenty-five centuries. This is twenty-five centuries of the elaboration of ensemblist-identitarian logic, which means the logic of separation, distinction, attribution. In fact, we find among the Greek philosophers, from the start, both the first clear formulation of the principles of ensemblist-identitarian logic and their explication, their elaboration, their in-depth study. It's clear, for example, that enormous work is deployed to extract and assert this entirely essential idea: No property is valid absolutely, *haplōs,* as Aristotle would say and as was already said before him. All properties and all attributions, all enunciations are valid only "with respect to," *pros ti*. This is a "with respect to" that can refer to aspects of the thing, to relations in which it's sunken, to the one who looks upon it, and so on. This isn't by any means obvious, although it might appear obvious in everyday matters. The proof is that still today in 1983—and frequently—people from the most naïve to the most sophisticated are unreasonable because they forget the *with respect to,* they forget in relation to what such and such a statement is true, and they forget the conditions of validity. If they hadn't forgotten it, then there wouldn't have been so many errors of reasoning in what they said. Yet, much too often—and I'm hardly exaggerating—what they're saying is just made up of chains of errors of reasoning. You should really go and have a look; you'll find nothing otherwise. And I'm not talking about conversations at a bistro; I'm talking about people who in principle reflect and then write and publish.

A huge effort is thus made by the first philosophers to show that statements—or properties since that comes down to the same thing (a statement is always attribution, a putting into relation)—are always "with respect to," *pros ti*; and this effort starts at least with Heraclitus and culminates in Aristotle.[276] Ensemblist-identitarian logic is there; and if it's true that it's not there in an entirely explicit way, nevertheless it's no longer there merely in the way we can say it's there as soon as there's human language or, at another level, in the way an immanent logic is quite obviously present in such and such behavior

---

276. *Eds.*: See, for example, Aristotle, *Sophistical Refutations,* 25, 180a25: "For it is impossible for contraries and opposites [...] to belong to the same thing without qualification; there is, however, nothing to prevent each from belonging in a particular respect or relation or manner, or to prevent one of them from belonging in a particular respect and the other without qualification" (trans. W. A. Pickard-Cambridge, in Barnes, *Complete Works*).

of a dog.[277] Here's a question: Why were tens of thousands of years needed for an explicit elaboration of the requisites of ensemblist-identitarian logic, of this dimension of all discourse, to be able to come about? That's an initial problem that I can merely posit here and for which there's no simple response. It correlates with the set of questions we're discussing, and with the creation of philosophy in Greece. A second important point is that this philosophy had to confront simultaneously, from the start and up to and including the Stoics in the fourth century and even later, a double task: on the one hand, the foundation, the explication, and the elucidation of ensemblist-identitarian logic as such; on the other hand, the inauguration of a thinking that goes very much beyond that logic, i.e. of thinking proper, if you will. This doubtless factored very heavily into its constitution, into the type of ontology elaborated most of the time, and thus also in later philosophy. We can already see this in Parmenides, whose ontology in large part—regardless of what moderns, Heidegger etc., say about it—comes down in the end to an elaboration of the principle of identity. Being is, non-being isn't; and one must not say that being is not or that non-being is. In response to which one can say, moreover: Non-being is, at least as much as is necessary for one to be able to say that it is not; and if it's just a figment of discourse, it at least appears there without any doubt. But let's get back to the problem that occupies us. From Parmenides on, thus, the necessity for the elaboration of identitary logic is already there; it's doubtless a fundamental co-determinant of ontology. This remains true of course for Plato, up through the moment when he, in his last period (in the *Parmenides*, the *Sophist*, etc.), in effect calls into question the possibility that simple ensemblist-identitarian logic could truly grasp what is. And he ends by admitting that one must—parricide—kill Parmenides and say that, in a certain sense, non-being is and being is not. Let's add that in Aristotle the distinction between ensemblist-identitarian logic and thinking is likewise fully established, both for us and for the thing itself. In a well-known passage of the *Nicomachean Ethics*, he makes a very marked distinction between *logos* and what he calls *nous*.[278] *Logos* is what proceeds by demonstrations, by a discourse on things which always takes other terms into account. But there

---

277. *Eds.*: On the ensemblist-identitarian dimension of language, see especially chapters 5 (specifically pp. 237–244) and 7 (pp. 345–353) of Castoriadis, *Imaginary Institution*. On the existence of an "embryonic system of ensidic logic" at work in animal behavior, see Cornelius Castoriadis, *Sujet et Vérité dans le monde social-historique* (Paris: Seuil, 2002), pp. 90–93.
278. *Eds.*: Aristotle, *Nicomachean Ethics*, VI, 12, 1143a25–1143b10. Also see the discussion in Castoriadis, "Discovery."

couldn't be a demonstration for the first and the last terms. They escape from ensemblist-identitarian logic. It's only among the terms in the middle that demonstration can operate. It's only *nous*—thinking—that can gain access, on the one hand, to the principles one couldn't demonstrate and to *ousia* (i.e. to the very essence of the thing) and, on the other hand, to the sensible or concrete givens.[279] The latter are not susceptible to demonstration either; all logical discourse in effect presupposes the possibility of coming to an understanding at least regarding a presentation of what we're speaking about; and you can never force a sophist to accept that a white table is white or the equivalent in other contexts if he says that it's black and doesn't want to let up. Thus, it's clear that Aristotle already recognized the distinction between ensemblist-identitarian logic and thinking: for us, it's in the distinction between *logos* and *nous*; for the thing itself as well, it's through the distinction between the *ousia* and the attributes of the thing. I don't want to get into this problem—it would lead us too far astray—but let's indicate in passing that in its central elaboration the *Metaphysics* doesn't escape from the identitary scheme, at least in the sense that Aristotle puts aside everything that is or appears to him as contradictory or in any case as not satisfying the principle of identity. If Aristotle does not have the illusion, like others, that he can derive everything from an ensemblist-identitarian principle like the principle of identity, he does think that everything, at least, must conform to this principle. When we speak of Greek philosophy we therefore shouldn't forget about this influence of the elaboration of ensemblist-identitarian logic. Nor, for that matter, when we speak about philosophy in general up to German Idealism, Hegel included.

I'm now going on to another point, i.e. the search beginning with Thales (insofar as what the doxographers tell us about this is credible) and then with Anaximander, Anaximenes, and so on, for what is truly the *archē* (the term is probably later), which means origin, principle, or *stoicheion* (element). We can say, first of all, that what these philosophers are looking for—at least according to the formulation of their thought in the doxographers, since for the Milesians, for example, we have almost no fragments—is, in modern language, a minimal generative set or element that accounts for the maximal set of what's observable. That's what the search for the principle, the *archē*, is. And what's thus proposed—to find the minimal element that accounts for the maximum of observables—is the very spirit of all Greco-Western science, up to and including today. But there is, of course, something else

---

279. *Eds.*: Aristotle, *Nicomachean Ethics*, VI, 12, 1143a25–1143b10; V, 9, 1142a25–30; VI, 6, 1140b30–1141a10; and especially *Posterior Analytics*, I, 1–2 and II, 4–10 and 19.

there which makes it such that we're not dealing with simply the first manifestation of the spirit or, if you will, the imaginary of the physical sciences. For, the idea of *archē* refers—beyond the generative element *within* the chains of consequence–causation—to an active generative principle. What's sought is a source, principle, or foundation no longer for the consecutive terms of the series but for the series itself as such. This is what appears clearly in Simplicius's statement where one finds the fragment that we discussed last time. The principle Anaximander is looking for is neither water nor any of the other elements; it is of a different nature, indeterminate. This is thus about the search for something that, being outside of all the terms of the series that are given and of the series itself, being the condition of the series, would only be immediately given and is by definition unrepresentable.

We've already seen that this implies a rupture with mythical thinking. One of the characteristics of all mythological explication of the world—indeed whether it's an issue of Greek theogonies and cosmogonies or those of other peoples—is that there wouldn't be any essential difference between, on the one hand, both the terms of the series and the series itself (i.e. a series of terms and events which is a narrative, e.g. generation of the gods, production of the egg from which the world springs, intervention of a hero who…) and, on the other hand, something other than the series which it presupposes. Let's repeat: In a mythical narrative, the first authors and their fundamental acts are included in the series, and if there's a difference in the mythical narrative of origins between the set of the narrative and the origin itself, it's not of the same order as the difference between a set of events and something which is not an event. Without getting into a genuine examination of mythical thinking but so that you can better grasp this difference, let's say that in a mythical account of what is, there's always a sort of presence of the founding moment. The event, which has always taken place *in illo tempore*—in a mythical past, precisely—is at the same time always there among the living, and it's always a foundation of what is. Indeed, it goes on to be repeated constantly in the rite, which is a ratification, a reassurance of the fact that what was founded is always well founded and will continue to exist; for, what thus gets repeated, even in a figural or weakened way, is the moment of the foundation, of the origin. Yet, this rupture between the series of events and that which is the condition for the series also inaugurates philosophical thinking, which doesn't search for a first event, but for something else. And since we talked about the profound relationship between certain elements of the imaginary grasp of the world by the Greeks as it appeared in their myths and the birth of philosophy, let's recall that this separation, this distance between a set of events and a *moira*, a *heimarmenē*, a universal law that imposes itself on the gods themselves, is already there in Homer, for example.[280] If Zeus at a given moment weighs the lot of the hero in the balance, it's difficult to believe that it's only at this moment that *moira*'s decision is made. Here, we meet again with the radical division between a set of events and a law or universal necessity that imposes itself on all beings. Let's add to this that in the first philosophers and indeed in every philosophical enterprise, there's an essential difference between the principle sought and a properly divine principle; and this is so, despite the vocabulary that they sometimes employ. For, even in monotheistic religions, the God-principle is at once person and enactor of an event, in the sense that what is so is so because *at a certain moment* a god created the world. It's only with rational theology that the question of a god who would be other than the enactor of an event would start to be posed, with the aporias we're aware of.

I dwelt on the fragment of Anaximander because, of the three Milesians, by all evidence it's him who truly accomplished the rupture. We saw that when Thales or Anaximenes says that the *archē* of beings is water or air, the rupture is and is not accomplished. It's true that if Thales's water is something representable in general, it's certainly not any water whose existence could be empirically observed. There's thus, in effect, a straying from the facts, and we could say the same thing about Anaximenes's air. But with Anaximander the rupture is completely accomplished. When he says that the principle of beings is the *apeiron*, the indeterminate, we have here a total rupture with the representable and perhaps even with the thinkable since what he displays is effectively an abyss. If that which is is truly indeterminate and indeterminable, then as such the determinations of what I call ensemblist-identitarian logic, which is precisely a logic of determinacy, are surpassed. But what likewise gets destroyed, if I may say so, is the way the imaginary and thought are anchored in figurability as well as in "making sense" for someone. That's destroyed along with all the density that can accompany this "making sense," which means the way it's an object of desire for us or a complement to our existence. If what is truly is *apeiron*, not only is this not something figurable but at the same time it's also something we can conceive of as most foreign to us. And if we can attribute an ultimate sense to what is as *apeiron*, this meaning is free for us; it doesn't provide us with anything. And in another way it's also un-meaning.

But there's also something else in this rupture. Here, thought appears for the first time as uniquely determined or interested by its own interest as thought. Or, if you will, it appears as completely disinterested. For, what Anaximander says, strictly speaking, serves no purpose; it can't be inserted into whatever chain of functions, of tendencies. It takes into account neither

---

280. *Eds.*: See Seminar V, pp. 82 ff.

the interest of the thinker as a human being nor that of the community to which he belongs; it would in no way facilitate a social activity. There's a principle, the *apeiron*, and it's about understanding. That's it. Or rather, it's about trying to understand this incomprehensible thing, i.e. how the *apeiron* can be the principle of a *kosmos* and how we get from there to whatever *peras* would exist for us, whatever determinacy. Thought thus appears as interested by its own proper interest, creates itself as interest of itself. That's what philosophy is. And we can say that in the same act it creates the truth, not in the empirical or factual sense, not the truth of the statement "This table is white," but the truth which is always at the same time an interrogation. Beginning with Anaximander, in the philosophical statement, the criterion of the truth—or rather of the rectification of statements—as conformity to the canonical relations between the statement and the referent of the statement no longer subsists except in an entirely partial way. This conformity becomes instrumental and subordinated and undergoes, above all, an essential alteration in its terms. That is, the statement can no longer be univocal, and the referent itself is problematic and in large part indeterminate. It's indeterminate or—what's more or less equivalent—surpasses the socially instituted world, surpasses reality such as it exists by and for the instituted society. Yet, there are univocal statements only inasmuch as there are determinate referents, and the referents are not and cannot be determinate except inasmuch as they refer back to the functional-instrumental dimension of the social institution of the world and human activities. We know, or we should know, that even within this socially instituted world, and even in this functional-instrumental dimension, statements are never univocal except in relation to need/use. In the human being such as he is socially fabricated, there's always incorporated therein the possibility or the faculty that's actually employed to abstract from ambiguities, i.e. from all the other possible meanings of a statement, and to retain only what corresponds to this statement's functional-instrumental integration in the life of society. But if you start by posing questions about the meaning of statements that are, for all that, entirely univocal in their functional-instrumental use, the result is immediate: You enter into the world of *Alice in Wonderland*, i.e. a world populated by characters who, when Alice says something very plainly that's entirely understandable, endlessly raise questions about the meaning of the terms she uses, about the statement's ambiguities, which create in principle no problem in real life. The dialogues of *Alice in Wonderland* often bring out the completely absurd character that can adorn—if we put ourselves for a moment in the perspective of, let's say, a sophist who would also be a poet—the language that we constantly use, which is of course perfectly sufficient for communication and cooperation in everyday life. This univocity is thus a property not of language in general but of the social use of language and likewise the result of an apparatus—this is of course a metaphor—incorporated into each one of us, which teaches us to not pose certain questions. For example, when you want to know where to find object *x*, and someone tells you it's on the table, you don't ask whether this has to do with a multiplication table or with a table of Mosaic law, since it's obviously the kitchen table if you're in the kitchen or the dining table if you're in the dining room. This univocity is tied to *chreia*, i.e. to social use/need, and it's necessary and it's sufficient that the statements are univocal with respect to it. Yet, as we've said, philosophical statements don't aim at something that's in the socially instituted world, nor even at something that can be instituted in general; they're not univocal and cannot be. Their referent surpasses the socially instituted world. It's thus problematic, and it can only offer itself as indeterminate. And in the end one must say that this referent—but here we're perhaps at the limit of what's thinkable—is created by thinking. Nobody can guarantee that being is *apeiron*, or *logos*, or *idea*, or *energeia*, or God, or Absolute Spirit, or matter, since in each case these terms are just the starting point for a series of never-achieved attempts at determination. This means that there's an essential indeterminacy here, and that we're very much dealing with a creation. But in opposition to other types of creation, like political creation for example, philosophy aims always at a certain relationship with what is, and with its mode of being. This is not simply reinterpreted but really reposited and therefore recreated into a new relation with an imaginary schema, like that which Anaximander gives us with the *apeiron*, or like what Hegel will later give us with the idea of Spirit passing through stages of its dialectical development. It's an imaginary schema, certainly, but one that does not exist "for itself" from this point of view, i.e. which always aims at a certain relationship with what is, without, of course, this being a matter of a relationship of scientific exactitude.

To give a response of this kind about what truly is—whether it's "water" or, to an even greater extent, the *apeiron*—is of course immediately to posit a separation between what is and what appears, *einai* and *phainesthai*. Thales says all is water, but I see wood, human beings, and mountains, not water. But in truth this wood is water; water is its genuine being. This water doesn't appear; hence, what appears is other than what is. What's the relationship between the two? Here's yet another digression to avoid misunderstandings. It's clear that the distinction between being and appearing, wholly like the truth–opinion distinction, must have always existed in a certain way in all languages and all societies. I've always thought that a language in which one couldn't say, "You believe that, but it isn't so," quite simply cannot exist as a human language. But in this distinction between belief and truth, we have something narrowly demarcated, i.e. the distinction is valid only from within the instituted domain. For every society and for every language there are things that exist and things that don't exist and canonical ways of perceiving things that exist and of saying what is. We certainly have the idea here that the human being can be wrong, that he can thus say what is not. But "what is not" means, in this case, that which is not, relative to what the society has posited as being. We recognize that there can be false belief, but at bottom this bears on secondary things. It's for this reason that even in the most archaic societies we'll find procedures—like divination or trial by ordeal—that allow one to decide what's true given the prospect of error or perplexity. But, once again, this bears on what's defined by the social institution. The rupture in the Greek case consists in that the idea of being as opposed to appearing, or of truth as opposed to opinion, surpasses the instituted domain and suddenly, if you will, pits itself against this social institution itself; and henceforth it's the instituted domain that tips over or risks quickly tipping over onto the side of appearance. This is what we can see already very clearly with Xenophanes, whom we're going to speak briefly about now.

Xenophanes was, according to tradition, the first of the Eleatics, and he's supposed to have thrived in around 540.[281] The doxographers tell us a lot of things about him and discuss many aspects of the doctrine they attribute to him, but we're going to examine them only with respect to the problems that have occupied us up to this point. Let's notice, first, that according to Aristotle in the *Metaphysics*, Xenophanes, having considered *ton holon ouranon* ("the whole heaven," i.e. the whole world, universe), "said that the One is god."[282] Xenophanes thus rejects the Homeric and Hesiodic polytheism and calls god One. This idea of a One was doubtless already there before him, but not in the form of a grand, transcendent principle, of a principle of being. This is the start of what would become the problem of rational theology in philosophy, a problem that would jeopardize—but could it do otherwise?—its development and in any case would come to haunt philosophy up to the present day. But what interests us above all is that with Xenophanes the critique of the instituted representation—that of the Greek tradition as well as that of the *doxai*, i.e. the opinions in general—begins and at once immediately attains its

---

281. *Eds.*: Plato, *Sophist*, 242d (= DK 21A29); Aristotle, *Metaphysics*, I, 5, 986b18; and for skeptical commentaries on this point see Kirk, Raven, and Schofield, *Presocratic*, pp. 164–166.

282. *Eds.*: Aristotle, *Metaphysics*, I, 5, 986b21; see also Burnet, *Early Greek*, pp. 126–129, and Kirk, Raven, and Schofield, *Presocratic*, pp. 169–172.

highest point. First of all, without trying to offer a genuine translation of them, I'll present you with some of his fragments (and I follow Diels's numbering). In fragment 11 one finds his celebrated critique of Homer and Hesiod, who are accused of having attributed to the gods all the shameful sorts of things that happen among men, e.g. lying, adultery, duplicity. He returns to this critique in fragment 12: These poets impute to the gods acts that are *athemistoi*, i.e. contrary to what one must do, contrary to the law. Then in fragment 14 he goes much further since he criticizes all anthropomorphic religion: Mortals believe that the gods are born, that they wear clothes, and have a voice and body wholly like themselves. For the first time, we find a clear and, in some sense, definitive statement condemning the projective character of representations of divinity in all the known religions. This critique is made more precise and deepened in fragment 15: If cattle, horses, and lions had hands and could draw or sculpt like humans can, they would represent the gods as having the shape of cattle, horses, or lions. And in fragment 16: For the Ethiopians, the gods have pug noses and black skin; for the Thracians they have blue eyes and red hair. The critique couldn't be made more clearly, and we shouldn't underestimate its audacity. Xenophanes opposes to this his own conception of the god (DK 21B23 and 26), i.e. a god who, he says, wholly sees, thinks, and understands (DK 21B24), and who is comparable to morals neither in body nor in thought (DK 21B23). We see immediately the importance of the idea, even from the point of view of Christian theology. But this aspect isn't going to hold us up any longer; I'll perhaps come back to it when I speak about the origin of theology, properly speaking.

Two other fragments especially interest us here. We won't linger over the first (DK 21B32), where we find the beginnings of a critique of language as such: What men call Iris (the rainbow) is a cloud, purple, red, and green.[283] Xenophanes is wrong of course; the rainbow isn't, from the point of view of physics, a cloud; but we can see the meaning of the critique. He goes much further in fragment 34, the reach of which is considerable. No man, he says, knows or will ever be able to know anything certain concerning the gods,

---

283. *Eds.*: See Mario Untersteiner, *Senofane. Testimonianze e frammenti, Introduzione, traduzione, e commento a cura di Mario Unstersteiner* (Florence: La Nuova Italia Editrice, 1955), p. 142: The common denomination of things is rejected because at its basis there is a false representation; in fact, for archaic thinking, denomination and concept are identical, and whoever rejects denomination rejects the concept as well. (See Heinimann, *Nomos und Physis*, pp. 48–49, who brings together the fragment by Xenophanes with the DK 31B9 fragment by Empedocles, about "what is called (*kaleousi*) death.") Against this interpretation, see Karl Deichgräber, "Xenophanes *Peri Phuseōs*," *Rheinisches Museum*, 37 (1938), pp. 1–31.

nor, for that matter, concerning anything else. And even if someone, he adds, were to succeed in saying the most true or exact thing possible, he himself wouldn't know it.[284] It's a thinking that has indisputable truth, and one we can still develop. The man with the most critical mind doesn't know whether the most rigorously demonstrated things that come out of his mouth are true, and this is not in a relativist-historical sense but due to the fact that he can never harness, explicate, and found the set of presuppositions for this truth that he enunciates. Nobody, ever, can have the knowledge and the certainty of knowing in an absolute way, even when asserting that two and two make four. We find at the end of the fragment this astonishing half-verse that only, unfortunately, carries all its force in Greek: *dokos d' epi pasi tetyktai*. *Dokos* is an Ionian form of *doxa*, opinion. It's the *doxa* or a *doxa* which *tetyktai* (is constructed) *epi pasi* (over all things). It's always the construction or the fabrication of a *doxa* (of an opinion, of what to you *appears as*) which is projected over all things, for men.[285] There you have Xenophanes, in 540 approximately. In a certain sense, everything has been said; and at the same time everything is beginning.

There's one last point regarding the very heavy political implications—this time, in the very narrow sense of the term—of the critique of mythology by Xenophanes, i.e. a contemporary of the great upheavals of the sixth century and of the democratic movement. To call into doubt the very existence of anthropomorphic gods committing adultery is to call into question the legitimation of aristocratic families. For, the ancestors claimed in general by these families are those heroes who issued from the union of the gods with

---

284. *Eds.*: Against the interpretation of the 21B34 fragment as a first manifestation of "skepticism" (common since antiquity), see Hermann Fränkel, "Xenophanes' Empiricism and His Critique of Knowledge (B 34)," in Mourelatos, *Pre-Socratics*, pp. 118–131, for whom *dokos* here means "probable" opinion and not "illusory." Gigon, *Ursprung*, pp. 179–191, essentially follows Fränkel's interpretation, even if he focuses, above all, on the opposition between what man can know and the "absolute" knowledge of god. For Deichgräber, "Xenophanes," pp. 23 ff. (cited in Kirk, Raven, and Schofield, *Presocratic*, pp. 179–180), Xenophanes merely develops the poetic theme of the contrast between the relative ignorance of the poet and the absolute science of the Muse, whom he calls to intervene (see, for example, Homer, *Iliad*, II, 458 ff.). Lastly, according to Kirk, Raven, and Schofield, *Presocratic*, p. 180, Xenophanes revives "the traditional doctrine of human limitations" in order to combat the excesses of speculative dogmatism.
285. *Marg. C.C.*: Xenophanes on *doxa*, Guthrie I <i.e. Guthrie, *History, Volume I*>, pp. 385–401, especially p. 399. Also, a first "historical" point of view <regarding the problem of knowledge>, fragment 18: "The gods did not reveal all things to men from the start, but with time, research, men find [...]."

women.[286] If Zeus had not committed adultery with Alcmene, mother of Hercules, then the Heraclides, kings of Sparta, would not have descended from Zeus. This is the conclusion anybody could draw from this critique. Moreover, we find other indicators in the poetry of the era, but I'm not going to focus on that.

I'm turning now to Heraclitus, who is from thirty or forty years later and thus writes at the end of the sixth century. Here as well we have fragments that we've been interpreting for twenty-five centuries, and each interpretation in turn is caught up in a different context. By the admission of the specialists themselves, to exhaust the bibliography on Heraclitus would be a life's work.[287] It goes without saying that the wretch who would devote his life to this task would be, at the end of the day, so totally mind-numbed that he would be prevented, by definition, from understanding Heraclitus. All the more so since one would need to make an additional effort, which is to understand where Heraclitus is situated and from where he's speaking. In effect, the *doxa* covers over everything here, and there isn't—we should be aware of this from the start—any non-debatable response to the problems that interpretation poses.[288] We must take risks here too while certainly showing the greatest awareness of the responsibilities involved but also by keeping in mind, as Xenophanes said, that even if one were to say the truth, one wouldn't know it, and one wouldn't know why one is saying it. If it's necessary to summarize in

---

286. *Eds.*: See Moses I. Finley, "Myth, Memory and History," *History and Theory*, 4:3 (1965), pp. 281–302 on the role played by these families in the survival of some traditional tales (pp. 297–298). And see François de Polignac, "The Hero and the Political Elaboration of the City," in *Cults, Territory, and the Origins of the Greek City-State*, trans. Janet Lloyd (Chicago: University of Chicago Press, 1995), pp. 182–149.

287. *Eds.*: If one wishes to be convinced, one may browse Evangelos N. Roussos, *Heraklit-Bibliographie* (Damnstadt: Wissenschaftliche Buchgesellschaft, 1971), containing around 1,300 references; Francesco de Martino, Livio Rossetti, and Pierpaolo Rosati, *Eraclito: Bibliografia 1970–1984 e complementi 1621–1969* (Naples: Edizioni Scientifiche Italiane, 1986), containing around 1,700 references; Léonce Paquet, Michel Roussel, and Yvon Lafrance, *Les Présocratiques: Bibliographie analytique (1879–1980), tome I: Des Milésiens à Héraclite* (Paris: Les Belles Lettres, and Montreal: Bellamin, 1988), containing 610 pages and 839 references. For just the essentials, see Philip Wheelwright, "Appendix D: Bibliography," in *Heraclitus* (Oxford: Oxford University Press, 1999), pp. 159–172.

288. *Eds.*: This does not stop some from thinking that "Heraclitan studies is—must be—a science"; see Serge Mouraviev, "Comprendre Héraclite," in Jules Vuillemin, ed., *L'Age de la science, 3: la philosophie et son histoire* (Paris: Odile Jacob, 1990), p. 181. This wish is all the more noteworthy, given that, for the same author, "After 180 years of philosophical work and exegesis, Heraclitan studies cannot yet deliver any real success. Heraclitology still has not been constituted as a science and has long been going through a deep and chronic crisis" (p. 232). Recall that Serge Mouraviev is the latest of the editors of Heraclitus.

one word why Heraclitus is important, I would say that he's in a sense a compendium of the philosophical effort preceding him and that he also brings along his own response. You know that they tend to present Heraclitus as an isolated thinker, willfully obscure and having no concern for the opinions of others, and that they sometimes make of him a haughty aristocrat, a sort of "stiff-necked philosopher." I will explain later why I don't believe in this image at all. From the 130 or so fragments that remain with us—even their number creates specific problems—something unfolds which is coherent enough as a whole, although Heraclitus is at times very obscure. It's an obscurity that's aggravated, to be honest, by those who have refused to look at his integration within a history, which is nevertheless sufficiently visible. Heraclitus talks about others and says that they know nothing. Have we really made a sufficient effort to understand the points on which he thinks others see nothing or don't understand what he means? You know that Jean Bollack and Heinz Wismann published an edition of his fragments some years ago with a translation and commentary, *Héraclite ou la séparation*.[289] I can't praise enough the science and erudition of Bollack and of Wismann, but I confess that I feel myself to be at an infinite distance from the orientation of this genre of work. It's a good example of this tendency of certain moderns—one certainly couldn't confuse Bollack and Wismann with Heidegger, about whom they are very critical, but what they're doing comes back to the same thing—to find in the fragments, whatever the cost, a non-trivial meaning that's suited to them. For all that, it's important to mention the book's restoration of certain fragments, which is quite welcome since the collection by Diels that we continue to use is at once aged, imperfect, and heavily marked (including in the very rendering of the texts) by the philosophical prejudices of Diels and his era, i.e. the end of the nineteenth century. Typically, philologists judge that they have no prejudice of a philosophical order, but we wonder how a philologist would go about judging the validity of a correction in a fragment of this type without having at least a tiny philosophical idea in the back of his mind. It simply doesn't hold up. Diels had philosophical ideas, and it's not difficult to discover them in this work of reconstructing the fragments, which he draws from testimonia that, as for what's essential, date from ten centuries after Heraclitus.

---

289. *Eds.*: Jean Bollack and Heinz Wismann, *Héraclite ou la separation*, 2nd edition (Paris: Éditions de Minuit, 1972). See also Jean Bollack, "Réflexions sure les interprétations du logos héraclitéen," in Jean-Francois Mattéi, ed., *La Naissance de la raison en Grèce* (Paris: PUF, 1990), pp. 165–185.

Let's go back to Heraclitus himself. He incontestably begins from the opposition between being and appearance already established by Xenophanes, who's someone he knows and criticizes. These are not his terms—he doesn't speak of *einai* and *phainesthai*—but the substance is there. It's of course absurd to believe that there could be thought without language, but it's also entirely stupid to say that an idea isn't there because the technical term to designate it isn't yet there. Heraclitus is of course aware of this separation. He's not writing in a void. And what he wants to establish is that the appearances or appearing, on the one hand, and being or what's true, on the other hand, aren't separated; but men only see appearances or else, in the best case, when they do succeed at observing that what's at stake are appearances, they go no further than this radical separation between what appears and what is. This is, very summarily, the nugget of what Heraclitus's thought is for me. I believe that if we consider all the fragments that are really worth the effort, we can arrive at this conclusion, regardless of the order into which we assemble them. I won't go into the study of the different attempts at their assembly since for me the best way to go about it is still to maintain a division into two parts, i.e. a critical part and a positive part. As an aside, I believe it's incontestable that Heraclitus actually wrote a book and that what we have are fragments of this book. Aristotle is perfectly explicit about this point.[290] You're also aware of the anecdote that Diogenes Laertius passes down: Euripides, after having given Socrates an example of Heraclitus's book, asked him what he thought of it, and Socrates responded, "You'd need a Delian diver."[291] So as not to drown, surely. Some modern philologists, of course—Kirk for example—can be found to assert that Heraclitus never wrote a book.[292] I don't want to be irreverent, but this is what earns a living for the philologist, i.e. to try to show that such and such a text is inauthentic or that such and such a thing we believe in, naïvely, something venerated by everyone, never existed.

In the group of fragments that we can call critical, Heraclitus sometimes corrects what we find in Xenophanes, even if he sometimes borrows from him.[293] On this issue he perhaps isn't fair, since sometimes in what he says there is manifestly a critique of the absurdity of the tradition, like what's found in Xenophanes; and he doubtless also thought what Herodotus

---

290. *Eds.*: Aristotle, *Rhetoric*, III, 1407b11–18.
291. *Eds.*: Diogenes Laertius, *Lives and Opinions of Eminent Philosophers*, II, 22. See also IX, 11–12.
292. *Eds.*: See G. S. Kirk, *Heraclitus: The Cosmic Fragments* (Cambridge: Cambridge University Press, 1959), p. 7. See the less categorical formulations found in Kirk, Raven, and Schofield, *Presocratic*, pp. 183–185.
293. *Eds.*: See DK 22B40.

repeats, i.e. that the Greek believe in innumerable stupidities, indeed on the most important subjects.[294] We can of course establish sub-groups within this critical part: the falsity of conventional wisdom; the relativity, or rather ambiguity, of human language; the falsity or relativity of sensuous givens. There's a last sub-group that one could quite equally classify within the "positive" part; it concerns, let's say, the objective aspect. It concerns the difficulties pertaining to the thing itself, i.e. that which acts as an obstacle to knowing what is, independently of all tradition, of all language, and even of sensuousness, i.e. independently, if you will, of the subjective aspect. I'm saying that this sub-group straddles somewhat, or forms a bridge over to, the positive part since we find in it statements not only about our knowledge but especially about what, according to Heraclitus, is. These are the ones that show, for example, that a predication is always "with respect to," relative to, never absolute, and also that for us there's a quasi-necessity for separation, which corresponds to a violence done to the thing itself. We can add in here the assertions relating to the unity of contraries, and those formulas in which everything is summarized, which talk about the violation, or rather self-violation, of *physis*, and in particular the celebrated fragment which says: *physis kryptesthai philei*, i.e. *physis* loves to hide.[295]

In the positive fragments, it's said that there's a way of searching to find what is and that it's open to all men. In Heraclitus we will find the first assertion in all known history regarding the universal capacity of all human beings, whoever they are and without any restriction, to have access to the truth. They all actually participate in the *logos*, and this serves as a counterpart to his accusations and permanent critiques of human errors, of frivolity of mind, and, in a word, of stupidity. These two contradictory assertions thus take on all the more force. We thus find here a search for what's true; an assertion of the universal capacity of humans to access the truth; and in the end, the assertion, by way of the idea of the unity of contraries but also the idea of "fire," that there's a world which is the same for all, and a unity of what appears and what's behind appearances, and that in this perspective all is one.[296] "All is one": a sublime and mysterious statement, and perhaps one that's completely empty. *Hen panta*, says Heraclitus, and he's thus opposing himself to the dispersion of myth or of communal representation, in which

---

294. *Eds*.: See for example Herodotus, *Histories*, II, 45, and there was already Hecataeus of Miletus, fragment 1a, in Felix Jacoby, ed., *Die Fragmente der griechischen Historiker. Erster Teil: Genealogie und Mythographie* (Leiden: Brill, 1995), pp. 7–8.
295. *Eds*.: DK 22B123.
296. *Eds*.: DK 22B50.

there's this, then that, then still another thing. But doubtless he's also opposing himself to three-quarters of the explicit philosophy of the century, which separates what appears from what is, all while Heraclitus asserts the unity of everything and proposes a metaphor for thus unity: *pyr*, fire. For, it's clear to me in this context that this is a metaphor, a metaphor both of the communicability, indeed of the universal communicability, of—and this is an aspect that we find in Anaximander, but which is, in truth, a fundamental element of the Greek imaginary—a generativity that is at the same time destruction since fire exists only through devouring things, even if this devouring is also light.[297] And over this One that is *pyr*, which is fire, there incontestably reigns, here again, a *dikē* and a *nomos*, a justice and a law.

I don't intend to discuss in depth this or that fragment, like with Anaximander. I would simply like to show you next time that the fragments, assembled and interpreted as I will go about it, make sense, and indeed that few things remain outside of and resist the interpretation. Heraclitus, of course, is merely perhaps the tenth philosopher whose name is passed down to us and the second, after Xenophanes, from whom we have a number of non-negligible fragments. And yet, with him we have the impression that there's already a history of philosophy, i.e. that Heraclitus considers a whole evolution, a whole problematic—what the Germans call a *Problemgeschichte*—within which the distinction between being and appearance

---

297. *Eds.*: Some interpretations of this central notion of *pyr*, or fire, make us able to see how Heraclitus's thought is difficult to formulate in a modern language. Recall that the starting point is found in Aristotle—i.e. the element or principle for Heraclitus is fire (*Metaphysics*, I, 3, 983b6–984a8)—and that antiquity will see this fire as a "substance." For Burnet, *Early Greek*, p. 145, we are still dealing with a "new primary substance" in the same way that "air" was for Anaximenes. For Gigon, *Ursprung*, pp. 207–224, whose own definition is followed by a long discussion on the opposition and the unity of fire and the world, fire is "the secret essence of everything" (p. 206). Similarly, for Fränkel, *Early Greek*, p. 439, "fire" is indeed "the principle that configures the world, but it is not an *archē* (origin, beginning) in the temporal sense." For Kirk, in Kirk, Raven, and Schofield, *Presocratic*, p. 198, "Fire is the archetypical form of matter. [...] Fire cannot be an originative stuff in the way that water or air was for Thales or Anaximenes," even if it might be "the continuing source of the natural processes [...]." Lastly, see also Marcel Conche, ed., *Héraclite: Fragments* (Paris: PUF, 1991), pp. 279–305, and specifically, p. 284: "Fire 'being always alive' is Fire as intelligence conceives of it so as to account for the life of the world. However, there are not two fires: the intelligible Fire is just the sensible fire insofar as it is understood by intelligence. The sensible fire is the immediacy of the intelligible Fire. Sight grasps no more than this. But *noos* grasps, in that which is for sight merely a sensible fire, a cosmic principle and a power of eternity." We may also consult Jean-François Pradeau, ed., *Héraclite: Fragments (citations et témoignages)* (Paris: Flammarion, 2002), pp. 127–132 and notes on pp. 236–245.

is posited; and he asserts that it's impossible to remain there, i.e. that one must try to reunify what appears as radically opposed. He thus represents a new stage in thinking, compared with the efforts of Anaximander. And he already fully demarcates what one could call the Greek domain by asserting this universality of *logos*—a position that's fundamentally democratic, regardless of whatever the political origins or opinions of Heraclitus may be. For, it's true that with him there are statements like, "for me one is worth more than 10,000, if he is better."[298] And that is, by the way, self-evident: One intelligent man is worth more than 10,000 imbeciles, if it's a matter of discussion, for example. Historians and modern interpreters make a big deal about this genre of statement: Heraclitus is an aristocrat, indeed he's born into a family of aristocrats, and so on.[299] Let's admire these people who are in the know about who Heraclitus—permit me this anachronism—voted for in elections. We don't know who he voted for. We do know by contrast what he said as a philosopher, namely that the possibility of accessing truth belongs to all men.

Questions

You said that, owing to the nature of its referent, the philosophical statement is not univocal. Does this particularity properly belong to philosophical language? Or is there something in all language that permits misunderstanding, non-univocity?

The non-univocity of philosophical language does not trace back solely to its referent but also to the attitude of philosophy. It's true that all statements are non-univocal—I mentioned *Alice in Wonderland* on this subject, though I could have cited a thousand others—but there's a social use, and in a given social body, a *bona fide* use of language. If, in a discussion between mathematicians where it's a question of mathematics, one pronounces the word "group," everybody knows that this is about a well-defined mathematical notion and not of a political group or otherwise. In social use or in the use of corporations, non-univocity is no longer there because there's a species

---

298. *Eds.*: DK 22B49.
299. *Eds.*: See for example Theodor Gomperz, *Greek Thinkers: A History of Ancient Philosophy, Volume I*, trans. Laurie Magnus (London: John Murray, 1920), p. 62; Gigon, *Ursprung*, pp. 198–199. See the more nuanced perspective in Lloyd, *Polarity*, pp. 222–223, who insists on the non-coincidence between cosmological representations and political attitudes in both Heraclitus and Empedocles. See the criticism of the received ideas regarding Heraclitus's "purported aristocratism" in Rudolf Schottlaender, "Heraklits angeblicher Aristokratismus," *Klio*, 43–45 (1965), pp. 23–29.

of tacit proposition always present which makes it such that everyone tries to understand the intention of the other and to attribute to the sentence or statement the meaning appropriate in such a practical context. We don't quibble; we try to understand one another as quickly as possible, and without even thinking about it we put aside all the other possible meanings of the statement that aren't adapted to the situation.

Philosophers would thus be the only ones who don't try to reach an understanding between themselves.

Well, in a sense that's true. But I don't think that this is sufficient to explain the importance of the eristical element in the history of philosophy. There, there's neither a determined context, nor a practical intention that would permit one to avoid non-univocity. The context is much vaguer, vaster, and we see this each time we try to understand a philosophy. In the case of the Presocratic fragments, it's much worse; the context is a field of ruins. We find torsos of statues, but we're familiar neither with the temple where it was found nor the ceremony in which it was supposed to preside. We happen suddenly upon splendid shoulders without knowing, sometimes, whether they're from a feminine or masculine divinity. Moreover, when we're dealing with complete texts, with works of authors from other eras, we also meet with problems—certainly of a different order—that are tied to the labor of the thought of the philosophy itself and to interpretation. The absence of a particular determinable referent and of a practical-instrumental sequence makes it such that it isn't easy and, in the last resort, that it's wholly impossible to avoid non-univocity. Someone asked me last time, you recall, a question about Anaximander's *chreōn*, and I responded that we can't define it by referring to other terms, any more than we can do so with *einai* or *alētheia* and that it's an issue, precisely, of terms from out of which a whole series of things become possible and comprehensible. This isn't to say that they don't signify; but this signification can be defined neither in the habitual way, through a proximate genus and specific difference as Aristotle would say, nor by establishing equivalencies. It can only be made explicit. But we never have the assurance that this explication is achieved, and we thus never have the assurance of univocity.

What is the relationship between chreōn, *the universal law that we couldn't surpass, and creativity? If* chreōn *is first, and if the last word must always come back to it, mustn't one say that creativity is, at bottom, just an illusion?*

Caution: we cannot juxtapose in this way notions like that of creativity with the thought of the Presocratics, or even with the primary deposit of the Greek imaginary, i.e. *chreōn*, *moira*, and so on. There's no idea of creativity in Anaximander. But the problem that you're posing nevertheless has a meaning. In the fifth century, we indeed see there appear—at the same time as the unfolding of philosophical and political activity, i.e. of democracy—the idea of human creativity, even if it isn't formulated *expressis verbis* or in terms that I myself use. It's present in what Aeschylus's Prometheus says. It's also there in the celebrated *stasimon* of *Antigone* which we'll comment on, which begins by: "Lots of things are terrible but nothing is more terrible than man." Here it's very precisely a question of the instituting capacity.[300] This is also there in the Sophists (let's remember that the Sophists are not properly "sophists" but very great thinkers). It's already there in the "Funeral Oration" of Pericles. It seems indisputable that the Greeks of the fifth century, in light of their own experience of political and philosophical creation, succeeded practically in formulating, besides the idea of history, that of creation. But one must not forget that this comes, in a sense, as a counterpoint to their initial articulation of the world: *chaos/kosmos* and *moira*. I'm telling you this because lots of stupidities have been written about the cyclical conception of time in the Greeks, and so on.[301] Yet, the problem is not that of knowing whether time is cyclical or linear; in the primary grasp of the world—*moira*, *chreōn*, perpetual genesis and destruction, and so on—there's no place for this alternative. We know what's going to come about as a counterpoint to this primary grasp in the fifth century. And then Plato and the failure of democracy draw near, along with the false lessons he draws from it; one curtain falls, and another history begins for thinking. The false lessons are, moreover, still with us.

---

300. *Eds.*: See Castoriadis's comments in "Aeschylean Anthropogony."
301. *Eds.*: For criticism of the commonplace view according to which the Greeks conceived only of "cyclical time," see: Victor Goldschmidt, "Théologia," in *Questions platoniciennes* (Paris: Vrin, 1970), p. 171; and Pierre Vidal-Naquet, "Divine Time and Human Time," in *Black Hunter*, pp. 39–60, which refers to two important studies published later, namely Arnaldo Momigliano, "Time in Ancient Historiography," *History and Theory*, 6 (1966), pp. 1–23, and Jacqueline de Romilly, "Thucydide et l'idée du progrès," *Annali della Scuola Normale Superiore di Pisa. Lettere, Storia e Filosofia*, 2:25 (1966), pp. 143–191. With similar themes, see G. E. R. Lloyd, "Views on Time in Greek Thought," in Louis Gardet, ed., *Cultures and Time* (Paris: UNESCO, 1976), pp. 117–148, especially p. 117: "[It] must be emphasized at the outset that there is no such thing as *the* Greek view of time. [...] The so-called 'cyclical' conception of time meant, as we shall see, quite different things to different Greek writers. More decisively, there is clear evidence of linear as well as cyclical conceptions in Greece." See also Castoriadis's remarks in *Sujet et Vérité*, pp. 350–351.

On the third opposition, physis/nomos, does the problem of non-univocity present itself in the same way for descriptive statements and prescriptive statements?

We'll revisit this question when we speak more specifically about the opposition *physis/nomos*. Let's say immediately that one must, here again, establish a distinction homologous to that which we posited for descriptive statements. For prescriptive statements within the framework of the instituted, there isn't any non-univocity, at least *pros tēn chreian*, with respect to need/use. It arises as an opening of interrogation pertaining to ultimate prescriptive statements or to what lies at their foundation. It's not at the point when we say that murder gets punished. We can certainly in that case debate, What is murder? You're perhaps familiar with the anecdote reported by Plutarch: Pericles has a discussion for a whole day with Protagoras in order to figure out who should be held to be the responsible party for the accidental death caused by a javelin thrower at an athletic event, i.e. the javelin, the one who throws it, or the judges of the ordeal.[302] Who's culpable? Is there a transgression of the injunction, one must not kill? Non-univocity can be overcome here; that's the labor of jurists. But one meets up with it again at the ultimate level: What is law, what is just law, when is a law just? There's non-univocity there because we're at the limit of the institution, because we are posing here the problem of the root, of the foundation of the institution. This is the question, among others, to which Sophocles's *Antigone* tries to respond.

---

302. *Eds.*: Plutarch, *Pericles*, 36, 3. Also, a similar textbook case is studied by the author of the *Second Tetralogy*, known under the name of Antiphon. See Kenneth J. Maidment, ed., *Minor Attic Orators, Volume I: Antiphon, Andocides* (Cambridge, MA: Harvard University Press, 1941). See also the comments in Williams, *Shame and Necessity*, pp. 61 ff.

XII. Seminar from March 2, 1983

Today we will once again turn, as with Anaximander, to the texts themselves, with this difference, namely that instead of analyzing a single passage in a deep way, I will try to collect and comment on what remains with us from Heraclitus, namely a bit less than a 140 fragments (I'll come back to this).[303] If I wanted to take up Heraclitus here, it was for several reasons. First of all, it's because it interests me passionately. Next, it's because this is the first philosopher in Western history whose transmitted corpus allows for a work of interpretation that goes beyond the exercise of divination about a singular fragment or (as with Xenophanes) about a handful of lines. Thirdly and above all, it's because with him we already find ourselves fully within philosophy, with all its splendor and indeed its obscurity. And this is especially because, as I told you last time, in this perpetual circle that philosophy and simply thinking travel, Heraclitus marks the achievement of a first movement; he completes—forgive me if I abuse the image—a first turn. For, let's repeat that Heraclitus, the same as Anaximander, didn't write in a void, as lots of interpreters seem tacitly to presuppose, particularly Heidegger.[304] He takes full account of the world that surrounds him and of all that preceded him, all while separating himself very strongly from it. We could say that he made a sort of synthesis out of it in the Hegelian sense, i.e. what he denies isn't ignored by him but—while being refuted and abolished—is implicitly contained in his own thinking. Heraclitus arrives at a crucial moment, which is (to take up the traditional terminology, which is inadequate in my view)

---

303. *Eds.*: On the number of fragments: There are 72 in Schleiermacher's edition of 1808; 130 in Bywater (1877); 129 in Diels-Kranz (1903–1934); 111 in Marcovich (1967); 136 in Conche (1986); and so on.

304. *Eds.*: See especially: Martin Heidegger, "Logos (Heraclitus, Fragment B 50)" and "Aletheia (Heraclitus, Fragment B 16)," in *Early Greek Thinking*, trans. David F. Krell and Frank A. Capuzzi (New York: Harper & Row, 1975), pp. 59–78 and pp. 102–123; Martin Heidegger and Eugene Fink, *Heraclitus Seminar 1966/67*, trans. Charles H. Seibert (Evanston: Northwestern University Press, 1993); Martin Heidegger, *"Heraclitus: The Inception of Occidental Thinking"* and *"Logic; Heraclitus's Doctrine of the Logos"*, trans. S. Montgomery Ewegen and Julia Goesser Assaiante (London: Bloomsbury Academic, 2018).

at the end of the archaic period and the start of the great classical period. According to the doxographic tradition, he was born around 540 and thrived around 505–500. He is thus about forty years old at the turn of the century. To situate things, I'll remind you of some other dates: Xenophanes was born around 570 and died around 470; Pythagoras was born around 570 and died around 490; Aeschylus was born around 525 and died in 456; Pindar was born in 518 (or 522); Parmenides, around 515; Herodotus, around 485. Thus, when Heraclitus was writing, all the great figures who were building—inasmuch as individuals may have this role—the great, classical century, i.e. the fifth century, were already there. And I remind you that in Athens, it was in 508 that the *dēmos*, led by Cleisthenes, introduced democracy in the full sense of the term.[305]

Let's have one word, just the same, about the textual problem. So, there remain about 140 fragments of Heraclitus, which are found for the most part either in the doxographers who were writing starting in the first century AD, or in Christian authors who, in order to prove the truth of their religion, were trying to find among the ancient philosophers the announcement of the truth revealed by Christ. One must also deal with the Stoics (the Stoic school is founded in the third century BC), who were inspired by Heraclitus and—we have the testimonial of Plutarch on this—quoted him while accommodating him to their own views.[306] We thus have, as with other Presocratics, not an authentic text but a series of statements or fragments of statements inserted into the text of an author. A formula of the type "as Heraclitus said" is followed by a certain number of words which we suppose are from him, often without us knowing exactly where they begin or where they end. All of those doing the quoting are starting from their own preconceptions, yielding a considerable bias in the selection of fragments, among which certain of

---

305. *Eds.*: See Seminar III, pp. 42 ff.
306. *Eds.*: See, for example, Plutarch, *The Obsolescence of Oracles*, 415 F. Also, Burnet, *Early Greek*, p. 142, notes that Schleiermacher (1808) already drew attention to the fact that most of Heraclitus's commentators mentioned by Diogenes Laërtius (*Lives and Opinions of Eminent Philosophers*, IX, 15) were Stoics and points out, "The word *synoikeioun* is used of the Stoic method of interpretation by Philodemos (cf. *Dox.* 547 b, n.), and Cicero (*N.D.* i. 41) renders it by *accommodare*." On the Stoic interpretation of Heraclitus, we may consult Émile Bréhier, *Chrysippe et l'ancien Stoïcisme* (Paris: PUF, 1951), especially pp. 135 ff. and pp. 176 ff. See, however, Gigon, *Ursprung*, p. 223, who warns against a "hypercritical" attitude in this regard. That a theme or a term has been used by the Stoics does not suffice to show that they would not be Heraclitean. Similarly, see A. A. Long, "Heraclitus and Stoicism," in *Stoic Studies* (Cambridge: Cambridge University Press, 1996), pp. 35–57.

them, for that matter, consist of three words.[307] The longest, which is first in Diels's collection, takes up seven printed lines. <Assuming about two lines per fragment>, this makes for an approximate total of 280 lines, hence about seven pages in a "Budé" edition. Yet, Heraclitus wrote a book.[308] What size might it have been? According to tradition, Empedocles (who is later) wrote a poem, *On Nature*—a title that's not authentic, doubtless—which counted 2,000 lines. Of course, one must account for the difference between prose and poetry and also the incredible density of Heraclitus's style. No matter what, 2,000 lines would represent about fifty pages. (A Plato dialogue of average size takes up about seventy pages in the "Budé" edition.) We would thus have at most a tenth of Heraclitus's book in the form of discontinuous extracts. To help you put yourselves in this situation, let's take an important book from modern philosophy, the *Critique of Pure Reason* or Spinoza's *Ethics*. Let's suppose that of the 700 pages of the former, eighty remained, or thirty of the 300 of the latter. Not pages that are in sequence, but pages cut from here, from there, the cuts being those belonging either to anti-Kantian or anti-Spinozist philosophers polemicizing against these philosophers; or to members of a later philosophical school trying to exploit Kant or Spinoza for its own ends, twisting their words; or, finally, to those faithful to a religion that appeared five or six centuries later, who would like to see in them the precursors of their faith. Starting from this, you'd be put to the task of understanding what Kant or Spinoza truly said. We're exactly like that with Heraclitus. For my part, I believe (this is perhaps my own prejudice) that we can, despite everything, collect these fragments to obtain articulated unities, ones that

---

307. *Eds.*: See, for example, DK 22B119 and 123. On the problems of Presocratic doxography in general, see the recent study by Jaap Mansfeld, "Sources," in A. A. Long, ed., *The Cambridge Companion to Early Greek Philosophy* (Cambridge: Cambridge University Press, 1999), pp. 22–45; and see the commentary in Jonathan Barnes, ed., *Early Greek Philosophy* (Harmondsworth: Penguin Classics, 1987), pp. 24–31. On Heraclitus, also see the notes accompanying Pradeau's translation, *Héraclite*, p. 23, where he says he tried to "reconstitute what the different or successive uses were which ancient authors made of Heraclitus's sentences." His book has the advantage of providing passages of the doxography that are more extended than those found in other editions.
308. *Eds.*: On this debated point, and on the question of the form of Heraclitus's writing, see Pradeau, *Héraclite*, pp. 16–23. According to Glenn W. Most, "The Poetics of Early Greek Philosophy," in Long, *Cambridge Companion*, p. 350, Heraclitus wrote "in a prose evidently shaped by various poetical techniques." On this point, Most refers to Karl Deichgräber, *Rhythmische Elemente im Logos des Heraklit* (Mainz: Verlag der Akademie der Wissenschaften und der Literatur, 1963). According to Fränkel, *Early Greek*, pp. 257–258 (especially note 9, p. 257), the works of the Presocratics were intended to be read aloud and discussed in public.

make sense today for us (and we shouldn't forget that we're always the ones talking). It certainly will not be a matter of systematic unity in the German sense, but we will nevertheless be dealing with a thinking that's perfectly coherent in its central grasp and in its articulations, a thinking that traces out for itself its own approach. And if this is possible without, in order to explain it, assuming sophistry on the part of the maker—which I exclude by hypothesis—we'll have here an extraordinary testimony to the power and the unity of Heraclitus's thought.

In the unities that I've constructed, and which seem to me quite obvious, I left aside as uncertain or non-pertinent eleven fragments out of the 140. There are, furthermore, thirteen that fall under what I would call the physico-cosmology of Heraclitus. I won't speak about the latter since they don't make up part of our topic. Let's notice that for Heraclitus as for the Greeks of his era, up to and including Aristotle, physics and cosmology—to speak in contemporary terms—made up (rightly) a part of philosophy. These fragments pose, moreover, a problem I will return to in the end. That said, they do fit perfectly within his general conception.

Here, I'll make a side point. As I told you last time, very often moderns choose fragments that suit them. This is especially so with Heidegger, who seizes upon the statements of Heraclitus that could have been written by Hölderlin, which simplifies the task enormously. In Bollack and Wismann, who set out to interpret all the fragments, we find an interpretive one-upmanship which consists in rejecting the obvious meaning whenever it presents itself, which happens quite frequently. Such an attitude rests on the postulate that it's impossible for an author as profound as Heraclitus to have meant to say that two and two make four, or that's it's false that two and two make five. So, if he writes that, then a second, hidden sense will have to be found. Thus, there begins a game with the text in which the interpretation frequently runs contrary to the syntax and the lexicon, the semantics of the language. Once again, there's a mass of things that appear obvious to us today, but which weren't and couldn't have been so at the end of the sixth century BC. We'll encounter a number of them. Western ethnocentrism has been well criticized; but we forget one of its most powerful forms, which consists in considering that what's obvious for us is obvious for everyone. The opposite is the truth: Never, nowhere on earth, is it a self-evident thing to criticize the beliefs of one's own community. This holds still today here and there, and in some cases we now shut people away in psychiatric hospitals, which already represents a rather evolved stage. We have to be wary of this attitude.

I was telling you last time that Heraclitus initially criticizes tradition. This includes the popular tradition, which means the set of instituted beliefs, as well as the lettered tradition represented by those who wrote before him, poets or others. He thus says that instead of honoring corpses we should throw them out of the cities, even more than excrement (DK 22B96). Against the sacred character of the corpse and the duty to bury it in accordance with rites, he asserts that the corpse is fetid, that it's no longer a man. People, he further says, purify themselves with blood for blood crimes, which is something as crazy as if, soiled with mud, they were to go into the mud to wash up (DK 22B5). And he adds that they adore statues and pray before them, as if they were talking to a house, in ignorance of what gods and heroes truly are (DK 22B5). Statues, of course, hear nothing; they cannot grant requests that they cannot hear, and yet the Greeks talk to them. And also, they don't know that Dionysus and Hades are the same thing (DK 22B15). Heraclitus appears likewise in an anecdote that they sometimes tell about Xenophanes (one only borrows from the rich), and it accords entirely with his spirit. Meeting with Egyptians who were crying during the ceremony commemorating the death of Osiris, he's supposed to have said: If it's a god, why cry? If you're crying, this means that you don't take him for a god.[309] Men believe that their lives are regulated by the gods or by *daimones* (divine beings), but you have the famous statement "the *daimōn* of man is his *ēthos*" (DK 22B119), which means the interior disposition that makes him act in such and such a way rather than another way. Lastly, the rejection of the tradition is explicit in this fragment cited by Marcus Aurelius, where Heraclitus says that one must not think and act as the child of one's parents (DK 22B74), an expression that in Greek could suggest something like "daddy's boy" but with reference to the intellectual attitude. One cannot leave it to one's father, or to one's ancestors, to find the right way to live. It's in this perspective that one must read the fragment "the eyes are better witnesses than the ears" (DK 22B101a). We have all heard certain stories told from our childhood: Are we going to take them as hard cash? No. We must examine or inspect it for ourselves.

As for the lettered tradition, Heraclitus lays into the poets and lyric poets who propagate the epic and poetic tradition in Greece. He thus says that Homer must be thrown out of the games and struck blows with a stick and Archilochus likewise (DK 22B42), and that most people have Hesiod for a master and believe that he knows many things, i.e. someone who didn't even know what day and night are (DK 22B57). Heraclitus in fact asserts the identity of day and night, while Hesiod, in the *Theogony*, makes night

---

309. *Eds.*: Aristocrites, *Theosophy*, 68–69, as reconstructed in Pradeau, *Héraclite*, pp. 186–187. (Compare the preceding to DK 22B5, which cuts short the quotation.)

and day two different divinities.[310] The Greeks also believe in the genius of Homer, who was so stupid that he didn't know how to solve a riddle posed by children. According to the tradition Heraclitus follows, it was thus formulated: "What we've caught, we no longer have; what we haven't caught, we still have" (DK 22B56). Homer is incapable of responding, and we would be too, I think. It's quite simply a matter of fleas the children had. They killed those that they had been able to trap, but they still had those which had escaped them. Heraclitus further says that one should distrust the thinking and intelligence of men since they believe what the lyric poets say and take the crowd as master, unaware that the majority of men are bad and that the good are rare (DK 22B104). This is one of the fragments they could take as pretext for defending the idea of an aristocratic and contemptuous Heraclitus. Another attack on Hesiod is that he divides the days into favorable and unfavorable, unaware that the nature of all the days is one (DK 22B106). Pythagoras is treated—Heraclitus doesn't mince words—as the first among imposters (DK 22B81). What's targeted with him is a whole lettered tradition that the first philosophers were part of; they believe—this is a fundamental vice—that *polymathiē*, as Heraclitus calls it, which means the fact of knowing many things, can replace thinking. Here we have a proclamation of the essence of philosophy. Philosophy does not specifically have to do with knowing about such and such object; it has to do with the activity of thinking, which of course couldn't be separated from all knowing, but which is something other than a simple knowing. Knowing a lot of things, he says, doesn't educate thinking, otherwise, it would have educated Hesiod and Pythagoras and also Xenophanes and Hecataeus (DK 22B40) and would have prevented them from saying stupid things.

In this double critique of tradition, the treatment of popular tradition is, by far, the most important, to the extent that it necessarily lays into the instituted representations and significations. We saw it in a first form in Xenophanes; but here it gains all its momentum and, beyond even what is instituted, draws on highlighting the relativity of immediate givens. Men, says Heraclitus, are mistaken with respect to their familiarity with things manifest (*ta phanera*), and it's this statement that introduces the anecdote of Homer and the children (DK 22B56). In effect, immediate, unreflective perception is misleading. Men possess, as we will talk about today, a sense apparatus that contains in itself the capacity for error; they have, furthermore, the presumptuousness (*oiēsis*) of believing they know, which is as catastrophic as that "sacred disease," epilepsy (DK 22B46). The capacity for error belonging to the sense apparatus is fully

---

310. *Eds.*: Day is the child of Night, per Hesiod, *Theogony*, 123–125. See Seminar VIII, p. 146.

at play whenever it isn't controlled by the interior power of reflection and of thinking which Heraclitus calls—as a whole tradition will do after him—the soul (*psychē*). This is why he says (DK 22B107) that the eyes and the ears are very bad witnesses for men, if they have "barbaric," uncultivated souls that don't craft the brute givens of sensuousness.[311]

I'm going into an aside here so as not to have to come back to it. You'll notice that I often happen—I have emphasized this myself—to use modern vocabulary and conceptualization in this commentary on the fragments. This presents a problem, which I'll return to; but even so I would like to signal that this vocabulary and this conceptualization could only be elaborated thanks to the work of Heraclitus and numerous thinkers who came after him. It is impossible, in my view, to ignore that the whole problematic of the relativity of sense givens is found posed *inter alia* in Heraclitus. To deny this, one would need to violate the texts, as in the appalling style of Heidegger. But even as violated, the texts continue to bear witness to this concern.

Let's go back to "presumptuousness." In another passage (DK 22B131), Heraclitus says that it signifies the halt of progression. That's a tautology, but quite important. If you believe you already know, it's not worth it to work or think. Yet, at the root of presumptuousness—and we have here a much more profound way of describing it, which is a major discovery/creation by Heraclitus—lies what he calls *idia phronēsis*, own-thinking, or private thinking. Fragment 2 says that most people live as if they had their own intelligence, even though the *logos* is *xynos*. People make out as if their thinking belongs to them properly, as if it had particular properties; but in reality, the *logos* is common. Short of diving into a linguistic discussion, I would point out to you that *xynos* is a very rich word, full of resonances. Firstly, it's the Ionian form of *koinos* (common).[312] But we also hear the word *xyn* (together, associated), which goes back to a distinct etymology. There thus exists a *logos* which is common to everything and yet to everything with an articulation between human beings and the whole (I'll come back to this); and faced with this, there are people each of whom persists in positing their thinking as separate and capable in itself and in its particularities of finding the truth. This is why (DK 22B17) most people, even when they have to confront things, don't think in kind (i.e. as they should); and when they've learned of them, they don't know them distinctly but simply believe they know them (implied: and

---

311. *Eds.*: See the commentary in Conche, *Héraclite*, pp. 266–268.
312. *Eds.*: See Pierre Chantraine, *Dictionnaire*, especially the entry on "ξύν" (pp. 767–768), which refers to some occurrences in Homer, Hesiod, and Herodotus; and see its bibliographical references on the "concurrence of *koinos* and *xynos*."

this is the worst). Heraclitus calls the people *axynetoi* (which suggests a very interesting comparison with *xynos*); in Attic dialect one would say *asynetoi*: the unintelligent. They're like surds, even after having understood; as the proverb says, they're "present absents" (DK 22B34). The example *par excellence* of this private thinking is sleep. For most men (DK 22B1), what they do awake escapes them in the same way they forget what happens during sleep. Yet, it's precisely due to this *idion*, to this ownness, that (DK 22B72) men find themselves in constant opposition even to that with which they are constantly in contact, namely the *logos*, and that the things they confront every day appear to them *xena*, foreign, or one could even say strange. Moreover, the *idia phronēsis* doesn't concern only individuals but humanity as a whole. There's a critique here, whether direct or allusive, of anthropomorphism. Asses, he says in a derogatory way, prefer straw to gold (DK 22B9). The asses are the humans, who don't know the true value of things. They think that some are just and others unjust, all while for the gods everything is just and beautiful. The beliefs of men are rattles, children's toys (DK 22B70).

Another very important point, which the fragments establish with certainty but on which they do not allows us to elaborate much, is the inadequacy of language. Men speak; they cannot do otherwise. The term *logos* that Heraclitus utilizes has quite a multitude of significations that communicate between one another; this is doubtless one of the most extraordinary terms in the Greek language and perhaps in any language. It signifies at once thinking, calculation, discourse, and speech. Heraclitus himself uses it in different senses.[313] In some passages *logos* manifestly means discourse; in others it's an issue of the first principle (we'll return to this). So, men exist in language; it's an inadequate language because it separates. Thus, the god who is, not mysterious, but no doubt a hidden being—and in any case a reuniting of opposites—receives, he says (DK 22B67), a name according to the pleasure of each.[314] In truth, the god accepts and doesn't accept a determinate name.

---

313. *Eds.*: Against the idea that *logos* has a technical sense in Heraclitus, see Jonathan Barnes, *The Presocratic Philosophers, Volume I* (London: Routledge, 1979), p. 59. But Kirk in Kirk, Raven, and Schofield, *Presocratic*, p. 187 says, "[It] cannot be simply Heraclitus' own 'account' that is in question (otherwise the distinction in [fragment 50] between *emou* and *tou logou* is meaningless), although the Logos was revealed in that account and in a manner of speaking coincides with it." See also Fränkel, *Early Greek*, pp. 371–373, who, while insisting on the absence in Heraclitus of a desire to elaborate a "technical" language, still admits a double meaning (explanation/order of the world) of *logos*, especially in fragment 1.

314. *Eds.*: We generally understand, in developing the image of the fire that burns different kinds of incense or spices, that the god is named "after the scent of each of these" (Pradeau,

This is the famous fragment 32, where we read that the One, which is alone wise (*sophon monou*), accepts and doesn't accept the name of Zeus. The name of Zeus belongs to the established religion, which places the god into a divine genealogy, mythology, and hierarchy. In this respect, it isn't suited to the One. But it could be suited to it, if one were to consider what the name of Zeus symbolizes, i.e. absolute excellence or ultimate mastery. Heraclitus's statement remains, not in ambiguity, but in the incompleteness of thinking. We can understand it if we link it to another one (DK 22B48) where he says that men give the bow (*biós*, which is one of the Greek names of the bow besides *toxon*) the name of life (*bíos*), even though it is an instrument of death. This play on words calls attention to the conventional and inadequate character of a word; but, more profoundly, it shows that language is obligated to fix or arbitrarily separate the predicates of the things from the being.

This leads us to a second great unity, which a modern would wrongly consider to be banal: the relativity of all predication. Here we're no longer envisioning the aspect of language but that of the things themselves. Predication is obligated to separate, and thereby it doesn't correspond to what is. Moreover, it's necessarily relative to, *pros ti*. But the risk is always present for men to forget this character and to transform a relative predicate into an absolute predicate. Here, from out of a multitude of fragments, I'll mention just one of them. You recall the one that talked about the seawater being beneficial to fish but fatal to men. It's impossible to attribute to the sea a property without saying *in relation to what*. We find the same idea in comparative mode: "The most beautiful monkey is ugly in comparison with humankind, and the wisest of men compared to the gods appears like a monkey in wisdom, beauty, and all the rest" (DK 22B82 and 83). I won't get into the details of the interpretation; it would require the same work we did with Anaximander. Similarly, what doctors do in cutting and burning and so on would be a crime if anyone else did it; they do it and even demand to be paid for it (DK 22B58). Similarly, again, men in the course of festivals in honor of Dionysus do the most indecent things (and here Heraclitus is alluding to the processions with the large *phallos*). If they were to act in this way outside of this circumstance, everyone would see in that the most extreme indecency (DK 22B15). But

---

Héraclite, p. 192), i.e. using a single term for the different pairs of opposites (day/night, winter/summer, etc.) that the fragment quotes. We know that *pyr* is missing from Hippolytus's text and was introduced there by Diels, who is, on this point, followed by Burnet, Kirk, and Conche in his commentary on fragment 67, in *Héraclite*, pp. 379–383. For another interpretation, see Bollack and Wismann, *Héraclite*, p. 221, according to which "the comparison links the distinction of the forms of the divine to the arbitrariness of language."

this relativity of predicates results from or rather is founded in something that surpasses it. We must really see how, here, we're no longer dealing simply with the problem—which is fundamental—of the elaboration of ensemblist-identitarian logic. Let it be said as an aside that this problem will henceforth shape all of Greek philosophy, which is blithely ignored by a number of modern interpreters among the most profound. It was starting from these considerations by Heraclitus, and Parmenides as well, that the whole of the fifth century became fascinated by the question of knowing under what conditions we can state something true, or even under what conditions statement is possible. This went so far that there was at least one philosopher who refused to speak because speaking implies positing limited determinations as if they were unlimited, a problem that we find in Plato, Aristotle, and even the Stoics.[315] But beyond this logical, ensemblist-identitarian aspect, we find an ontological consideration. There's not only a relativity of predications, but also, at the end of the day, a merger of things that appear to men in their discourse as irreconcilable. One can't yet speak of contradictory terms; the notion will appear only later, in Plato and Aristotle.[316] These irreconcilables, thus, in fact coexist in being; they're the very faces of one and the same reality. The structure of being is contrariety; being would not be if it didn't contain contraries, at the same time and in the same respect. Of course, these are not Heraclitus's terms, but we're obligated to say it this way. The great work of Aristotle would consist in saying that a thing cannot not be identical to itself at a given moment and in a given respect. Naturally, this thing can change; we can look at it from a different point of view. A trivial example: a cube that's white on one of its faces and black on the opposing one. X says the cube is white. Y says the cube is black. Contradictory statements? No, since the cube is not at the same time white and black in the same respect. Yet, Heraclitus implicitly ignores this distinction. For him, contrariety is precisely contained within being in one moment and in the same respect. Hence: "God is day and night, winter and summer, war and peace, fullness and famine" (DK 22B67); "night and day are one" (DK 22B57); "the living touch death and the waking, sleep" (DK 22B26); and so on.

But—and this is the second great moment—we cannot say that this contrariety exists, full stop. On the one hand, it's inherent in being. From this point of view, it ends up of course in an indeterminacy (no need to remind you, here, of Anaximander's *apeiron*). But it's not on this point that

---

315. *Eds.*: This is the position of Cratylus, follower of Heraclitus, as Aristotle presents it in the *Metaphysics*, IV, 1010a7–15.
316. *Eds.*: See Lloyd, *Polarity*, pp. 96–102.

Heraclitus places the emphasis. Far from being a simple passive coexistence of contraries, contrariety is at the same time an ontological determination and an active principle, struggle, discord, war. All that exists is in conflict, not only with other things, but with itself. Hence (DK 22B80), one must know that war is universal (*xynon*), that justice (*dikē*) is conflict, and that everything arises according to conflict, according to necessity. And again: War is father of all and king of all. This is the splendid fragment 53, which continues with the fundamental statement, to which we will return when we speak about politics and slavery in Greece, namely: It's war that has designated (*edeixe*) some as gods and others as men.[317] The distinction between men and gods was thus revealed by war, which means that in a sense it was already there. War has made some slaves, others free men. I'm drawing your attention to this because we have here the central philosophical thesis of the Greeks on slavery, which will remain constant with the sole exception of Aristotle. It's a thesis that's philosophical but also political, practical, and one that's true. There are no slaves nor free men by nature, but it's war, violence, that makes them thus. Of course, for the man–god distinction here, we could think of a sort of initial indifferentiation after which conflict breaks out, displaying immediately what god is and what man is.[318] Here again, the error of men is to see in conflict only conflict, even though it's also a principle of unity and of coexistence, and in the end of harmony, which is Heraclitus's term. Men, he says (DK 22B51), don't understand (*ou xyniasin*) how what is opposed to oneself (*diapheromenon heautō*) accords (*homologei*) with oneself. As I just underscored, it's not a question here of a purely exterior conflict, between X and Y. And Heraclitus continues <with this oft debated and difficult to translate expression>: *palintropos harmoniē*. I will, for my part, say "oscillating harmony," a harmony that has two opposed vectors, like that, as he says, of the bow and the lyre.[319] To pull a bow taught, two opposed forces must in

---

317. *Marg. C.C.*: Πόλεμος πάντων μὲν πατήρ ἐστι, πάντων δὲ βασιλεύς, καὶ τοὺς μὲν θεοὺς ἔδειξε τοὺς δὲ ἀνθρώπους, τοὺς μὲν δούλους ἐποίησε τοὺς δὲ ἐλευθέρους.
318. *Marg. C.C.*: The inequality of power between gods and men is essential and permanent. That between the free and slaves is a contingent result (if the slaves take up arms, etc.).
319. *Eds.*: Some authors (Bywater, Diels, Bollack/Wismann, Conche, etc.) retain the *palintropos* that is found in Hippolytus's text, but others (Zeller, Burnet, Reinhardt, Kirk, Marcovich, etc.) lean towards the *palintonos* in Plutarch (*De Iside et Osiride*) and in Porphyry (*De Antro Nympharum*). The term *palintropos* can be rendered as "adjustment through actions in the opposite direction" (Conche), *palintonos* by "tending equally in opposite directions" (Kirk). See the discussion in Wheelwright, *Heraclitus*, pp. 106–119, 128–129, and 153–154; by Kirk in Kirk, Raven, and Schofield, *Presocratic*, pp. 192–193; Bollack and Wismann, *Héraclite*, pp. 178–181; Conche, *Héraclite*, pp. 423–429; and

effect be in play. This is what men don't understand whenever they consider contraries as fixed and separate entities and contrariety as negative and destructive; whereas (DK 22B8) what opposes itself accords with itself, the most beautiful harmony is that which is produced by entities in conflict, and everything arises according to *eris*, discord and dispute.

Beyond this opposition of self against self which is *polemos*, i.e. a war that is at the same time harmony—two great principles of the constitution of being—we must mention yet another aspect of contrariety: flux. You're aware that this theme had an enormous influence on numerous currents of later philosophical reflection, the Sophists, Democritus, Plato, and so on. You're all familiar with the maxim *panta rhei* (everything flows), which isn't properly speaking from Heraclitus.[320] And you know the assertion, "One cannot bathe twice in the same river" (DK 22B91). We may cite other passages: "the sun is new every day" (DK 22B6); and "we go and don't go into the same river; we are and are not" (DK 22B49a), which goes even further into negation of fixed attribution and identity. And fragment 126 enunciates the intimate connection between contrariety and flux: "What is cold becomes hot; what is hot becomes cold; the wet becomes dry; and the dry gets wet."

There you have the three great theses, or significations, that Heraclitus poses for the understanding of being. Of course, they contradict all that men habitually think. They in effect establish, between what appears and what truly is, a divorce that Heraclitus characterizes as the violation of nature by itself: *physis kryptesthai philei*, "nature loves to hide" (DK 22B123). It's from this perspective, and in connection with other points I'll talk about soon, that one must understand this other fragment, according to which "the king whose oracle is in Delphi (Apollo) neither speaks nor conceals, but signifies" (DK 22B93). The prophetess at Delphi, the Pythia, transmits statements all

---

Pradeau, *Héraclite*, pp. 151–152 and 269–270. The translation of *harmoniē* also poses problems. See Guthrie, *History, Volume I*, pp. 435–437 on the meaning of *harmoniē* and pp. 439–440 for discussion of fragment 51, especially note 3. To understand the image, he explains that, for him, things stand with the bow as they do with the lyre: the instrument is *at rest*.

320. *Eds.*: Simplicius, *Commentary on Aristotle's Physics*, 887, 1. Diels and Kranz do not retain this reference in the fragments but provide in the testimonials a neighboring form of it told by Diogenes Laërtius (DK 22A1, 8). The expression—and its Heraclitan authenticity—has sparked many controversies. Against the idea of a "doctrine of flux" in Heraclitus, see especially Reinhardt, Cherniss, Marcovich, and Kirk. The last—i.e. G. S. Kirk, "Natural Change in Heraclitus," in Mourelatos, *Pre-Socratics*, pp. 189–196 and 189–198—follows Reinhardt's interpretation. But for another point of view, see Guthrie, *History, Volume I*, pp. 446–469; Wheelwright, *Heraclitus*, pp. 29–36; and Conche, *Héraclite*, pp. 463–466.

the more deceiving as they seem to be clear. Thus, when Croesus consulted the oracle to know whether he should fight the Medes or give up on the war, the Pythia replied to him that if he crosses the Halys (the great river that divides Asia Minor in two), he'll destroy a great empire.[321] Based on this, Croesus quite joyfully sets off to war and gets defeated. It's his own empire that was destroyed by the Medes. The statement was perfectly precise, and Croesus only needed to bring it down upon himself. Heraclitus, of course, couldn't but appreciate the style of the Delphic oracles. With respect to the king at issue in the fragment, it's a metaphor for being but also for the sage. Furthermore, there's nothing in this dissimulation of being that's diabolical. Einstein will say: I can believe that the good God is clever, but not that he would be perverse (*boshaft*), i.e. that he built the laws of nature in such a way that we could never discover them.[322] We have the same idea here. Being is not made in such a way that all its messages would only be veiled and deceptive; but at the same time what appears of it, what offers itself, is not a clear saying. It *signifies*, which is direct translation for a modern like me of the verb *sēmainei*; one could also render it by indicates, which would be closer to the original meaning, "give a sign, show by pointing." A historian could write for example that a king signified (*esēmane*) an order with a hand gesture. So, being indicates or signifies what it is, without saying it clearly. And we could of course say something similar about true discourse on being, which without seeking to dissimulate, will never, for all the reasons we've said, be capable of saying being, at least in an articulated, deductive, and univocal *logos*. Put simply, the truth of being can be indicated in the discourse of the sage, hence in that of Heraclitus himself (and, let's hope, in ours perhaps as well). There's another aspect of the veiling, which we'll return to, which is not a total obscurity; it's in what he says about the soul and the depth of its *logos*.

Let's recapitulate. We considered a first group of fragments, those which we could call the propaedeutic critique, or the destructive part, as Bacon says in the seventeenth century. They establish the falsity of the tradition and critique sense givens, the presumptuousness of private- or own-thinking, and language. A second part speaks of being; it establishes the

---

321. Eds.: Herodotus, *Histories*, I, 53–56.
322. Eds.: "*Raffiniert ist der Herrgott, aber boshaft ist er nicht.*" Or: "The Lord is subtle (and therefore the world is complex), but he is not perverse (he has not deliberately created an unnecessarily complicated world)." On the circumstances in which Einstein pronounced these words in 1921, see Lewis S. Feuer, *Einstein and the Generations of Science* (London: Routledge, 1982), p. 104. This formula was used in the title of the biography by Abraham Pais, *Subtle is the Lord: The Science and the Life of Albert Einstein* (Oxford: Oxford University Press, 2005).

relativity of predication in the properties of being and, among these properties, contrariety, *polemos*, the harmony resultant from contraries and flux. The consequence is that being can be thought, but only through signification and not in an ensemblist-identitarian *legein*. We can now move on to a third group of fragments that concern the condition of man before finishing with a fourth, which constitutes a great return to being.

To designate the habitual, banal condition of "private" man, Heraclitus resorts to the metaphor of sleep, a metaphor that for him is almost a reality. In a sense, all men are continually sunken into sleep; and yet even this isn't enough to make them escape the One-All (*hen-pan* or *to xynon*) since, as he says in a splendid phrase, "even those who sleep contribute to the existence of the world" (DK 22B75) and are doubtless also always subject to what happens to the world and in the world. Yet, "we must not act and speak as men asleep" (DK 22B73). Dreadful banality? What does Heraclitus mean by men asleep? Those who are turned towards their proper, private world. You recall the fragment that says that the *logos* is common to all, but the majority of men have a private thinking (DK 22B2). What Heraclitus means here is that if you remain enclosed within what you already think, you're like a man who sleeps. In effect, everybody, when he's sleeping, lives in a world that's proper to him; and one who lives in his own world sleeps. But for those who are awake, says Heraclitus (DK 22B89), there exists a unique and common world. To be awake is to live in this world, not of course like a set of material objects, trees, earth, and so on, but as a world that's common from the point of view of the *logos* that traverses it and in which men participate. It would have yet been necessary here, if we'd had the time, to address other fragments that concern the disposition requisite for getting to the bottom of things, the exigencies of knowing.

Let's return to this famous *logos xynos*. Short of seeking to exhaust all of its significations, the *logos*, in Heraclitus, is just as much human as cosmic. We should take these two acceptations separately since the human *logos* doubtless can be *logos* only to the extent that it participates in the cosmic *logos*, of which it is an aspect or a realization. That this is indeed an issue of a distinct reality is what fragment 1 shows, which some have wanted to see as the proem, i.e. the introductory paragraph of the whole book (something that seems to me to be highly doubtful).[323] In any case it's the longest fragment:

Yet, true discourse being this ...

---

323. *Eds.*: This hypothesis is based above all on a remark by Aristotle in the *Rhetoric*; see Seminar XI, note 292, p. 194.

—namely, what will follow—

> ... men always render themselves unintelligent both before hearing it and once they have heard it. For, even though all things arise according to this discourse ...

—i.e. this *logos* that I'm going to exposit, but here we already see the semantic oscillation: this theoretical discourse is at once a *logos*-law—

> ... they resemble ignorant men although they have the experience and the sayings and the acts, such as I myself do develop them, dividing each thing according to nature and saying how it is. But what other men do awake escapes from them as much as ...

—i.e. as also escapes from them—

> ... what they forget while sleeping.

We encounter the metaphor of sleep, which will come to have an immense philosophical fortune, used to designate the life of man, i.e. the awakening of the man who sleeps, waking up to thinking, to examination, and so on. Kant will thus say that Hume awakened him from his dogmatic slumber, pulled him from his private, Wolffian world.[324] But what this fragment tells us is also that there exists a *logos* which is that of men, this *logos xynos* of fragment 2. We must bring it together with fragments 113 and 116, which assert respectively that thinking (*phroneein*) is common to all and that it belongs to all men to know themselves and to think correctly (*sōphronein*). This expresses, once again, the fundamentally democratic position of philosophy, in any case of Greek philosophy and of Heraclitus when he speaks *qua* philosopher.

I would like to make an incidental point, which as usual isn't really incidental. We've seen (DK 22B107) that sensuousness was a source of errors. But at the same time one must say that it makes up part of reality, that there always exists a certain correspondence between it and all that is. Put differently, thanks to sensuousness men can never be totally deprived of access to reality; this is what this statement refers to: "If all things were to become smoke, we would (still) distinguish them by the nose" (DK 22B7).

---

324. *Marg. C.C.*: The *dogmatische Schlummer* is the sleep of dogma, which means presumptuousness. — *Trans.*: For Kant's reference to Hume, see Immaneul Kant, *Prolegomena to any Future Metaphysics*, ed. Gary Hatfield (Cambridge: Cambridge University Press, 2004), p. 10.

The idea of the *logos xynos* is found in other fragments, formulated differently. We thus read (DK 22B114): "If one wants to speak with intelligence, one must fortify oneself with what is common to all, like the city does with the law, and even more so." And here we pass on to another point, essential for the philosophical anthropology of Heraclitus, specifically the soul. We can, I believe, link it with the *logos* in a non-artificial way, thanks to fragment 115: "There is a *logos* of the soul that grows (or: grows itself) of itself." There exists a discourse of the soul ("of the soul" here is a subjective genitive, i.e. a discourse that the soul does), or a thinking, a reason of the soul. But if the *logos* of the soul grows of itself, this refers precisely to the soul as self-activity. And this is where all the threads that lead to the way (*hodos*) come together, because this soul, for Heraclitus, all while being an example of the nature of what is—a privileged example for us because commensurable with what is—presents this particularity of having a *logos* that grows of itself, the depth of which is inexhaustible, which becomes the condition for our access to the universal *logos*. That's what fragment 45 talks about: "The limits of the soul (*psychēs peirata*), you will never discover, even if you traverse the whole path, so profound is its *logos*." Of course, we must here understand the term *peirata* in the sense of "spatial" boundaries since it's an issue of traversing a path. But these are also—I cannot help but think of this in this context—*determinations*. We could not discover determinations of the soul—in any case, its ultimate determinations—even when traversing the whole path (or "all the paths," as Bollack and Wismann translate). But the *logos* of the soul is perhaps so profound only because, precisely, it grows of itself. The soul is thus an incommensurable profundity and at the same time energy proper, spontaneity, self-unfolding. And this is where the work of the philosopher comes in, which consists in waking men. For this, he himself offers an example: "I explored (*edizēsamēn*) myself" (DK 22B101). He doesn't say that he went looking for himself, or that he questioned himself. He's this explorer who wanted, without achieving it, to traverse all the paths likely to lead to the limits of the soul; but in this exploration he could observe the depth of his *logos*, the fact that this *logos* feeds on itself, and doubtless also that the movement of his research was itself also a manifestation of this self-growing of the *logos* of the soul.

There's a whole series of conclusions to draw from the fragments that concern man. The most important, in my view, is that Heraclitus contrasts investigation with tradition, that he establishes very firmly the necessity of the law for the political community: "the people must fight for the law like for their walls" (DK 22B44). And, at the end of the day, for him, the only *daimōn* to which we would be subject would be our own *ēthos*, i.e. our disposition, attitude, or way of being—the English would say *tuning*, as with the tuning of a piano—in relation to the world.

We will end, as promised, with some considerations that are both ontological and cosmological, although I will not deal with cosmology for itself. First of all, Heraclitus posits the unity of everything. "Hearing not me but the *logos*, it is wise to acknowledge that all is one (*hen to pan*)" (DK 22B50). What gives itself as more than diverse, what gives itself in contrariety and flux, is one. Of course, flux and contrariety couldn't be reduced to a simple deceptive appearance in the most superficial sense; Heraclitus insists too much on their importance. What's deceptive is to see only, each time, one of the aspects present; or else to hold contrarieties to be exclusive, irreconcilable oppositions; or finally to postulate an absolutizing and absolutized separation of appearance from reality. For, in truth, appearance makes up part of this one which is being. Being cannot be without appearing; that's what Heraclitus says, following the Milesians and others. One must acknowledge that all is one, and for this same reason one must also acknowledge that "the way going up and going down is the same" (DK 22B60). This is also why he says: "How could one elude what never hides?" (DK 22B16). What is it that never hides? In Homer, for example in the third book of the *Iliad* (v. 277), it's Helios, the sun. It's traditional to address the sun by saying "you who have your eye on all." It's a formula—the sun able to see all things, even hidden crimes—that we'll find in all folklore. But here we're not dealing with the sun since we know that day and night, light and darkness, are the same thing. What never hides (*to mē dyon pote*) is the soul, it's being, and that's what we cannot elude. And it's this same one, as I already said, that accepts and does not accept the name of Zeus. This one is also the world, "this world, the same for all, which was created neither by a god, nor by a man…." (In a certain sense this clarifies the meaning of the expression "does not accept the name of Zeus.") "[But it] always was, is, and will be eternally living fire which kindles according to measure and extinguishes according to measure" (DK 22B30). The one is thus the cosmos, and at the same time it's fire. Naturally, there's a problem here. This is not an issue, as I already told you, of an empirical fire. I think, for my part, that it's a metaphor for being, in its concreteness and activity. We read in fragment 90: "All things are exchanged for fire and fire for all things, like merchandise for gold and gold for merchandise." Those of you who have read *Capital* will see fire as playing the role—a horrible anachronism!—of what Marx called the universal equivalent. In what sense could we say this? Doubtless because it produces at the same time as it consumes, and it's eternally changing all while remaining the same. It's an ontological universal equivalent.

But this idea of fire has another side, which is connected to Heraclitus's cosmo-physiology. It has to do with the thirteen fragments that I evoked at the beginning, which one cannot be rid of based on the pretext that we find in them the trace of Stoic ideas. The doxographical tradition describes for us a Heraclitean physical cosmology centered on fire, in which the dry and the wet (that which was heated to the point of drying out, and its opposite) play the role of first elements. It must be said that the Stoics had conceptions very close to those of Heraclitus; they went so far as to attribute to him their own idea of *ekpyrōsis*, i.e. of a general conflagration of the universe in periodic intervals, followed by its rebirth. Such a conflagration doesn't exist, as far as we know, in Heraclitus.[325] What exists is a physical cosmology in which fire is no longer a simple metaphor but plays the role of a sort of element or origin at the same time as of a metaphorical place to which all things that exist return. I'm not going to talk about that aspect here. The birth of physics and cosmology in Greece is a separate chapter. What interests us, I remind you, is the creation and the institution of society. Whatever it may be, fire is of course also a metaphor *par excellence* for the process through which all things differ and everything is one, through which all things change while being eternal since the cosmos which is eternal is itself subject to the law.

There exists a divine law, a *chreōn*, said Anaximander, which nourishes all human laws. This is what fragment 94 says: "The sun itself cannot surpass the (or his) measures; otherwise, the Erinyes, helpers of *dikē*, will find him out." This is a statement that could be applied to a criminal: *he will be found out*. Here there is thus posed, anew and despite the *hen to pan*, the question of a division between being and its law. It seems to me that Heraclitus perceived this resurgence of division and that his ultimate aim was to unify the two through the identification of the one with fire but also with the *logos* which is *nomos*. This is precisely, for me, the meaning of fragment 41: "One thing is wise, which is to know the *gnōmē* that governs all things in all respects." Here, *gnōmē* is thinking (Bollack and Wismann translate it by "intention"; the word

---

325. *Eds.*: The doctrine was attributed to Heraclitus by most scholars in the nineteenth century (Zeller, Diels, Gomperz, etc.), the most notable exceptions being Schleiermacher and Lassalle. See Burnet, *Early Greek*, pp. 157–163, which poses the question, "Did Heraclitus teach a general conflagration?" and responds in the negative. The other, affirmative position is still being defended nowadays by Charles H. Kahn, *The Art and Thought of Heraclitus: An Edition of the Fragments with Translation and Commentary* (Cambridge: Cambridge University Press, 1979), pp. 134 ff. It is also defended by Denis O'Brien, "Héraclite et l'unité des opposés," *Revue de Métaphysique et de Morale*, 95 (1990), pp. 147–171, which, moreover, embodies the bitterness of certain polemics. For the opposed view, see Kirk, Raven, and Schofield, *Presocratic*, pp. 185 and 198.

can have this sense, but I don't believe that that's the case in this passage). Yet, the fire is *logos*, or it's thinking, and thinking is fire. Therefore, it's a question of knowing fire, the fire whose light comes from its consumption of the matter that nourishes it. We could commentate at length on this idea.

Questions

Regarding unity, is there not a fragment in which Heraclitus says one must conceive of the logos *as separate from all things?*

We in fact have fragment 108, which is quite obscure and seems entirely isolated compared to the others. This is the one that, most likely, Bollack and Wismann took as the starting point for their interpretation (though we don't see well, for all that, where they are headed). Regardless, this is it:

> *Hokosōn logous ēkousa oudeis aphikneitai es tauto, hōste ginōskein ho ti sophon esti, pantōn kechōrismenon.*

> Of all those from whom I have heard discourses, none arrives at the point of knowing what is wise (*sophon*), separate from all.[326]

Bollack and Wismann translate it as:

> Of all that about which I have listened to discourses, not one arrives at the point that it distinguishes the thing that, separate from all, makes artful.[327]

The "thing that makes artful" is from *ho ti sophon esti*. It's true, *sophos* can designate someone astute, very capable, the possessor of a know-how. That said, I find this interpretation indefensible, even on the grammatical level. But this is not the place to talk about that; we're not in a philology seminar. According to my interpretation, Heraclitus says that none of the men he's heard speaking succeeds in knowing what is *sophon* (meaning the truth) considered in itself (*pantōn kechōrismenon*), i.e. not in the sense of a thing that would be "separate from all others" but rather "by putting all else aside." It's thus an issue of knowing what is wise, what is true, *considered as such*, to make use of modern terminology.

---

326. *Trans.*: Castoriadis's French: "*De tous ceux dont j'ai entendu les discours, aucun ne parvient au point de connaître ce qui est sage (sophon), séparé de tout.*"
327. *Trans.*: Bollack and Wismann, *Héraclite*, p. 305: "*De tout ce sur quoi j'ai écouté les discours, pas un ne parvient à ce point qu'il distingue la chose qui, séparée de toutes, fait l'art.*"

Allow me a bit of perspective building here. You're aware that the reference edition for the Presocratics is the collection by Diels. Yet, all serious philologists agree in recognizing the pressing need for a new edition of these fragments, firstly because we have discovered others, and then because the authenticity of some of the fragments already known has become very doubtful for different reasons; and finally and above all it's because—as I already mentioned to you—Diels's work is strongly reliant on the ideas of his era. Whenever one seeks to establish an ancient text, it's a matter of making it understandable. Understandable for whom? What is it that can be understood? What is it that's obvious? What's understandable for Henri Estienne has nothing to do with what is so for Diels.[328] Nor does what's understandable for Diels have anything to do with what is so for Heidegger. Following from the reading of the manuscripts, a certain number of ideas come to orient the choice of retained lessons and potentially to suggest corrections; and one translates consequently upon that. Here's how Diels translates fragment 108 (I'm translating from German):

> Of all those from whom I have heard (or: perceived) words, none arrives at the point of knowing that the wise one (i.e. a neuter expression) is something separate from all others.[329]

What is this "wise one" that's separated from all others, unless it's the God of a canonical monotheistic theology, or of a canonical philosophical idealism?[330] We hear the spirit of an era in this expression, i.e. 1900, with the terms belonging to Wilhelmian Germany, when the idealists dominated the Univer-

---

328. *Eds.*: Henri Estienne gave us the first printed edition of Heraclitus—i.e. Henricus Stephanus, ed., *Poesis philosophica* (Geneva: Henricus Stephanus, 1573)—in which fragments and letters attributed to Heraclitus are gathered next to excerpts by diverse "philosophical" poets (Empedocles, Xenophanes, Parmenides, Cleanthes, etc.).
329. *Trans.*: Diels and Kranz, *Fragmente*, DK 22B108 translation: "*Von allen, deren Worte ich vernommen, gelangt keiner dazu zu erkennen, daß das Weise etwas von allem Abgesondertes ist.*" Castoriadis's French: "*De tous ce dont j'ai entendu (ou perçu) les mots, aucun ne parvient jusqu'au point de connaître que le sage (expression au neutre) est quelque chose de séparé de tout le reste.*"
330. *Eds.*: Hermann Diels, "Heraclitus," in James Hastings, ed., *Encyclopedia of Religion and Ethics, Volume VI* (Edinburgh: T. and T. Clark, 1913), pp. 591–592: "Heraclitus is the profoundest thinker before Plato, and is a joint-founder with him of the Idealism which under the influence of Plato and Christianity has prevailed over other systems. It is to the profundity of his thoughts that the misunderstanding of them is due, both in his own times and down to the present day. The positive character of 19th cent. thought especially has shown itself incapable of grasping the daring transcendency of his view of the Cosmos."

sity; but, beyond that, twenty centuries of philosophy end up at the idea that what is wise must be separate from all. Yet, we cannot interpret this fragment alone by itself, by going against the dozens of fragments that say all is one. If all is one, there's no place for something the existence of which is separate from all else. We're thus obligated to give the expression *pantōn kechōrismenon* a different sense. I proposed one for you. Or otherwise we would need to say that brave Stobaeus, whose *Florilegium* contains our passage, was sleeping or was thinking of something else while he was recopying the quotation, or at least that he added a bit that came from elsewhere. But we cannot contradict what Heraclitus repeats all the time. I thank you for having given me the opportunity to make this point explicit.

How exactly should we understand contrariety?

On this subject, one would first need to be very conscious of the positions of the fragments that we are examining, upstream from a certain number of distinctions that philosophers and logicians were able to establish down the line.[331] You're aware that even in Plato we don't find the distinction, explicit since then, between contraries or opposites and contradictions. Aristotle was the first to establish it, by writing that it doesn't amount to the same thing to say "white and black" versus "white and non-white."[332] We therefore cannot interpret Heraclitus based on later logico-philosophical concepts. We really have to see that the contrarieties he enumerates in fact constitute what, starting with Aristotle, we call, not contradictories, but contraries, which means oppositions of polarity, i.e. hot and cold and so on. This is so even if we must also take account of what is particularly dense and tough in his style. For, you'll find in him oppositions that don't belong to the same logical level placed on the same level. For example, to oppose in one and the same way hot and cold, life and death, gods and men, or even day and night would be (from the later point of view) to mix up categories, i.e. to pass from one category of discourse to another. Hot and cold are properties of material things; gods and men are categories or classes of beings; day and night—at least if these aren't metaphors designating light and darkness—are something different

---

331. *Marg. C.C.*: Fernando Gil, *Libre* <i.e. "Opposer pour penser," *Libre*, 5 (1979), pp. 129–182>.
332. *Eds.*: See, for example, Aristotle, *De interpretatione*, 6, 17a33–37 on the definition of contradictory propositions and *Categories*, 10, 11b32–37 on the nature of opposition between black and white.

still. What we have here are simple contrarieties, established principally from out of locatable qualities. I remind you of Hegel's famous statement, in his lessons on the history of philosophy, which claims to have not left out a single fragment of Heraclitus in the *Science of Logic*.[333] In my view, anyway, he's talking a big game; there are certainly fragments he didn't consider. Regardless, we can't make of Heraclitus a dialectician in the Hegelian sense. We have to resist that genre of temptation, even if, of course, we are perched atop more than twenty centuries of philosophical elaboration, which makes it very difficult for us to grasp the specificity of a conception at such a distance. We must put in the effort to place ourselves back into the spirit of an era in which thinking is discovering, not banal oppositions, but the coexistence of contrary attributes.

It's thus in fact an issue of a constitutive difference?

Yes, since Heraclitus doesn't limit himself to saying that there's contrariety of attributions but asserts that this contrariety is constitutive of what is. This is the important point. Once this is achieved, the discussion of this position identifies strictly with the twenty-five centuries of philosophy that followed; you're free to take it up further, if you feel you've got the courage and the capacities. In any case, it has lost none of its actuality. The flux, for example, returns in Zeno's paradoxes: It's impossible to assert what this is because the same thing, in the same moment, is in contradiction with what it is. There exist at present some naïve people, some mathematicians for example, who believe that we've done away with Zeno's paradoxes. That's absolutely false; the debate is far from being finished.[334] And when interpreters try to say

---

333. *Eds.*: G. W. F. Hegel, *Lectures on the History of Philosophy, Volume I: Greek Philosophy to Plato*, trans. Elizabeth S. Haldane (Lincoln: University of Nebraska Press, 1995), p. 279: "Here we see land; there is no proposition of Heraclitus which I have not adopted in my Logic."

334. *Eds.*: See M. Schofield in Kirk, Raven, and Schofield, *Presocratic*, pp. 263–279, especially p. 279: "Of all the Presocratics, Zeno has most life in him today." See also Gregory Vlastos, "Zeno of Elea," in Paul Edwards, ed., *The Encyclopedia of Philosophy* (New York: Macmillan, 1967), pp. 369–379, which focuses on Zeno's place in the history of philosophical *argumentation*. And see the discussion in Lloyd, *Magic*, pp. 71–79, which also contains notes referring to previous works (Tannery, Cornford, Raven, Fränkel, Owen, Vlastos, etc.). See also the recent study by Richard D. McKirahan, "Zeno," in Long, *Cambridge Companion*, pp. 134–158. Maurice Caveing, "Zeno," in Jacques Brunschwig, G. E. R. Lloyd, and Pierre Pellegrin, eds., *Greek Thought: A Guide to Classical Knowledge* (Cambridge: Belknap Press, 2000), p. 785–795, especially pp. 791–792 ("Resolutions of

something new, they assert that the history of philosophy leads one astray. In effect, either one identifies the discussion of Heraclitus's doctrine on contrariety with the whole later history of philosophy, of abstract thought, of logic, or one asserts that another interpretation is possible and true, and then the whole history of philosophy in question appears like a deviation, a misunderstanding. They'll say that this history is based on a bad understanding of Heraclitus through imputing problems to him that were not his own. That's doubtless true; and we ourselves risk doing likewise, to the extent that we're condemned to a perpetual back-and-forth between what was important for Heraclitus and what's important for us. If need be we could perhaps say—since our interest is not of an archaeological nature—that if the questions that mattered for Heraclitus are of concern for us, it's only insofar as they already mattered for us. Once again, this posits the whole problem of interpretation. Very briefly, I believe that the history of philosophy, in relation to what preceded it, is at every moment in a sort of deviation but that this permanent deviation is rightly a philosophical creation. This means that Plato—and already Socrates—did violence to Presocratic ideas and Aristotle to those of Plato and that, in a sense, if they hadn't done so, then there would be no Aristotle and Plato. But, at the same time, if the preceding texts give the starting point to this movement, and if the latter takes nourishment from them, then they nevertheless retain their proper signification, which isn't exhausted by later philosophies. This is what motivates the return to the texts. There's a circulation of ideas in a *logos xynos*.

Do you consider as interpretable this fragment (DK 22B52) that talks about time as a child who plays with pawns? Can one give it a cosmological reading?

There's no fragment that I consider as uninterpretable. I said that there are some for which the signification is uncertain, or else which are so mutilated that one could make them say nearly everything and its contrary since their interpretation depends on a context lost for us. The fragment you cite makes up part, for me, of those that one could call, in a word, relativist. It is quite

---

the Aporias"), considers the problem to be resolved. Castoriadis returned to the subject in "Remarks on Space and Number," published posthumously in *Figures*, pp. 244–259, especially pp. 254–256 ("Digression on Zeno"), which mentions in this regard the names of Russell, Whitehead, Peirce, James, Whitrow, and also Alexandre Koyré, "Remarques sur les paradoxes de Zénon," in *Études d'histoire de la pensée philosophique* (Paris: Gallimard, 1971), pp. 9–35.

close to another fragment (DK 22B124) that I didn't have time to mention, according to which this world, which is the most beautiful of all, is just a mass of things thrown together randomly. Here again, it's a question of the solidarity of contraries. This randomness according to which things are thrown together produces the most beautiful harmony, the most beautiful order (*kosmos*). Atlan, Progogine, or Varela could make this fragment an epigraph to their works.

XIII. Seminar from March 9, 1983

Today we are going to wrap up our examination of problems posed by the birth and the first development of philosophy. And if, in this affair, I have taken Heraclitus as the nodal point, it's because, all while completing in a sense a first cycle of philosophical elaboration, his oeuvre also contains the germs for all that would follow. I remind you that Heraclitus thrived in about 500 BC, and that in this era we already have seventy-five years of explicit philosophy, nearly three centuries of great poetry (Homer, Hesiod), and two centuries of lyric poetry, even if it's in the sixth century that the latter became developed. And from the start lyric poetry, far from being a simple expression of affects or sentiments, also presents statements of philosophical and political reach. Such is the case with a celebrated passage of Archilochus (second half of the seventh century), which is absolutely surprising in this respect. There's this career soldier, perhaps a mercenary, who one day fled the battlefield, leaving his shield behind—the most shameful act of cowardice in ancient Greece—and he writes, "I threw down shield; I can always buy another."[335] This is a frontal assault against the common belief about what virile virtues are, i.e. the bravery of the soldier. Moreover, we would find in lyric poetry, if we had time to pause here, more than an analogical statement implying a critique of the instituted beliefs and norms.[336]

---

335. *Eds.*: See Archilochus, fragment 5, in West, *Iambi et Elegi, Volume I*. West translates it—in M. L. West, ed., *Greek Lyric Poetry* (Oxford: Oxford University Press, 1999), p. 14, as: "Some Saian sports my splendid shield: I had to leave it in a wood, but saved my skin. Well, I don't care—I'll get another just as good."

336. *Eds.*: See, for example, Xenophanes (DK 21B2), who, enumerating the honors reserved to the city's winners in the games, opposes this publicly acclaimed value to that of his own poetry. That is, the athletes' exploits do not contribute in any way to a just political regulation (*eumoniē*), and "do not fatten the city." Or see Sappho's lines—see Edgar Lobel and Denys Page, eds., *Poetarum Lesbiorum Fragmenta* (Oxford: Clarendon, 1955), fragment 16—which define "that which is the most beautiful" (*kalliston*): Against all those who pretend to find it in "the army of horsemen" or "infantrymen" or in "a war fleet," she declares, in her proper name, that it is "that which everyone desires" (*kēn' ottō tis eratai*). See also the beginning of Pindar, "Olympian 1," in *Complete Odes*, lines 35–59: He tells the myth of Tantalus differently than tradition has done before him, because "it is proper

One of the results of this first unfolding, i.e. of the first three-quarters of a century of philosophy, is the separation in and by this movement between being and appearing, between what is and what gives itself to us *qua* human beings. This is a necessary result of the research in which the Ionians were already engaged when they wanted to find a principle, an *archē*, as Aristotle would say down the line in writing (or rewriting) this history, which is in effect *allo ti para tauta*, i.e. something else alongside what appears.[337] This obviously implies a critique of representation (which Xenophanes made, as we've seen); and to the division being/appearing there is immediately added the division *alētheia/doxa* (truth/opinion) as well as a conception of the human fabrication of *doxa*, clear already in the Xenophanes fragment. This is the famous *dokos epi pasi tetyktai*, i.e. an opinion or a belief that things are so (*dokos*) is fabricated (*tetyktai*), covering all things (*epi pasi*).[338]

Before going into the third opposition, between *physis* and *nomos*, I would like to go back over and finish with Heraclitus and what will follow him, especially since we won't be approaching any more philosophical works this year. Heraclitus, thus, who is familiar with the difference between being and appearing, wants to overcome it; the formulations like *hen to pan*, "all is one," aim at this as much as do the fragments on unity, on the identity even of contraries, and on the negation of every essential difference between being and becoming. How, then, can it account for the fact that not only do we live in a world divided but also that in a sense we are necessarily in this division since there is error and truth since we cannot think without this constant movement of a critique of our own ideas, a movement that Heraclitus himself

---

that a man should speak well of the gods" and "I cannot call any of the blessed gods a cannibal." In these examples and elsewhere, the contestation aims each time at an ethical position (and possibly political, even aesthetic) that has been embodied in an earlier or contemporary poetic discourse, which is designated as rival. (Thus, the military images at the beginning of Sappho's passage obviously allude to the *Iliad*; and all the argumentation of the poem calls into question the warrior values of the epic.) The quarrel of ideas is coupled with a debate between concurrent genres. In this regard, see the analyses by Jesper Svendro, *La Parole et le marbre: Aux origines de la poétique grecque* (Lund: Studentlitteratur, 1976), which focus especially on what the message of a type of poetry owes to the material and social conditions of its production. See also Philippe Brunet, "Conclusion: Un naissance agonistique?" in *La Naissance de la littérature dans la Grèce ancienne* (Paris: Librarie générale française, 1997). On the anti-aristocratic elements in "lyric" poetry, see also Walter Donlan, "The Tradition of Anti-Aristocratic Thought in Early Greek Poetry," *Historia*, 22:2 (1973), pp. 145–154.

337. *Eds.*: According to the formulation of Simplicius, cited in Seminar X, p. 163. See also Aristotle, *Metaphysics*, I, 3.

338. *Eds.*: DK 21B34; see the commentary in Seminar XI, pp. 189 ff.

of course accomplishes? The error and the misery of man is that he introduces a separation without seeing that it is he who introduces it. First, it's due to his presumptuousness, his stupid belief in his own-thinking, the *idia phronēsis*, i.e. that which separates him from the *xynos logos*, from the reason that subtends and traverses all that is and nourishes it as well. Next, it's due to his language since in order to be able to speak man must effectuate distinctions between things that are not really distinct.[339] Not to read too much into Heraclitus or to steal the spotlight, but I believe that we already have here, in germ, both the recognition of the inescapable characteristic of the ensemblist-identitarian dimension—i.e. of the logic of distinction and determination—and the certainty that this logic could exhaust neither what is nor what can be said.

There's therefore a particular point of view that the human being introduces by his presumptuousness and his language; we find it incorporated into each being, in any case into each animate being. From this comes the apparently banal statement according to which asses prefer hay to gold; they have their proper point of view as asses, for which hay has a privileged value.[340] It thus belongs to the structure and the organization of all things that there would be what's particular and that each particular would have a point of view on everything that it is not. I don't think it's too much of a modernization of Heraclitus to attribute that to him. But if this introduction <of the particular into the whole> takes effect for the other beings in the universal circulation, i.e. in the fire which ceaselessly changes all that is into something different, then for man there's an additional division: He rears up, comes to revolt against this universal exchange by wanting to impose his *idion*, his particular point of view. At the same time—and this is the other dimension of this division—through his *phronein*, man can overcome his *idia phronēsis* and, by thinking, find himself in the truth of *hen to pan*, wherein one thing is the whole and the whole is just one.

Having reached this point, are we going to conclude that with Heraclitus the problem of philosophy is resolved, that all of what should be said was said, and that the representation is finished? No, of course. Despite the grandeur of a thinking which sees where the problems are and tries to surpass them, Heraclitus reintroduces the division that he wants to abolish. For, even if the universal *logos* merges into being and indeed into "fire," it calls for being said.[341] And in order to say, man must overcome his *idia phronēsis*. With him, therefore, there always subsists this sort of doubling; i.e. the work of thinking,

---

339. *Marg. C.C.*: It's not by chance if "Heracliteans" equates, more or less, to "skeptics."
340. *Eds.*: DK 22B9.
341. *Marg. C.C.*: Truth is discourse (±?).

which always tends to fall into the private and into the particular, is itself required for him to overcome this very failure. And this work of thinking thus necessarily reintroduces a double separation. The first is between the one who puts in the effort of thinking and the masses who don't think like him. We could recall here all the statements of Heraclitus about the many (*hoi polloi*) who believe that such and such, who have the illusion of thinking that such and such. But there's also a division within the philosopher, who's forced to recognize that he himself does not simply and directly have access to the unity of the whole and to the universal *logos*, but rather that for him a constant work of thinking is necessary.[342] He does this without being guaranteed—far from it—not to reproduce illusion, *doxa*, error, division.

All of that of course is not Heraclitus but a commentary on Heraclitus. But it allows us to understand why there's a history of philosophy and why philosophy, and thinking in general, is an interminable enterprise in the strictest sense of the term. For, twenty or thirty years after Heraclitus, with Parmenides, the movement restarts with what seems to be a retrograde step but which, in fact, differently integrates what has already happened, although it's by no means an issue of a cumulative development or a dialectic in the Hegelian sense. Parmenides, in effect, is familiar with Heraclitus.[343] He alludes to him in order to criticize him and reestablish an absolute separation (in English, one would say it's *unbridgeable*, something across which we can't build a bridge). There is being and there is non-being; between the two there is no communication. Indeed, non-being cannot even be (and must not be) said.[344] This is a non-being that, for him, is more than non-being; it comprises all of that which, in one way or another, would make what is participate in what is not: movement, difference or alterity, multiplicity itself. All of that is not and cannot be. We see here how from this point forward the grasp of being operates not under the sign of presence, as Heidegger says, but under the sign of determinacy. The determinate alone is; and if it must be fully determinate,

---

342. *Marg. C.C.*: ἐδιζησάμην ἐμεωυτόν <and> ψυχῆς πείρατα (…) <DK 22B101 and B45>; see Seminar XII, pp. 216 ff.
343. *Eds.*: For the opposed view, see Gigon, *Ursprung*, pp. 244–245, for whom Heraclitus and Parmenides pose different problems and ignore one another, as well as Reinhardt and von Fritz (per the references in Guthrie, *History, Volume II*, pp. 23–26). For Jacob Bernays (1885), it is indisputable that Parmenides criticizes Heraclitus, about which see Burnet, *Early Greek*, pp. 179–180, who follows him on this point. After retracing the polemic from Bernays forward, Guthrie, *History, Volume II*, p. 23, concludes: "There is no external evidence to help: we can only say it is possible, but not certain that Parmenides had read the other's book."
344. *Eds.*: DK 28B2, 7–8.

it can be only a single thing. Rejected as non-being are thus movement, diversity, multiplicity, alteration, and so on, which, if they were to exist, would introduce indeterminacy. Further, even if Parmenides knows that he thinks being, he cannot admit that being and the thought of being are two, except by reintroducing division and finally multiplicity. It's thus necessary for him to assert the unity of being and thinking. As he says in a line of his poem: what is, is the same thing as that of which there exists thinking.[345] It's pointless to focus on the terribly constraining character of such a discourse; you only need to reflect on this to be convinced of it. The fact that there would be two things rather than one already introduces an insurmountable aporia: we would need to think of them as one from a different point of view, and so on.

Parmenidean argumentation against multiplicity or, if you will, against the different figurations of determinacy, will be reprised and elaborated by Zeno of Elea; and we'll find it in the fifth and fourth centuries in the arguments of certain Sophists and Megarians. For, there's something like an internal necessity of thinking—or at least something like a natural slope since we can think differently, and we have in fact thought differently—to hold on to these assertions that the one alone is and thinking and being are thus the same, in order to end up 2,000 years later, in Germany, for example, with the statement: being is Spirit. But we already have in Parmenides the germs of what will be, across the centuries, theological philosophy or rational theology.

Obviously, in this absolute form, the situation is untenable. Parmenides asserts in his poem that there exist two ways: that of the truth, and another, deceptive one, that of opinion, of *doxa*.[346] But, try as he may to reject all of

---

345. *Eds.*: DK 28B3. Also, see Burnet, *Early Greek*, pp. 169–182; Guthrie, *History*, Volume II, pp. 14–20; and Kirk, Raven, and Schofield, *Presocratic*, pp. 244–248. On the translation of *to gar auto noein estin te kai einai*, M. Schofield, in Kirk, Raven, and Schofield, *Presocratic*, p. 246, translates it as, "For the same thing is there both to be thought of and to be," while mentioning that "other authors interpret it as 'thought and being are the same.'" Cordero, *Les deux chemins*, p. 34, has "thought and being are the same thing [*penser et être sont la même chose*]." Denis O'Brien and Jean Frère, in Pierre Aubenque, ed., *Études sur Parménide, tome I* (Paris: Vrin, 1987), p. 19, have: "It is in fact one and the same thing that one thinks and that is [*C'est en effect une seule et même chose que l'on pense et qui est*]." Marcel Conche, in Parménide, *Le Poème: Fragments* (Paris: PUF, 1996), p. 87, has: "For the same thing is at once thinking and being [*Car le même est à la fois penser et être*]." Barbara Cassin, in Parménide, *Sur la nature ou sur l'étant* (Paris: Seuil, 1998), p. 78, has: "A same is in fact at once thinking and being [*Un même est en effet à la fois penser et être*]." These works permit one to have a rather complete view on the state of Parmenidean studies. We would also mention the essays in the edited volume Mourelatos, *Pre-Socratics*.
346. *Eds.*: DK 28B2. Also, on the "two ways," see Gigon, *Ursprung*, pp. 250–255, and Kirk, Raven, and Schofield, *Presocratic*, pp. 244–246. On the different interpretations of

what is multiplicity, diversity, or alteration by relegating it to the world of *doxa*, in a certain way (*pōs*, as one says in Greek, i.e. *somehow*), as soon as one speaks of it, this *doxa*, this illusion, exists. It's thus necessary to introduce a new division between the truly true—the genuinely being—and illusion, which is only an appearance. We don't have the time to dig into all of what will be elaborated from the fifth century onwards; but the lineage of Parmenides leads through Anaxagoras into Plato, who, by means of the famous parricide in the *Sophist* and then the developments of the late dialogues, is led to recognize the existence of the multiple, of change, even if it means conferring upon it an ontological dignity less than that of genuine being, the *idea*, the *ousia*, i.e. idea or essence. Furthermore, he has to kill Parmenides at another level, a purely logico-ontological level, since to refute the assertion "being alone is, and non-being is not" is also to admit that being and non-being, in a certain way, become mixed and determined one by the other. That is, for everything of which one can say that it is, one can also say in an infinity of ways that in other respects it is not. And this inter-crossing of determinations, and of determinacy and indeterminacy (because non-being, in the *Sophist*, is also indeterminacy), doesn't simply concern beings, or the empirical, concrete beings, but also the categories themselves, the supreme genera. The fact remains that, in Plato, the surpassing of the absolute opposition between being and non-being, as also that between *alētheia* and *doxa*, imparts to the thinkable, to the idea, to *ousia*, a fundamental ontological privilege. (We can, moreover, wonder whether the idea in Plato coincides with what the moderns call thinkable. Doubtless not.) *Ousia* is genuine being; the world of phenomena and *doxa*, and the material world doubtless as well, is *hētton on*, has a lesser being.

The other philosophical lineage, starting from the Parmenidean aporias and made fully explicit through the arguments of Zeno on the impossibility of movement and division would pass through the rather singular and very important figure of Empedocles (whom we won't be able to discuss), who renews and radicalizes the Milesian cosmology and philosophy, in order to end up—passing by way of the Sophists, then Leucippus, Democritus, and Epicurus—with a different recognition of the multiple, with an new interpretation of the relationship between the sensible and the intelligible. The essential point in my view with these thinkers is their refusal of the fundamental thesis of philosophical theology or rational theology, namely the ontological privilege accorded to *nous noētos*, to the purely thinkable. And it's

fragment 2 and in particular the problems posed by the translation of *estin*, see Conche, *Parménide*, pp. 75–86, as well as the other works cited above.

not by chance if in the final analysis it's very much in this philosophical lineage that one finds the germs of reflection on democracy and on what I call historical creation or human creation, an idea that is absolutely foreign to Plato and even, to the extent that he is familiar with it, one that is radically condemned by him.

At the end of this evolution there's Aristotle. We would be tempted to say that he's in the middle, in this *mesotēs*, this mean that he so prized, indeed going so far as to make of it the definition of virtue; but I would rather say that he is somehow beyond this melee. As such, he succeeds in integrating what's essential from the reflection that precedes him, making use of this *phronēsis*, this fantastic faculty of measure, of "prudence" (a word that's honestly ridiculous), i.e. this philosophical judgment proper, which is something that places him entirely apart. For, the philosopher must not be only and not especially a great spectator; he must above all be someone who in facing concrete things, as in facing the most obscure theoretical problems, keeps a cool head and a sturdy judgment. Whereas the poetical element in the true sense of the term, which is present in every great philosopher, tends often to unfold in a movement of thinking in which it follows its inspiration or the force of words incautiously, Aristotle remains, himself, always on the side of the things as they are, the things real or the things thought, the things of thinking. But we will revisit at length Plato and Aristotle when we talk about democracy. Here, I simply want to evoke this crossing of paths that presents itself starting with Heraclitus, which will divide Greek philosophy and then later philosophy, and note that in this division the "onto-theological" current, as Heidegger calls it, has always been dominant, i.e. a current which Heidegger himself belongs to, but that's another story.

Let's go now to the opposition between *nomos* and *physis*. As a first remark, we've talked about the birth of philosophy as an *explicit* activity, but we must not forget that there's in fact a double birth of philosophy. In the Greek cities, doubtless in the seventh century and before Thales himself, there emerged a philosophy *ergō* (in act), and not simply *logō* (in speech), as a political struggle in the interior of the community. It's philosophy in act because the stakes of this struggle aren't first of all to obtain such and such a privilege—it's not an issue of extracting a salary augmentation or of imposing a lowered retirement age—but to call into question the instituted order: Who lays down the law of the city, the *nomos*? And based on what criteria? This is a question to which the *dēmos* begins to respond by self-defining itself as source of the law, by claiming responsibility for this positing, even if, in this first historical phase, it doesn't completely succeed. In any case, it's starting from the question of the *nomos*, posited in act by political activity, that the oppositions being/appearing and truth/belief will adopt in Greece their acuity and their specific profundity. As such, as I've already discussed with you, these oppositions could only exist everywhere and always since they're inherent in all human language, which must always be able to make out the difference between "it is so, in truth" and "it seems it is so; it's your opinion." But what isn't inherent in language is the distinction between a nature and a *nomos* conceived (since *nomos*, like *logos*, presents a very large spectrum of significations) as a positing of a rule both instituted (constituted) by a community and instituting (constituting) it.

Second remark: One must distinguish in this *physis/nomos* opposition the aspects that are explicitly thematized, philosophical, or locatable from a philological perspective, from the opposition as it is laid out in deeds. Its first thematized appearance is found in a statement attributed to Archelaus, the first known Athenian philosopher, about whom we know few things other than that he would have been the master of Socrates, the latter being born in 469, which permits us to situate Archelaus and his teaching at around 450. As Diogenes Laertius reports, this statement asserts that "the just and the unjust (*to dikaion kai to aischron*), exist not *physei* but *nomō*."[347] These two words are in the dative, this marvelous case that has been the subject of numerous doctoral theses; its significations are so manifold and impossible to render into French. I'll translate them, for my part, as "not in and by nature, but in and by the law"; or "by means of, in virtue of, as a function of, etc. the law." We also have a fragment of Archelaus, passed down by Hippolytus, according to which "men are distinguished from other animals/beings in constituting/instituting (*synestēsan*) leaders, laws, arts, cities [...]."[348] Even if the order of enumeration isn't from Archelaus but from Hippolytus, we have practically everything in this statement: leaders (power); laws (the fact that this power is never purely arbitrary); arts; and cities. We could equally cite here a passage of the Hippocratic treatise *On Airs, Waters, and Places*, where some have seen the first appearance of the opposition. But this treatise is probably from the era of Herodotus, thus posterior to Archelaus.[349]

---

347. *Eds.*: Diogenes Laertius, *Lives*, II, 16 (= DK 60A1). See Kirk, Raven, and Schofield, *Presocratic*, p. 389.
348. *Eds.*: Hippolytus of Rome, *Refutation of All Heresies*, I, 9 (= DK 60A4). See Kirk, Raven, and Schofield, *Presocratic*, pp. 387–388.
349. *Eds.*: See Heinimann, *Nomos und Physis*, pp. 13 ff. The text can be found in English as "Airs, Waters, Places," in G. E. R. Lloyd, ed., *Hippocratic Writings*, trans. John Chadwick and W. N. Mann (London: Penguin Books, 1983). In French, see Hippocrates, *L'Art de la médecine*, trans. Jacques Jouanna and Caroline Magdelaine (Paris: Flammarion, 1999). The latter observe in this text "the oldest kept testimony of the opposition between *nomos/physis*" (p. 280). Also see Jacques Jouanna, ed., *Hippocrates*, trans. M. B. DeBoisie

But beyond the thematization of the terms, the *physis/nomos* opposition present in the collective political activity is already there implicitly, and not only in Presocratic philosophy but even in Hesiod. For example, there's a passage of the *Works* where it's said that Zeus posed for men a *nomos*: The animals can perfectly well devour one another since there isn't any *dikē* among them; but to men he gave *dikē*, "the first of goods."[350] If it's true that the term *nomos* is not opposed here to a *physis*, this *nomos* is nevertheless already present as the object of a positing, even if it's divine; but, conceived as something overarching, it amounts, on the one hand, to homophagy and absence of justice for the animals and, on the other hand, to *dikē* for humans. Xenophanes, in turn, through criticizing *doxa*, in fact takes it out on the *nomos*, in the sense of social institution, through the intermediary of terms like *ta nomizomena* (from the verb *nomizō*), i.e. that which a category, a society, or even all men believe, profess, or share.[351] But it's with regard to the critique of language that the opposition *physis/nomos* will be very precisely formulated. Here, again, this starts with Xenophanes, who, in fragment 32, which we already spoke about, reproaches men for giving the name of a goddess, Iris, to the rainbow, which is for him just a physical phenomenon of the same order as the cloud.[352] And we could find similar statements in Anaxagoras as well as Empedocles, for example, when the latter states that men call death *potmos*, that which is just a separation of elements. But it's by convention-institution—by habit, if you will—that they use this word, and Empedocles tells us that he himself also obeys the usage.[353] For he knows well that in order to speak, men of a community cannot use just any old word, nor invent a personal vocabulary. There are words that impose themselves, and language is a law. And we've seen that Heraclitus criticizes language many times over, inasmuch as it conventionally separates what should remain one. Let's not forget Parmenides, to whom we'll not return here.

In the middle of the fifth century, and on this critical basis, the famous question will again gain all its momentum, namely, whether language is *physei*, by nature, or rather *thesei*, by positing, *nomō*, by law or institution-convention.[354] Certainly, its maturation must have begun long before

---

(Baltimore: Johns Hopkins University Press, 1999), p. 224. For Guthrie, *History, Volume I*, p. 58, the Archelaus passage "is probably earlier, and in any case the first known mention [of the distinction] in an ethical context."

350. *Eds.*: Hesiod, *Works and Days*, 276–280.
351. *Eds.*: DK 21B2 and 13.
352. *Eds.*: See Seminar XI, p. 190.
353. *Eds.*: Plutarch, *Adversus Colotem*, 113 A–B (= DK 31B9).
354. *Eds.*: See Guthrie, *History, Volume II*, pp. 474–476.

Archelaus and the Hippocratic texts. For, the singular critique of language necessarily had to end up in the problem of its conventionality and of its naturalness. When a philosopher said, "We give such a name to such a thing, but, in truth, we shouldn't call it thus," the implication was that there is a true name for each thing, hence something like a natural correspondence. But, at least since the eighth century, the Greeks traveled, and they knew well that other peoples named, let's say, "itou" what they themselves named "table." How could one then pretend that the Greek language was alone true? And even within Greece, between the different dialects, differences of pronunciation and lexicality existed. This discussion was thus very probably present from the sixth century on, and it seems to me the best proof of this is the clear and definitive response in favor of *nomō* which the immense Democritus provided, in a fragment on which we'll briefly comment.

Democritus is approximately a contemporary of Socrates, and we can situate his maturity at around 450–440. The fragment we'll occupy ourselves with was first transmitted to us by Proclus.[355] The latter reports that according to some, including Pythagoras, names have a natural correspondence with the beings they designate. Yet, Pythagoras was aware that words are human creations, imposed upon things. Insoluble contradiction? No, because the only one who can name things, he said, is the wise man who, through thinking, knows their true nature. There is thus a human legislator who posits for each being the true name that refers to it. And this is an idea that we couldn't dismiss with a shrug of the shoulders. Let's recall what has been written about the privilege of the poet in naming things. There's Mallarmé, in *The Tomb of Edgar Allan Poe*: "to give a purer meaning to the words of the tribe"; and Rilke says the poet gives things their name.... After having thus exposed the Pythagorean conception of language by nature, *physei*, Proclus follows up by presenting the opposed argumentation, hence that of Democritus. On this point I can only advise you to reread the *Cratylus* by Plato, this dialogue on the conventionality or naturality of language, which makes explicit and criticizes the two positions, but without arriving at any conclusions. Nevertheless, it's a dialogue of a mature nature, not a rhetorical exercise; but it remains problematic and aporetic. It's very much like the *Theaetetus*, moreover, which deals with epistemology (with true knowing), passes through a review of the different definitions, refutes them, and then wraps up with a "we'll try to do

---

355. *Eds.*: The fragment is DK 68B26, transmitted in Proclus, *On Plato's* Cratylus, trans. Brian Duvick (Ithaca: Cornell University Press, 2007). For Proclus, Democritus's position was close to that of Hermogenes in the dialogue.

better next time." As Proclus presents it, quite to the contrary, the demonstration of Democritus is exhaustive and definitive. The four arguments that he presents on the conventionality of language seem to me, I'll say in passing, richer and more fecund than those of Saussure, who, in his *Course in General Linguistics*, in order to introduce the principle of the "arbitrariness of the sign," is satisfied with pretty much noticing that in France one calls "*boeuf*" that which one calls "*Ochs*" across the Rhine. The last of Democritus's arguments is, moreover, a quasi-refutation by anticipation of structuralism. But let's take them one by one. He begins with homonymy, i.e. if different things bear the same name, how could the name exist by nature? For language to be *physei*, one would need at least one name per thing. And there must be only one, which is the second argument, synonymity, which Democritus—or Proclus perhaps—calls polyonymy. Here again, the naturality of language should exclude that several names apply to one and the same thing. We already see the fecundity of these two first arguments, which concern the absences of bi-univocal correspondence, term-by-term correspondence, between names and things, but which one can generalize to the whole of language. That is, one same description can very well apply to several processes, and a single sequence of facts can be described in an indeterminate number of ways. Without this universality of language, moreover, we could not speak. If the same word, the same description, couldn't apply to indefinite occurrences, we would have to ceaselessly invent new complexes of words to describe an unprecedented event or an identical event in another place. The sophistical derivation of this argumentation, like that of the Megarians, will be grafted on here: This seminar from March 9, 1983, of course, is not the seminar from March 2; but no more is it the same as the one from fifteen minutes ago, and in ten minutes, it will be a different seminar. By wanting to define it, by making it enter into the universality of the term "seminar," we've eliminated its proper reality, which was this-seminar-here, in this-moment-now. The conclusion of philosophers interested in the substance of things—not in eristics, even if not all the latter is solely about controversy—is as follows: Since we can never speak except in universal terms, we must admit that the individual is ineffable, that one can never truly speak the individual. The third argument against the naturalness of language, which Democritus or Proclus calls the *metathesis onomatōn*, the displacement of names, is the most ordinary. It's just simply that we can change the name of a thing without affecting this thing at all. We can thus call Aristocles Plato, and Tyrtamus Theophrastus—two examples that cannot be from Democritus since these authors both lived in the fourth century—and change nothing in the nature of these personages. We're obviously in full convention.

The fourth argument, modestly entitled *ek tēs tōn homoiōn elleipseōs* (from out of the lack of similarities), in fact goes much further than it seems. How is it, asks Democritus, that *phronēsis* in the substantive (i.e. right thinking, judgment, prudence, etc.) corresponds to the verb *phronein* (i.e. to judge well, be in your right mind, etc.), whereas from the name *dikaiosynē* (i.e. justice) no verb is derived? In one case, we have a logical and organic connection, inherent in thinking and in the thing itself between a process, an action, and a categorical property; in the other case, there isn't. To what nature could such an incoherency correspond? Where is the logic in this affair? Nowhere. Such dissymetries and anomalies can only be due to decisions, human positings.

You can very well see why this argument goes much further than it seems, i.e. that it's in fact a refutation by anticipation of structuralism and all logicism. For, it can be applied to all stages of language, already at the elementary level of phonology. The latter teaches us that there are, in language, concatenations of permitted phonemes and others forbidden, which cannot form lexemes, words. This logic, which Jakobson himself by the way rightly qualified as totalitarian (i.e. whatever is not forbidden is obligatory), would require that all forms of permitted concatenations of phonemes become realized, forming just that many lexemes in the language in question. Yet, this isn't so. "*Vèche*," for example, would be a perfectly legitimate word in French, but it doesn't exist. You could fabricate innumerable words in this way, far more than actual French deals with. These words would be, from the phonological perspective, perfectly allowable. And, at the lexical level, derivation and production do not operate solely according to an internal logic that would require such and such a mode of composition according to the cases; it instead presents a kind of "accidentality," this dependency both on historicity and on the connotative (and, in the end, magmatic) aspect of the signification that Democritus already signaled by way of the disequilibrium between *phronein-phronēsis* and (null)-*dikaiosynē*.

I would like to comment very briefly on a different fragment of Democritus, reported by Diogenes Laertius, which says: *nomō thermon, nomō psychron*, i.e. the hot and the cold are by means of the *nomos*, by convention-institution.[356] This proposition obviously isn't about language; it's not the words *thermon* and *psychron* that are called into question. Nor is it about the simple relativity of sensuous impressions, nor for that matter about what philosophy later called "secondary qualities," i.e. things—taste, color, and so on—that would depend on the human being's sensorial organization while the form or the mass would be "primary qualities." In my view, what

---

356. *Eds.*: Diogenes Laertius, *Lives*, IX, 72 (= DK 68B117).

Democritus asserts here in saying *nomō* is that there's a social constitution of the hot and the cold, and hence more broadly of sensible qualities, color, sweet, bitter, and so on. This is not a social construction of the elementary sensation but rather of what we would call the perception of things, which means the insertion of the elementary sensation into a vaster organized complex, outside of which it doesn't exist. (For you know that isolated elementary sensation doesn't exist; it is always caught up in a sensorial flux and, above all, constructed by the subject.) Just after these four words, Diogenes Laertius cites another statement of Democritus, which is wholly extraordinary: *etēi de atoma kai kenon* (in reality there are only atoms and void), *etēi de ouden idmen* (and we know nothing), *en bythō gar hē alētheia* (since truth is always in the deep of the ocean, at an unfathomable depth). Galen, who takes up this same passage, completes it by showing how Democritus sees the equilibrium between phenomena and sensations, on the one hand, and thinking, on the other. First, he tells us, Democritus *diebale ta phainomena*, i.e. calumniates the phenomena, accuses them of being deceivers. Color, sweetness, or bitterness are so only by convention, *nomō*. After this, he attributes to the senses this response: "Poor (or: miserable) thinking, having drawn beliefs (*tas pisteis*, i.e. that which you can believe in, which is also perhaps proof of your beliefs) from us, you are trying to demolish us; but your victory would be for you your own downfall."[357] Let's risk a parallel. Take Kant in the Preface to the *Critique of Pure Reason*: Concepts without sense material are empty; sensations without concepts are blind. For Democritus, sensations are a source of error, but the senses say to thinking: It's from us that you get that which makes you believe and the test and proofs of this belief; and if you try to abolish us, our abolition will be your own ruin. There's no contradiction there, but precisely the capacity to see both aspects of the question at once.

My final remark on this *physis-nomos* opposition concerns the single word *nomos*, which contains in summary what I call the human creation among the Greeks. All of this is tied to the famous question of cyclical time, to the eternal return, to unawareness of progress, which are themes—I've already alluded to this—that are not specifically Greek, at least not as one typically presents them.[358] We could even find numerous testimonies proving that the Greeks didn't have a purely cyclical conception of time, among which the most decisive is, from very early on, this idea of a humanity separating itself from animality, then constructing itself as humanity by its own proper acts and creations. Numerous historians of philosophy (for example, the

---

357. *Eds.*: Galen, *De experientia medica*, XV, 8 (= DK 68B125).
358. *Eds.*: Seminar XI, p. 200.

excellent Guthrie, author of a history of Greek philosophy up to Aristotle in six volumes that are very useful, a bit dull perhaps, but complete enough) talk, on this issue, about an anthropological theory of progress. And I would agree well enough with this expression, on the condition that one rightly detaches the term "progress" from its nineteenth-century connotations. What's at the core of the Greek conception is the understanding, quite early on, that there's a separation between humans and nature (the animals, for example), which is not a natural given but the product or the result of human acts, acts which posit this separation, which constitute it, and which are of the order of the *nomos*. The word is not yet employed, and the term "creation," or *poēsis* in ancient Greek—a rather ambiguous term, by the way—is never pronounced in this context. But this vision is already there in Xenophanes, for example in the fragment describing for us men, ignorant to begin with, who by dint of searching "find in time what is best." It's also there in Protagoras, according to all we know of his oeuvre, and even according to what's said in the dialogue of Plato that bears his name. We encounter it again in other authors in prose, as in the anonymous extract from Iamblichus's *Protrepticus*.[359] The essential testimonies for our topic are yet three passages—among the most striking ones—from tragic poets.[360] The first is in lines 442–468 and then 478–506 of *Prometheus Bound* by Aeschylus, the date of which is not precisely known, but only that it's one of the first works of the author, who died in 456.[361] In this tragedy, we already have quite clearly a separation between a pre-human state and a genuinely human state, even if it's a god, Prometheus, who's responsible for this rupture by having given to men the arts and the *nomoi*, the institutions. (We can, moreover, read a development of the same order in lines 201–213 of Euripides's *The Suppliants*, dated to around 420.) But less than a generation after Aeschylus, in about 440, in Sophocles's *Antigone* (in lines 332–375), there arrives this fantastic hymn about the creative power of human beings, who institute cities, who give themselves laws, who create language, arts, and so on. This is the famous chorus that begins with the

---

359. *Eds.*: In 1889 Friedrich Blass showed that about ten pages in the work by Iamblichus dedicated to the opposition between *physis* and *nomos* came from another work, by an unknown author from the fifth or the fourth century BC (and it has been called since then the *Anonymus Iamblichi*). In French, see Jean-Paul Dumont, ed., *Les Sophistes, Fragments et témoignages* (Paris: PUF, 1969), pp. 224–231. See also Guthrie, *History, Volume I*, pp. 314–315; Kerferd, "Sophistic Relativism," in *Sophistic Movement*, pp. 103–104; Jacqueline de Romilly, *The Great Sophists in Periclean Athens*, trans. Janet Lloyd (Oxford: Clarendon, 1998), pp. 168–170 and 205–210.
360. *Eds.*: On Aeschylus and Sophocles, see Castoriadis, "Aeschylean Anthropogony."
361. *Eds.*: See Seminar V, note 109, p. 84.

line: "Numerous are terrible things, but nothing is more terrible than man." Terrible here, which attempts to translate the word *deinon*, has the same meaning as in Rilke's "Every angel is terrible." That is, he's not describing fear, horror, or flight but the presence of an incoercible power that, as soon as it appears, makes the everyday collapse. We'll then find in Critias, or in the Hippocratic writings, numerous texts focusing on this separation of man in relation to a natural state, i.e. on that which is, in my language, the self-positing of humanity. But if the three tragedians seem to me, once again, privileged witnesses in this respect, it's because their genius was also in their expressing with a fantastic acuity what one could call the *topoi* of the era, the ideas, the problematics, as we would say today, which are discussed, which are in the air at the time. That's what the relationship of a great poet with his time involves. Think of John Donne or Shakespeare. I'm not saying that they transcribe the newspapers, but they know how to take up what's there in society, what's being discussed, how to give to these themes a form and an intensity that will project them far beyond their era. I believe, therefore, that the positing of the *nomos*, as equivalent to the self-constitution of humanity, is an idea that at the turn of the sixth to fifth centuries, between 500 and 450, is starting to be perceived. It will be entirely explicit later on with Protagoras, the Sophists, and so on, only to become central in the "Funeral Oration" of Pericles, in the second book of Thucydides. But we'll see all of this when we talk about Athenian democracy and of its consciousness of itself. I would add, likewise, that this understanding of the *nomos* as the self-creation of man was necessarily nourished by the political struggles that, from the seventh century onward in the cities culminated in modifying, sometimes overturning, the *nomoi*. Even if this political creation was exercised at a level infinitely less radical since the instituted framework was always preserved, it certainly also contributed to the philosophical radicalization of this idea that humanity separates itself from animality by positing its *nomos*.

Questions

My question doesn't have a direct connection with what you were just saying, but I'm not fully grasping what, at bottom, your critique of Heidegger is. For him as well what's tragic in philosophy, starting at a certain moment, is to have been a thinking of determination. And this is why he wants to find what he calls the path of being.

That really isn't the subject, but I can't blame you for it. I'm not about to go on a digression, and I myself have mentioned Heidegger several times, whose positions on the ancient Greeks couldn't be neglected, even if I consider them radically false. I'm not going to pretend to be surprised that he doesn't interpret Greek thinking like me, in terms of a struggle against chaos, or a confrontation between appearance and being, truth and *doxa*. What I reproach him for is for seeking to put this thinking into a Procrustean bed so as to eliminate all of what doesn't agree with his view of what Greece is, this truth of being that arises in a clearing…, which I persist in calling a pastoralism. If he hadn't mutilated the texts in this way, he couldn't have written those monstrosities we can read, for example in "The Age of the World Picture," about Protagoras's "man is the measure of all things."[362] For Heidegger, this statement in no way expresses the relativism that has been read in it down the line—and that Protagoras, for all that, confirmed elsewhere—but rather means approximately (I'm quoting from memory): "Man is measure of the presence of things present, of the non-presence of those that are not." That's just pure Heidegger, who turns Protagoras on his head. And that's just one example among many others, i.e. a symptom, if you will. For, Heidegger never succeeds in seeing in Greek culture either this fundamental conflict <between being and appearing>, or the tragic—the word is weak—dimension of its imaginary grasp of the world. We'll speak again about this with regard to his interpretation of the famous chorus of the *Antigone* mentioned just previously, which is also wholly aberrant, and which mutilates the text and the thing itself—Greece in this case—as much as in the interpretation he gives of the statement of Protagoras.

---

362. *Eds.*: See Martin Heidegger, "The Age of the World Picture," in *Off the Beaten Track*, trans. Julian Young and Kenneth Haynes (Cambridge: Cambridge University Press, 2002), p. 78:

> "Because we have long been accustomed to understand Greece in terms of a modern humanistic interpretation, it remains denied to us to think being as it opened itself to Greek antiquity, to think it in a way that allows it its ownness and strangeness. Protagoras' statement reads:
>
> πάντων χρημάτων μέτρον ἐστὶν ἄνθρωπος, τῶν μὲν ὄντων ὡς ἔστιν, τῶν δὲ οὐκ ὄντων ὡς οὐκ. (cf. Plato's *Theaetetus* 152a)
>
> Of all things (those, namely, that man has around him in use and usage, *chrēmata chrēsthai*) man is (in each case) the measure, of what presences, that it so presences, of that, however, to which presencing is denied, that it does not presence.
>
> The being whose being is up for decision is understood, here, as that which is present in the sphere of man, arriving in this region, of itself."

Heidegger, ultimately, says that the Greeks interpret being as presence, and that this is at once the profound truth of philosophy <and perhaps also the origin of its deviation>. No. For the Greeks, being isn't presence but *peras*, determinacy. And presence is just a modality of determinacy. That's why, you recall, I started this year with the idea of chaos, always there in Greece, which comes back in philosophy as *apeiron*, or as matter, or as the *chōra* of the *Timaeus*. Once again, to privilege the grasp of the world as presence is to miss what's essential, the nucleus of the ancient Greek world, and thus to distort the meaning of the texts one interprets. This is what Heidegger does from the beginning with Homer and the famous line on Calchas in the *Iliad*, Calchas who knows what is, what will be, and what has been; and this becomes, in Heidegger, what is present, what will be present, what has been present, indeed with no regard for philological accuracy.

But what separates me most profoundly from him is his central thesis, which he calls the ontological difference, i.e. the question of the being [*l'étant*] as radically distinct from that of being [*être*]. Heidegger belongs to the onto-theological tradition precisely in virtue of this distinction between being [*être*] and the being [*l'étant*], which he wants to make central, and which is foreign to the Greek world. For the Greeks, there's no question of being [*être*] separated from the question of the being [*être*] of beings [*étants*], and this is why one doesn't ask *ti to einei*, which would be entirely possible grammatically speaking, but rather *ti to on*, what is being/the being [*être-étant*].[363] And Plato and Aristotle therefore pose the question in this way, even if, for the latter, his vacillation on the meaning of what he calls *prōtē philosophia* has troubled many interpreters. For, sometimes he seems to say that first philosophy speaks of being [*être*] as such, without considering any being [*étant*] and sometimes that it speaks of the being [*étant*] *par excellence*, i.e. that which fully realizes what we call being [*être*] and which is for Aristotle thought self-thinking itself, which he also calls god. But Heidegger's distinction cannot exist for Aristotle; never does he separate being [*être*] in this way, nor indeed as a simple term that would apply simply to all things like an abstract universal, as Hegel would say. Lastly, this Heideggerian ontological difference is nothing other than an embodiment of the central thinking of theology, which enforces an infinite distance between something, God, and everything else, creatures.

Do we have an idea of the relationship that might have existed between Buddhist thought and Greek thought? Were there correspondences?

---

363. *Marg. C.C.*: Τὸ δ'εἶναι οὐκ οὐσία οὐδενί, Aristotle <*Posterior Analytics*, II, 7, 92b13>.

We know nothing, at least nothing positive. Certainly, in the Hellenistic era, when religion took on mystical, orientalizing aspects, stories began to circulate about the voyages of Pythagoras to the Indies, the resemblances between Heraclitus and Zarathustra (Zoroaster), and so on. Doxographers are full of them; I don't remember which one makes Plato into a Greek Moses.[364] And the philosophers who followed the campaigns of Alexander certainly also played their role in this affair. But, like Guthrie and already Burnet, I believe that if there was influence, it's a lot more logical to think of a Greek influence on Hindu thinking, precisely because of Alexander's campaigns. We know the results of this influence on statues: it's the famous Greco-Buddhist sculpture and its Buddhas that resemble *korai*. But that doesn't change anything regarding the originality of what unfolds in India and in China as well in the fifth century, i.e. during Jaspers's famous "axial age," the age of cultural creations with religious and philosophical tonality, although without connection to some kind of political activity, i.e. to the establishment of a public space for thinking, of a public synchrony and diachrony, open to all. You'll find immense literature on this question of influences and origins since it's a sport that has always inspired people, even if, beyond a certain threshold, it no longer makes any sense.[365]

364. *Eds.*: Numenius of Apamea, a Neoplatonic philosopher of the third century, wondered what Plato could be other than a "Moses who spoke attic." See fragment 8 in Atticus, *Fragments*, ed. Edouard des Places (Paris: Les Belles Lettres, 1973). See also Burnet, *Early Greek*, p. 16; and Walter Burkert, "Oriental Wisdom Literature and Cosmogony," in *Babylon*, pp. 49–51.

365. *Eds.*: This is especially so if it ends up in a veritable suppression of the object itself as, for example, in Hesiod's case. It is undeniable that there are Eastern sources in Hesiod's cosmogony as well as Sumerian, Babylonian, Phoenician influences, and so on. See Kirk, Raven, and Schofield, *Presocratic*, pp. 43–46; Kirk, *Myth*, pp. 288 ff.; Vernant, *Origins*, pp. 110–112 and bibliography p. 135; West, *Theogony*, pp. 19–31 of the introduction ("Prolegomena"), as well as the bibliography on "Hesiod and the East," pp. 106–107. But such observations end up sometimes in "extremist" formulations such as the following one from Jacqueline Duchemin, *Mythes Grecs et sources orientales* (Paris: Les Belles Lettres, 1995), p. 100: "The Hesiodic poems have received so much from the Near East that one can, at the limit, consider that everything in them comes from the lands of Asia Minor, and that their essential role, in the history of literary works and myths, consisted in introducing into Greece the content of great mythological poems developed, since Sumer, by the great civilizations and ancient religions of near Asia."

Supplemental Materials (1979–1999)

Translated by María-Constanza Garrido Sierralta

Appendix A. Reports on Teaching

Cornelius Castoriadis

1980–1981 and 1981–1982: Institution of Society and Historical Creation

During the two years of 1980–1981 and 1981–1982, the seminar was dedicated to the question of the specificity of the social-historical as a region of being.

An introductory framing sketched out the limits and aporias that the exact and natural sciences (mathematics, physics, biology) are encountering in the present stage of their development, i.e. the shock rendered against the dictatorship of ensemblistic-identitarian logic and deterministic closure. Without seeking confirmations through "positive" knowledge—nor fearing refutations by it—it is important to notice that the idea of creation, formerly scandalous, no longer seems irreconcilable with the state of this knowledge in its privileged domains.

Society can only be thought of as creation of itself, i.e. as creation once and for all (institutions, social imaginary significations) and as continued creation (history in a narrow sense, social regimes, and particular historical entities).

At the beginning of this creation there is a "contingent" fact, namely the emergence of the human species with its aberrant (or monstrous) biological particularities. The unfitness for life which is characteristic of the human *qua* simple living being results from the rupture of the living being's functional regulations due to the emergence of the human psyche and its singular features. These include: the reign of the radical imagination, which breaks with the ensemblistic-identitarian "understanding" of the animal; the disassociation of psychical pleasures and bodily pleasures; and the defunctionalization of pleasure. The psyche is a monad that is self-centered and riveted to the pleasure of pure representation.

After the fact, the institution of society appears as the response that allows for the survival of the human species; but, obviously, this could not provide us with any "explanation." The social-historical is a field of creation that makes itself exist while making exist the institution and the social imaginary significations that incarnate it. The individual, resultant from a process of social fabrication, is possible only by means of the violent imposition of forms on the psychical monad, i.e. forms for which no production or deduction, whether formal or material, is conceivable: language, rules, values, objects, reality, world.

While indissociable, psyche and society are irreducible to one another. The attempts to derive the social from the psychical or, inversely, to see in the psychical merely the effects of the social are failures. We see this concretely through the analysis of what the institution of society must obligatorily provide to the psyche for it to survive and of what the psyche must obligatorily accept in order to enter into the world. These reciprocal constraints provide—trivialities aside—the only invariants, the only universals of institutions in history.

Among these universals, the most important is that the institution of society must provide *meaning* to the psyche. This is one of the "functions" of social imaginary significations. To the extent that this meaning is presented and imposed as incontestable and not open for discussion, society institutes itself as heteronomy. It then also provides an extra-social (intangible and inaccessible) guarantor of meaning, which it posits at the same time as the source of the institution. It turns out that society creates itself, almost everywhere, almost always, as heteronomous, or religious, society.

Heteronomous or religious society is not necessarily divided in the strong sense of the term (i.e. in an asymmetrical and antagonistic way). The appearance of the social division—or of the state's domination, which amounts to the same thing—represents in turn a new historical creation. It presupposes the positing of significations that are not causally produced, nor logically or metaphysically derivable.

Nor does the reality of domination cause the struggle against domination, and even less so the struggle for an autonomous institution of society.

The appearance of societies that challenge and call into question, even partially, their own institution represents an ontological creation of another degree: it is an *eidos* that transforms *itself qua eidos*.

1982–1983 and 1983–1984:
Institution of Society and Historical Creation

The seminar spanning the previous years had tried to show that with the appearance of societies that challenge and call into question, even partially, their own institution, we witness an ontological creation of a new type, i.e. of an *eidos* that transforms *itself qua eidos*.

The seminars from the years 1982–1983 and 1983–1984 have focused on putting this idea to the test, making it explicit, and elucidating it based on the decisive example of ancient Greece and, specifically, of the creation of democracy and philosophy. Inseparable in the fact of their genesis, democracy and philosophy are in fact also indissociable at the level of signification. In both cases, the dominance of the inherited institution—gods and tribal representations, or the law which is simply found there—is challenged and called into question. In both cases, a new relationship is instituted between both man and truth—i.e. the opening of a public space of discussion, the creation of an individual who makes his or her thinking the measure—and, similarly, between man and law—i.e. the human positing of the law after the deliberation and decision of the *dēmos*. In both cases, a movement without possible closure is inaugurated, i.e. boundless interrogation regarding truth and interminable contestation regarding justice. Finally, in both cases, human activity explicitly recognizes that it cannot have recourse to an external jurisdiction; even if political activity or philosophical activity come to posit "external" criteria for justice or for truth, they recognize that *they* are the ones who posit them.

The "causes" habitually invoked to "explain" this creation do not explain anything at all. No meaning may be attributed to the expression, "the state of productive forces in the fourth century explains the theory of predication in Aristotle." Moreover, these "explanations" contravene the elemental principles of scientific explanation by passing over in silence the major counter-examples that can be brought forth in opposition to them. Greece did not have a monopoly on slavery; but it did indeed have one on democracy and philosophy. The hoplite phalanx was equally present in both oligarchic and democratic city-states. According to all attributable "conditions," Rome *could have been* another Athens. But it was not another one, nor the opposite; between their two worlds there is no relationship (except obviously that of influences).

Even prior to the emergence of the *polis*, we may discern the germs of its creation in the first imaginary grasp of the world and of life by the Greeks, inasmuch as it is expressed in religion and myths. We find enough of a prefiguration there of what would become explicit afterwards in the creation of both politics and philosophy for us to be able to say that the Greek myths are, quite simply, true. Hence, we have the theogonic myths: what exists arises from out of Nothing (void, i.e. Hesiod's chaos); all power, even divine, is arbitrary, founded on force, and transient; there is no conflation of being and value. Hence, likewise, we have the positing of the monstrous, of the non-human, as one who is ignorant of laws and deliberative assemblies (Cyclopes). Hence, lastly and especially, we have the categorical refusal of the illusions of *post mortem* salvation, indicated by the miserable status of the souls in the underworld (*Nekuia*).

Among the representatives of this inaugural phase of philosophy, the seminar highlighted Anaximander and Heraclitus, who were discussed at length both because they were the closest to the imaginary core of the Greek grasp of the world—with genesis and destruction being subject to a law that is beyond human meaning and non-meaning—and because they exhibit as of the sixth century the accomplished freedom of spirit.

The institutions of the democratic *polis* were analyzed based on those of the Athenians, considered not as a "model" or a finished form but as translating a process of explicit, continued self-institution throughout almost four centuries. The Athenian direct democracy implies that the political body legislates and governs in person; it requires an effective participation of the citizens in all the affairs of the *polis*, i.e. a participation that is in turn encouraged and stimulated by explicit measures and by the general ethos of the community. This goes hand in hand with the refusal of "representation," of "political expertise," and of the constitutional illusion. Finally, the democratic *polis* does not have and is not a "State," in the modern sense of the term; it *is* the community of the citizens. "Athens" is a geographical expression; the political term is "the Athenians."

Through its refusal to found itself on extra-social norms, the institution of democracy encounters the question of the criterion for the laws as an interminable question, and it can know no other limit than its *self-limitation*. This self-limitation of the people's sovereignty—both *de facto* and *de jure* unlimited—even has formal institutions to make itself effective, such as the *graphē paranomōn*. But the properly political dimension of tragedy (which certainly is not the only dimension of it) is to be found in its function as an institution of self-limitation, which is illustrated by a detailed analysis of *Antigone*.

The calling into question of the institutions proper to the tribe, their relative relativization, is the condition for an observation of other tribes which would be capable of seeing in them similar or equivalent things. In the same way, the elimination of actions by supernatural agents is the condition for a reasoned research regarding the past. Thus, it was with Herodotus that ethnography and history became possible for the first time; and this is why it would take more than two millennia for them to become so again.

Appendix B. Political Thought[366]

Cornelius Castoriadis (1979)

Here is the central point of the matter: there has not been, up to the present, any genuine political thought. There has been, during certain periods in history, a real political activity and the thinking implicit in this activity. But explicit political thought has only been political *philosophy*, that is to say, the

---

366. *Eds.*: The text that follows, which has been succinctly introduced in the Editors' Introduction to this volume, is found in the Castoriadis archive in a box containing the essential research dating from the end of the 1970s to the 1980s used in the seminars at EHESS. It consists of fifty-six typed pages in three copies dated by the author as being from 1979. These different drafts have various handwritten annotations: some are common to all three (changes to some of the terms, moving some portions of text); others (marginal additions, references, corrections, etc.) are found in only one of these drafts. Some handwritten pages containing up to twenty lines were inserted in one of the duplicates; these were additions to be included into the body of the text. Finally, in other boxes of the same series, some only partially drafted, handwritten pages contained numbered references corresponding to the calls for footnotes in the typed text. These are explanations or simple references, sometimes incomplete, which we have almost always included as footnotes. These handwritten notes are obviously just rough outlines; some have posed problems for reading that we have been unable to solve. Our work consisted in merging these three versions (visibly contemporaneous) while integrating the inserts and notes. The undecipherable passages are indicated by ellipses in angle brackets <...>; the sections reconstructed by the editors are also in <angle brackets>, as in the main body of the seminars. Other handwritten annotations by the author in the body of the text have been placed in [square brackets].

To what has already been said about the context, it might be added that the during the summer preceding the seminars at EHESS, Castoriadis had been invited to Greece by the "Ionian Center of Chios" to give a series of lectures on "The Genesis of Democracy and Political Philosophy." These lectures, drafted and dictated in Greek, were followed by a public discussion. The content of these lectures largely overlaps with those of the seminars on Greece and the text we are about to read. Among the other presenters at the conference that summer, Olof Gigon should be noted in particular, with whom Castoriadis maintained an ongoing intellectual and friendly relationship; his remarks had Heraclitus as their main theme.

province of philosophy, subordinated to it, enslaved to metaphysics, chained to philosophy's non-conscious assumptions, and strained by its ambiguities.

This assertion may appear paradoxical. It will appear less so if we recall that by political I mean the lucid activity that aims at the institution of society by society itself, and that such an activity has a meaning as a lucid activity only within the horizon of the question: What is society? What is its institution? *With a view to what*, this institution? However, the answers to these questions have always been tacitly borrowed from philosophy, which in turn has dealt with them only by violating their specificity through beginning with something else, i.e. the being of society/history as beginning with the divine, natural, or rational being; creative and instituting activity as beginning with conformity to a norm given from elsewhere.

But the paradox is real. Philosophy is born in Greece simultaneously and consubstantially with the explicit political movement (democracy). These two emerge as calling into question the socially instituted imaginary. They arise as interrogations that are profoundly joined through their object: the established institution of the world and of society and its relativization through the recognition of *doxa* and *nomos*, which in turn also leads to the relativization of this relativization, in other words, to the search for an internal limit to a movement that is, in itself and in principle, interminable and indeterminate (*apeiron*). Take the question, "Why is our tradition true and good? Why is the power of the Great King sacred?" Not only does it not arise in an archaic or traditional society; it *cannot* emerge, and it does not make sense. Greece makes exist—creates *ex nihilo*—this question. The socially established *image* (representation) of the world *is not* the world. It is not simply that what appears (*phainetai*) banally differs from that which is (*esti*); this is something every primal human knows, as they also know that opinions (*doxai*) differ from truth (*alētheia*). Rather, as soon as it is recognized in a new depth—as soon as this new depth is, for the first time, excavated—this gap between appearance and being, between opinion and truth, becomes unbridgeable and is perpetually reborn of itself. This is so because we make it exist by our simple existence itself. We have access, by definition, only to what appears; and every appearance owes something to us. This is also the case for any organization of appearance or signification conferred upon it. "If horses had gods, they would be equine," said Xenophanes, Parmenides's master (DK 21B15). It is not necessary to be Greek to understand the implication: if our gods are "human" (anthropomorphic), it is because we are humans. And if we take away from the gods, from God, or from anything the canine, equine, or human "attributes"—i.e. Persian, Greek, Ethiopian, etc.—what remains? Does anything remain? Nothing remains, said Gorgias (and Protagoras); there remains the *kath' hauto*, the "in itself and for itself," said Plato, i.e. that which *is*, *as* it *is*, separately and independently of any consideration, of any "view" (*theōria*). Both answers are equivalent, rigorously speaking. Both abolish discourse and political community. This is irrelevant for Gorgias, but not for Plato. For the latter we must also find someone who may *see* what *is* without having this view add or subtract something essential in what is seen, nor alter the *that* which it is. Of course, this requires the abolition of any sensory relationship—"vision" is a pure metaphor—and of any perspective of vision and thus requires its actualization outside of space and outside of time; it requires, above all, a kinship or even, rigorously speaking, an essential identity between the one who sees and what is seen. In fact, it is only on this condition that what the seer would bring to the seen in his vision, which would come from himself, would not alter what is to be seen. This type of seer is the soul, once "purified" and recondensed to its divine nucleus. [*Manuscript addition*: Then one must re-descend and validate as much as possible the discourse, the mixture, the appearance, etc., which is an enterprise that is nearly impossible, even though for Plato this becomes an extraordinary, fertile ground that would nourish twenty centuries of reflection.[367]]

As Xenophanes's statement here cited shows, the gap in question (between appearance and being, between opinion and truth) is not rooted solely, and not completely, in individual subjectivity (which became the modern philosophical interpretation until the rediscovery of ethnology and "cultural relativism"). The differences between appearances and opinions, as with subjective differences, have always been able to be resolved in both archaic or traditional societies by recourse to the opinion of the tribe or to that of the community backed by tradition and identified automatically with truth. The peculiarity of Greece is the recognition that the opinion of the tribe does not guarantee anything: the opinion of the (Greek) tribe is but its *nomos*, its posited law, its "convention." This is convention, not in the sense of a contract (it is not in those terms or in that category that the Greeks thought the social) but in the sense of a positing, of an inaugural decision, of an establishing. (The opposition in the related discussions between *physei/nomō*, i.e. by nature/by law, is entirely homologous with the opposition *physei/thesei*, i.e. by nature/by a positing that results from a decision. These two terms are united in the

---

367. See, for example, Plato, *Timaeus*, <34b, 36d–e> on the <constitution> of the soul by the demiurge. The passage discussed at length in the treatise *De Anima* by Aristotle (Book III, <2, 425b 25: "the act of the sensible and that of sense (perception) is one and the same">) on *nous* refers back to the same idea, namely that a part of *nous* is the same in essence as the <existents>.

act of denomination by the legislator, *nomothetēs*, i.e. the one who establishes the law.) This *nomos* is without a doubt, in some of its aspects, the feat and the peculiarity of such and such city, tribe, or ethnic group. But it is perhaps also, in its most widespread aspects, the feat and the peculiarity of the human tribe in general: *nomō thermon, nomō psychron*, said Democritus; hot and cold exist only in and by "law," by "positing" (DK 68B117).

It is evident that this recognition is possible only through a radical rupture with the traditional attitude towards tradition. This attitude, which is an integral part of tradition itself, consists of the positing of the tradition, of one and only one tradition—ours—as sacred and saintly, not open for discussion, unquestionable, untouchable. Our tradition—religion, gods, God, etc.—is the only true one; all others are false (their gods are regularly defeated by ours). This positing is no longer tenable as soon as this tradition is recognized as being simple tradition, the transmission of an initial positing across generations that could be modified by a new positing. If the law is the law because it has been posited as law, we may posit another. This rupture is thus a *political* rupture, in the most profound sense of the term: the recognition by society of its possibility and of its power to posit its laws. And of course, this goes hand in hand with the arrival of another question: *Which* laws? What is a good law, or a just law, when the quality of the law starts being dragged into the realm of discussion?

Let us recap the main lines of the movement. For countless millennia, human societies institute themselves, and institute themselves without knowing it. Shaped by the obscure and silent experience of the Abyss, they institute themselves not to be able to live, but to hide this Abyss, the Abyss external and internal to society. They do not recognize it, in part, only so as to better cover it over. They posit at the center of their institution a magma of social imaginary significations, which "account for" the being-thus of the world and of society (but in truth, they *constitute thus* this being-thus), and which posit and fix orientations and values of individual collective life, which are closed for discussion and unquestionable. In fact, all discussions, all questioning of the institution of society and those significations which are consubstantial to it would reopen broadly the interrogation of the Abyss. Thus, the space of questioning opened by the emergence of society is closed as soon as it is opened. There is no questioning except of the factual sort; there is no questioning regarding the why and for-what of the institution and signification. They are exempt from being questioned and from contestation by the fact that they are posited as having an *extra-social source*. The Abyss has spoken, it has spoken to us; it thus is not—it is no longer—an Abyss. (Christians remain ever here.) And this remains true, whether it is an issue of an "archaic" society, without an asymmetric and antagonistic social division and without a State, or whether it is an issue of historical societies ("oriental despotism") that are strongly divided, involving a State, and are in fact always more or less theocratic.

The rupture takes place in Greece. Why in Greece? There is nothing fatalistic about it; it might have not taken place or might have taken place elsewhere. It also did take place, in part, in other places—in India, in China, around the same era. But it remained on the way. I can say nothing, I know of nothing to say about the reasons for the occurrence of this rupture among these people and not others, at this particular time and not at another. However, I do know why it was only in Greece that it almost went to the end, why it was there that history was put in motion in a different way, why it is there that "our" history begins and that it begins as a universal history in the strongest and fullest sense of the term. It was only in Greece that the work of this rupture was inseparably linked to and supported by a political movement and that interrogation did not remain a simple questioning but became *interrogative positing*, which means the transformational activity of the institution that at the same time "presupposes" and "entails"—therefore, does not fail to presuppose and does fail to entail but is *consubstantial* with—the recognition of the social origin of the institution and of society as a perpetual origin of its institution.

This political dimension both binds together and brings to their most acute power—within a totality that is at the same time coherent and conflictual, torn, and antinomic—the other components of the imaginary creation which the Greeks constituted and which constituted them as Greeks. This is an issue of their "experience," or better put: of their ontological-affective positing; of their positing of universality; of their liberation with regard to discursive questioning, which is to say that this questioning does not recognize any closure and likewise turns in on itself, interrogates itself.

The Greek experience, or their ontological-affective positing, is the discovery or de-concealment of the Abyss. This is without a doubt the nucleus of the rupture and without any doubt its absolute, transhistorical signification, i.e. its henceforth eternal character of truth. Here, humanity climbs onto their shoulders to look beyond itself and to look at itself, to notice its inexistence and to set itself to making and to the making of itself. There's a banality that must be repeated forcefully because it is constantly being forgotten and re-covered-over: Greece is first and foremost a tragic culture. The Western pastorals attributed to Greece in the seventeenth and eighteenth centuries, like Heidegger's profound commentaries, all amount to the same thing from this point of view. All of Heidegger's edifying fables on Greek philosophy are beside the point; he speaks of them like someone who has never read or understood a single tragedy, nor even Homer, who amounts to tragedy and anticipates all of them, i.e. Homer "the educator of all of Greece." What makes Greece is neither measure nor harmony, nor an obviousness of truth as "unveiling." What makes Greece is the question of *non*-meaning or of *non*-being. This has been stated in black and white since the beginning, even if the plugged ears of the moderns cannot understand it, or do understand it only by way of their Judeo-Christian consolations or their philosophical advice columns. The fundamental Greek experience is the unveiling, not of being or of sense, but of irremissible non-meaning. [*Manuscript addition*: The Greeks assert so strongly that being is, only because they are obsessed with the (obvious) certitude that, likewise, being is not, i.e. that its being is inseparably chained to non-being.] Anaximander (DK 12B1) stated this, and it is in vain to cleverly gloss his statement in order to obscure its meaning, which is that simple existence is *adikia*, "injustice," excessiveness, violence. Simply by the fact that you are, you offend against the order of being, which is therefore, likewise, essentially the order of non-being. And faced with this, there is no recourse and no possible consolation. The grinding wheel of impersonal *Dikē* tirelessly crushes all that comes to be.

The Greek gods—as Hannah Arendt rightly recalled—are "immortal," not eternal: Zeus is himself, according to Prometheus, destined to dethronement, and this was publicly displayed in Athens around 460 BC.[368]

For Anaximander, being is also *apeiron*: indefinite and indeterminate, indeterminable, unlimited, and without form, without term, and outside measurement. Greek term, measure, and harmony were created and conquered over and against this fundamental and originary Greek experience, which is by no means that of the Romans, nor that of Çakya Mouni, who had already answered by *accepting* Nothingness.

Certainly, this experience includes as a counterweight, or is weighed down by, an experience which is just as pervasive and strong of *physis* as a living and sensible order, i.e. as a regular self-generation, as a power carrying itself into act as Aristotle would say later, as a "natural" harmony and beauty. This is an experience that is condensed into the very term designating the world, i.e. *kosmos*, order, good order, form; this is that world that Plato describes in the *Timaeus* as an animal or again as a "blessed god" (*eudaimona theon*) and one that we can see as such still today and perhaps not for long, in August, at midday, from the summit of the Patmos, from "Homer's grave" at Ios, from

---

368. Aeschylus, *Prometheus Bound*, 907–910, 947–948, and 958–959.

a thousand other places in the country. But one would have to be vapid not to see that the supernatural beauty of this nature, the immeasurable laughter of this sea, the pacifying brilliance of this light render even darker the certainty of somber Hades, just as the azure translucency of the islands and mountains resting on the shimmering sheet renders even more unbearable the obscure and incessant agitation of our passion and of our thought. It is against the strongest possible experience of the plenitude of *physis*, against the phantasmatic nostalgia for the status of a dolphin in the Aegean, of a horse in Thessaly, of a cicada at Delphi, of our own plenitude if we could simply remain stretched out on the sand, drinking through every pore the heat of the sun, watching the huge wheel turn—and it is starting from the realization of our non-accord, i.e. of our strangeness, of the excess of being and of non-being which we represent in a *kosmos* that is self-sufficing—that the Greek world constitutes itself. What we have so often and so naïvely considered as its "natural" harmony is the most advanced and most extreme of artifices, which achieves through artistry the erasure of the traces of artificiality. It is as such that the Greek temple is cleverly planted there where it appears as having always been, from all eternity, called forth by the landscape. It renders itself, after the fact, a natural and indispensable part of it.

Anaximander's statement expresses in a language that is already philosophical but also still poetic—like that of Heraclitus, of Parmenides, of Empedocles—what is amply present in the tragedy that the *Iliad* is, and in the bundle of tragedies that the *Odyssey* is (in which we also find, for the first time, theater within theater and story within story). This is the eternally restarted cycle of injustice, of excessiveness, and of outrage leading to catastrophe and destruction. For, it is only in this way that order may be reestablished by *Dikē* and *Nemesis*. For the most part, this is also the point of view of Hesiod in the *Theogony* (eighth century BC). Such is the first reserve from which this culture constitutes itself, i.e. its first imaginary grasp of the world, which is found, throughout its mythical symbolization, to coincide with the truth of the world. Greek mythology is true; it is more than a mythology.[369] It is also from out of this reserve that the Greek response to the question—i.e. the question that this ineliminable non-meaning poses and poses to us—is constructed. It is a response that is developed in feats, in the activity of the people, the expression of which we find in the first philosophers as well as in the poets of the

---

369. For example, it is impossible not to see the universal truth in the myth of Narcissus, Oedipus, the struggle of generations throughout the *Theogony*, etc. In the myth of Narcissus, it is the whole of humanity that looks at itself and voices itself.

fifth century. This response is that which puts *self-limitation* at the forefront, both for the individual and for the people (*dēmos*), i.e. self-limitation which has the name law and justice. "The *dēmos* must fight for the law even more than for the walls of the city" (DK 22B44), said Heraclitus (end of sixth century). The Orphic versions of mythology in the same era and even in Pindar provide the same lesson, which is formulated in its most elevated form in *Prometheus* and the *Oresteia* (458 BC, when Socrates was twenty years old and Plato was to be born only thirty years later).[370] Politically (likewise ethically) everything had already been said.

But this first reserve also already contains another decisive component in this imaginary grasp of the world: universality. This is something we know, but Hannah Arendt was right, here again, to recall it recently: In the *Iliad* there is no privileging of the Greeks over the Trojans, and in truth the most human, most moving hero is Hector rather than Achilles, i.e. Hector who suffers a radically unjust fate and is deceived by a goddess (and not just any one, i.e. Athena) at the very moment he is about to die. Centuries later, a like attitude can be seen in *The Persians* (472 BC), where there is not one depreciating word directed at the formidable enemy who wanted to reduce Greece to slavery. The Persians and the Greeks are rigorously placed at the same level. The main character, the most moving and the most respectable in the play, is Atossa, the mother of the Great King. And what gets condemned and "punished" is the *hybris* of the individual Xerxes. (There's no need to bring up Euripides's *The Trojan Women*, 415 BC, where the poet presents his people to his people as a group of ignoble and demented criminals, without faith or law; and he wins second prize.) Again, in *The Persians*, I do not think we have noticed as of yet the immense importance—philosophical and political and beyond—of the definition of the Athenians given by the poet. When Atossa asked (even though the war was not yet over, since the Battle of the Eurymedon took place in 468 and peace was not concluded till 449) to be instructed on Athens and its people, the chorus's brief response culminated in this line: "They are neither slaves nor subjects to other men" (v. 242). This is the definition of the Athenians by an Athenian, through which we can condense today and for all time a political program for the whole of humanity.

This universality is also expressed not only through the interest in the lives and customs of other people but through the impartiality of the gaze, which

---

370. It is obvious that "literary" testimonies have a completely different role for understanding Greek culture than, for example, contemporary culture. Literature was not *separated* but was truly like the most direct expression of the spirit of the people. I am not speaking here of a *description of a reality*, but the *expression* of the social imaginary, of norms, etc.

of course presupposes a relativization of laws, of norms, of the very words of the tribe. It would take twenty-five centuries for Western "scientific" history and ethnology to be able to regain a portion of Herodotus's objectivity.[371] From the outset, it places on a same footing the "memorable actions of both Greeks and barbarians"; describes the customs and institutions of the latter without ever emitting a value judgment; and is eager to show that a particular deity or Greek practice was borrowed from the barbarians. But already before Herodotus by 150 years, Hecate, Thales, and Solon carried out "philosophical" voyages.

The Abyss is Abyss, and it is vain to try to pass over it. The recognition of this fact goes hand in hand, virtually, with the recognition of this other fact, namely that *our* institution of the world—which means our way of living with the Abyss and our impossible and inevitable compromise with the Abyss—contains a relative, arbitrary, and conventional component. It is only from there that interest in other societies' institution is authentically possible (i.e. that geography becomes something more than entomological curiosity or instrumental knowledge in the service of trade or war) and that impartiality becomes possible with regard to them.[372] But it is also by means of this positing—here again, there is no logical or real priority (i.e. it is a circular implication)—that there can arise *interrogation* (i.e. philosophy and thinking in the strong sense of the term) as the questioning both of what is capable of not being conventional, arbitrary, or relative in our institution of the world and of society—including in appearances, as also in our opinions, in our laws, and in our language—and as a questioning bearing on what is to be done. In both cases, this is a search for a limit to arbitrariness, or for the possibility of relativizing the relativization.[373] We are always within *doxa* (opinion). However, if there is *only* opinion, there is no longer any opinion (and even this is impossible to say with certainty: that we are always within opinion). To nature (*physis*), infrangible and immutable even in its changes, are opposed the laws of human communities (*nomoi*), contingent, conventional, and arbitrary, whose extreme variability does not prevent the survival of people who believe in them, nor of the opinions of such people that they are good

---

371. Let us not hastily qualify this judgment as excessive: most French, English, and German historians write a French, English, and German history respectively.
372. *Marginal Note*: The same situation in the West in the seventeenth and especially in the eighteenth century.
373. Quarrel over the *phusei* or *thesei* character of language: <...> Heidegger wrote, "Greek is not a language, but the language." A Western hyperbole that ignores the following: It is because the Greeks recognized that Greek is *only a* language <...> that they were Greeks.

and the only ones who are good. Yet, we cannot live without law; and as soon as we have ceased to grant a thoughtless privilege to our law, we cannot live without asking ourselves: What law is good, and what is law?

But what produces Greece is not the simple contemplative recognition of appearance as appearance and opinion as opinion; it is not a variant of a Buddhist vision. Just as essential as the recognition of the Abyss is the decision and the will to confront the Abyss. *There is something to do*, and *there is something to think and to say*, in a world where nothing assures in advance the value of doing or the truth of thought and speech. And this practical-effective dimension of the Greek institution of the world and of society, the *activity* that is expressed in the creation both of mathematics and of legislation, brings us to the political roots of the constitution of the Greek world.

For, it is not from out of a philosophical reasoning and by means of it that the posited law, the tradition, the received institution are called into question in Greece. If democracy in Athens is not fully established until Cleisthenes, around 510, this was the culmination of an effective social and political movement that was already old, in many of the city-states and in Athens as well, going back around two centuries. The period is obscure and my objective here is not history. What matters is the calling into question, the contestation by the people's movement of the traditional oligarchic regime, whose signs were clearly there as of the beginning of the seventh century. The *dēmos* struggles against power's instituted forms; it struggles against tradition. This struggle is already implicitly a "philosophy"; that is, it unveils the essence of political tradition as *simple tradition*. From this point of view, what matters is not the complete formation and acquired victory by democracy but rather the questioning, which is raised and practically asserted, of the validity of a simply inherited political order.

The chronological and even essential priority of this political jolt on the philosophical movement in the narrow sense is not something doubtful (we place Thales's maturity at around 585). But in a different sense, there can be no question about priority. Before the philosophers, the *dēmos* did philosophy in action. It did not do so in the general sense, in which all people in responding to the question of the meaning of the world do philosophy. Rather, it did it by contesting in and through its actions—which do not and cannot function without discourse and discussion, argumentation and reflection—the idea of a law given once and for all and sacrosanct because simply given. And thus, it did it by raising the question of both the content and the source of the law and by desiring to respond by defining itself as this source, the seat of effective power, of legislative capacity, and of the exercise of justice.

The beautiful formulation by J.-P. Vernant is that Greek reason is the daughter of the city.[374] This is without a doubt true, if we take reason in a relatively restricted and "technical," almost professional sense. However, in a more originary sense, we must say that city and reason were born together and can only be born together. In order to transform the *polis* from a simple enclosure and fortified shelter into a political community, the *dēmos* must create *logos* as a discourse exposed to control and critique by everyone and by itself, and must not lean back upon any authority that is simply traditional. And reciprocally, *logos* can be effectively created only to the extent that the movement of the *dēmos* establishes in action a *public and common space*. This is a space in which for the first time in the history of humanity (insofar as we are aware) there become possible and real: display of opinions, discussion, and deliberation; the equality without which discussion would have no meaning and the discussion which achieves this equality (*isēgoria*); and the freedom that these presuppose and entail (*parrhēsia:* responsibility and obligation to speak). Without this public and common space, a condition that is not material or external but essential and fundamental, philosophy in the strict sense could not have been born, or would have remained a servant of a religion or of an established institution of society, as was the case in the East. And this public space is not only synchronous; it is also and above all diachronic, temporal, *historical* in the strong sense. This is the creation of a public time of thinking, in which a continuous dialogue with the past is made possible, in which the present is neither absorbed in the simple repetition of a tradition, nor condemned to only possibly emerging through new foundations that are inspired or revealed and must be kept withdrawn from discussion. It is a space that will remain, by right, forever indestructible. The last solitary philosopher who, hiding his thoughts, would survive under a global totalitarian regime would be a philosopher inasmuch as he would continue to dialogue ideally and effectively with the line of philosophers that begins with Greece and, more generally, so long as he would situate himself by postulation in this public and common space of the search for truth, of confrontation, of reciprocal control and sifting of opinions that have been opened up or, more exactly, created for the first time and forever by the *dēmos* of the Greek cities. What is at stake in this space is not in fact solely what is to be done here and now but what the law should henceforth be; not just the establishment of the facts or

---

374. Jean-Pierre Vernant, "The Formation of Positivist Thought in Ancient Greece," in *Myth and Thought among the Greeks*, trans. Janet Lloyd and Jeff Fort (New York: Zone Books, 2006), p. 397.

the opportunity for such and such act or application of the law, but rather the goal of these acts and the law as such in itself.[375]

This political activity, this self-institution of the city—a partially explicit self-institution for the first time in history—is at the same time thought.[376] It is not only and not entirely the thought of philosophers and by philosophers; it is thought of the people and by the people. Here again, in considering this phase of history, we must take into account the heavy censure to which the autonomous activity of the people is always subjected by the "official" memory, which is more or less the only one, of history.[377] We must reconstruct what is essential from the echoes that we find not in the philosophers but in the poets and the historians, i.e. in Aeschylus (in *The Suppliants, The Persians, The Oresteia*), in Sophocles (*Antigone*), in Herodotus, or in Thucydides, to cite only the most important examples. Herein lies the decisive proof in my view. What Herodotus posits—during the famous discussion on the respective merits and demerits of the three regimes (Book III, 80), i.e. monarchy, oligarchy, democracy—as the definition of democracy, as expressed by Otanes, is the *drawing of lots* for those who must exercise any office. This is a fundamental and accurate idea that I plan to return to but also an *idea that could never have crossed the mind of a philosopher as a philosopher*, i.e. an idea the popular origin of which is obvious. Similarly obvious is the non-learned origin of the other decisive idea of democracy, i.e. of the power to be located "in the middle" (*en mesō*), whose origins we have been able to trace back far prior to the birth of explicit philosophy.[378] The pinnacle of this thinking of democracy and of politics is obviously Pericles's "Funeral Oration" in Thucydides (Book II, 35–46). It does not matter whether Thucydides's text is literally faithful to Pericles's speech (it is certainly faithful to his spirit) or whether Thucydides invented it from *a* to *z*. It is an Athenian from the late fifth century who is speaking (Thucydides, himself a general in 424, probably

---

375. This aspect, which to me is obviously the most important, is not taken into account by H. Arendt's analyses, which are otherwise admirable, e.g. in Arendt, *Human Condition*; in *On Revolution* (New York: Viking Press, 1963); and in the essays in *Between Past and Future* (New York: Viking Press, 1961), especially "What Is Authority?"
376. See Vernant, "Geometry and Spherical Astronomy in Early Greek Cosmology," in *Myth and Thought*, pp. 203 and 206.
377. I have highlighted this point since 1964, i.e. see "Le rôle de l'idéologie bolchevique…," collected in *L'Expérience du mouvement ouvrier* (Paris: UGE, collection "10/18"), pp. 385–416, and in *Quelle démocratie? Tome 1* (Paris: Éditions du Sandre), pp. 191–212.
378. See Jean-Pierre Vernant and Pierre Vidal-Naquet <see texts cited in this volume, note 22, page 27>.

APPENDIX B. POLITICAL THOUGHT   261

died around 400) and who shows that these thoughts could be thought and plausibly exposed to a people who could recognize itself therein.

The culmination of this movement is Athenian democracy, which during the century of its maturity was home to a creation without analogue in what preceded it and in what followed it, up to today. And it knows and affirms itself as such, ("[...] in summary, I say that this city is the educator of all of Greece [...] we have no need for any Homer to laud us," says Pericles in Thucydides, Book II, 41, 1; 41, 4). This democracy tragically fails; it fails because of *hybris*, because it overlooks itself, because it does not succeed at self-limiting itself or universalizing itself. It is defeated in the Peloponnesian War, after which the city, despite its efforts, despite an intense political and spiritual life, enters the path of decline. It itself planted the germs of this war, of its defeat, by restricting freedom, equality, and justice to the narrow space of the city.

This defeat of Athens, equivalent in fact to the historical defeat of democracy, had incalculable historical results—and as for what concerns us here, it fixed the course of political philosophy for over twenty-five centuries. Explicit and developed political philosophy began with Plato and up through the present remains within Plato's orbit, within his manner of posing problems even whenever it challenges the solutions. Yet, Plato and his political philosophy—and his philosophy in general (but here I can only make certain allusions)—are the result of the defeat of Athenian democracy. Plato's political philosophy does not "arise" from Socrates's conviction as such.[379] This conviction, for an incomparable genius such as Plato—no matter what feelings of pain or anger there might have been—could only be at most a sign, a sign that he interpreted among many others. But it carried an immense weight in the context that followed 404, and even 416, in the proliferation of a host of other signs that were all seen as bearers of the same signification, namely the incapacity of democracy to find in itself its own measure and limits, or what amounts to the same, to effectively achieve justice. Despite the beauty of Péguy's statement—a city where a single man suffers injustice is an unjust city—a mind such as Plato's would have never condemned a man, a city, or a regime over a single act of injustice.[380] Plato condemns Athenian democracy

---

379. Here, I profoundly disagree with H. Arendt <...>, for reasons that we will see in what follows in this text.
380. Plato's greatness in this respect is proven once again, if one needs more proof, by the sublime role he gives to Aristophanes in the *Symposium* (around 380? [*sic*]), who nevertheless had also been <...>, in a sense, responsible for Socrates's conviction, as it clearly says in the *Apology*. <Péguy's statement referred to above is from *De Jean Coste* (Paris: Gallimard, 1937), p. 32: "[...] if one single man is knowingly held or, what amounts to the same thing, knowingly left in misery, that is enough for the entire civic pact to be null;

due to its defeat and on that basis. Certainly, this is not a cynical Hegelianism, but it is based on what he believes he can extricate as the causes of this defeat and as the profound connection of these causes along with the very nature of the democratic regime. If you will allow me the argument, i.e. a fiction for purposes of illustration: Plato's political philosophy would have been inconceivable in an Athens that would have extended up through the year 350 the life that was its own up through 430. The condition under which Plato would become Plato, and under which philosophy in general (and political philosophy in particular) would thenceforth definitively take on the orientation that would predominantly characterize it, is this failure of democracy. It is not because Plato introduces a new interpretation of truth as the adequacy of representation with its object that his philosophy, and philosophy as such, thenceforth takes a peculiar path, as Heidegger would have it.[381] It is rather because Plato must (or believes he must), when faced with this failure, seek out an indubitable object by which to regulate both the representation as well as the norm for action (individual and collective). The conception of truth as adequacy with… is merely an implication. And what this conception—which is incontestable in the small affairs of knowledge just as in the domains already constituted, and is paradoxical to the extent of being unsustainable (but ineliminable, in the end) in the big businesses of knowledge—is opposed by is not an *alētheia* as the "unveiling" of Being, but the truth that *brings itself about* in and by the instituting movement of the city, in all its manifestations. These extend from the legislating activity of the people to the creation and exposition (representation) of tragedy; from the contradictory deliberations by the *dikastēria* to the construction of the Parthenon; from the sophists' exhibitions to discussions between philosophers and citizens in the *agora* or in the gymnasiums. Plato's ontology and political philosophy bring themselves about—certainly also as dependent on other contributions and factors—by means of the occultation and closure of the political problematic, which are themselves effects of the effective historical failure of democracy. To put it bluntly, with Pericles's "Funeral Oration," political thought, politics itself, reaches its summit and its provisory and interminable end. With Plato, there begins something else entirely, i.e. a political philosophy that is no longer political thought because it is immediately beside the question. In fact, its condition of possibility is a disregard for the fundamental fact that defines

for as long as there is a man outside [the pact], the door that is closed in his face encloses a city within injustice and hatred.">
381. See Martin Heidegger, "Plato's Doctrine of Truth," trans. Thomas Sheehan, in Will McNeill, ed., *Pathmarks* (Cambridge: Cambridge University Press, 1998), pp. 155–182.

the possibility of political thinking: the self-institution of society. The self-instituting activity of the *polis* had exploded into the world for almost three centuries and had done so explicitly. Plato's philosophy is possible only on the basis of the repression of this experience—a repression conditioned by what is considered its failure.

To see this more clearly, it is necessary to return to the origins of the creation of the Greek imaginary world. The primordial grasp is, we have seen, that there is no guaranteed signification of the world and of existence; or, rather, it is that the sole guaranteed signification is the non-meaning constituted, for each human being, by death's certainty (*Odyssey*, Book XI, <488–491>) and, for every being in the *kosmos* (gods included), by the *Dikē* which assures that being's destruction when the time comes. This, which I have called the discovery of the Abyss (or Chaos, *chasma*), goes hand in hand with the unleashing, the liberation of *hybris*, i.e. excessiveness, violence, insolence, outrage, insult, and injury. These two are inseparable (as some seem to be rediscovering today). We could even say that each one conditions the other.

However, there is more than a deep convergence; there is an essential identity between this imaginary grasp of the world and the Greek political (and philosophical) activity. It is because they perceive the world as Chaos that the Greeks construct Reason. It is because no law is given that we must establish our own laws. Greek *paideia* is something that is won against *hybris*.

What is the condition of *hybris*? That no meaningful norm is imposed; or, if we prefer, that no external limit, except catastrophe, comes by itself "naturally" to restrain human projects, aims, and activities. This is such that *hybris* cannot be foreseen and can only be corrected, redressed, and erased by catastrophe.

Chaos is not simple disorder. In the depths of the world there is a Chaos as an unspeakable disorder.[382] However, there is order in appearances, in the constituted world. This order is that of birth–destruction in their endless succession, and this order is un-meaningful. Further, as the expression of the chaotic, non-normed essence of human depth, *hybris* forms part, in a sense, of the mechanism of the restoration of order since by driving to excess, it provokes the catastrophe that reestablishes things. However, this reestablishment is neither consolation nor expiation. It simply is what it is. There is no connection between Greek *hybris* and Judeo-Christian sin. *Hybris* does not

---

382. The roots of the world stretch out towards a Chaos, sinking into an infinite without limit: Xenophanes, DK 21B15 and 16 [sic] [— Trans.: See DK 21B28]; Hesiod, *Theogony*, 726; Vernant, "Space and Political Organization in Ancient Greece," in *Myth and Thought*, p. 232.

transgress any commandment or law, human or divine. Polycrates did not violate any rule by being at the height of happiness. Only, he had too much of it, without even infringing upon others. Then in what sense did he have too much? He *was* too much; ultimately, he was, quite simply. As Anaximander says, simply existing is *adikia*, non-justice. The transgression we are dealing with here is transgression of an ontological condition of coexistence. There is multiplicity; there is succession. A being [*étant*] cannot take the place of all others, neither synchronically nor diachronically. If—to insert a subsequent thought here—each being [*étant*] tends to persevere in being [*être*] and in its being [*être*], even this (which would define the ontological consistency of each particular being [*étant*]) would be in contradiction with the ontological condition of coexistence of beings [*étants*], i.e. it would be *adikia* or *hybris*. Beings [*étants*] can only be together if the space for each—its place—and the time for each—its duration—has been measured out for them. *Dikē* takes care that this measure is respected. It lifts the contradiction and assures the continuation of coexistence by means of the continual destruction of particular beings [*étants*].

Human generations themselves provide a striking illustration of this: How would a human world be conceivable if immortal generations were added to immortal generations? This obvious point is mythically projected in the *Theogony* as well. Ouranos, then Chronos, since they procreate, must yield their place. Being is begetting; and begetting is condemning oneself to die, or if we are immortal by nature, to being dethroned. And this is independent of any "injustice" in the moral sense, of any foresight, of any preventive action. Chronos eats his children in vain. His *hybris* simply consists in that, having himself taken his father's place, he refuses to yield this place to his children.

Yet, what is sketched out on the basis of this fundamental grasp—and I repeat that this is *true* considered in itself—is, starting with Hesiod, and within the simultaneity and the consubstantiality with the political struggle in the city-states, another answer to the question of the order of the world and of society, an answer that is *creation*. Mythically and religiously, it is the development of a new conception of *Dikē*, which is brought about by way of the poets, first with Hesiod, the orphic cult, the philosophers; we find its full expression in Aeschylus and Pindar, nearly a century prior to Plato's maturity. Put briefly, it is the conception of *Dikē* as self-limitation, as *sōphrosunē*.[383] [*Marginal Note*: φρόνησις.] At the strictly political level, it is the creation of an institution

---

383. This is the meaning of Aeschylus's trilogy of *Prometheus*, in which Zeus himself becomes just only after a <long period of time>. See Mazon's commentary on *Prometheus*. See also Pindar <for example, the beginning of "Pythian 8," lines 1–15, or "Olympian 13," lines

where the struggling forces in the city no longer simply balance each other by their simple juxtaposition and violent opposition and the periodic catastrophes that result from them, but rather by a self-limitation by means of which power can no longer belong to one person or one particular category, but belongs to everyone and no one, i.e. is both placed "at equal distance" from everyone and can no longer be an object of appropriation. But also—and we must highlight this point just as strongly—it is equally "participated in" by all; and this is so in a way that is *simultaneously* collective (it is the *dēmos*, in its Assembly, i.e. *ekklēsia*, that legislates over all, and it is from the *dēmos* that the judicial assemblies, i.e. *dikastēria* and even, at least starting in the fifth century, a certain number of "civic priesthoods", are brought about by drawing lots) and individual.[384] (That is, every Athenian citizen may be assigned by drawn lot to be the president of the Republic, *epistatēs tōn prytaneōn*, for twenty-four hours. The statistical probability of being chosen once in a lifetime, during the Classic period, was of the order of 25 or 30%; and taking into account all the functions to which he may be nominated by drawing lots, he is guaranteed to exercise public functions several times during his life.) Thus, power is essentially demythified and desacralized, and democracy is concrete; it is in no way reduced to an abstract equality before the law. Strictly at the level of thought and philosophy, in the end, it is the simultaneous search, in the *kosmos*, for an order other than that of the simple succession of emergence and destruction and, in the *logos* that may say all things and can apparently show forth all things or at least render all things plausible, for the internal limits that may regulate its usage.

In short, there is at once: a discovery and dis-obstruction of the Abyss, of Chaos, as the experience of how the sole ultimate order that reigns in being is the un-meaningful succession of emergence and destruction; a recognition of how this same un-meaningful order rules (or would rule, left to itself) human affairs by means of *hybris*, *adikia*, and a *Dikē* that is only catastrophe; and an assertion of and will for how there is something to do and to say, the creation of another order, which can be founded only on the search for and imposition of a limit, which is thenceforth necessarily self-limitation.

The creation of democracy is, philosophically, a response to the un-meaningful order of the world and the departure from the cycle of *hybris*. It is so only because it contains simultaneously and consubstantially the recognition of how no other nature or tradition (or divine prescription) provides the

---

1–10, where *Dikē* is associated with *Eunomia* and with *Eirēnē* [Peace], with all three opposed to *Hybris*>.

384. See Vernant, "Space," pp. 235–262.

norm that could regulate human affairs. The *polis* establishes and creates its law, through a contingency that knows itself as such, and which asserts itself through acts, since the law (resulting from deliberation) is itself always subject to discussion and liable to amendment or repeal. This is the contingency of every particular law and the non-contingency of the very *fact* of the law.[385] In this way, this response is something completely different than a closure. The movement of the *dēmos* is *ipso facto*—just like, at the same time, additionally and identically, philosophy—an opening, although the word is precisely deceptive; it is *creation* and *constitution* of a public space of interrogation about being and appearance, truth and opinion, nature and law. This is not explicitly considered as in technical works; it is a thought in action, a thought that brings about, and brings itself about through bringing about. (Although its degree of explicitness as shown by what we see in Herodotus and Thucydides is considerable, despite not being the topic there.) But what the Greek world built itself up upon, as of seventh century, was these certainties: There is always a need for the law and always a questioning of the law; and as soon as there is a questioning of the law, there is a possible action aiming to amend the law. There is no reasoning or prioritizing here; there is a positing of an originary articulation that one can traverse in one direction or another. We can just as well say that we want to amend the law, and as soon as there is action aiming to amend the law, there is a questioning of the law. If we wish to amend the law, then we have already put it into question; and if we have put it into question, then we already want to amend it. In any case, we cannot live without law; but it is we ourselves who give ourselves the law, and whichever law. The law is a human work; it is the work of *anthrōpos* by which *anthrōpos* makes itself *anthrōpos*. *Anthrōpos* makes itself *anthrōpos* by giving itself a law, which means by instituting itself when its nature has no internal or natural limitation. *Anthrōpos zōon politikon* does not simply mean that the human is a "social" animal in a vague sense (or, to be precise, Aristotle obviously knew about hives and anthills, but he did not define the bee or the ant as "political animal"), as it has practically always been made out to say. What Aristotle says, in modern language, is that the human is an *instituting* animal, which exists only by its appearance and its participation in an instituted community and one that institutes itself (gives itself its laws).

In fact, when Marx defines the human as an animal that produces itself through labor, we can and we obviously must notice the anchoring of this conception in the era and the imaginary of capitalism, and observe that Aristotle's

---

385. This is so from Homer (*kuklōpes athemistoi*, at *Odyssey*, IX, 112–115) to Aristotle (*zōon politikon*, etc., *Politics*, I, 1253a4).

conception is both deeper and more universal. But we must also highlight that what Marx does in reality is to erect a particular institution—labor—into being the source-institution of all the others. But he can do this only because, precisely, he disregards the fact that labor itself is an *institution*, no matter its particular social-historic form, and because—although he cannot say it clearly—he sees in it a natural particularity of the biological species *Homo*, which comes to take on a central position in the social life of the latter, thus providing it with a "natural-rational" determination. By this very fact it is also provided with the apparent possibility of breaking the circle of reciprocal determinations of the different sectors of social life and the solidarity of the different dimensions of its institution.

And, of course, there is a co-substantiality of this definition of the human as "political animal" with the other definition—i.e. as *zōon logon echon*, the animal possessing *logos*—since there is only *logos* in and through the *polis*, and a true *polis* only in and through the *logos*.[386] There is no *polis* without the creation of a public space of questioning and of mutual checks; and such a space *is* already the *logos* in its effectiveness. This is clear from Heraclitus (*logos xunos*, DK 22B2) up through Aristotle, i.e., "That is why we do not give power to a man, but to *logos*" (*Nicomachean Ethics*, Book V, 6, 1134a34–35).[387] A statement that, however late it may be, can be understood only if from the start we take the terms literally. To whom, then, did the Athenians, and among them lived Aristotle (and he lauds their regime in the *Constitution of the Athenians*, as we will see), give power? Was it to a book that contained the *logos*, or to a High Priest of it? It was to their own legislative and deliberative assemblies, in which the *logos* was both, as speech and argumentation, the medium of the coexistence of citizens as citizens and, as proportion, measure, and reason, the only possible rule for this coexistence and for the activities that it founded. As, and as more than, an impersonal Reason, *logos* in this statement is the discourse that circulates between humans, which everyone participates in equally by right, and which, by means of this partitioning and this circulation, risks least of all being fixed once and for all in one place and being put in the service of a personal *hybris*. The *logos* here is the effective truth such as it makes itself in and by the city, i.e. as a common truth and also

---

386. Among the recent authors who have insisted on the relationship of the two aspects, we must again cite H. Arendt.
387. *Trans.*: On the debate about whether to read the term *logos* or *nomos* in this passage, see C. D. C. Reeve, "Notes," in Aristotle, *Nicomachean Ethics*, trans. C. D. C. Reeve (Indianapolis: Hackett, 2014), p. 266, note 374. Thanks to Enrique Escobar for assistance on this point and for correcting the French version's reference.

as a deployment of truth and not as the possession of a truth given once and for all.

During the ascending phase of this movement, philosophy in the strict sense accompanies it without pretending to replace it and without claiming for itself a sovereign place. Political activity opens the interrogation, and it responds to it. It lives, it gives a proof for movement by moving, it institutes the democratic city-state, defeats the Persian invader, builds the Parthenon, and creates tragedy, in which a man of genius, carried by the genius of a people, defines for all eternity what man is: neither slave nor subject of another man (Aeschylus, *The Persians*, v. 242). In its very activity democracy finds its certainty, the only kind possible. This is a certainty, moreover, that likewise philosophy alongside it, as not yet separated from "science," seeks out; and in some domains it establishes it, by creating rigorous demonstration: Thales, Pythagoras, Democritus.... But it is not due to a deficiency, a distractedness of mind, or a slowness or delay necessary for the progression of knowledge that no one or almost no one conceived, during this period, of extending the field of these rigorous demonstrations to include political affairs.[388] This is the wisdom that Aristotle would make explicit after Plato and expressly against him, namely that the rule of rigor in politics is not the same as in mathematics.[389] Aristotle is much more "classical"—and even, if we dare to say, more "Greek"—than Plato on this point and on many others.

Indeed, the struggle for the establishment of democracy and its victory opened up the problematic of the institution. They showed through actions that the source of institution is the instituting activity of the people. The city itself posited its own laws. It was perfectly able to endure the discussion and amendment of them. It showed itself capable of living and accomplishing the most difficult undertakings and the most sublime works during a period that was something quite other than a phase of historical tranquility. And this went hand in hand with—and in fact was made possible by—the recognition that nothing can determine in advance the content of the law, that there exists no extra-social norm by which one may regulate this content.

This is the practice of democracy. This is also the meaning of the famous dialogue between the spokespeople of the Athenians and the Melians, reported by Thucydides.[390] To the Melians, who argued that the action of

---

388. With the exception of Hippodamus of Miletus, whom Aristophanes mocks in *The Birds* <v. 1000–1009>, and who without a doubt played a role for Plato, notably in the *Laws*.
389. Aristotle, *Nicomachean Ethics*, I, 1, 1094b11–26.
390. <Thucydides, *History of the Peloponnesian War*, V, 85–111.> Here again, the literal fidelity of Thucydides's text does not matter. The discussion obviously summarizes the arguments

the Athenians—who wanted to force them into their coalition—was unjust, the Athenians responded that the question of just and unjust can only arise between equals; between unequals, force prevails. We are in the habit of reading this passage negatively, if I may say so—i.e. the negation of the possibility of a right embracing unequals—while its positive meaning is just as important, namely that between equals, right—and not force—must prevail and that reciprocally where right prevails, there is equality. Between equals, there is a discussion about right, and where there is discussion about right, there is equality. But what is this equality, where does it come from? Certainly, the boundary of democracy—and, in this precise case, the *hybris* that would lead to its defeat—is the refusal to ask, or even to envision this question beyond the frontiers of the city, i.e. between cities. (Nevertheless, quite obviously, there already existed an "international right": the relations among cities, even during times of war, were regulated in multiple ways. And it is certainly not for the twentieth century to boast of even the slightest progress in this respect.) The argument by the Athenians about the prevalence of force in the relations between unequals remains, of course, the expression of a reality, and the aporia of international right is still the same and by no means masked by the farce of the League of Nations or the United Nations, etc. Who establishes the rules of international right? Where does the *force* reside which would penalize potential transgressions—which today are more than ever a reality—of the rules of international right? But we cannot forget—nor assume such a forgetting by the Athenians—that this equality was something that democracy established, i.e. instituted "arbitrarily" as its own law inside the city, between people who had started out by being unequals, and who indeed remained so from every point of view *except* that of participation in power and their position before the law. How can there be a determination of *who* is equal, except based on an instituting action that posits equality and the category of individuals among whom this prevails? And how, once these equals have been defined, can there be a predetermination of the outcome of their discussion and deliberation on what right is? Where can the substantive, fixed, and once-and-for-all determined criteria be found? Who are the equals, what is right, and on what basis can the latter be determined? In truth, neither Plato nor Aristotle would be able to respond to these questions any better than democracy did in its actions; and, moreover, they did not respond at all. Plato *thinks* he responds by establishing a source and norm that is extra-social

---

and the political thought of the period. Let us recall the essential facts <...>: The Melians' arguments in the end tended to show the Athenians (a) that their action is unjust; (b) that it would go against their interests.

relative to the social norm, which means that he damns himself to radically overlooking what the social is and to dragging expressly along with him in this damnation twenty-five centuries of philosophy. Aristotle's superiority over Plato on this precise point consists in his explicit recognition that these questions can only remain open. That is, <in some matters>, "there is no just and no unjust in the political sense; because this latter (namely, the just and the unjust) is according to law and is for those for whom there is by nature law. These are those for whom there is equality as to the fact of governing and being governed" (*Nicomachean Ethics*, Book V, 10, 1134b12–14). The just and the unjust are defined by the law; in order to say that such and such political constitution is just or unjust, there would have to already be prerequisite law that this constitution would respect or would transgress.

But who would posit this law? A law can be posited only by someone (an individual or a collective body) that the political constitution, precisely, authorizes to posit laws. Any justification (or criticism) of the institution moves in a circle. The instituting power is originary; it is pointless to seek an external norm for it. The "by nature" of Aristotle is here a pure invocation of *fact*. "Those for whom there is equality as to governing and being governed" are not determined "by nature" in the sense that women carry children or birds fly. Aristotle knows quite well that "equality as to the fact of governing and being governed" was established before his eyes—the eyes of his memory— by a succession of historical acts, which he himself describes in detail in the *Constitution of the Athenians*, i.e. of all free citizens; and he knows that elsewhere it exists only for an oligarchy or for a single man, "equal" to himself. The political person says *who makes* the law, and this is necessarily "prior" to any law. The political person says who is equal with regard to the political, and in what way.[391]

Democracy means that the people *posits itself* as people who are equals in terms of power and the law. It thus also signifies that the people posits and declares right. On what basis? Let us recognize—and let us also recognize the greatness of democracy which consists in recognizing in action—this ineliminable feat: The people posits and declares right on the basis of itself, which means, in a sense, on the basis of *Nothing*. This means radically from nothing, if the Something that would be opposed to the Nothing here were supposed to be something guaranteed and determined outside of the self-determining activity of the people. (Quite obviously, recourse to a Something

---

391. Aristotle had already defined the just as "the legal and the equal" (*nomimon kai ison*). The aporias of how to define legal before the law, and of how to define equality, underlie the entire fifth book of the *Nicomachean Ethics*.

of this kind is pure illusion since, were this Something to exist, it would still be effective only inasmuch as it would be taken up in and by the self-determining activity of the people.) Democracy is the recognition of this fact, namely that to be free means understanding that one has no recourse counter to oneself. To be free is not to live in risk (the choice is denied to us on this matter, anyway) but to recognize that we are the only risk to ourselves and to accept as a matter of fact our being so. ("I fear much more our own mistakes than the devices of our opponents," says Pericles in Thucydides, Book I, 144, 1.) Democracy is the regime that has nothing to fear but its own mistakes and in which we have renounced complaining to anyone about what happens because we are (as far as is humanly feasible, i.e. *kat' anthrōpon*) the author of it. Democracy is effectively the regime that is at risk by its own deed. It has no guarantee against itself. The other regimes do not know the risk; they are always in the certainty of servitude. They are no more guaranteed against themselves than democracy; but they do guarantee slavery to all. Contemporary stupidity would like for the political to be the domain of existence, the only one, and one in which uncertainty would be absent. It emits terrified screams because nothing would come to limit, in the absence of transcendent norms, what a democratic and revolutionary regime could do, as if we were unaware that history in essence is filled with monstrosities committed by regimes laying claim to such norms. So this is where we are, after twenty-five centuries of political reflection.

Democracy is, in other words, the recognition of how the institution of society is always self-institution, how the law is not given to us by anyone but is made by us. It renders this fact *open*; it is explicitly self-institution since nothing limits the legislating power of the people, and since any limit that would be imposed on this power would again result from an act of this power (and could also be amended by such an act). (It is again legislative acts that, in Athens just as during the French Revolution, often prohibit in advance this or that proposal for law or threaten with penalties those who would formulate them.)

However, from another point of view, the only thing essential once we put aside infantile, made-up stories (for it is an infantilism which tries to find in a Constitution, whatever it may be, or in a series of divine commandments, whatever these may be, a guarantee of society against itself) is that democracy is the *only* regime that tends to realize—and in principle can, as much as humanly feasible, realize—the only limits realizable in the indeterminacy of society, namely internal limits, i.e. self-limitation. I will return to this question in the final chapter of this book. What must be recalled here is the putting to work of this self-limitation within Greek democracy—in particular the

Athenian case because it was the one that went the farthest, and it was the one that was historically the most important, and also for this reason, namely that it is the one about which we are least incompletely informed—and within the particular institutions in which it was embodied.

The first such institution, which moreover cannot even be qualified as a particular institution since it is equivalent to democracy itself, is the creation and constitution of a genuine *public space*. I already spoke about this above. But one could never emphasize enough this fact and its paramount importance to us today in modern conditions. Democracy is the only regime in which a real public space exists. Every other regime makes up part—and generally, the most essential part—of that which imports into the society a "secret of power." That is, should it concede even certain freedoms (of press, of opinion), not only are these genuinely *granted* and able to be revoked according to the good will of those who govern; but also, by the very fact that these are something gratis, they have, if I may say so, very little use. There exists a real public space only to the extent that there exists a *vital interest* of the citizens in this public space, and this interest exists only as part of or as bearer of their vital interest in the public reality—the *res publica*, i.e. *ta koina* as opposed to *ta idia*—which in turn can exist only to the extent that they *can* do something with respect to this public reality. A public space is not an entity created once and for all that functions on its own once a few freedoms of expression have been granted. I am certainly not disregarding the difference between a regime where freedoms exist and another where they are abolished; not only is it preferable to live in the first of these rather than the second, but politically important things are possible in one and not in the other. However, as the experience of most contemporary "democratic" societies shows, a formal public space loses its importance and signification to the extent that citizens are, by this or that process or mechanism, rendered passive in relation to the public reality; and they are fatally in this position to the extent that they rightly believe that they can do nothing or not much about it. At the limit—i.e. a limit that we have practically reached today—the public space, in these conditions, only serves the dissemination of pornography (sexual pornography is, of course, the least important; I am speaking of political and ideological pornography). This pseudo public space and the contemporary role of the media go hand in hand. The public space and the *agora*, as they existed in Athens, were driven by the active interest of citizens, something indissociable from what these same citizens were going to have to decide the next day on this or that law, on this or that public construction, on this or that foreign policy, or on peace and war, which they would have to carry out themselves.

It is only by means of such a public space, which is not something gratis, that procedures of discussion, of challenge, of checks, and, finally, of deliberation take on their meaning. This deliberation, which took place in the *ekklēsia*, has worth because the *agora* and the incessant discussion of common affairs exist. And conversely, it is because they know that there will be deliberation, and want it, that the Athenians discuss these affairs seriously. The intermediate condition here, which is in fact crucial, is *direct democracy*. We passionately discuss public affairs because we will have to decide for ourselves. There is no sense in discussing such things, with or without passion, if it is to elect "representatives" who, once elected, will be able to—and regularly do—do whatever they like. "Representative" democracy, which is in fact a negation of democracy, is the great political mystification of modern times. "Representative" democracy is a contradiction in terms, which conceals a fundamental deception.[392] And, hand in hand with this mystification goes the mystification of elections. Elections are not a democratic institution or procedure. It does not cross Herodotus's mind to present elections as a characteristic of democracy; democracy is defined, *inter alia*, by the *drawing by lots* for the magistrates. The first English trade unions would rediscover this profound truth in the nineteenth century, i.e. that the positions to be filled are filled on a rotational basis, which comes to the same. The Athenians draw by lot their magistrates. The elective positions for the most part are limited to generals for whom, by the nature of things (i.e. matters of the conduct of armies and military operations), a (collegial) unity of command is indispensable and an expertise and a skill make sense. This has a profound wisdom standing exactly opposite to contemporary senility: elective positions essentially concern tasks of technicality and expertise. It is not the experts who decide about who is an expert; it is the people who, quite rightly, decide: they have seen them at work. (Today, we know what the designation of "experts" by "experts" gives us.) But for political affairs there is, by definition, no particular expertise. (It is Plato who, as we know, would launch and "found" this deadly deception of a particular expertise, knowledge, or science that would enable one to govern humans. And he would do this, which aggravates his case, with full knowledge

---

392. We know that Rousseau—based on more or less objectionable considerations about the general will—saw and said, "The English people thinks itself free; it is greatly mistaken. It is so only during the election of the members of Parliament; as soon as they are elected, it is slave, it is nothing" (Jean-Jacques Rousseau, *Social Contract* <Book III, Chap. XV ("On Deputies or Representatives")>. I myself have written: "To decide who is to decide already is not quite deciding for oneself" ("On the Content of Socialism, II," <in Cornelius Castoriadis, *Political and Social Writings, Vol. II*, trans. David A. Curtis (Minneapolis: University of Minnesota Press, 1988), p. 98>).

of the facts, as the *Protagoras* and Protagoras's myth show, which indeed expresses, in mythical guise, the philosophy in act of democracy.)

This is not to say that democracy disregards differences of intelligence or political judgments that may exist between individuals: it <knows how to> *listen* to them and it is the sole regime assuring them that they will at least be heard. It is even more than that: democracy can and does confer on them not power but authority. The fact that democracy has admitted political men of the caliber of Miltiades, Themistocles, Aristides, Cimon, Ephialtes, and Pericles, and that it allowed them to play the role they played, this again is one of the unparalleled achievements of this regime. Democracy did not flatten things out into an equality of indifferentiation. Just as she was able to crown Aeschylus, Sophocles, Euripides, or Aristophanes rather than other competitors, and just as she was able to select Ictinus and Phidias for the construction of the Acropolis, so too was she able to recognize the political greatness of individuals she had herself fed from her bosom. We can be certain that the quality of silence on the Pnyx when Pericles rose to speak had to change. Thucydides went so far as to write, speaking of the Pericles years, that the regime was "democracy in words, but in fact the power of the first citizen" (*logō men dēmokratia, ergō de prōtou andros archē*, Book II, 6, 9). However, Pericles never exercised nor wanted to nor thought about exercising power outside and beyond the limits democracy traced out; he spoke in front of the people, he convinced them by giving them *reasons*. Applicable to him is, with more truth no doubt, Michelet's beautiful statement on Robespierre: "He desired authority; he never desired power." This is a border we will consider uncertain and permeable, certainly. However, here again, it is vain to seek absolute assurances. The authority of Pericles never, despite Thucydides, degenerated into power exercised by a one alone, bestowed upon him, incontestable. The Athenians were able not to have followed him in such and such circumstance; his political opponents were always able to act freely.[393] To the genius individual, democracy again offers the ideal field of action and realization, since it forces the individual to overcome himself, for it imposes onto the individual, as a counterweight and an antagonistic force to rise above, the criticism and the check of everyone.

This creation of a public space that supports deliberation and is supported by it is also a creation, as I have already said, of an *explicit diachrony*. The fact that there has not been any genuine history as explicit, documented, and critical collective memory except in two eras, and solely in those (and the

---

393. The generals were <moreover> "subject to repeal;" see the trial of the Arginusae.

rest of the time, only more or less intelligent and skillful chroniclers)—i.e. in ancient Greece and in modern times since the eighteenth century—is neither by chance nor a simple coincidence resultant from the fact that these two periods would also have been, besides, periods where knowledge was constituted and developed.[394] Democracy and history condition one another reciprocally. It is only in democracy that there can be explicit history, and democracy created both the *possibility* and the *need* for such a history. [*Marginal Note*: See Russian historians, for example, or even Chinese!] For, reciprocally, an explicit and critical historical memory is in turn a condition for the functioning and for the very existence of democracy. This memory is one of the institutions of the self-limitation of democracy and one of the manifestations of its search for relative points of reference for its actions, as soon as it is recognized, more or less overtly, that neither divine law, nor natural law, nor rational law, can dictate to society its law. In other societies, there is either ahistorical tradition, or else a chronicling supported by scribes, priests, or monks in secret for the exclusive use of theocratic or despotic (usually both) bureaucracy. What marks out the limits—and does so independently of any consideration relating to "progress" or otherwise of the "scientific spirit"—is that these pseudo-histories, these chronicles, can only be dynastic, princely, or caliphal genealogies, i.e. the *res gestae* of royal or sacerdotal potentates and the dominant circle surrounding them. According to tradition, Herodotus read his *Histories* during the Olympic Games in front of the Greeks all together.[395] And this history speaks about the actions of the Greeks and the barbarians, of the institutions of the ones and of the others. Even if it is teeming with stories and anecdotes related to kings and exceptional people, it is necessarily the history of the *people*. And modern historiography would become, once again, a historiography great and worthy of its name only when the French Revolution would force it to become, anew, the history of the people.

The people creates the law. I said that it creates it from out of itself, which is to say, in a sense, from out of Nothing. This itself implicitly brings with it, in any case, its own past. Obviously, each time, the people is already something; it is what it has made itself be so far. In a sense: Nothing. For, what it is does not provide any extra-social norm as to what it should do. It is not because the French have so far been accustomed to live this way that what they would

---

394. The great Roman historians, especially Tacitus, are obviously inconceivable without the Greek heritage, *and* also <progeny> of the Republic, even if they come much later.
395. See Pherecyde—and Thales congratulates him for having <poured into the community>, *en koinō*, the first work in prose (Vernant, "Geometry," p. 205).

do from this habit and this mentality would necessarily be good, i.e. good for them or good in general. "Nothing," also in another sense, i.e. because the people would be nothing if there were no power of creation, no instituting source. And what lies within this source, we can neither determine nor discern. But also, from another point of view, this Nothing is everything, i.e. everything that can be grasped as already determined at the moment of the creation of the law. The moment when I have to decide what I have to do, I am Nothing; from what I have already been, I cannot draw anything absolute and definitive as to what I have to do; and if I am truly doing, then I am doing something else. But also, I do what I do by means of my own history, i.e. what I have already made of myself, including as a capacity and possibility for doing, and this history is there, in any case implicitly. But, if it were there only implicitly, as buried, mute, and incarnated in what I am, then I would be fully non-conscious and alienated. Each time, I am in this specific and indescribable relationship with my own history—i.e. in the thickness of what I have already done and what I have made of myself—but I can communicate with that history. The same is true, *mutatis mutandis*, of the life of a people. Under despotism or under oligarchy—and even under the restrained, partial "democracy" under which we live—a people is condemned to not have a memory, or to endure a fabricated pseudo-memory, which amounts to the same, if not something worse. This memory—in other words, the diachrony of the public space of thought, or explicit, recorded, and critical history—is not a guide, nor does it include school lessons as to what is to be done. But it is a reference point, in the sense that it establishes a silent dialogue of the people with its only possible *alter ego*: its own past. It is not a response to the problems of the present, but experience and ballast; it is the diffused light that bathes historical creation, which prevents each new historical act from being an instantaneous, disjointed fulguration tearing apart with no further effect a Cimmerian night. That "those who ignore history are condemned to repeat it" does not mean that by knowing history one avoids falling back into the same errors, in a utilitarian and pragmatic sense. The blinding and obscure fact is that the rupture of historical repetition—this mummification of the past in the form of a perpetual present that tradition in the strong sense of the term effectuates—goes hand in hand in Greece as well as in the dawn of modern times with the explosive birth of what appears to be turned to the past but is rather precisely the opposite of tradition, namely explicit historical memory. Not only do they not exclude one another, but they imply and demand one another. Perhaps we will understand this less poorly if we recall—while amending it—Husserl's statement, "All tradition is forgetting of origins." All tradition is forgetting of *the* origin. It is not a forgetting of such and such determined origin, seeing as the tradition founds and secures itself by invoking *a* determined origin, which it makes into the *only* origin and the origin, period. Rather, it is forgetting of the fact that there was, *and there is always*, here and now, here in front of us, a possible origin and an actual origin, i.e. that we have the possibility of being origin. As the opposite of tradition, history as saving from oblivion the multiple origins that the past has been, is in truth a liberation of the present and opening up of the future.

Just how much democracy was aware of this function of history is shown by the French Revolution—I will return to this—as well as by the "Funeral Oration" in which Pericles retraces the history of the city and attributes to previous generations their due in order to link their work to that of the generation presently in the prime of life (*en tē kathestukeia hēlikia*, II, 36, 3) and calls on the young not to show themselves to be inferior; which in the context clearly means not to *innovate* less and less well than those who preceded them.

[*Manuscript addition*: *Paideia pros ta koina* <education with a view to common affairs>]

[*Manuscript addition*: Ostracism and *graphē paranomōn*. (The profundity of political thought implied by this arrangement makes Plato seem like a child.)]

Thus, democracy is the regime that establishes itself as a permanent, explicit self-institution and which, at the same time, knows that it can be limited only by itself, institutes the conditions of its own self-limitation, and attempts to achieve mastership over a *hybris* that does not belong to it in its own right but belongs to all that is human.[396] Plato himself, its fierce enemy, would recognize the greatness of the initial period of the Athenian democracy, in which, according to him, *dikē* (justice) and *aidōs* (shame) still reigned (*Laws*, <III, 698b, 699c-d>).

---

396. Self-limitation. Obviously, I am not unaware that the self-institution of democracy is not "total" and "radical," or in other words, that it, on the one hand, experiences limitations coming from elsewhere (religion, morals, etc.). Nevertheless, it should not be forgotten that, as M. Finley said, religion in Greece and in Rome "was a function of the political organization [...] whereas in the Near East government and politics were a function of the religious organization" <Moses I. Finley, "Between Slavery and Freedom," *Comparative Studies in Society and History*, 6:3 (1964), p. 246; quoted in Vernant, "Space," p. 239, note 9>. I am reminded that even some priestly positions were (by Clisthenes already, perhaps) assigned through the drawing of lots. On the other hand, there was the <practice> of "slavery." The ineptitude of the Marxist vulgate (and even of Marx himself) states that Greece did not stay alive off politics. True, but it did not stay alive off slavery *either*. See Vernant and here also Marx himself. The condition for the existence of the ancient city was the small peasantry (and handcraft), *not* slavery.

However, no more than any other human endeavor, democracy does not in itself entail the automatic guarantee of its continued success. And it does not entail an absolute assurance against *hybris*, its own excess. Democracy is a response to *hybris*, but it is not and could not be—any more than any other regime—the extinction of *hybris*. Democracy provoked its own essential defeat through the Peloponnesian War and even did so in a repeated way throughout this war (from which it could have emerged victorious several times, were it not for its own mistakes, its own excesses). What matters here is not this war itself but what its causes—as well as the reasons for Athens's defeat—express, i.e. the limits of universality, the refusal to extend the domain of justice (*dikē*) to the relations between cities (manifested already long before the war by the reduction of allies into the status of protégés and subordinates). This story is itself a tragedy: the hero can do nothing but walk towards fatal actions, whatever the warnings and advice given to him by the chorus; the Athenians continued their ascent towards the domination of Greece, despite the clear lessons given by their own poets, whom they coronated, from *The Persians* by Aeschylus up through *The Trojan Women* by Euripides and in multiple plays by Aristophanes.

The failure of democracy seemed to show that the people is not capable of positing and declaring the law, nor of deciding correctly what is to be done and not to be done, i.e. of governing itself, limiting itself. Democracy ruined itself in potentiality even before having formally disappeared due to its double excess, internal and external. It is to this situation that Plato wanted to respond, by bringing in an external measure to society. It was a false and even vapid response. It could not be otherwise. There can be no external barrier to the possibility of human *hybris*. No one and nothing can guarantee them against themselves. *Nihil timeo nisi me ipsum.* No one and nothing—not a "rational" theory any more than a "holy lie," like those invented by Plato, or any kind of theological fiction—can guarantee society against itself, as the whole historical experience shows. To say that democracy is the regime of freedom is also to say that it is the regime under which the risks of social and historical existence are most *explicit*, which in no way means that they are the greatest there, but quite the contrary. This is something contemporary illusionists gloss over, as they must, when they condemn the risk in revolution that things may go awry (revolution is democracy that never stops, i.e. continuous democracy). Democracy can actually go awry; but other regimes cannot, because they have already gone awry. An observer and critic as acute as Aristotle did not fall into these puerile confusions. Speaking about the "final" democratic regime of Athens, whose functioning he had observed and lived at length (i.e. the "eleventh revolution" as of Thrasybulus in 403), he said, "For the people has made itself master of everything, and everything is regulated by decrees (*psēphismata*, i.e. decisions of the People's Assembly) and by tribunals in which the people dominate. Indeed, even the judgments that once belonged to the *Boulē* are now in the hands of the people. And it seems that we have done the right thing: for the small number is more easily corruptible than the large, both by money and favours" (*Constitution of the Athenians*, XLI, 2). Aristotle did not say that the people are incorruptible (or infallible) but that they are less so than the few, the *oligoi*, which is true. He sees and knows well that here there is no absolute for which to search.

It is this absolute that Plato seeks. He wants to find the measure for law, the extra-social standard for society, the norm of the norm. He will finally place this measure in the "god" himself (see the *Laws*: "It is the god who is the measure all things"), in order to trace out the model of a city that one can rightly call theocratic.[397] Plato's genius is that he was actually able to find and make explicit the only other term of the alternative opposite to democracy: theocracy or ideocracy (which are the same thing, really). Obviously, in historical reality theocracy and ideocracy can never be anything other than the power of a particular social category, i.e. the Church, the party, etc. If God were personally interested in human affairs, we would have known so for some time.

In the background of Plato's political philosophy there is the other tragedy, namely the trial, conviction, and death of Socrates. I have already said why I do not think that this injustice alone could have motivated Plato's attitude towards democracy. However, on this subject, which has been debated for so long and condemned evermore to obscurity—since most of what we know about Socrates has forever become indistinguishable from what Plato wrote—some remarks directly related to the problem discussed there seem useful to me.

The conviction of Socrates was not a judicial crime. It was a tragedy. In this tragedy, Socrates is neither more nor less innocent than the hero of another tragedy. Socrates was unquestionably a *hybristēs*, i.e. someone who infuriates and offends others by his excessiveness. This excessiveness, here, is the perpetual *exetasis*, the "dialectical" examination, which unveils the false or pretended knowledge of others. He says it himself in the *Apology* (21b–e, 30e, 37d–e); Plato calls him *hybristēs* two or three times (see *Symposium*, 219c).

---

397. Pierre Vidal-Naquet, "Plato's Myth of the Statesman, the Ambiguities of the Golden Age and of History," in *Black Hunter*, pp. 295–297. (Vidal-Naquet here reemploys a formula from V. Goldschmidt.)

And, of course, Socrates knew that, and he knew the risk he was running. To those who offered him before his trial an "apology," he replied that he did not need one, having spent his life thinking about how he would respond if someone ever brought accusations against him. This is a strange idea, which certainly has two sides (since we can say that with it the discourse on the "dialogue with the soul with itself" begins), but which also and above all incontestably reflects the knowledge that his activities could be judged by others as transgressing the rules of coexistence in the city. (That the mere *existence* of someone who has not committed any formal offence can be felt by the city as provisionally dangerous may seem unacceptable to us today, *but* it was something self-evidently accepted by all Athenians: ostracism means exactly this). And, *hybristēs* he remained until the end, proceeding with his proposal, after being found guilty, that the city should give him free meals in the Prytaneum, which means that the city ought to treat as it treats its own benefactors someone it has just declared, wrongly or rightly, to be guilty of impiety and corruption of the youth.

And yet, at the same time, Socrates is still a citizen, in the full sense of the word. It is perhaps no coincidence that Plato in the *Symposium* glorifies him through Alcibiades for his acts of endurance and military bravery, i.e. something a Lacedaemonian or even Persian soldier could just as well have accomplished. It comes to pass (*sumbainei*) that the fictitious date of the dialogue did not allow him to mention the most eminent act of bravery of the already old Socrates (at sixty years old), i.e. his presiding over the assembly and refusing, against a furious crowd, to put to a vote the illegal and iniquitous accusation against the ten generals who were victorious at the Arginusae. As Clemenceau would say in another time speaking of Zola, "Men have been found to resist the most powerful monarchs and to refuse to bow down before them, but few indeed have been found to resist the crowd, to stand up alone before misguided masses, to face their implacable frenzy without weapons and with folded arms to dare a no when a yes is demanded. Such a man was Zola!"[398] Socrates is not only the one who teaches that it is "better to suffer injustice than to commit it." He is also the one who knows that there is justice only in and by the city. To accept exile before his conviction or to propose it as punishment after it certainly would not have been an injustice. However, what Plato himself conveys to us as coming from his mouth (*Crito*) is like a Leibnizian theodicy of the democratic city and its laws. That is, if we want the justice that only the city and its laws can guarantee, then we must also accept

---

398. Bruno Weil, *L'Affaire Dreyfus* (Paris: Gallimard, 1930), as quoted in H. Arendt, <i.e. Hannah Arendt, *The Origins of Totalitarianism* (San Diego: Harcourt, 1973), p. 114>.

the individual injustices that can be produced. Socrates knows—he says it explicitly—that it is the city that has made him who he is. This is the strict truth, to which we may add that it is the city that allowed him to *think* as he did. (This is a consideration to which Plato would pay no attention, i.e. this man whom the city, by a strange irony as M. Finley points out, allowed to open a school and to carry out a teaching profession for decades. Let us add that this teaching profession was immediately forbidden, not to mention inconceivable, in his worshipped Sparta.)

Socrates participates in the life of the city, while Plato takes his leave. And this manifests itself in the very form of their activity. Plato founded a more or less closed school, while Socrates came and went in the *agora* and became a gadfly for all citizens. Obviously, Socrates believed that citizens may be awakened to the truth; for Plato, both his actions and his theory (despite the *Meno*) show that he did not believe in that.

In the condemnation of Socrates there was a *hybris* of both protagonists. As for the *hybris* of the city—represented by a small majority of heliasts—and the injustice committed, it is useless to go back over it. But Socrates's *hybris* is found not only, and not very much, in his behavior. (We would love to see how the various intellectuals who today mourn the death of Socrates would carry themselves when faced with Socrates at a Parisian dinner, and to see whether they would accept to be invited a second time with him.) It touches upon an extremely fine and ambiguous point, which constitutes the tragic dimension of the whole affair. Put briefly, democracy is a regime that is based on the plurality of opinions (*doxai*) and functions through them. Democracy makes its truth through the confrontation and dialogue of *doxai*, and would not exist if the idea (i.e. illusion) of a truth acquired once and for all were to attain social efficacy. This confrontation implies and demands the most acute reciprocal criticism and checks; but this is precisely *reciprocal*. That is, everyone fights *for* an opinion he believes to be just and politically pertinent. If he demolishes the opinions of others either for the sake of nothing and by not putting anything in its place, or in the name of an absolute and definitive Truth, he puts himself out of play regarding the city, and he therein transgresses a law, which while not being written, is perhaps nothing less than the most fundamental of all. (Besides, it was in a sense written. That is, the one who during an internal conflict of the city did not take sides was struck by *atimie*, i.e. dishonor and privation of civic rights.) Pericles refutes the opinions he believes to be false and gives an exposition to his own. But what does Socrates do? He refutes everyone's opinions; he shows everyone that they do and speak and decide as if they knew, while in truth they know nothing, and in any case, no more than him, i.e. he who knows nothing. (The same would apply if, as in Plato's post-Socratic dialogues, he were to have actually given birth to *the* Truth.)

Socrates combats the *doxai*. In doing so, he is within democracy; democracy produces him and needs him. But Socrates also fights *doxa* as such, whether in the name of an *ouden oida* that dissolves action and the city, or in the name of an absolute Truth that would dissolve them just as much. How do we judge this? Socrates's *exetasis* is the extreme point of the internal questioning of democracy, for which, once again, democracy is to be credited. Socrates is inconceivable elsewhere than in Athens. Is a democracy—and, moreover, *any form* of political organization—possible if one assumes that strictly no one knows what they are saying? And yet, democracy must be able to assume the very risk of such a demonstration. In Socrates's case, the Athenians did not accept him (although they had accepted him in many other cases). Socrates knew he ran this risk. His tragedy is the tragedy of a philosopher who was also a citizen. Plato's will only be that of a writer.

Plato would resume the fight against *doxa* as such, and he would fully endorse the conclusion that no one knows what they say, unless they have followed the Platonic path. There is eternal truth, i.e. a vision or view (*theōria*) of being "in itself" (*kath' hauto*). No truth emerges in the activities, discussions, or deliberations of the city; these only generate error, and all existing cities are sick. What appears implicitly in Greek thought and practice in the sixth and fifth centuries, and which is affirmed through actions by the establishing and legislating activity of democracy—i.e. namely the recognition of the conventional character (i.e. by positing, *thesei*, and not by nature, *phusei*) of the law, of the institution, of language, and therefore also, implicitly, of social-historical human creation)—is brutally set aside. The only creation that the community would be capable of is the creation of corruption; the only history it knows is the cyclical repetition of regimes. There exists one and only one just city (which is ideal, in the modern sense of the term), whose law is not and cannot be posited by humans, even if it is mediatized by the action of some of them. Philosopher kings do not create and do not posit anything; they regulate the life and the order of the city according to timeless truth to which they have access *qua* philosophers. If there is a timeless being, which is also essence (and even beyond essence) and norm (i.e. the *agathon*), the city cannot be enabled to lay down just laws. Conversely, if the city is in fact incapable of laying down just laws, and since laws are needed, there must be a timeless being who is both essence and norm. Plato's politics thus contributes to determining an ontology that would definitely be that of the Greco-Western tradition, i.e. being as timeless (*aei*) and fully determined (*eidos* and *peras*); the exclusion of Time; the covering over of creation. The

Platonic God is himself subject to uncreated Ideas; the *Timaeus*'s demiurge creates nothing but rather he produces-arranges a world according to an eternal Paradigm.[399]

Thus, there reappears—and this time in reflective and "rational" form—the positing of an extra-social source of institution; and this is so not only with regard to the institution in the strict sense—the law of the city, the political constitution—but also with regard to the institution in general, i.e. the institution of the world. The rootedness of the being-thus of representation, for example, in the conventional and arbitrary being-thus of the *doxai* and the *nomoi* of the tribe, glimpsed by the Eleatics, and clearly and strongly asserted by Democritus and then by the great sophists, to whom I alluded above, is concealed solely to the benefit of the search for the conditions of correct or true representation (i.e. *doxa orthē meta logou*, or correct or right opinion including reason, although the *meta logou* is truly untranslatable), which would owe everything to being as it is in itself and nothing to anything else.

---

399. This is so despite an ontological *hapax* in the *Republic* (i.e. God creates the idea of *bed*). But it is a bed that is at stake here, i.e. a composite "object." It is almost a "technical invention." It is difficult to see what meaning there could be in the Platonic ontology—and in any ontology—for the idea that God creates, for example, the Idea of One, the Idea of Being, or even (and perhaps especially) of the Other (in the sense of the *Sophist*).

Appendix C. Castoriadis and Ancient Greece

Pierre Vidal-Naquet (June–July 1999)

Castoriadis was a theorist of self-creation; and self-creation, which he himself came to exemplify through his life and work, is what he found in the Greek *polis*, particularly, of course, in Athens.[400]

In presenting Cornelius Castoriadis's candidacy to the School for Advanced Studies in Social Sciences [EHESS] several years ago, I told the following anecdote. A famous professor of Roman law was one day in Ferney when d'Alembert was there. Wanting to express his admiration for Voltaire, he said the following to the editor of the *Encyclopedia*: "It is only in Roman Law that I find him a little weak." "That is exactly my opinion," replied d'Alembert, "with regard to mathematics." I made it clear that such was not my opinion with regard to the relationship Castoriadis had with ancient Greece. I could discuss Plato and Aeschylus with him on equal footing.

I became acquainted with the journal in which he wrote, *Socialisme ou Barbarie*, towards the end of 1956 or at the beginning of 1957 following the Hungarian revolution and the repression that brought about its end.[401] But it was a bit later before I understood that what Castoriadis meant by "socialism," and what he later called the self-institution of society, owed much to the ideal of Athenian democracy as represented in a positive manner by the *Funeral Oration* that Thucydides gives to Pericles; or by the narrative developed by Protagoras in the Platonic dialogue named after this great sophist; or, in

---

400. In this presentation in which memories and analyses are blended, I have retained the oral character that belonged to it when I presented it on the occasion of the "Journées Castoriadis," on June 24, 1999 (Paris, EHESS). I would like to thank Stella Manet for her enthusiasm and friendship. — *Eds.*: This essay was first published in French as Pierre Vidal-Naquet, "Castoriadis et la Grèce ancienne," *Esprit*, 259 (December 12, 1999), pp. 131–143.
401. I wrote some casual memories about this subject in "Mélanges Castoriadis," in G. Busino, ed., *Autonomie et Autotransformation de la société, la philosophie militante de Cornelius Castoriadis* (Geneva: Droz, 1989), pp. 17–26. These "Mélanges" were published in *Revue européenne des sciences sociales*, 86 (1989), pp. 16–26.

a negative way, by the *Constitution of the Athenians* by Pseudo-Xenophon, whom we label the Old Oligarch in our jargon.

It was 1958 when I first made contact with the group that edited the journal. And it doesn't really matter that these members later became "dissidents," seeing as they were Jean-François Lyotard and Pierre Souyri. I must admit that back then I considered Athenian "democracy" as largely bogus, since it did not include women, metics, and slaves. Souyri then told me: "You know that the Athenian peasants, when something that really interested them was being debated, all came to the people's assembly, the *Ekklēsia*." Incidentally, the same Souyri wrote some extremely remarkable analyses of Mao's China in the journal, and he first introduced me to K. A. Wittfogel's book *Oriental Despotism*, a book I then had to get translated and introduce with a preface, not without provoking a stir.[402]

A few years later, during the winter of 1963–1964, in a group that took the name "Saint-Just," I got to know a little better the two founders of *Socialisme ou Barbarie*, Castoriadis and Claude Lefort, who thus transitioned from myth to reality. Three experts on ancient Greece, J.-P. Vernant, François Châtelet, and myself, had been invited to debate on the theme of ancient democracy. At the time, Lefort and Castoriadis had rediscovered, beyond Marxism, the democratic idea, in particular the idea of direct self-instituting democracy. If we actually reread the Castoriadian utopia entitled *On the Content of Socialism*, we will notice that there is indeed a close link between the idea of direct democracy and the radical concept of self-management that is the focus of the text, with the obvious difference that Athenian democracy developed in a pre-industrial world and that the question of the management of factories or banks had never been asked.[403] On many occasions Castoriadis used the term "germ" to characterize Greek democracy, and I believe that on this point we can say he was right.[404]

I will set up my presentation under a "triple hat" expressed in three words: the word *polis*, the word *historiē*, and the word *poiēsis*. These are three Greek words, of course, since Castoriadis was profoundly "Hellenic." However, contrary to some contemporary Greeks, he did not believe that because he spoke Greek, he was exempt from studying the Greek authors. He dove into

---

402. These are mentioned in my book *La Démocratie grecque vue d'ailleurs*, 2nd edition (Paris: Flammarion, 1996), pp. 267–276.
403. See Cornelius Castoriadis, "On the Content of Socialism I–III," in *Political and Social Writing*, trans. David A. Curtis (Minneapolis: University of Minnesota Press, 1988), *Volume I*, pp. 290–309, and *Volume II*, pp. 90–192.
404. See for example Castoriadis, "The Greek *Polis*," especially p. 105.

them, conducting a close reading of the great texts from Homer to Aristotle, becoming a poet among poets, historian among historians, philosopher among philosophers, all in all keeping an indispensable reflexive distance. His commentary on Plato's *Statesman* by itself is a testament to his expertise.[405] I am not asserting that he was always right, or that in all cases I agree with him. But very often he brings a new interpretation to such and such lines of Aeschylus, to such and such an analysis of Aristotle, which, though these may sometimes be debated, are largely as valuable as those of all the professionals combined.

The Transformations of the City

First, there is the *polis*. We translate this word as city with good reason, contrary to the Anglo-Saxons, who call it *city-state*. The latter has the disadvantage, rightly condemned by Castoriadis, of making one believe that this is a state or the embryo of a state.[406] In 1978, Castoriadis began the series *Carrefours du Labyrinthe* by asking: "What political insights would Plato and Aristotle have been capable of if the Greek people had not created the *polis*?"[407] Therein lies the heart of the Castoriadian way of thinking; we are dealing with creation or an invention. Castoriadis writes: "The Athenians did not find democracy amidst the other wild flowers growing on the Pnyx, nor did the Parisian workers unearth the Commune when they dug up the boulevards."[408] The socialist idea, and likewise the democratic idea, are inventions. The Greek city was born three centuries prior to democracy. And this is also an invention. There were cities in Phoenicia before there were any in Greece, but these cities did not profess a collective name.

Castoriadis rightly marveled at the *edoxe* ("it pleased the people") in the classical and Hellenistic inscriptions. But before the *edoxe* there was the *efade* at Dreros in Crete in the seventh century BC. There was an emergence of the city just as there was an emergence of democracy or tragedy three centuries later. Nevertheless, we can complete what Castoriadis wrote by showing, as M. I. Finley and J.-P. Vernant and multiple others do, that if the city was born in the Greek world, the Greek person was not born a citizen. Before

---

405. See Cornelius Castoriadis, *On Plato's* Statesman, trans. David A. Curtis (Stanford: Stanford University Press, 2002). See also Cornelius Castoriadis, *Figures of the Thinkable*, trans. David A. Curtis (Stanford: Stanford University Press, 2007), where you can find the texts on Aeschylus, Sophocles, and Sappho to which I shall later return.
406. See Cornelius Castoriadis, "Power, Politics, Autonomy," in *Philosophy*, pp. 156–158.
407. Castoriadis, *Crossroads*, p. xxii.
408. Castoriadis, *Imaginary Institution*, p. 133.

the emergence of the city, there was the modest incarnation of "oriental despotism" called the "palatial" world of Knossos, Mycenae, Malia, Tiryns, among others. Some, like Henri Van Effenterre, already saw therein a functioning city. This heroic hypothesis is what drove this historian to write the book entitled *La Cité grecque des origines à la défaite de Marathon*.[409] Of course, we could refine this point further, as authors like Claude Bérard or Anthony Snodgrass have done.[410] François de Polignac has suggested that the city rests on a sort of alliance between the *agora* at the center, representing the civic area, and the temple, delimiting its borders.[411] For instance, we see in Eretria on the Euboean Gulf a royal tomb transformed into place for heroic worship. With the city, we witness the birth of what some, including me, call the "civic space." What Castoriadis wrote about this period is particularly subtle and sophisticated. Civic time was born at the same time as civic space; and time, which is itself also part of the imaginary, is denied and created at the same time. Castoriadis says, "[The] social institution of imaginary time [...] tends to cover over, to conceal and to deny temporality as otherness-alteration."[412] Furthermore, he maintains, "It would not even be enough to say that the description or analysis of a society is inseparable from the description of its temporality, the description and analysis of a society *is* obviously the description and analysis of its institutions. And among these, the first one is that which institutes it as being, as being-society and *this particular* society, namely the institution of its own temporality."[413]

In a text from 1990, Castoriadis wrote, "For me, the Greece that matters is the Greece extending from the eighth to the fifth century BCE. This is the phase during which the *polis* created, instituted, and in approximately half the cases transformed itself more or less into the democratic *polis*. [...] [Important] things still happened in the fourth century and even afterward [...]."[414] I must say that this "even afterward" causes me problems. If for

---

409. Henri Van Effenterre, *La Cité grecque des origines à la défaite de Marathon* (Paris: Hachette, 1985). — Trans.: The provocation contained in the title is found in its reference to the Greek city's "defeat" at Marathon, which inverts the common narrative.
410. See Claude Bérard, *L'Hérôon à la porte de l'Ouest, Eretia: fouilles et recherches III* (Berne: Éditions Francke, 1970); and Snodgrass, *Archaic Greece*.
411. François de Polignac, *Cults, Territory, and the Origins of the Greek*, trans. Janet Lloyd (Chicago: University of Chicago Press, 1995).
412. Castoriadis, *Imaginary Institution*, p. 131.
413. Castoriadis, *Imaginary Institution*, pp. 127–128.
414. Cornelius Castoriadis, "The Greek and the Modern Political Imaginary," in *World in Fragments: Writings on Politics, Society, Psychoanalysis, and the Imagination*, trans. David A. Curtis (Stanford: Stanford University Press, 1997), p. 90.

Castoriadis the fourth century is the century of what he calls "the second birth of philosophy"—Plato and Aristotle after Anaximander, Parmenides, and Heraclitus—it is evident that in his eyes (as is the case for an entire historiography starting with Thucydides and extending from Plutarch to Toynbee), it is the fifth century—from the Greco-Persian Wars to the fall of Athens—that is the Great Century. There is truth in this judgment; it's the century of tragedy, of the pediments of Olympia, of Phidias, of the *Funeral Oration* attributed to Pericles by Thucydides (which we never tire of saying is an apology for the generation of Pericles, more than for those ancestors that the fourth-century orators will honor).[415]

There is actually something prodigious in the rhythm of the change that occurred in the fifth century. Let us reflect on what separates Aeschylus from Euripides, or the pediments of Olympia from the Erechtheion. We quite rightly cannot speak of a neoclassical art in the fifth century, nor even of a "neo-archaic" art. In order to illustrate this new rhythm of the interiorization of social-historical time by the Athenians, Castoriadis relied on a famous text written by Thucydides (1,70) in which the Corinthians explain to the Spartans what the differences are between them and the Athenians:

> They [i.e. Athenians] are innovators, swift in invention as well as in the execution in actions of that which they decide upon. Whereas you [i.e. Lacedaemonians] are satisfied with conserving what you have, invent nothing, and do not even complete everything that is necessary. Again, they are daring beyond their power, and seek danger beyond what's reasonable, and remain full of hope in the face of hardship. Whereas for you, you stop short of enacting all your power, mistrust even what is certain, and believe that you will never be released from your ills. They are indefatigable, while you limit your efforts; they easily thrive as expatriates, while you cannot be separate from your country. For, in leaving they believe they'll acquire something, and you only think of the damage that could be done to what you already have [...].[416]

In this transformation of Athens, in this incredible series of abrupt mutations, what is the specific place of the fourth century, i.e. the century of philosophy? Evoking this historical moment in a few words,

---

415. Regarding the funeral oration as a genre and as an institution, I recommend the book by Nicole Loraux, *The Invention of Athens: The Funeral Oration in the Classical City*, trans. Alan Sheridan (Cambridge, MA: MIT Press, 2006).

416. See Castoriadis, *Imaginary Institution*, p. 208 (translation modified). Referring to *The Imaginary Institution of Society* in 1975, "Corneille" (a nickname of Castoriadis) had drawn my attention, with a pretense of nervousness, to his translation of Thucydides in these pages. Naturally, they are the ones I am quoting.

Castoriadis defines this as the era when "the philosopher ceases to be a philosopher-citizen (Socrates) and, 'extracting himself' from his society, speaks *about* it (Plato)."[417]

This is an assertion that raises several questions. Is it true that there is a breach in the history of Athens at the very end of (what nobody then knew we would later call) the fifth century, more precisely, let's say, after the crisis marked by three major events: the fall of Athens in 404; the government of the "Thirty Tyrants"; and the democratic restoration in 403? Following Nicole Loraux, I would concentrate on the importance of one of the clauses of the agreement reached under the archon Eucleides (403/402): μὴ μνησικακεῖν, "It is forbidden to reproach anyone for his past."[418] This was, in effect, to install forgetting in the heart of the city. Thus, I think the breach was real, and I am not the only one making that judgment, though it does not seem obvious to me that this breach was positive, as some people believe. See, for example, Martin Ostwald, in an important book entitled *From Popular Sovereignty to the Sovereignty of Law*.[419] For him, it is no longer the people who are kings but the law. And it is true, as Castoriadis says, that democracy presupposes the right of the people to err heavily, for instance by voting for the fatal expedition to Sicily, or by behaving even in a criminal way as in 406 during the Arginusae affair, when the public decided to summarily execute the generals prevented by storm from recovering the drowned citizens or those in danger of being so after the victory.

Xenophon makes us hear the cries of the crowd: δεινὸν εἶναι εἰ μή τις ἐάσει τὸν δῆμον πράττειν ὃ ἂν βούληται, "It is abominable to prevent the people from doing what they want."[420]

Aristotle also thought that this turning point during the reign of archon Eucleides was one of the eleven *metabolai*, one of the eleven transformations that marked the history of Athens. He even thought that it was the most important since it was in his view the last one.[421]

---

417. Cornelius Castoriadis, "Une interrogation sans fin," in *Domaines de l'homme, Les carrefours du labyrinthe II* (Paris: Le Seuil, 1986), p. 245.
418. Aristotle, *The Athenian Constitution*, 39, 6; and see Nicole Loraux, "To Forget in the City," in *The Divided City: On Memory and Forgetting in Ancient Athens*, trans. Corinne Pache and Jeff Fort (New York: Zone Books, 2006) pp. 15–44.
419. Martin Ostwald, *From Popular Sovereignty to the Sovereignty of Law* (Berkeley: University of California Press, 1986).
420. Xenophon, *Hellenica*, I, 7, 12.
421. Aristotle, *The Athenian Constitution*, 41 [or XIV, 3]. Allow me to use this reference to say, following Castoriadis and others, that the title from which the quote is cited is absurd. The correct title would be: *The (Political) Regime of the Athenians*.

APPENDIX C. CASTORIADIS AND ANCIENT GREECE 291

Let's say the following as an aside. I think, as does Castoriadis, that the *metabolai*, or at least the most important of them, are not changes just for laughs. After Solon, at the beginning of the sixth century, it was understood that one could not be both slave and Athenian. The Cleisthenian revolution, which I worked on with Pierre Lévêque thirty-six years ago (and which, thanks to David Curtis, saw an American edition come from the French some thirty-two years later), established the framework of Athenian democracy for a long time.[422] Positively, the institutions are imitated by the democracies that develop after Athens, based on its example. Negatively, the unknown legislator who created the Boeotian confederation that functioned from 471 to 386, which we know about from the *Hellenica Oxyrhynchia*, wanted to appear as anti-Cleisthenian. Here, where the Athenians emphasized the numbers of 3, 5, and 10, the Boeotians divided themselves up by numbers of 4, 6, and 11 and did so in a way that seemed as artificial as those used by Cleisthenes in Athens towards the end of the sixth century. The oligarchic legislator thus faced off against the legislator who created democracy. And Plato, at the end of his life in the *Laws*, transposed the Cleisthenian space into the time of the gods. The ten tribes, the ten *prytaneis* became twelve, a number borrowed from the religious calendar that Cleisthenes had previously set aside.

But let us return to this breach at the end of the fifth century which sets up the regime described by Aristotle. The fourth century, taken roughly, is the century of written philosophy (Socrates, who wrote nothing, drank the hemlock in 399); it is the century of the *nomos*, of the law, even if the idea of the *nomos* as master or king is an ancient idea.[423] It was also the era, in its middle, when those moderates so dear to Jacqueline de Romilly had great influence.[424] When I was a young assistant at the Faculty of Literature in Caen, in 1956–1957, I explained one day to my students that the most prestigious of these men, Eubulus, was as much of a democrat as Antoine Pinay was a republican. That wasn't saying much, really.

The century of written philosophy is *par excellence* that of the philosophical hatred of democracy. Certainly, Plato had the honesty not to disfigure Protagoras, the only thinker, along with Democritus, for whom there remains something more than just traces. For Democritus one must deal with Latin

---

422. Pierre Lévêque and Pierre Vidal-Naquet, *Cleisthenes the Athenian: An Essay on the Representation of Space and Time in Greek Political Thought from the End of the Sixth Century to the Death of Plato*, trans. David A. Curtis (New York: Prometheus Books, 1997).
423. Marcello Gigante, *Nomos Basileus*, 2nd edition (Naples: Bibliopolis, 1993).
424. Jacqueline de Romilly, "Les modérés Athéniens vers le milieu du IVe siècle, échos et concordance," *Revue des études grecques*, 67 (1954), pp. 327–354.

(Lucretius) or Byzantine (Tzetzès) texts and for Protagoras, the theorist of democracy and the social contract, with Plato's *Protagoras* and *Theaetetus*.[425] Nevertheless, the real issue raised by Castoriadis's writing is that of knowing when we are to see the democratic city as dying. Should we think that the tragedy of Athens, the one Thucydides narrates and Xenophon completes, is likewise a tragedy of institutive democracy? Or should we think, as the great majority of historians do today, that the fourth century, and to an even greater extent the Hellenic epoch (dominated no longer by νόμος but by τύχη), prolongs the civilization of the *polis* for several centuries?

It is not easy to respond, but in fact Castoriadis was not really interested in the Hellenistic era and little in Rome. A malicious observer might say that if Castoriadis and most of us here are reading and discussing Aeschylus, this is thanks to professors from the Roman period who went to the trouble making selections from among his pieces, which ended up coming down to us.

As for Aristotle, dearest of all to our friend Corneille, we can read him either by looking back upstream as Corneille does (all the while noting, with him, that Aristotle no longer understands Athenian tragedy) or else by looking downstream, i.e. by holding him (i.e. Aristotle, tutor of Alexander) as the one who inaugurated the era of Hellenistic philosophy. To say that he was a democrat, as did Castoriadis, is undoubtedly excessive.[426] He was a man of measure who bordered on what he himself called absolute monarchy, the παμβασιλεία, without going too far into it.[427]

At the Birth of History

The second field of reflection is history. Castoriadis perceived Herodotus and Thucydides in their true greatness, and, as he said, he perceived the "extraordinary rhythm of intellectual creation in democratic Athens."[428] From Herodotus to Thucydides, there is the same transformation with historical invention as there is from Aeschylus to Sophocles with tragic and anthropological invention, and this occurred in barely twenty years. It begins with

---

425. See Thomas Cole, *Democritus and the Sources of Greek Anthropology* (Cleveland: Western Reserve University Press, 1967). This book was known by Castoriadis, as one can see in *Figures of the Thinkable*.
426. Cornelius Castoriadis, "The Greek and the Modern Political Imaginary," in *World*, p. 88. One will also find the comment regarding the incomprehension of tragedy there.
427. Aristotle, *Politics*, III, 16, 1287a8.
428. I am quoting here from "Aeschylean Anthropogony," p. 1.

Hecataeus of Miletus, the first historian, from whom we at least know the opening address: "Hecataeus of Miletus recounts what follows and what he judges to be true, for the words (*logoi*) of the Greeks are, as it seems to me, many and laughable."[429]

Herodotus ridicules him, in turn—in light of Hecataeus's proud claim to be the sixteenth-generation descendant of an Egyptian god—by describing the temporal immensity of the Egyptian era.[430] Thucydides takes over the reins by critiquing his predecessor, sometimes on minute details, and showing his lack of accuracy (*akribeia*).[431] One must admit that in this domain as well the breach at the end of the fifth century is a true cut. Far from distancing himself from Thucydides, Xenophon completes his work by taking up his narrative in the *Hellenica*, preceded by a mere μετὰ ταῦτα, "after this." It took two and a half centuries and the arrival of the great Polybius in order to surpass Thucydides by looking not toward the origin of the Greco-Persian Wars, nor toward the causes of the Peloponnesian War, but toward how, around 220 BC, the Mediterranean world became unified in the perspective of the historian. And, on this point, I admit with Robert Bonnaud that it was unfortunate that Castoriadis completely ignored Polybius.[432]

Perhaps one could also say that Castoriadis neglected another dimension of Western historical consciousness: the biblical dimension. I often explain to students that at the origin of historical consciousness there are two sources, the Greek source that seeks truth and the Jewish source that is a reflection on human ambiguity. Consider what Pierre Gibert says about the episode mentioned in 2 Samuel 11–12: From his roof, David sees Bathsheba naked. He later learns this is the wife of one of his officers, Uriah the Hittite. He sleeps with her, she gets pregnant, and David sends Uriah to war so he can be killed. Nathan informs David that he has sinned and that Yahweh will kill the child he had with Bathsheba. However, David and Bathsheba will have another son, and this is Solomon, "in all his glory," the ancestor, according to Christian tradition, of Jesus of Nazareth.[433] The Messiah is therefore the descendant of a sinful king. This ambiguity nourishes the thought of the last great Roman theorist of history, Saint Augustine. Marrou showed long ago that there is in

---

429. *Trans.*: We have directly translated from the French Vidal-Naquet's rendering of the Hecataeus quotation.
430. Herodotus, *Histories*, II, 143–144.
431. See Thucydides, *History of the Peloponnesian War*, I, 20, 3, which corrects—without ever naming—Herodotus, *Histories*, IX, 53 regarding the claimed "Pitanate battalion."
432. Bonnaud's conference presentation came before mine on June 24, 1999.
433. Here, I am loosely following Pierre Gibert, *La Bible à la naissance de l'histoire* (Paris: Fayard, 1979).

Augustine no City of God that purely and simply opposes the terrestrial city, one that mere mortals could easily separate, but rather that the two cities (the two kingdoms) *perplexae sunt et permixtae,* i.e. are intertwined and mixed with one another.[434] In other words, not everything was negative with regard to the surpassing of the Greek city, and, on this point as well, I am tempted debate with Corneille. This topic would lead us into multiple reflections.

The Greek city at its apogee, as seen by Castoriadis, is not in the least an "ideal" city in exactly the utopian Platonic sense, nor in the sense of Thomas More's *Utopia*. The city is not ideal because it incorporated the socio-historical and the radical imaginary, all things that Plato himself hated. For Plato, φαντασία has only essentially negative connotations, in contrast with Aristotle, as Castoriadis saw him.[435] Even though our friend was impassioned by Plato, it's because this enemy of the imaginary and of poetry was also one of the greatest creators of myths known to universal thought. Consider the myth in the *Statesman* that Castoriadis carefully analyzed in the seminars conducted in February, March, and April of 1986, about which he rightly states that Plato, in presenting an inverted time, inaugurated science fiction.[436] This is also what Plato did by creating the myth of Atlantis, which is essentially a charge against the Athenian democracy assimilated to oriental despotism, a myth that inspired many poets Castoriadis passionately loved, such as William Blake, but also many crooks and imposters. Atlantis is one of the great creations of the Western imaginary, Aristotle being one of the few thinkers to completely escape its spell, a spell that exists to this day.[437] Finally, I am getting to my last point of disagreement with Castoriadis. We— Castoriadis, Pierre Lévêque, and I—debated this at length at the Centre Pompidou (thanks to Stéphane Barbery, David Curtis, and Pascal Vernay), on March 27, 1992. The event was held in commemoration of the 2,500th anniversary of the Cleisthenian reform.[438] What Castoriadis disputed was Finley's

---

434. Henry-Irénée Marrou, *L'Ambivalence du temps de l'histoire chez saint Augustin* (Montréal and Paris: Institut d'études médiévales and Vrin, 1950), referring to *City of God*, 1, 35.
435. Cornelius Castoriadis, "The Discovery of the Imagination," in *World*, pp. 213–245.
436. Cornelius Castoriadis, *On Plato's* Statesman, trans. David A. Curtis (Stanford: Stanford University Press, 2002). We can find an analogous myth in… Elsa Triolet, where the baroness lives her life backwards, from death until birth. See Elsa Triolet, *Qui est cet étranger qui n'est pas d'ici? ou Le Mythe de la baronne Mélanie* (Paris: Éditions Pierre Seghers, 1944).
437. See my essay on this topic, "Athens and Atlantis: Structure and Meaning of Platonic Myth," in *Black Hunter*, pp. 263–284.
438. See Cornelius Castoriadis, "The Athenian Democracy: False and True Questions," in Lévêque and Vidal-Naquet, *Cleisthenes*, pp. 119–27.

famous formulation: "An aspect of Greek history is the advance, hand in hand, of freedom and slavery."[439]

One can naturally debate this, and Castoriadis did not hold back about it, emphasizing that at the time democracy came into being slaves were probably few and that if democracy made slavery and its development possible, the reverse is not true. Nevertheless, between the one and the other there exists a relationship that we can legitimately call dialectical. More remarkable is the fact that when Protagoras, in the Platonic dialogue that bears his name, grounds the legitimacy of democracy, he grounds it on the possibility proper to man (*anthrōpos*, not *anēr*) to possess the know-how that allows him, *vis-à-vis* the technicians, to decide on more strictly political questions, i.e. for naval carpenters to build triremes, but for the people to decide on what shall be built.

My last comment on this topic is to say—and here I have a major disagreement with Castoriadis—that Athenian slavery was radically different from what took place in Sparta and elsewhere in the Greek world, or even what existed in Athens prior to Solon. This liberation of the peasant-owner, which—according to Jefferson, Marx, and Castoriadis—was characteristic of ancient Greek democracy (and which I have happened to call the true Greek miracle), was made possible by commodity-slavery, by *chattel slavery*. I am not ready to back down from this statement. According to an adage borrowed from Aristotle, *amicus Cornelius, sed magis amica veritas* (or at least what I believe to be the truth).[440]

Thinking Poetry

To conclude, here are a few words on poetry, on the ποίησις that is creation. I will situate myself relative to an expression by René Char on the last page of *Hypnos*, a sort of journal of war and of the poet's resistance: "In our shadows, there is not one space alone for Beauty. The whole space is for Beauty."[441] I heard these words resonate over Char's open grave, and it was different words by Char that concluded my *ēpitaphios* for Corneille in December 1997:

---

439. This can be found in the conclusion of Moses I. Finley, *Slavery in Classical Antiquity*, 2nd edition (Cambridge: Heffer and Sons, 1968).
440. Or, as John Philoponus in the sixth century would have said, φίλος μὲν ὁ Κορνήλιος, φιλτέρα δὲ ἡ ἀλήθεια. See John Philoponus, *De aeternitate mundi contra Proclum*, 144, 21, which concerns Plato, of course, recalling Aristotle, *Nicomachean Ethics*, I, 6, 1096a11–18.
441. *Trans.*: René Char, "Leaves of Hypnos," in *Furor and Mystery and Other Writings*, trans. Mary Ann Caws and Nancy Kline (Boston: Black Widow Press, 2010), p. 215.

"Minuscule death of summer / relinquish me enlightening death / now I know how to live."[442] If I quote Char here it is in a way to oppose the Heideggerian reading of Greek poetry. I know that Char met Heidegger in Provence and thought they spoke the same language. Char and Heidegger believed themselves to be the heirs to the Greeks, in particular the Presocratics. However, Char spoke with regard to Heraclitus about tragic democracy. As Castoriadis shows, Heidegger spoke of a Greece without *polis*, whose poets spoke the purest Heideggerian language.[443] In fact, they neither spoke this language nor the language of Freud. Let us note in passing: Corneille was a psychoanalyst and knew that each of us is "a well without bottom." He wrote about Greek poetry, but never did he think to put Antigone or even Oedipus on the couch. I am grateful to him for not doing that, since those who have crossed this forbidden line have written such loads of nonsense.

Ποίησις. To think creation is to think poetry. Anyone who has taken an interest in poetry knows that poetry is somewhat by definition polysemy, i.e. a play on different layers of meaning. Nevertheless, there is an exception to this norm. There once was a professor of literature to whom we owe the following remark: "For one not to search for a meaning and a single meaning in an utterance, whether in prose or poetry, in high or low literature, grave reasons, which have yet to be discovered, would be called for"; or further: "One must look for the letter before looking for the spirit. Texts have only one meaning or they have no meaning at all."[444] The same professor translated Nerval's *Chimeras* into French, under the title *La Clé des Chimères et autres Chimères de Nerval*. I was going to omit—well, not really—his name, Robert Faurisson.[445] Now, Castoriadis's close friends knew that poetry was part of his personal universe: the poetry of Rilke, Hölderlin, Hugo, but also and more

---

442. *Trans.*: Vidal-Naquet is quoting from René Char's "En trente-trois morceaux," which can be found in *En trente-trois morceaux et autres poèmes* (Paris: Gallimard, 1997).
443. See Castoriadis, "Greek *Polis*," p. 104, and in particular the study mentioned above on Aeschylus and Sophocles. Castoriadis describes the Heideggerian Greece according to the following formula, in Cornelius Castoriadis, "The 'End of Philosophy'?," in *Philosophy*, p. 15: "Here we have the bizarre spectacle of a philosopher talking interminably about the Greeks, and whose thought draws a blank in the place of *polis*, *erōs*, and *psyche*."
444. *Trans.*: This statement is by Robert Faurisson, a known Holocaust denier who is frequently criticized by Vidal-Naquet. The translation is drawn from an identical passage in Pierre-Vidal Naquet, "A Paper Eichmann," in *Assassins of Memory: Essays on the Denial of the Holocaust*, trans. Jeffrey Mehlman (New York: Columbia University Press, 1992), pp. 1–64, quotation p. 45.
445. For these references, see Serge Thion, *Vérité historique ou vérité politique?: Le dossier de l'affaire Faurisson: la question des chambres à gaz* (Paris: La Vieille Taupe, 1980), p. 54. Also, Faurisson's "translation" of Nerval was published by Pauvert in 1976.

APPENDIX C. CASTORIADIS AND ANCIENT GREECE   297

importantly Greek poetry from Homer to Cavafy. Greek poetry was for him what art was for another philosopher, who, like him, also came to France at the end of 1945 on the RMS *Mataroa* but died young in 1981, i.e. Kostas Papaioannou.[446] Greek art was for Kostas what Greek poetry—Homer, lyric poetry, tragedy—was for Corneille. Many will discover this by reading the posthumous volume of *Carrefours* where [Castoriadis] grapples with Sappho, Aeschylus, Sophocles, and Shakespeare in an attempt, with regard to poetry, to make the respective means of Greek and English come face to face with one another.[447]

Let us conclude, as he does, with a tiny poem attributed to Sappho:

Δέδυκε μὲν ἀ σελάννα
καὶ Πληΐαδες, μέσαι δὲ
νύκτες, παρὰ δ' ἔρχετ' ὤρα,
ἔγω δὲ μόνα κατεύδω.[448]

As Corneille shows, the poet plays with light and darkness, the moon (φεγγάρι in Modern Greek), and the Pleiades, this constellation whose heliacal setting occurs in the spring. Ὥρα (ὤρα) is at once the season, youthfulness, and the beauty of spring, to which the solitude of the sleeper is opposed. We could translate this as follows: "The moon has sunk and so have the Pleiades. The nights are in their midst and the beautiful hour is approaching, but I sleep alone." We can, I believe, echo this by noticing that the sinking is death, whether provisional or definitive. Homer's heroes die and sink into Hades. The *Tomb of the Diver* in Paestum, one of the rare frescoes that testifies to what great painting was like in the fifth century, sinks precisely towards the doors of Hades, a motif appropriated so often for a tombstone. This was decisively shown by Bruno D'Agostino and Jesper Svenbro in a masterful article.[449]

This moon with its brilliance in turn echoes a famous line by Parmenides, perhaps one of the most beautiful lines in Greek literature. It is more or less

---

446. See Kostas Papaioannou, *The Art of Greece* (New York: H. N. Abrams, 1989). I drafted his biography in the preface to its French re-publication in 1993 with Mazenod.
447. *Trans.*: Cornelius Castoriadis, *Figures du pensable, Les Carrefours du labyrinthe VI* (Paris: Le Seuil, 1999).
448. *Trans.*: For a recent translation and discussion, see Diane J. Rayor, "Note on Translation," in *Sappho: A New Translation of the Complete Work*, trans. Diane J. Rayor (Cambridge: Cambridge University Press, 2014), p. 21: "The Moon and Pleiades have set—half the night is gone. Time passes. I sleep alone."
449. See Bruno D'Agostino, "Le Sirene, il tuffatore e le porte dell'Ade" and Jesper Svenbro, "Appendix," in *Annali dell'Istituto universitario orientale di Napoli. Sezione di archeologia e storia antica*, 4 (1982), pp. 43–50.

the only debt that I owe to Jean Beaufret, who one day wrote on the board when I was in foundational literature course:

νυκτιφαὲς περὶ γαῖαν ἀλώμενον ἀλλότριον φῶς

Luminous at night, wandering around the earth, light coming from abroad.[450]

If one makes this line resonate, if one analyzes its overtones, as Corneille would say, we will find in it the wandering that strongly moves us at the beginning of *Oedipus at Colonus*. There, Oedipus is a beggar wandering with his daughter Antigone. We find this light coming from elsewhere, and it reminds us that the city is not an island, any more than a human being is according to John Donne: "No man is an island, entire of itself; every man is a piece of the Continent, a part of the main." This text, as we know, was used as an epigraph by Hemingway to introduce his novel *For Whom the Bell Tolls*.

In the preface to *Crossroads in the Labyrinth*, where he quotes four admirable lines from the first of the *Sonnets to Orpheus*, Corneille writes, "The immeasurable laughter of the Greek sea can be heard no more."[451] And he adds, still being polemical against Plato, i.e. the Plato of the allegory of the cave (that first representation of the cinema): "To think is not to get out of the cave; it is not to replace the uncertainty of shadows by the clear-cut outlines of things themselves, the flame's flickering glow by the light of the true Sun. It is to enter the Labyrinth; more exactly it is to make a Labyrinth exist and appear when we might have stayed 'lying among the flowers, facing the sky'" (Rilke).[452] Is this immeasurable laughter truly inaudible? It seems to me, on the contrary, that Corneille still makes us hear it.

---

450. This is fragment XIV in Barbara Cassin, *Parménide, Sur la nature ou sur l'étant—La langue de l'être* (Paris: Le Seuil, 1998). Our contemporary, J.-P. Vernant, thought he had rediscovered the Greek moon: "It's Selene (Goddess of the moon), but as I said, nocturnal, mysterious, and bright." And he recalls a bit later that for the Greeks, "Light is vision, vision is luminous." See Jean-Pierre Vernant, *Entre mythe et politique* (Paris: Le Seuil, 1996), p. 202 and p. 216. — *Trans.*: See Hermann Diels, *Die Fragmente der Vorsokratiker*, ed. Walter Kranz (Berlin: Weidmannsehe Verlagsbuchhandlung, 1952), DK 28B14. The English above translates Cassin's French.
451. Castoriadis, *Crossroads*, p. ix (translation modified). The "immeasurable laughter of the waves" is an expression from Aeschylus, in *Prometheus Bound*, 89–90.
452. Castoriadis, *Crossroads*, pp. ix–x (translation modified).

Index

Abyss, 119, 149, 155, 252, 253, 257, 263, 265
acculturation, 45–46
Achaeans, 83, 90, 91, 108, 132
Achilles
   critique of heroic world, 71
   critique of royalty, 130
   and death, 72–73, 75–76
   and the gods, 108
   and human sacrifice, 113
   and justice, 131–132
   and *moira*, 82, 85
   and the tortoise, 50
   and tragedy, 68–69, 71
   and universality, 92–93
Achilles Tatius, 150–151
Achsenzeit, 29
action, 68, 69–70
actualization, 50–51, 53, 251
adikia, 165, 166, 170, 171, 173, 179, 254, 264, 265
Adorno, T. W., 78
Aeschylus, 133–134, 202
   The Persians, 256, 268, 278
   Prometheus Bound, 84–85, 110–111, 238
   Prometheus Unbound, 84
affect, 98, 100–101
Agamemnon, 70–71, 89–90, 113, 114, 127, 130
agora, 61, 104, 125, 127, 127–128, 262, 281, 288
alētheia, 4, 7, 180, 198, 226, 230, 250, 262; *see also* truth
algebra, 48–49
Alice in Wonderland, 187
Amasis, 174
American Indian myth, 141–142
analytic school, 57
Anaxagoras, 233
Anaximander, 7, 84, 163–164, 185, 196
   apeiron, 150, 186–187, 188, 254; and Milesian cosmology, 175–177
   chreōn, 218

existence, 264
   Fragment DK 12A9/B1, 161, 166–175, 179–180: Heidegger's translation, 164–166, 169; time in, 177
   injustice, 255
Anouilh, J., 68–69, 69n81
anthropogony, 116–119, 121
anthropomorphism, 106–108, 109–110, 118, 190, 191, 208
Antigone (Anouilh), 68–69, 69n81
Antigone (Sophocles), 162, 199, 238–239
apeiron, 150–151, 154, 161n247, 163–164, 167, 171–173, 175–177, 186–188, 210, 241, 250, 254
apophatic theology, 119
appearance/appearing, 4, 7, 180, 188–189, 194, 217, 226, 240–241, 250–251; *see also phainesthai*
archaeological finds, 112
archaeology, 35–36, 40
Archaic Greek period, 40
archē, 150, 163, 167, 172, 176, 184–185, 186
Archelaus, 232
Archilochus, 205, 225
Arendt, H., xxvi, 5, 12, 87, 90, 99, 129n200, 254, 256, 260n375, 261n379, 267n386
Aristarchus, 56
aristocratic families, 191–192
Aristodemus, 94–95
Aristotle, 7–8, 231, 268, 270
   apeiron, 154
   Constitution of the Athenians, 267, 270, 279
   contrariety, 221
   democracy, 278–279
   einai/being, 166, 210, 241
   ensemblist-identitarian logic, 182, 183–184
   human beings, 266–267
   ideal objects, 50
   love, 98–99
   on myth of Pandora, 156–157
   Physics, 163

in Plato dialogues, 37
praxis, 68, 70
Simplicius on, 163
theory of predication, 247
on Xenophanes, 189
art, works of, 12–13
Asiatic monarchy, 4, 39
astronomy, 45
Athena, 70, 82, 85, 104, 108, 113, 123
Athenian democracy, xxi, 202, 248, 261–262
Athenian tragedy, 5
Athens, 42, 43, 58, 109, 136
athetesis, 56
Auschwitz, 11
autonomous society, 24–25
autonomy, tradition of, 3, 3n1
axial age, 29

Babylonians, 27, 47–48, 52, 73
barbarians, 33, 92, 134–135, 257, 275
Battle of Kosovo, 62
Battle of Marathon, 16
Battle of Platea, 94
Battle of Thermopylae, 94
being
    Anaximander on, 166–169, 254
    and contrariety, 210
    and non-being, 228–229, 230
    v. appearing, 4, 7, 180, 188–189, 226, 240–241, 250–251: in Heraclitus, 194, 217
    see also einai; existence; non-being
Bérard, V., 59
Bethlehem, 120–121
Bible, 59
Big Bang, 176
binary logic, 138
Blegen, C. W., 36
blindness, 175
Bollack, J., 193, 204, 219
borrowing, 44, 45–48, 52–53
Bourbaki, N., 48
Buddha, 10, 29
Buddhist thought, 241–242

Cadmus, 47
cannibalism, 112
Castoriadis, C., xi
    The Imaginary Institution of Society, xviii
    interest in Greek heritage, xx–xxv
    La Création humaine, xvii–xviii
    "Political Thought", xix–xx, 249–283

Castoriadis, Z., xxvii
Chadwick, J., 43
chaos, 118, 144, 145–151, 162, 172, 263
Chinese philosophy, 29, 30
Chios, 31, 42
choice, xxv, 9, 11, 12, 17, 93–94
chōra, 152, 241
chreōn, 164–165, 170–171, 172, 175, 177, 179–180, 198–199, 218; *see also* law
Christianity, 80, 89, 93, 98, 99, 106, 113–114, 118
Christians, 59
Chronos, 84, 85, 111, 148, 264
Cicero, 46
classical tragedy, 69
Cleisthenes, 43, 60, 202, 258, 291
collective warrior *see* phalanxes
colonization, 31–32, 40
community, 60, 132–133
Confucianism, 29, 30
Constant, B., 19
Constitution of the Athenians (Aristotle), 267, 270, 279
Constitution of the Athenians (Pseudo-Xenophon), 286
contemporary culture, 61–62
contrariety, 210–212, 214, 217, 221–223
Corinth, 16
cosmic space, 51
cosmology, 175–177, 218
creation, 44–45, 47–48, 116, 118, 121, 238, 245–248
Création humaine, La (Castoriadis), xvii–xviii
creative imagination, 67–68
creativity, 7, 198–199
Cretan tablets, 38–39
Crete, 39, 40, 42, 101, 112
Critique of Pure Reason (Kant), 203, 237
Critique of the Power of Judgment (Kant), 12–13
Croesus, 213
cryptography, 38–39
cultures, 8–10
    borrowing from each other, 44, 45–48, 52–53
    contemporary, 61–62
    Greco-Western, 9–12
    Greek, 8–9, 28–30, 58–60, 63–66
    see also societies
Cyclopes, 60, 92, 111, 123–126, 128, 148, 248

dactylic hexameter, 62
Daoist tradition, 30
Dark Ages, 40, 64n75, 65, 81, 128
de Coulanges, F., 19
death, 65–66, 72–76, 80–81, 83, 84, 85–87, 104, 113, 233
decasyllables, 62
Delphic oracles, 212–213
democracy, xxiii, 4, 5–6, 109, 202, 231, 265–266, 270–279, 281–282
 definition, 260
 direct, 248, 273
 and gender, xxi
 in Greece v. other cultures, 28–29
 and philosophy, xviii, 143, 156, 247, 250
 and political institutions, 23–25, 268–269, 271
 and politics, 26
 and tragedy, 27
democratic institutions, 42–43; see also political institutions
democratic tradition, 3
Democritus, 7, 234–237, 252, 283, 291–292
destinal hope, 143–144
Detienne, M., 27n22, 28n23, 117, 121, 141–142
Diels, H., 193, 220
dikē
 Anaximander on, 162–163, 166, 169, 170, 172, 254, 255
 Heraclitus on, 196, 211
 Hesiod on, 233
 in Homeric poems, 131, 132
 see also justice
Diogenes Laertius, 194, 232, 236, 237
direct democracy, 248, 273
discourse, 141–142
Discovery of the Mind, The (Snell), 55–56
divine presence, 120–121
divinization, 121–122
division of labour, 42
documentary sources, 16–17
Dodds, E. R., 88n120, 114, 117
dogma, 115, 116
Dörpfeld, W., 36
doxa, 250, 257, 282
 Heraclitus on, 192
 Parmenides on, 229–230
 v. *alētheia*, 4, 7, 180, 226, 240
 Xenophanes on, 191, 233
 see also opinion
Draco, 42

drama, 68–69
Dreros, 42, 287
Dumézil, G., 102, 139–140

eclipse, 31
editors, xxvi
Egyptians, 47–48, 52, 73, 123, 134–135, 205
eidos, 12, 13, 19, 247
einai, 4, 7, 146, 166–169, 188; *see also* being
Einstein, A., 213
elections, 109, 273
Eleusis, 103, 104
Empedocles, 203, 230, 233, 255
ensemblist-identitarian logic, xiii-xiv, 181–184, 186, 227
enthnocentric prejudice, 55–56
ethnogolization, xxiii
epical-religious poems, 102
equality, 5–6, 94, 269, 270
eran, 99
essence, 168–169, 184, 230
ethics, 98
Ethics (Spinoza), 203
Euclidean geometry, 52
Euclidean space, 51
Euhemerus, 36
Euripides, 77, 120, 194, 238, 256, 274, 278, 289
European cultures *see* Greco-Western cultures
Evans, A., 38
existence, 167–168, 264; *see also* being

falsifiability, Popperian, 33–34
families, 191–192
fascism, 11–12
fate *see moira*
feminist movement, xxii
Ferguson, A., 19
Finley, M. I., 24, 35, 43, 57, 64–65, 66, 91, 103, 105–106, 107, 110, 111, 113, 114, 277n396, 281, 287, 294
fire, 196, 217–218
flux, 212, 217, 222
formulas, 60–62
France, xxi, 12, 17
Freud, S., 138
"Funeral Oration" (Pericles), 43, 199, 238, 260–262, 277

Gadamer, H.-G., 19–21
Galen, 237

gender, xxi
gendered language, xiii
genius, 12, 13
germ, xiv, xviii, 8, 32, 66, 81, 83, 128, 132, 139, 225, 227, 229, 231, 247, 261, 286
Geometric period, 40
geometry, 47–48, 51, 51–52
glory, 129–130
God, 98, 99, 106, 118, 120–121, 154
God Without Being (Marion), 106
gods
    Cretan tablets, 39
    Heraclitus on, 208–209, 211
    in Homeric poems, 82–85
    immortality, 254
    and men, 36, 99, 106–114, 117, 118–119
    "national" character of, 122–123
    powers of, 95
    Xenophanes on, 189, 190, 191–192, 250
Gorgias, 250–251
Greco-Western cultures, 9–12
Greece, xx
    arrival of Greeks in, 37–38, 39
    rediscovery of, 46
Greek colonization, 31–32, 40
Greek creation, 44, 47
Greek grasp of the world, 23, 25, 65
    chaos and cosmos, 136
    Homeric poems, 68–71, 79, 80
    law, 175
    and philosophy, 143
Greek heritage, xx–xxv
"Greek miracle", 44, 47, 142
Greek myth, 67–68, 86, 116, 118, 142–143, 144, 157–158, 247–248
Greek poems, 58–59
Greek polytheism, 3n1
Greek religion, 97–114, 119–121
    Homeric religion, 97, 103–114, 155
    idolatry in, 119–120
    "national" character of gods, 122–123
    no anthropogony in, 116–119
    no immortality in, 121–122
    no revelation in, 115–116
    pre-Hellenic elements, 101–103
    as social phenomenon, 100–101
    Western perception of, 97–99
Greek society and culture, 8–9
    in Homeric poems, 63–66
    importance of Homeric poems for, 58–60

Greek thought, 4, 136, 282
    and Buddhist thought, 241–242
Greek tradition, 3
Gulag, 11

Havelock, E., 43, 167, 168
Hebraic world, 116
Hebrews, 45, 59, 74, 98
Hector, 69, 71, 82, 90, 93, 113, 131, 162, 251
    as hero, 75–76, 91
Hegel, G. W. F., 23, 78, 93, 184, 188, 201, 222, 228, 241, 262
Heidegger, M., 35, 183, 193, 220, 257n373, 262, 296
    being and time, 177
    critique of, 239–241
    on death, 75
    Greek poetry, 296
    Greek language, 257n272
    Greek philosophy, 46, 253–254
    Heraclitus, 201, 204, 207
    meaning, 143
    onto-theological current, 231
    preconception, 19
    presence, 168, 228
    translation of Anaximander, 162, 164–166, 169, 171
    unveiling, 21
Helios, 217
Hellenic Middle Ages, 40
Hellocentrism, xxi, xxii
Heraclitus, 7, 192–197, 225, 226, 248, 256
    contrariety, 210–212, 217, 221–223
    cosmo-physiology, 218
    critique of tradition, 204–207, 213
    ensemblist-identitarian logic, 181–182
    god of Delphi, 22
    inadequacy of language, 208–209, 233
    logos xynos, 214–216, 227
    men asleep, 214–215
    moira, 84
    private thinking, 207–208, 213–214, 227–228
    relativity of all predication, 209–210
    relativity of predication, 214
    unity of everything, 217, 219–221
hermeneutic circle, 19–20
hermeneutical position, 19–20, 21
Herodotus, 10, 92, 134–135, 174, 175, 202, 260, 273, 275

heroic combat, 41
heroic world, critique of, 71–72, 79, 132–133
Hesiod, xxi, 41, 82, 111, 112, 118, 130, 190
   Theogony, 145–149, 205–206, 264
Hindu philosophy, 29–30
Hippolytus, 120, 232
Hisarlik, 36
"historical event" interpretation, 36–37
historical memory, 275, 276
historiography, 5, 15–18
   and hermeneutical position, 19–20, 21
   and understanding, 20–22
history, 8, 13–14, 100–101, 276–277
Homer, 43, 190, 205–206
Homeric man, xxv
Homeric poems, 31, 32, 40–41, 43, 217
   critique of heroic world, 71–72, 79, 132–133
   critique of royalty, 130
   death, 72–76, 80–81, 85–86
   definition, 80
   enthnocentric prejudice, 55–56
   era referred to in, 63–66
   existence, 168
   importance for Greek culture, 58–60
   individuation, 87–90
   interpolations and additions, 56–58
   justice, 130–132
   mode of composition, 60–63
   moira, 81–83, 85–87, 110
   Muses and Mnemosyne, 66–68
   spectators, 77
   tragic grasp of the world, 68–71, 80
   universality and impartiality, 90–93
   values, 129–130
   see also IIliad; Odyssey
Homeric religion, 97, 103–114, 155
Homeric research, 35–36
homoioi, 94
homonymy, 235
Hop-o'-My-Thumb, 140
hope, 143–144, 156–157
hoplite revolution, 41–42
hoplitic phalanxes, 63, 247
human beings, 266–267
   creation of, 116, 118, 121, 245
   divinization of, 121–122
   v. non-humans, 123–128
   see also Homeric man
human community, 60
human sacrifice, 112–113

humanist Hellenism, 142
Husserl, E., 48, 276
hybris, 6, 263–265, 267, 269, 277–281
   in Anaximander, 144, 162, 170–171, 173, 175
   in Homeric poems, 70–71, 85, 86
hyper moron, 83
hyper-tragedy, 68–70

ideal objects, 50, 52
ideal space, 50, 51, 52
ideality of numbers, 50, 51, 52
idolatry, 119–121
Iliad, 32, 40, 58
   agora, 127
   being and appearance, 217
   composition, 62, 65, 68
   death, 72–73
   glory, 129
   gods, 107, 108, 110, 111, 112
   heroes, 76, 79, 114
   human sacrifice, 113
   hyper moron, 83
   impartiality, 91, 92–93
   individuation, 87–88, 89–90
   justice, 131–132
   moira, 82, 85
   "national" character of gods, 123
   royalty, 130
   themes, 61
   tragedy, 69–71
   universality, 256
Imaginary Institution of Society, The (Castoriadis), xviii
imagination, 67–68
immortality, 85–86, 99, 104, 121–122, 254, 264
impartiality, 90–93
indeterminate, 150
India philosophy, 29–30
individualism, 132–134
individuals, 19
individuation, 87–90
infinite, paradoxes of the, 50
influence, 44, 45
injustice *see adikia*
intellectualization of history, 100–101
interpretation, 21
interrogative positing, 253
Introduction to the Iliad (Mazon), xxvi
Ionia, 42, 128
Iphigenia, 113

irrational numbers, 152–153
Isaiah, 119
Israel, 120–121

Jaspers, K., 29, 242
jazz, 61–62
Judaism, 89
judgment, xxv, 9–13, 157, 231, 274
judgment of taste, 13
justice, 130–132; see also dikē

Kant, I., 12–13, 98, 143, 203, 215, 237
Knox, B., xxiv, 76n95
kosmos, 145, 152, 162, 172, 254, 255, 263

labour, division of, 42
language, xii–xiii, 38, 190, 197–198, 208–209, 233–236
law, 12, 24, 24n20, 42, 49, 104, 145, 175, 252
   and democracy, 247, 266, 275–276
   Heraclitus on, 216
   in *Odyssey*, 126
   v. nature, 4
   see also chreōn; nomos
Lévêque, P., 39, 291, 294
Lévi-Strauss, C., 115, 140n221, 141, 157
Linear B, 35, 38–39
localization, 108
logic
   binary, 138
   ensemblist-identitarian, 181–184, 186, 227
logos, 183–184, 188, 195, 197, 219–221, 259, 267–268
logos xynos, 207–208, 214–216, 227
love, 98–99, 106
lots, drawing of, 109–111, 260, 265, 273, 277n396
lyric poetry, 225
lyric poets, 58, 60, 61, 62, 65, 205–206

magic, 49–50
magma, 22n16, 45, 47, 65, 67, 81, 101, 104–105, 112, 138, 142, 148, 236, 252
Mallarmé, S., 234
Marion, J.-L., 106
markings, xii
Marx, K., 42, 217, 266–267, 277n396, 295
Marxism, 35
Marxist historiography, 17

mathematical proof, 53
mathematics, 46, 47–49, 50–52, 153
mathematization, 154
Mazon, P., xxvi
meaning, xiv, 44, 72, 140, 142, 246; *see also* non-meaning
melodrama, 68–69
memory, 66–68, 275, 276
meta-tragedy, 68–70
Michelet, J., 274
Middle Helladic period, 39
Milesian cosmology, 175–177
mimēsis, 67
Minoan civilization, 39
Minoan-Mycenaean period, 43
Mnemosyne, 66–68
modernity, 78, 154
moira, 70, 81–87, 110, 118, 170, 185–186
Momigliano, A., 134–135
monotheistic cultures, 9–10
monotheistic position, 144
monotheistic religions, 3, 21, 116, 186
monsters, 134
morality, 98
multiplicity, 228–230
Muses, 66–68
Mycenae, 36, 40
Mycenaean civilization, 38, 39, 64
Mycenaean era, 62
myth, 137–139
   and discourse, 141–142
   Greek, 67–68, 86, 116, 118, 142–143, 144, 157–157, 247–248
   and tales, 139–141
mythical narrative, 185
mythology, 139, 154–155, 190–191

nature *see physis*
Nazism, 101
negative theology, 119
Neugebauer, O. E., 47
Nietzsche, F.W., 150n240
nomos, 250, 252
   v. *physis*, 4, 7, 179, 180, 200, 231–239
   see also law
non-being, 50, 147, 183, 228–229, 230, 254, 255
non-meaning, 142, 145, 158, 248, 254, 255, 263
numbers, ideality of, 50, 51, 52

Occident, 12

Odyssey, 40, 58
   composition, 59–60, 62–63
   death, 72–73, 85–86, 104
   distinction between human and non-human, 118
   gods, 111, 112
   humanity v. non-humanity, 123–128
   hyper moron, 83
   individuation, 87–88
   justice, 66, 131
   "national" character of gods, 123
   philosophy and politics, 31
   themes, 61
   Westernness in, 78
Oedipus, 140
Old Testament, 3, 21, 45, 59, 74, 98, 116, 119
Olympian religion *see* Homeric religion
onta, 172, 173
opinion, 18, 251, 281–282
   v. truth, 4, 7, 180, 189, 226, 229
   see also doxa
opposites *see* contrariety
oral poetry, 61–62
originality, 52
Orphism, 121, 122, 136
Otto, W.F., 49, 82, 85, 105–106
ousia, 168–169, 184, 230

palatial civilization, 39
Panathenaic festival, 58
Pandora, 144, 156–157
paradoxes of the continuum, 50
Parmenides, 183, 202, 228–230, 297–298
Parmenides (Plato), 151–152
Parry, M., 61–62
Peloponnesian War, 43, 278
peras, 151
Pericles, 43, 199, 200, 238, 260, 261, 262, 274, 277, 281
periodization, 40
Persian invasions, 43
Persians, 135
Persians, The (Aeschylus), 256, 268, 278
Phaeacians, 124–125
phainesthai, 4, 7, 188; *see also* appearance/appearing
phalanxes, 41–42, 63, 247
Pherecydes, 150–151
Philebus (Plato), 151
philein, 99
Philolaus, 151
philology, xxvi

philosophical language, 197–198
philosophy
   birth of, xix, 6–8, 26–28, 163, 185–188, 231
   and democracy, xviii, 143, 156, 247, 250
   by the *dēmos*, 258
   in Greece v. other cultures, 29–30
   history of, 228
   judgement and choice, 9, 12
   and mythology, 139
   and politics, 30–32
   and rational theology, 136
   validity of, 18
   see also political philosophy; Western philosophy
physical space, 51
physics, 17–18, 153
Physics (Aristotle), 163
physis, 195, 254, 255, 257
   as creative power, 13
   v. *nomos*, 4, 7, 179, 180, 200, 231–239
Pindar, 202
pitch, 52
Plato, 7–8, 58, 136, 282
   being, 230, 241, 251
   dialogue of the soul with itself, 76, 88
   Egyptians, 135
   on Homer, 68
   ideal space, 50
   kosmos, 254
   mathematics, 152–154
   ontological questions, 166
   Parmenides, 151–152
   Philebus, 151
   political philosophy, 6, 261–262, 269–270, 277, 279, 280–281
   Republic, 6, 37, 58, 283n399
   Seventh Letter, 50
   Sophist, 151–152
   Timaeus, 151–152, 241, 254, 283
Plutarch, 200
Poe, E.A., 23
poems, 58–59; *see also* Homeric poems
poet singers *see* lyric poets
polis, 4, 32, 41, 156, 259
political collectivity, 4–5
political institutions, 23–25, 268–269, 271; *see also* democratic institutions
political law, 12
political philosophy, 6, 7, 12, 249–250, 261–262, 279
political pluralism, 3n1

"Political Thought" (Castoriadis), xix–xx, 249–283
politics, 11, 25–26
　in Greece v. other cultures, 28–29
　and philosophy, 26–28, 30–32
Polycrates of Samos, 174–175, 264
polyonymy, 235
Polyphemus, 124, 125
polytheism, 3n1, 10
Popperian falsifiability, 33–34
Poseidon, 70, 108–110, 124
positing, xiv
praxis, 68, 70
pre-Hellenic religion, 101–103
predication, relativity of, 209–210
Presocratics, 31
presumptuousness, 207, 227
private thinking, 207–208, 227–228
Proclus, 234–235
progress, 238
Prometheus, 254
Prometheus Bound (Aeschylus), 84, 85, 110–111, 238
Prometheus Unbound (Aeschylus), 84
Protagoras, 238, 240
Protogeometric period, 40
Pseudo-Plutarch, 164, 171
Pseudo-Xenophon, 286
psyche, 246
psychoanalysis, 33
Ptolemaic theory, 34
public space, 266, 267, 272–273, 274, 276
Pylos, 36, 38, 39, 40, 62
pyr, 196
Pythagoras, 202, 206, 234
Pythagorean school, 52
Pythagorean theorem, 153
Pythagoreanism, 136

rational mastery, xxii
reason, 27, 27n22, 156, 259
　Ruse of Reason, 78
reconstitution-restoration, 17–18
reinterpretation, 35, 36–37
relativity of predication, 209–210
religion, 39–40, 80, 190, 252; *see also* Greek religion; monotheistic religions
religious thought, 29–30
Renaissance, 47
representative democracy, 273
Republic (Plato), 6, 37, 58, 283n399
revelation, 115–116

rhapsodes, 58
Robespierre, M., 274
Romanized transliteration, xiii
Romans, 46
royalty, 130
Ruse of Reason, 78

sacred, 155
sacrifice, 112–113, 117, 121
St. Louis Blues, 61–62
Sakellarakis, Y., 112
Sakellariou, M. B., 39
Saussure, F. de, 235
Schliemann, H., 35–36
Schulze, E., 169–170
sciences, 47
Scientific American, 176
seminars
　plan for publication, xvii–xviii
　transcriptions, xxvii
sensations, 237
sensuousness, 215
Seventh Letter (Plato), 50
Shakespeare, W., 59
signification, xiv, 22–23, 35, 44, 53, 58
Simplicius, 163, 171, 172, 185
sin, 113
slavery, in Greece, xi n1, xxi, xxiv, 6, 35, 41, 58, 94n136, 104, 211, 247, 256, 277n396, 286, 291, 295, 211
sleep, 214–215
Snell, B., xxv, 55–56
Snodgrass, A.M., 43
social-historical creation, xviii, 44–45, 47–48
social imaginary, 138–139, 143, 246, 252
social phenomena, 99–101
social representation, 115–116, 118
societies, 8–9, 13, 32–33, 245–248; *see also* autonomous society; cultures; Greek society and culture
socio-historical world, 157–158, 245–246
Socrates, 75, 81, 194, 279–282, 290, 291
solidarity, 133–134
Solon, 42, 86–87
Song of Roland, The, 65
Sophist (Plato), 151–152
Sophocles, 162, 199, 238–239
sortition *see* lots, drawing of
soul, 216, 217
sound, 52
space, 50, 51–52, 152; *see also* public space
Sparta, 94–95

spectators, 69, 70, 77
Spinoza, B., 203
stoicheion, 163, 167, 172, 184
Stoics, 154, 202, 218
subscripts, xxvii
substratum, 152–154, 163
sun, 217
supplementary notes, xxvi
synonymity, 235
Syria, 102
Syros, 150

tablets, 38–39
tales, 139–141
Talmud, 116
Tartarus, 148–149
taste, judgment of, 13
teaching, reports on, 245–248
technology, 42
Thales, 31, 163, 186, 188
theogonic myths, 247
Theogony (Hesiod), 145–149, 205–206, 264
thinking, 183–184
　private, 207–208, 227–228
　work of, 14
Thucydides, 43, 260, 268–269, 274
Timaeus (Plato), 151–152, 241, 254, 283
time, 164, 177, 199
　civic, 288–289
　public, 259
Titans, 148
tradition, 252, 276–277
　of autonomy, 3, 3n1
　critique of, 204–207, 213
　Daoist, 30
tragedy, 5, 68–71, 116, 253–254
　and democracy, 27
　spectators, 69, 70, 77
trans-social apprehension, 44–45
transcendence, 119
transcriptions, xxvii
translation, xiii–xiv, xxvi–xxvii

transliteration, xiii, xxvii
Trojan War, 63, 64
truth, xxvi, 195, 262, 267–268, 282
　and man, 247
　v. opinion, 4, 7, 180, 189, 226, 229
　see also alētheia

understanding, xiv, 20–22, 23, 32–33
Unitarians, 57
universality, 90–93, 256–257
US Declaration of Independence, 80

Ventris, M., 38, 43
Vernant, J.-P., xxv, 27–28, 74n93, 88n121, 117, 121, 138, 141, 144n225, 156, 259, 277n396, 286–287, 298n450
vested interest, 36
Veyne, P., 15, 16
Vidal-Naquet, P., xi, xxvii, 32, 41, 43, 57, 89n123, 91n131, 117, 133n213
von Ranke, L., 16

wars, 43, 211–212; *see also* Trojan War
water, 150–151, 186, 188
Western cultures *see* Greco-Western cultures
Western philosophy, 97
will, 88–89, 93–94, 98
Wismann, H., 193, 204, 219
Wolf, F. A., 57
women, in Greece, xi n1, xxi, xxiv, 6, 58, 286
work of thinking, 14
works of art, 12–13
World of Odysseus, The (Finley), 35, 64, 66
writing, 64

Xenophanes, 151, 189–192, 194, 202, 226, 233, 238, 250–251
Xenophon, 58, 135, 290, 292, 293
xoana, 119
xynos, 207

Zeno of Elea, 50, 222, 230